Mobile Cultures

CONSOLE-ING PASSIONS

Television and Cultural Power

Edited by Lynn Spigel

←→

Mobile Cultures

New Media in Queer Asia

EDITED BY CHRIS BERRY,

FRAN MARTIN, AND

AUDREY YUE

←→

Duke University Press   Durham & London

2003

Designed by C. H. Westmoreland

Typeset in Minion with Meta display

by Keystone Typesetting, Inc.

Library of Congress Cataloging-in-
Publication Data.

Mobile cultures : new media in queer Asia
/ edited by Chris Berry, Fran Martin, and
Audrey Yue.

p. cm. — (Console-ing passions)

Includes bibliographical references and
index.

ISBN 0-8223-3050-4 (cloth : alk. paper)

ISBN 0-8223-3087-3 (pbk. : alk. paper)

1. Gays—Asia. 2. Interpersonal
communication—Asia.

3. Communication—Technological
innovations. 4. Internet—Social aspects.

5. Computer networks—Social aspects.

I. Berry, Chris. II. Martin, Fran. III. Yue,
Audrey. IV. Series.

HQ76.3.A78 M63 2003

306.76'6'095—dc21

2002014236

Contents

Introduction: Beep—Click—Link
Chris Berry, Fran Martin, and Audrey Yue 1

I INTERFACES: GLOBAL/LOCAL INTERSECTIONS

I Knew It Was Me: Mass Media, "Globalization,"
and Lesbian and Gay Indonesians
Tom Boellstorff 21

Japanese Queerscapes:
Global/Local Intersections on the Internet
Mark McLelland 52

Guided Fan Fiction: Western "Readings" of Japanese
Homosexual-Themed Texts
Veruska Sabucco 70

Syncretism and Synchronicity:
Queer'n'Asian Cyberspace in 1990s Taiwan and Korea
Chris Berry and Fran Martin 87

Queerly Embodying the Good and the Normal
David Mullaly 115

II MOBILE SITES: NEW SCREENS, NEW SCENES

Singaporean Queering of the Internet: Toward a
New Form of Cultural Transmission of Rights Discourse
Baden Offord 133

Pop and *ma*: The Landscape of Japanese Commodity
Characters and Subjectivity
Larissa Hjorth 158

From Khush List to Gay Bombay: Virtual Webs of Real People
Sandip Roy 180

III CIRCUITS: REGIONAL ZONES

Queer Voyeurism and the Pussy-Matrix in
Shu Lea Cheang's Japanese Pornography
Katrien Jacobs 201

Sexing the City: Malaysia's New "Cyberlaws"
and Cyberjaya's Queer Success
Olivia Khoo 222

Paging "New Asia": Sambal Is a Feedback Loop,
Coconut Is a Code, Rice Is a System
Audrey Yue 245

Bibliography 267

Contributors 293

Index 297

CHRIS BERRY, FRAN MARTIN,

AND AUDREY YUE

Introduction: Beep—Click—Link

At utopia-asia.com, a leading Asian gay and lesbian Web portal, banners for *Time* magazine, BBC World Service, and *The Advocate* loom large.[1] In *High Tech Rice*, an answering machine connects a Filipina American as she lives between two cultures.[2] In Melbourne, Australia, Yellow Kitties, an Asian lesbian support group, comes of age with a logo that reconfigures an iconic character from Japan's Sanrio.[3] In New York City, a South Asian gay and lesbian "Jungli Boogie Bhangra Blow-Out" fundraiser spins house, hip-hop, chutney, soca, and reggae. At Rice Bar in Sheung Wan, near Central, Hong Kong GAMS (gay Asian males) seek out other Hong Kong GAMS.

The recent emergence of gay and lesbian communities in Asia and its diaspora is intimately linked to the development of information technology in the region. The July 1994 official introduction of the Internet in Singapore, the launch of China's English-language Web in 1993, and Malaysia's Multimedia Super Corridor gateway inception in 1996 have mediatized the region, with some 47 million Japanese currently with Internet access and half of Koreans over the age of 17 being regular Internet users.[4] Information has indeed sparked a revolution, transforming lives and lifestyles. More significant, information has enabled the expression of sexual identities in a region that is notorious for the regulation of both information and sexual conduct. Since the mid-1990s, gay and lesbian literature about Asia and Asian diasporas has emerged with titles such as *Gay and Lesbian Asia, Different Rainbows,* and *Q&A: Queer in Asian America.*[5] The fluidity and ubiquity of information, from storage and image to media markets, has increased with digitization, making it more powerful and accessible. Information has crossed national boundaries, enabled global gay and lesbian coalitions, and formed new queer cultures incorporating Asian imaginaries. These cultures foreground the historicity of the mediascapes of the West, Asia, and the Asian diaspora. They are characterized by the ephemerality of the commodity in late modernity. And they form a network connected by the technology of a speed-space, producing mobile and transient cultures. Hence our book *Mobile Cultures: New Media in Queer Asia.*

Time magazine reported in March 2001 that in the past five years the Internet had done to Asia's gay and lesbian communities what Stonewall enabled in the West over the past twenty-five years.[6] The 1994 introduction of the Netscape browser has played an important role in the types of information constitutive of emergent gay and lesbian identities in Asia, its diaspora, and its cyberspace. Beginning with a handful of file transfer (ftp) sites publishing bibliographic resources about Asian gay and lesbian literature[7] and Telnet ports hosting local bulletin boards, the user-friendly interface has transformed information from subcultural data to a "presentness" enabled by multimedia synergy. With it, interactive chats, self-managing listservs, and short messaging codes have proliferated on the bandwith alongside repertoires and libraries of imageworlds and signs. Information consumption has fueled information production and an increasing self-awareness, shifting subterranean bulletin board cultures and self-writing historiographies from shared interest minority groups and genealogical retrieval to a larger project of self-creation. This project asks questions both ontological (Who are we? Who we are may not be what we are) and epistemological (How do we know ourselves as the product of where we come from? Where we come from may not be what we know ourselves to be). In the process, it modernizes new kinds of connectivity and communities, online and offline. Mediated by displacement, Queer Asia uses new media to challenge the desexualization of the Asian gay man[8] and the anomaly of the Asian lesbian by indigenizing the global and producing mobile and contingent practices of self-inscription and self-identification.

If burgeoning Queer Asia and its digital facilitation is the object of study in the essays collected here, the anthology itself engages two emergent and rapidly growing fields of study. One is the globalization of sexual cultures; the other, the study of "new media." In relation to the first of these, it seems fair to say that if one single preoccupation has characterized both academic and popular discussions of sexualities over the past decade, it has been the globalization of sexual cultures. Indicative of the popular anxieties that arose over this question in the 1990s, for example, is an article on the rise of consumer culture in Vietnam that appeared in Melbourne newspaper *The Age*'s weekend supplement, *Good Weekend,* in 1998. The article notes: "Even what are considered subcultures in the West have permeated the increasingly porous membrane around Vietnam. In Ho Chi Minh City, at the Phuong Cac café, hundreds of gay men gather on Sunday mornings. The air shimmers with expensive cologne as the young show off their designer clothes and buffed bodies. Logos of designers like Versace and Calvin Klein abound . . . everything from the clothes, the pumped-up muscles, the haircuts . . . to the attitudes and confidently open manner have been sucked in from a gay culture that transcended all borders; the café could have been in San Francisco's Castro District."[9]

The language of this description is instructive. Employing a tropology all too familiar in post-AIDS discussions of homosexuality, the excerpt figures "Western gayness" as an unstoppable virus, permeating Vietnam's "porous membrane" to cause the mutation of Ho Chi Minh City into a city indistinguishable from San Francisco. With its lingering attention to the symptoms of middle-class commodity culture, the excerpt also shows the mixture of triumphalism and nostalgia that characterizes popular journalistic discourse on the crumbling of Eastern bloc communist regimes under the assault of global capitalism—which, like gay culture, "transcends all borders." This highlights the fact that any discussion about the globalization of gayness inevitably draws on broader debates over the effects of globalization in general. As a result, to begin talking about the global gay, it is necessary first to speak about debates over globalization itself.

Stuart Hall frames a central question on how best to think about globalization: "Is this just the old enemy in a new disguise? Is this the ever-rolling march of the old form of commodification, the old form of globalization, fully in the keeping of capital, fully in the keeping of the West, which is simply able to absorb everybody else within its drive? Or is there something important about the fact that, at a certain point, globalization cannot proceed without learning to live with and working through difference?"[10] Arjun Appadurai's now classic essay "Disjuncture and Difference in the Global Cultural Economy" is useful in classifying answers to this question. Appadurai delineates two critical responses to globalization: one that privileges homogenization and one that privileges heterogenization.[11] A homogenizing view of cultural globalization, which has been characteristic of much important Marxist writing on the subject, constructs the process as producing an overall reduction of cultural difference around the globe, as commodification proceeds hand in hand with cultural "Americanization." This view, adopted by neo-Marxist commentators such as Fredric Jameson and Masao Miyoshi, is one that, in a much simplified if also ambivalent form, underlies the weekend magazine description of Ho Chi Minh City's Phuong Cac café.[12] As Lisa Rofel observes in her incisive critique of Michael Hardt and Antonio Negri's book *Empire,* one danger with approaches that rest on an assumption of the universally homogenizing effects of global capitalism is that such approaches risk rhetorically reenacting the very violence they also denounce: the erasure of cultural difference.[13]

In fact, Hardt and Negri's book represents an interesting development in globalization studies, insofar as it appears in one way to take issue with the homogenization thesis by emphasizing plurality, hybridity, difference, and a polynuclear world structure. Squarely rejecting the "Americanization" thesis, the authors state emphatically, "*The United States does not, and indeed no nation-state can today, form the center of an imperialist project,*" and, taking their cue from Deleuze and Guattari, they insist that their notion of "empire" "manages hybrid identities, flexible hierarchies, and plural exchanges through modulating networks of command." However, as Rofel discusses in some detail, the authors' apparent appreciation of the effects of decentering and cultural dis-integration belies the deeply homogenizing impetus of their thesis as a whole, which casts a highly Eurocentric notion of empire as "a new form of global sovereignty"—even as "the sovereign power that governs the world"—and presumes a universal and undifferentiated "capitalism" that is the engine behind this new world order.[14]

Appadurai's heterogenizing view offers a different alternative. This view foregrounds the interactions between the Western and the non-Western that globalization enables and impels, and holds that as a result, cultural globalization challenges the global hegemony of the West, and indeed of any singular world order, as much as it reinforces or extends existing structures of cultural domination. Appadurai is suspicious of the presumption of homogenizing accounts to explain globalization as though it were a singular process reducible to a consistent or predictable logic; he prefers to emphasize precisely the unpredictability and instability—the "disjunctures"—that follow from the interaction of the different forms of flow that happen in and through globalization.[15] This more nuanced approach to the intricacies of cultural flow in the era of globalization does not claim that

Mobile Cultures

cultural forms and identities emanating from the United States have now altogether ceased to act as a compelling influence in cultures worldwide. Rather, it asks that we recognize that Americanization is not the *only* influence and that the effects of American culture are not felt equally or in the same way at every location. Such an approach, we believe, has much to contribute to the postcolonial project of "decentering the West" by challenging narrowly Eurocentric forms of knowledge. To take up this approach is not the same as simplistically privileging the local and the particular over the global and the universal while leaving that dichotomy squarely in place. Rather, as Ann Cvetkovich and Douglas Kellner suggest, such an approach means we must "think through the relationship between the global and the local by observing how global forces influence and even structure ever more local situations and ever more strikingly. One should also see how local forces and situations mediate the global, inflecting global forces to diverse ends and conditions and producing unique configurations for thought and action in the contemporary world."[16] As we discuss in detail at the end of this introduction, many of the contributors to this volume take up Cvetkovich and Kellner's challenge to articulate the global with the local and to attend to the ways each cross-cuts and problematizes the other in the realm of sexual cultures.

In a recent essay, Appadurai poses a crucial question researchers of global and regional cultures need to address: "In short, how does the world look—as a congeries of areas—from *other* locations (social, cultural, national)?"[17] Through detailed, microlevel engagements with specific cultural contexts, the contributors to this volume offer a range of necessarily varied and discontinuous responses to the crucial question. How does the world and the Asian region look from this specific point in culture and history? The heterogeneity of their responses underlines the insight of many scholars of globalization and regionalization that, despite the familiar rhetorics of "one world" and of "Asia" as a singular and coherent cultural region, in practice these processes do not produce one world or one Asia, but many.

Prior to the recent debates on the way sexual cultures and sexual knowledges become mobile in globalization, approaches to sexual cultures throughout the world could be divided into two broad camps. On the one hand, traditional anthropological and sociological work on sexual cultures tended to take an empiricist approach, addressing as their object sexualities as they are practiced as modes of cultural organization in diverse geographic locations. This work tended to emphasize the "cultural difference" of the "other" culture under investigation, projecting a discrete "cultural identity" and paying little attention to potential for intercultural communication and appropriation between contexts.[18] In contrast to this ethnographic tendency to appeal to the "otherness" of different cultural contexts stands work that tended rather to assume, and often celebrate, the cross-cultural sameness of "gay" or "lesbian identity." To take an extreme example, Judy Grahn's 1984 book *Another Mother Tongue* contains a chapter entitled "We Go around the World," in which she asserts that "people are Gay the world over" because "being Gay is a universal quality."[19] Neil Miller's 1992 book, *Out in the World*, in which his project was to "go out in the world . . . in search of gays and lesbians," similarly assumes in advance that "gays and lesbians" are what he will find, while also collaborating in the writing of a universalizing fantasy of a "gay globe."[20]

Later academic discussions of what has often been called "global queering," after a much discussed 1996 article by Dennis Altman, have tended to take up the terms of the broader debates on cultural globalization and transpose them onto the domain of sexual cultures.[21] Early interventions into these debates tended, like the article on gay commodity culture in Vietnam cited above, to emphasize the homogenizing power of gayness gone global. Posing a central question in these debates, and implying a response to it that comes down on the homogenizing side, Altman asks, "Is there . . . a universal gay identity linked to modernity? This is not to argue for a transhistoric or essentialist position . . . but rather to question the extent to which the forces of globalization (both economic and cultural) can be said to produce a common consciousness and identity based on homosexuality."[22] The position Altman indicates here, in which the globalization of Euro-American modernity results in a universal gay identity and "common consciousness" across the globe, was common enough in the mid to late 1990s to border on becoming a kind of "cultural commonsense" view of sexualities in the global age—as indicated by its reproduction in the piece of popular journalism about Ho Chi Minh City. But more recently, this view has been strongly challenged by new work that has begun to appear on the topic.

Since the late 1990s, a series of books and articles has challenged earlier presumptions that "globalizing" is synonymous with "homogenizing" in the realm of sexualities. This later work is marked by a number of characteristics. It is in general less speculative and makes a more active, research-based engagement with sexualities as practiced and represented in local contexts. Its detailed engagement with the micropolitics of sexualities situated in place leads in turn to a tendency not to see the global and the local as two arenas utterly separate and opposed, but to consider the mechanics and meanings of *glocalization,* or the localization and indigenization of globally mobile understandings of sexuality.[23] This is the approach taken by Lenore Manderson and Margaret Jolly in their introduction to *Sites of Desire, Economies of Pleasure: Sexualities in Asia and the Pacific.*[24] Eschewing both the universalist, essentializing view of "sexuality" as something shared and unitary across cultural divides, and also the simplistic relativism born of the reification of "cultural difference," Manderson and Jolly hope that their collection might "focus on cross-cultural *exchanges* in sexualities" in the colonial period and after. Comparably, the 1999 special issue of *GLQ* edited by Elizabeth A. Povinelli and George Chauncey on "Thinking Sexuality Transnationally" collects work on local and global sexualities that, in general, discards the conceptual opposition of the global and the local for an emphasis on the intricate weave of the *transcultural.* Lisa Rofel's essay in that volume, "Imagining Gay Identities in China," provides a succinct statement of this newly dominant conceptual paradigm: "Transcultural practices resist interpretation in terms of either global impact or self-explanatory indigenous evolution. Instead, they open inquiry into contingent processes and performative evocations that do not presume equivalence but ask after confrontations charged with claims of power."[25] Another instance of this turn away from the simplistic model in which the local and indigenous confronts the global and Western in a stark encounter where one must always eventually cede power to the other is Cindy Patton and Benigno Sánchez-Eppler's 2000 collection, *Queer Diasporas.*[26] This anthology proceeds from the assumption that mobility, rather than fixity or identity, is a defining characteristic of both actual bodies in diaspora and of desire and sexuality themselves.

The contributors to this volume are, in general, writing out of this recently ascendant paradigm in global sexuality studies that works in the interstices of the transcultural. Tom Boellstorff's essay, for example, argues that the Indonesian terms *gay* and *lesbi* are neither simply direct translations of gay and lesbian nor autochthonous and authentically "local" sexuality categories. Rather, he suggests, they are ambivalent signifiers of identity produced out of the messy transmission between the contexts of local Indonesian audiences and the Anglo-American cultures that produced "gay" and "lesbian" in the first instance. This messy transmission, in which the message received is never quite the same as the one that began the journey, is what he calls "dubbing culture." In the context of Malaysian politician Anwar Ibrahim's trial for sodomy, Olivia Khoo's essay examines how Malaysian women identifying as lesbian in local Internet cultures respond to the official discourse that produces sodomy as religious crime while at the same time subtly conflating it with both the homosexual and the Western. Here too, then, the situation is not one of a homogeneous "global lesbian" culture confronting local cultures of sexuality, but the significantly more complex situation of local women appropriating an ostensibly "global" signifier—"lesbian"—as a standpoint from which to critique a local official discourse that exploits religious law on sodomy both to dispose of a political threat and to reinforce a version of Malaysian nationalism that takes as its foil a "West" tainted by its association with homosexuality. Again, Berry and Martin's essay finds that models of sexuality deployed within lesbian, gay, and queer Internet cultures in Taiwan and South Korea bespeak the creative glocalization of Euro-American sexuality categories in these Asian contexts, rather than evidencing a simple takeover of the latter by the former.

In addition to the study of sexualities, this anthology also contributes to research on new media. Although new media can be understood broadly to cover everything from fax machines and satellite television to cell phones and pagers, there is little doubt that computer-mediated communications (CMC) ranging from email to the Internet come to mind as the most prominent example of new media for many people at the moment. Yet, as David Silver notes in his survey of writing on CMC, "while scholars from across the disciplines flock to the general topic of cyberculture, few have made their way into the margins to explore issues of race, ethnicity and sexuality online."[27] In addition to the absences listed by Silver, we would note the lack of work on the Internet and other new media outside the West. The essays collected in *Mobile Cultures* help to fill these gaps. But more than this, we hope they also challenge assumptions about what new media are, about their social position and function, as well as Eurocentric, heterosexist, and simply erroneous notions of what should be counted as culturally marginal and what as central in today's world.

The Asian societies written about in this anthology are highly diverse. They range from urban and middle-class societies like those addressed in South Korea, Taiwan, and Japan, where the use of media technologies is at least as widespread as anywhere in the West, to others that are more agrarian and less materially wealthy, like India and Indonesia, where even land-line phones and electricity are by no means ubiquitous. With these circumstances in mind, Tom Boellstorff points out in his essay on dubbing culture that what counts as new media in one place may not in another, and that the significance of what are conventionally understood as new media also varies widely. On the other hand, as Sandip Roy indicates when he recounts hearing by email from small town–based Indian men who have sex with men, one should not presume that what are conventionally under-stood as new media in the West have no significance in less affluent cultures elsewhere.

This observation in Roy's article underlines the importance of materially grounded research in efforts to understand the social position and function of the new media. All the work in *Mobile Cultures* shares this characteristic. Therefore, just as it contributes to work challenging the untested assump-tions underlying early writing on globalization and sexualities, it also joins other work challenging the equally untested assumptions underlying the early writing on the new media.

This earlier writing follows a well-established pattern. For, as the title of Carolyn Marvin's *When Old Technologies Were New: Thinking about Electric Communication in the Late Nineteenth Century* reminds us, what counts as new media varies from era to era as well as from place to place.[28] And, as Lynn Spigel noted in her study of the introduction of the then new technol-ogy of home television, despite all the changes, "the terms of the thinking about communication technologies are very much the same."[29] Initial re-sponses to the new media technology of the day have divided and continue to divide between rapturous utopianism and apocalyptic alarm. Both re-sponses are usually derived from the same characteristics: the new connec-tivity enabled by these technologies feeds hopes for global human commu-nity at the same time it feeds fears about damage to face-to-face local community. For example, James Carey traces initial responses to the tele-graph back to the eighteenth-century ideal of a universal "brotherhood of man."[30] Marvin notes the fears of social breakdown inspired by electrical communication.[31] And in her study of the origins of broadcasting in America, Susan J. Douglas also covers "the fevered expectations" that "wireless would bring world peace, freedom from the cable companies, a democratized communications system, transcendence over space and time."[32]

This bifurcated pattern has continued with today's new media. David Silver notes, "Early cyberculture often took the form of dystopian rants or utopian raves. From one side, cultural critics blamed the Internet for deteriorating literacy, political and economic alienation, and social fragmentation. . . . Conversely, a vocal group of writers, investors and politicians loosely referred to as the *technofuturists* declared cyberspace would bring down big business, foster democratic participation, and end economic and social inequities."[33] Clearly, this repeated pattern suggests ideological overlays. Furthermore, just as previous utopian hopes and apocalyptic fears have not been realized, there is every reason to expect a similar outcome for today's new media. However, this does not mean new media have no significant new effects at all. Certainly, the art practices of Shu Lea Cheang analyzed by Katrien Jacobs here are entirely dependent on the globalized connectivity produced by digital media, as are the specific transnational connections enabling the Western women's interpretations of YAOI culture considered by Veruska Sabucco.

What needs to be undertaken to achieve a more precise understanding of the real and novel social effects of today's new media is materially grounded research. Nancy Baym noted this lack in studies of Internet communications as early as 1995.[34] And even though queer people emerged early among the Internet's most enthusiastic users, this situation still prevails as regards research on lesbian, gay, and bisexual Internet use.[35] Beyond a small but growing number of fieldwork-based studies,[36] most writing on sexuality and new media has been theoretical and/or speculative, sometimes flirting with more sensational possibilities such as virtual transvestism and cyber-rape.[37] The essays collected in this volume make a valuable and timely contribution to materially grounded research into the deployment and effects of new media in lesbian, gay, bisexual, and transgender communities viewed within their specific cultural contexts.

Much of the very early work depended on contrasting new media with the existing material world and placing the media conceptually as though they were somehow separate from that world. In the case of CMC, this is clearly expressed in the rhetoric of the "virtual" and the "real." As Kevin Robins puts it, "The mythology of cyberspace is preferred over its sociol-

Mobile Cultures

ogy . . . it is time to re-locate virtual culture in the real world."[38] Indeed, this is precisely what has been occurring in the past few years. Responding to her own concerns about a lack of fieldwork, Baym's research contradicted earlier assumptions that CMC inhibits interpersonal communication and the formation of community. Her 1995 work showed that Internet users in the field overcome the lack of visual and aural channels and do form personal relationships and communities, often integrated with their lives off the Internet. This rethinking underlies a great deal of the work on new media being produced at the moment. For example, the essays collected in the *Race in Cyberspace* anthology are heavily focused on actual practices on and off the Internet and derive their theorizations from them rather than from abstract or formal properties of the Internet.[39] In this book also, many of the essays start from the assumption that the use of new media is not separate from but part of everyday life, conditioned by it in various locally specific ways and having particular effects on it. For example, Mark McLelland's investigation of YAOI and "newhalf" cultures on the Internet in Japan demonstrates how they extend and further enable existing and local cultures. And while Audrey Yue's essay shows that the Internet has enabled regional connectivity implicated in the discourse of New Asia for upwardly mobile Singaporean and Malaysian lesbians in a manner that is unprecedented, she simultaneously highlights how pager technology has enabled the extension and maintenance of altogether more local working-class lesbian communities in Singapore.

Finally, the particular focus on historical and social practice in an Asian rather than Western context is itself a distinctive feature of this anthology that also challenges much current thinking about new media. In much the same way that attention to the specific Asian contexts of "global queering" demonstrates that global connections are locally made and therefore variable rather than homogeneous, the essays here show that the appeal and uses made of new media are also highly locally specific. Larissa Hjorth's essay on the "character" dolls that Japanese consumers often hang off their mobile phones shows a very particular local adaptation and personalization of the hardware that, she argues, depends for its communicative effect on the heritage of the idea of *ma*, or the gap that opens up meaning. The implications of Berry and Martin's essay on South Korea and Taiwan and McLelland's essay on Japan challenge the usual characterization of CMC as "global"; in each case, the particular verbal languages preferred by users tend to localize rather than globalize Internet usage. Furthermore, Berry and Martin's essay, David Mullaly's essay on a Thai Web site that appropriates the idea of the gay gene to encourage local discussion, and Baden Offord's essay on Singaporean activism and the Internet all show how local concerns with social and/or legal visibility condition and stimulate local queer Internet use.

On the other hand, just as avid queer use of the Internet challenges the usual assumption that new media, like other technologies, are mostly toys for straight boys, so other essays in this volume challenge the idea that when global connections are made through the Internet, they are also dominated by forces dominant off-Net. Sabucco's essay shows how the global connections made possible by the Internet have enabled Western women's YAOI culture of *anime* interpretation and rewriting. Roy's article shows how the Internet and associated new media facilitate a transnational Indian queer activism that previously would have been far more difficult to implement.

These essays share an interdisciplinary approach to theoretical frameworks and highlight a self-reflexive practice of cross-cultural hybrid research. As such, they extend the hybrid oral/written language potential recently suggested by Mann and Stewart in their communications theory study on Internet research.[40] Roy's social movement account of diasporic South Asian gay identity incorporates ethnography with grassroots activism. Offord's political economy approach to the cultural transmission of sexual rights in Singapore's cyberspace and Khoo's media institutional study of cyberlaws and censorship in Malaysia point to interconnectedness between state imperatives and everyday life. Similarly, Yue examines the relationship of cultural policy to informational capitalism using cybernetics to problematize cultural citizenship. McLelland, Hjorth, and Sabucco explore the consumption of Japanese popular culture through fandom, art theory, and cultural history. These essays situate the queer consumption of new media within the uses of culture in Asia and its diaspora, from the effects of the distribution of resources, the processes of moral valuation, and the conditions of belonging to the logics of transnational exchange. Jacobs deploys postmodern film spectatorship to foreground the traffic in pornography, and Mullaly uses semiotics to locate the different postcolonial grammars of speech. Together, these essays, like Boellstorff's anthropology of cultural translation, exemplify the mediations between the virtual/real, digital/analog, and East/West. They engage the politics of representation surrounding us/them, self/other, researcher/researched, and draw attention to how meanings are embodied in practice, reflecting the partiality of knowledge claims. This contingency foregrounds the unrelenting attention given to stories, rituals, routines, and conversations using a wide range of interpretative tools, such as participant observation, fieldwork, email surveys, focus group interviews, and online questionnaires.[41] Like Berry and Martin's hybrid approach to data collection, showing how cyberspace is embedded within real social spaces in South Korea and Taiwan, these methods engage the circuits of distribution, regulation, and production to highlight how new media have indeed been embodied in real spaces and by emergent identities in the queer Asian imaginations.

Running through all the essays collected in *Mobile Cultures* are three highlighted features of new media: technology, transportation, and communication. Technology, from hardware to terminals and memory bytes, plays an important role as a link, a network, and a practice for mediating the divergence and convergence of queer 'n' Asian displacement. Mass transportation has facilitated the accelerated movement of both bodies and information, opening the way to new modes of navigation and travel that have restructured the grids of how we communicate and experience communities in our everyday lives. Communication, as a tool that transmits messages from one place to another, rides the information highway in the search for identity, a highway that may also be intersected by traffic lights and signals. Interwoven with the analytical practices of the essays collected in *Mobile Cultures* are queer stories about Asia and new media that speak of dot coms, crackdowns, and gaps and cracks in meaning. From sexual politics to cultural policies, the same browsers with different clicks drag icons to reveal the junctions and disjunctions where meanings crack, collide, and collude. In spite of and alongside the commercialization of sex from Net-order brides to online Asian gay and lesbian pornography, new media have become a crucial site for constituting new Asian sexual identities and communities.

These essays foreground the role of new media in the intricate interactions of local and global in constituting new forms of queerness, and can be considered as addressing three broad themes. Part 1, "Interfaces: Global/Local Intersections," groups together work that emphasizes the local appropriation, or glocalization, of globally mobile technologies and discourses. Mark McLelland examines how the availability of the Internet has changed Japan's YAOI and "newhalf" sexual cultures and simultaneously placed these very locally specific cultures in a framework of global accessibility. Chris Berry and Fran Martin argue against a view of cultural globalization that casts it as synonymous with cultural homogenization by drawing attention to local appropriations of Internet and BBS technology by emergent lesbian, gay, and queer communities in South Korea and Taiwan. Tom Boellstorff styles the Indonesian borrowing from and rescripting of global gay cultures as "dubbing culture," and David Mullaly shows how a scientistic discourse of gay genetics is reconceptualized at a Thai Web site through reference to traditional Buddhist notions of "the good person" and "the blameless life." Like McLelland, Veruska Sabucco also considers YAOI; however, her essay also considers glocalization "in reverse", analyzing the appropriation of homoerotic Japanese *manga* cultures by Western women fans who create communities through Internet technologies.

The essays collected in the second part, "Mobile Sites: New Screens, New Scenes," emphasize the local specificity of the contexts in which new media are used while also highlighting the role of new media mobility in reconstituting what counts as "locality." Larissa Hjorth's examination of the signifying (and nonsignifying) practice of hanging character dolls from cell phones in Tokyo foregrounds how constructions of sexuality in contemporary Japan differ in crucial ways from Euro-American contexts. Sandip Roy demonstrates the forging of new notions of what counts as "Indian" in the use of CMC among gay and lesbian communities in India and the Indian diaspora. Baden Offord highlights the utility of the Internet for the formation of resistant queer community politics locally in Singapore.

Part 3, "Circuits: Regional Zones," intimates some of the queer possibilities inherent in new discourses and practices of transnational Asian and Internet regionalism, which are themselves responses to globalization. Katrien Jacobs considers some of the implications of the transnationally mobile art practices of Taiwanese American filmmaker Shu Lea Cheang in making her latest work, a feature-length porn film made in Japan, *IKU*. In doing so, Jacobs demonstrates a specifically regional set of cultural flows (Taiwan-USA-Japan) and bespeaks a queering of Asia Pacific regionalism. Both Olivia Khoo's and Audrey Yue's essays are concerned with the rise of the rhetoric of New Asia and the ways local lesbian communities in Singapore (Yue) and Malaysia (Khoo) respond to the changed discursive conditions of culture and nationhood. The New Asian regionalism is for these authors first of all a strategy of power, but they draw attention to how it simultaneously

Mobile Cultures

enables novel tactics of resistance from local queer subjects who exploit the mobilities enabled by new media to extend lines of community and identity underneath and alongside the newly extensive lines of regional power.

We hope that the essays collected here excite more interest in this topic and inspire further research. For, extensive as the range of material collected here is, it in no way exhausts the possibilities. Indeed, we must emphasize that important new media uses in queer Asian cultures that we are already aware of are not included in this volume. These range from the chat rooms of Hong Kong to the mobile phone texting languages of Manila and the burgeoning queer Web sites of the People's Republic of China. These are omitted not by choice but because of lack of research, and we look forward to reading essays on these and other queer 'n' Asian new media practices in the near future.

Notes

We would like to thank everyone who has helped us to make the production of this anthology possible, in particular, Ken Wissoker of Duke University Press, the two anonymous readers, and the Console-ing Passions series editor, Lynn Spigel; our eagle-eyed bibliographer Salena Chow; and the diligent and patient authors of the essays collected here, all of whom tolerated a seemingly endless flow of editorial inquiries from us.

1   Utopia, *Utopia Homepage,* 13 December 1995, ⟨http://www.utopia-asia.com⟩ (1 April 2001).

2   Joanner L. Cabatu and Ekaterina Mirkin, dirs., *High Tech Rice,* USA/Russia, (1996).

3   Yellow Kitties can be contacted at yellowkitties@hotmail.com.

4   "Technology: Over 47 Million Japanese Have Internet Access," *Nando Times,* 24 April 2001, ⟨http://www.nandotimes.com⟩ (1 May 2001); "Korean Internet Users Tallied at 20.9 Million," *Korean Herald News,* 20 April 2001, ⟨http://www.koreaherald.co.kr/SITE/data/html_dir/2001/04/17/200104170032.asp⟩ (1 May 2001).

5   Gerard Sullivan and Peter Jackson, eds., *Gay and Lesbian Asia* (New York: Haworth Press, 2001); Peter Drucker, ed., *Different Rainbows* (London: Gay Men's Press, 2000); David Eng and Alice Yom, eds., *Q&A: Queer in Asian America* (Philadelphia: Temple University Press, 1998).

6   "Boys Night Out: We're Here. We're Queer. Get Used to it. Can Singapore Accept Its Gay Community?" *Time International* no. 157, (19 March 2001): 37.

7 See, for example, David Bedell, "International/Multicultural Bibliography on Gay, Lesbian, and Bisexual Concerns," in *Queer Resources Directory* (29 June 1995), ⟨http://www.qrd.org/world/misc/international.lgb.bibliography⟩ (30 June 1996); "Queer Asian Pacific Resources," in *Journal Articles of Interest for Gay, Bi, Lesbian, Transgender Asian/Pacific People* (29 December 1997), ⟨http://www.geocities.com/WestHollywood/Heights/5010/articles.html⟩ (30 June 1998).

8 Daniel C. Tsang writes that the sexually explicit dialogue of local bulletin boards have enabled the sexualization of the Asian gay male. "Notes on Queer'n'Asian Virtual Sex," in *The Material Queer,* ed. Donald Morton (Boulder, CO: Westview, 1996), 310–17.

9 Robert Templer, "Lennon v Lenin," *Age Good Weekend* (17 October 1998): 53.

10 Stuart Hall, "The Local and the Global: Globalization and Ethnicity," in *Culture, Globalization and the World System,* ed. Anthony D. King (London: Macmillan, 1991), 19–39. See also James Clifford, "Mixed Feelings," in *Cosmopolitics: Thinking and Feeling beyond the Nation,* ed. Pheng Cheah and Bruce Robbins (Minneapolis: University of Minnesota Press, 1998), 366.

11 Arjun Appadurai, "Disjuncture and Difference in the Global Cultural Economy," *Public Culture* 2, no. 2 (spring 1990): 5–6. See also Fredric Jameson, "Notes on Globalization as a Philosophical Issue," in *The Cultures of Globalization,* ed. Fredric Jameson and Masao Miyoshi (Durham, NC: Duke University Press, 1998), 54–77.

12 Fredric Jameson, "Postmodernism, or the Cultural Logic of Late Capitalism," in *Postmodernism: A Reader,* ed. Thomas Docherty (Hemel Hempstead, U.K.: Harvester Wheatsheaf, 1993), 65; Masao Miyoshi, "A Borderless World? From Colonialism to Transnationalism and the Decline of the Nation-State," *Critical Inquiry,* no. 19 (summer 1993): 726–751; Miyoshi, "'Globalization,' Culture, and the University," in Jameson and Miyoshi, 247–70.

13 Lisa Rofel, "Discrepant Modernities and Their Discontents," *Positions: East Asia Cultures Critique* (forthcoming).

14 Michael Hardt and Antonio Negri, *Empire* (Cambridge, MA: Harvard University Press, 2000), xiii–xiv, xii–xiii, xii, xi.

15 Appadurai, 6. See also Hall; Néstor García Canclini, *Hybrid Cultures: Strategies for Entering and Leaving Modernity,* trans. Christopher L. Chiappari and Silvia L. López (Minneapolis: University of Minnesota Press, 1995); Iain Chambers, "The Broken World: Whose Centre, Whose Periphery?" in *Migrancy, Culture, Identity* (London: Routledge, 1994), 67–92; Mike Featherstone, "Global and Local Cultures," in *Mapping the Futures: Local Cultures, Global Change,* ed. Jon Bird et al. (New York: Routledge, 1993), 169–88.

16 Ann Cvetkovich and Douglas Kellner, "Introduction: Thinking Global and Local," in *Articulating the Global and the Local: Globalization and Cultural*

Mobile Cultures

Studies, ed. Ann Cvetkovich and Douglas Kellner (Boulder, CO: Westview Press, 1997), 1–2.

17 Arjun Appadurai, "Grassroots Globalization and the Research Imagination," *Public Culture* 12, no. 1 (2000): 1–19, 8; emphasis added. For a critique of Appadurai's emphasis on the wane of America's cultural power in globalization, see Leo Ching, "Globalizing the Regional, Regionalizing the Global: Mass Culture and Asianism in the Age of Late Capital," *Public Culture* 12, no. 1 (2000): 233–57. The contents of *Public Culture* 12, no. 1 have been collected in Arjun Appadurai, ed., *Globalization* (Durham, NC: Duke University Press, 2001).

18 See, for example, Sue-Ellen Jacobs, Wesley Thomas, and Sabine Lang, eds., *Two-Spirit People: Native American Gender Identity, Sexuality, and Spirituality* (Chicago: University of Illinois Press, 1997); Thamora Fishel, "Extending the Limits of Social Construction: Female Homosexuality in Taiwan," *Historical Reflections/Reflexions Historiques* 20, no. 2 (1994): 267–86.

19 Judy Grahn, *Another Mother Tongue: Gay Words, Gay Worlds* (Boston: Beacon, 1984), 103, 105.

20 Neil Miller, *Out in the World: Gay and Lesbian Life from Buenos Aires to Bangkok* (New York: Random House, 1992), xiv.

21 Dennis Altman, "On Global Queering," *Australian Humanities Review* 2 (July–September 1996), ⟨http://www.lib.latrobe.edu.au/AHR/home.html⟩ (9 December 2001). See also Dennis Altman, *Global Sex* (Chicago: University of Chicago Press, 2001).

22 Dennis Altman, "Rupture or Continuity? The Internationalization of Gay Identities," *Social Text*, no. 48 (1996): 79.

23 The term "glocalization" originates from the Japanese concept of *dochakuka*, "the agricultural technique of adapting one's farming technique to local conditions," and referred originally to the strategy of global cultural industries' attempts to produce localized products for local markets. Roland Robertson, qtd. in Koichi Iwabuchi, "Idealess Japanisation or Purposeless Globalisation? Japanese Cultural Industries in Asia," *Culture and Policy* 7, no. 2 (1996): 34.

24 Lenore Manderson and Margaret Jolly, eds., *Sites of Desire, Economies of Pleasure: Sexualities in Asia and the Pacific* (Chicago: University of Chicago Press, 1997).

25 Lisa Rofel, "Qualities of Desire: Imagining Gay Identities in China," *GLQ* 5, no. 4 (1999): 457.

26 Cindy Patton and Benigno Sánchez-Eppler, eds., *Queer Diasporas* (Durham, NC: Duke University Press, 2000).

27 David Silver, "Looking Backwards, Looking Forwards: Cyberculture Studies 1990–2000," in *Web.Studies: Rewiring Media Studies for the Digital Age*, ed. David Gauntlett (London: Arnold, 2000), 27.

28 Carolyn Marvin, *When Old Technologies Were New: Thinking about Electric Communication in the late Nineteenth Century* (New York: Oxford University Press, 1988).

29 Lynn Spigel, *Make Room for TV: Television and the Family Ideal in Postwar America* (Chicago: University of Chicago Press, 1992), 182.

30 James Carey, "Technology and Ideology: The Case of the Telegraph," in *Communication as Culture: Essays on Media and Society* (Cambridge, MA: Unwin Hyman, 1988), 201–230.

31 Marvin, 64–65, 69–70, 85–87.

32 Susan J. Douglas, *Inventing American Broadcasting, 1899–1922* (Baltimore: Johns Hopkins University Press, 1987), 59–60.

33 Silver, 20.

34 Nancy K. Baym, "The Emergence of Community in Computer-Mediated Communications," in *CyberSociety: Computer-Mediated Communication and Community*, ed. Steven G. Jones (Thousand Oaks, CA: Sage Publications, 1995), 139.

35 R. McLean and Robert Schubert, "Queers and the Internet," *Media Information Australia*, no. 78 (1995): 78; David F. Shaw, "Gay Men and Computer Communication: A Discourse of Sex and Identity in Cyberspace," in *Virtual Culture: Identity and Communication in Cybersociety*, ed. Steven G. Jones (Thousand Oaks, CA: Sage Publications, 1997), 133–45.

36 Shaw; Tsang, 153–62; David J. Phillips, "Defending the Boundaries: Identifying and Countering Threats in a Usenet Newsgroup," *Information Society* 12, no. 1 (1996): 39–62.

37 Much of the theoretical work is collected in Jenny Wolmark, ed., *Cybersexualities: A Reader on Feminist Theory, Cyborgs and Cyberspace* (Edinburgh: University of Edinburgh Press, 1999). One of the more thoughtful monographs on the topic is Sue Ellen Case, *The Domain-Matrix: Performing Lesbian at the End of Print Culture* (Bloomington: Indiana University Press, 1997).

38 Kevin Robins, *Into the Image: Culture and Politics in the Field of Vision* (London: Routledge, 1996).

39 Beth E. Kolko, Lisa Nakamura, and Gilbert B. Rodman, eds., *Race in Cyberspace* (New York: Routledge, 2000).

40 Chris Mann and Fiona Stewart, *Internet Communication and Qualitative Research: A Handbook for Researching Online* (London: Sage, 2000).

41 On Internet ethnography, see Daniel Miller and Don Slater's Trinidadian study of how the Internet has interwoven into the fabric of everyday life: *The Internet: An Ethnographic Approach* (New York: Berg, 2000). Although this study examines the relationship of the Internet to nationalism and ethnicity, it does not locate how sexuality is embedded in its everyday practice.

↔ |

Interfaces

GLOBAL/LOCAL

INTERSECTIONS

TOM BOELLSTORFF

I Knew It Was Me: Mass Media,

"Globalization," and Lesbian

and Gay Indonesians

Introduction: Agency, Globalization, Authenticity

One long afternoon I sat on the cool tile floor of a lower-class home in Surabaya, in Indonesia's East Java province, speaking about *gay* life with Darta, a large man in his early thirties. We were alone in the main room, but family members, all Muslim like Darta himself, bustled about nearby. I realized that because we were speaking Indonesian, they could be listening in on the conversation, yet Darta did not seem bothered. I looked up at him, a typically gentle smile on his face as he reclined on a sofa, and asked, "Does your family know about you?" Darta answered, "Yeah, they know that I have sex with men. It's no problem. They don't say it's a sin or anything. After they read magazines, they knew and understood, and accepted me."

"What magazines did they read?" I asked.

"Women's magazines, like *Kartini*. Those magazines always have gossip columns. So that's how they knew."

"When did you hear about *gay* for the first time?"

"I also read about it from magazines. It was in fifth or sixth grade [ca. 1985], on the island of Ambon where I grew up. It was there that I first heard about *lesbi*. Earlier, you know, *gay* wasn't around yet [*gay belum ada*]. But *lesbi* was already in women's magazines . . . and I read lots of those magazines because Mom was a regular subscriber. Mom and I loved reading the articles on sexual deviants. I was always effeminate, and one day she even said I was *lesbi!* Because she didn't know the term *gay;* the term wasn't public back then. But eventually I learned the term *gay* as well [*dapat gay juga*]. That was also from a magazine. There was some story about historic English royalty . . . Richard someone. When I saw that, I thought 'There're others like me.' "

In my fieldwork in Indonesia, Darta's calling himself *lesbi* for several years before learning of the term *gay* is unique. However, the central role mass media played in the process by which he came to occupy a *gay* subject-position is typical. In relation to the rubric of this volume, it is particularly interesting to note that, like Darta, I find forms of ostensibly "old" mass media, particularly print forms such as magazines, more significant than "new" electronic or digital media in the dissemination of the *lesbi* and *gay* subject-positions in Indonesia. It is a truism that mass media are also crucial to "Western" queer sexualities; by definition, nonnormative sexual subject-positions are rarely discovered through "tradition" or the family. However, mass media in Asia have taken a variety of pathways different from Western ones, compelling queer Asians and their outsider allies (like myself) to query the role of new *and* old mass media in queer subject-positions, erotic sensibilities, and politicized identities. This is the problematic with which the various essays in this volume concern themselves in some fashion.

With this theoretical horizon in mind, in this essay I ask a specific question but proffer a broad answer. The question is: How do certain people in contemporary Indonesia, the world's fourth-largest country by population after China, India, and the United States, come to occupy the subject-positions *lesbi* and *gay*, which appear to originate in the West? The answer: what I call "dubbing culture." Extending the productive representation of cultural logics as "discourses," this labels a contingent process by which incomplete mass-mediated messages animate a sexual self felt to be fully modern and authentic, yet at a disjuncture from the local. I therefore pose the problem of *lesbi* and *gay* subject-positions in terms of translation, leaving *lesbi* and *gay* in italics. *Lesbi* and *gay* have their own history and dynamics: they are not just "lesbian" and "gay" with a foreign accent. Although shaped by globalizing mass media, these subject-positions are not simply "reruns" of Western ones.

Three issues are of particular importance to this discussion and the understanding of queer Asia more generally. The first has to do with implicit theories of agency that underlie many descriptions of mass-mediated erotics, desire, and pleasure in Asia (and elsewhere). Again and again a presocial erotic, desiring, pleasuring self is granted an assumed ontological priority: flipping open the newspaper, surfing the Web, and then secondarily entering into a transformative relationship with the mass media in question. The specific case of queer Asian sexualities provides a useful test case with which to explore questions of agency, as such sexualities seem so self-evidently to require a kind of voluntaristic gesture of choice vis-à-vis more normative sexualities. Notice the verbs: queer Asians are said to "appropriate," "resist," and "struggle." The tone is triumphant, the mood confident, the good and bad sides cleanly drawn, and the teleologies linear, marching resolutely toward global freedom.

I was a queer activist and HIV/AIDS educator in the United States, Russia, Malaysia, and Indonesia before I became an anthropologist, and I sympathize with the politics that underlie this kind of writing. Yet, are we really served by these notions of human agency, as if people live in terms of active verbs, with a clear set of "interests" always at hand? This is particularly ironic when "queer" is deployed as if its flexibility makes it inherently more liberatory than the supposedly rigid concepts of lesbian and gay. In a historical moment of "flexible accumulation," "flexible bodies," and "flexible citizenship," it seems premature to assume that flexible sexualities are oppositional; they lie eerily close to the sort of market-niche-ing selfhood demanded by late capitalism.[1] After all, it is only in the past 150 years, "and in a limited and localized geographical space, that a way of thinking emerges in which human being is understood in terms of persons each equipped with an inner domain, a 'psychology,' which is structured by the interaction of biographical experience with certain laws of processes characteristic of human psychology."[2]

If, in our desire to confront the violence, injustice, and oppression against sexual and gender minorities, we ascribe to Asians the voluntaristic, choice-making individuality required and presupposed by late capitalism, we impair our analyses and compromise our politics. By implication we presume that queer Westerners operate under such simplistic notions of the individual; we take capitalism's theory of the self at face value and lose sight of the multiplicity of selfhoods extant worldwide. Second, we cannot understand how sexual subjectivities emerge in unexpected ways; how could such an analysis explain how Darta saw himself for many years as *lesbi?* Finally, we short-circuit our ability to develop a culturally respectful queer politics.

Nowhere is this more apparent than in the darkly humorous trajectory of "human rights" discourse. In Indonesia as elsewhere in Asia, human rights has largely replaced development as the concept of choice to be applied unthinkingly to every circumstance of oppression, as if it were a transparent idea, with no history and no cultural assumptions built into it. As a good Western subject I love the idea of human rights; it makes sense to me because I was raised in a culture founded in the liberal ideology of the autonomous subject, with natural abilities and desires, that human rights also presupposes. In Indonesia, however, human rights is known as *hak azasi manusia,* referred to in both print and speech by its acronym HAM. This in an environment where 90 percent of Indonesians are Muslim (and thus forbidden to eat pork) and the meaning of English ham is so well-known that across Indonesia, McDonalds and other fast food chains refer to hamburgers as beefburgers.[3]

This anecdote points up a more foundational problem: for many Indonesians, human rights are seen as something Christians get, a conclusion they see confirmed in the inconsistent interventionist policies of Christian-dominated Western powers (including the United States, but Australia above all in the wake of the independence of Timor Lorosae, formerly East Timor). Indonesians are not paranoid; at times such governments (particularly the United States) voice a preference for protecting the human rights of Christians. The link between human rights discourse and totalitarianism, founded in the fact that human rights discourse requires assuming a "bare humanity" abstracted from social context, was first noted by Arendt half a century ago.[4] Without a notion of human rights that does not assume the Western liberal subject, I fear that human rights discourse in Asia will either become co-opted by state forces or rejected as incompatible with "Asian values." Similarly, without a more nuanced notion of agency, our analyses of sexuality and mass media will remain in a register of boosterism bearing little connection to the real-world experiences of queer Asians.

There seems to be no easy resolution: navigating between structure and agency remains one of the most vexing and productive dilemmas in social theory. It is with such orienteering in mind that in this essay I recount a recent debate concerning the dubbing of imported television shows into the Indonesian language. From this debate I draw the term dubbing, which I then extend metaphorically to think about how ostensibly "foreign" mass-mediated messages can be reconfigured at the point of what otherwise might be called "reception." Just as the dubbed television show in which "Sharon Stone speaks Indonesian" does not "originate" in the United States, so *gay* and *lesbi* subject-positions are distinctively Indonesian phenomena. Yet, just as the range of possibilities for a dubbed soundtrack is shaped by images originating elsewhere, so a "dubbed" subject-position, and the persons who occupy that position in some fashion, cannot choose their subjectivities just as they please. I move, then, from a literal, technical meaning of dubbing to a more speculative, analogical use as a way to approach the relationship between social actors and the modes of subjectivization by which such individuals come to occupy subject-positions.[5] I trace this metaphorical use of dubbing culture to the domain of mass media, but it is pertinent to questions about postcoloniality and authenticity more generally.

A brief aside on terminology. I speak of *subject-positions* (extant social categories of selfhood) and *subjectivities* (the various senses of self: erotics, assumptions about one's life course, etc. that obtain when occupying a subject-position [partially or completely, temporarily or permanently]). I use *identity, identify,* and *self-identification* in a more limited fashion, referring to explicit (often explicitly politicized) claims to membership in *lesbi* or *gay* as indices of community. In speaking of Indonesians who use the terms *lesbi* and *gay* (or close equivalents), de-emphasizing identity is useful because it helps avoid a behaviorist approach (frequent in studies of erotics and sexuality) that sees behavior as preceding and determining identity. Identity versus behavior is a false dichotomy: identity is not simply a cognitive map but also a set of embodied practices, and behavior is always culturally mediated through self-narrative. As a result, focusing on subject-positions and subjectivities turns attention to the total social fact of *gay* and *lesbi* selfhood.

One important advantage of this theoretical framework of subject-positions and subjectivities is that it cross-cuts and indeed deconstructs the identity/behavior binarism, as subject-positions and subjectivities each have both ideational and material aspects (a subject-position can be formed and sustained through not only ideology but also architecture; a subjectivity lived not just through belief but also through fashion). This is basically a Foucauldian framework that draws from the epistemological "break" between volumes 1 and 2 of *The History of Sexuality,* wherein Foucault shifted from an emphasis on "the formation of sciences" about sexuality and the "systems of power" inciting sexuality to "the practices by which individuals were led to focus their attention on themselves, to decipher, recognize, and acknowledge themselves as subjects of desire, bringing into play between themselves and themselves a certain relationship that allows them to discover, in desire, the truth of their being."[6]

I think of subject-position as a rough translation of *jiwa*, which means "soul" in Indonesian but often has a collective meaning; *lesbi* women will sometimes say "*Lesbi* have the same *jiwa*"; male-to-female transvestites (*waria, banci*) will say they "have the same *jiwa*"; and *lesbi* women and *gay* men will sometimes say they share a *jiwa*. I think of subjectivity as a rough translation of *pribadi* (or *jati diri*), both of which mean roughly "self-conception"; a *gay* man once distinguished *pribadi* from *jiwa* by saying that "every person possesses their own *pribadi*." Interestingly, *identitas* has a much more experience-distant, bureaucratic ring for most Indonesians: one *gay* man defined *identitas* as "biodata: name, address, and so on" (*biodata: nama, alamat, dan sebagainya*).[7]

This problem of agency underlies the second issue at stake in a dubbing culture analysis of queer Asia: the presentation of global capitalism as absolute, on the part of both global capitalism and its critics. Gibson-Graham, in a feminist critique of globalization narratives, note their similarity to rape narratives: both present a masculinized entity (the rapist, or global capitalism) as always already in a position of dominance, and a feminized entity (the rape victim, or the local) in a position of weakness.[8] This is more than a metaphorical parallel: as narratives about relationality and transfer, stories of sexuality are always also stories of globalization and vice versa.

Like Gibson-Graham, who hopes that "a queer perspective can help to unsettle the consonances and coherences of the narrative of global commodification,"[9] in this essay I present globalization "losing its erection" and susceptible to transformation. In queering globalization in this manner, we do not lose sight of the immense suffering and injustice it causes. Instead, we highlight that this suffering and injustice is caused not by a singular globalization but by a complex network of interlocking economic, political, and social forces, forces that are not always in agreement and not always in absolute dominance. In terms of the dubbing metaphor, we might say that the voice of globalization is powerful, but that voice does not "move" across the globe, it is dialogically reconstituted. It is in a constant state of dubbing.

As a result, the very notion of cross-cultural research must be rethought when the cultures in question have been "crossing" in advance of the ethnographic encounter.

A third issue at stake is that of authenticity. Most analyses of queer sexualities in Asia fall into one of two reductionisms: either queer Asians are seen as autochthonous bearers of "traditional" same-sex and transgendered identities masked by Western terms, or they are traitors to tradition, duped by the West and victims of global gay imperialism. Such a stark binarism harks back to the larger concerns with "derivative discourse" that appear in many discussions of postcoloniality and bespeaks the same liberal framework underlying assumptions about agency and globalization noted earlier.[10] It provides little help in understanding the richly textured relationships of affinity and opposition that characterize the bonds between queer Asians and mass media. In particular, what makes these relationships between sexuality and mass media theoretically compelling is not that the mass media in question are new (e.g., cell phones and the Internet versus print media), but the complex interface between sexuality and mass media on the one hand, and representation, reconfiguration, and authenticity on the other.

A theory of dubbing culture contributes toward a more grounded understanding of the imbrication of queer Asian subject-positions with mass media. It reframes these issues through a lens of translation, asking how the unintended reconfiguration of mass-mediated messages can result in subject-positions experienced as authentic even as they link with "distant" messages. For this reason, the social practice of dubbing is the key word of this essay. (Dubbing here means taking a "foreign" film or television show and adding a new spoken soundtrack, such as dubbing a French movie into English.)

As in any dub, I weave two things into one, bringing together *gay* and *lesbi* subject-positions with a debate over dubbing in Indonesia. I hope to provide a sense of my own serendipitous realization that these two issues are interlinked—and that dubbing provides a crucial clue to understanding the lifeworlds of *gay* and *lesbi* Indonesians. In the first section below, I examine the important role of globalizing mass media in their lives, and in the second juxtapose this with the 1996–1998 dubbing controversy. In the final section, I dub the earlier sections to arrive at a theory of dubbing culture, a theory that I hope will contribute toward understanding not only *lesbi* and *gay* subject-positions, but mass-mediated subject-positions elsewhere in Asia and beyond. The contribution of a theory of dubbing culture lies in better conceptualizing the mobility of cultural forms themselves—the ways in which the "movement" of culture takes place, is always already caught up in cultural logics concerning what counts as movement and an object for movement.[11]

The "Problem" of Gay and Lesbi Subjectivities

The most enduring Western stereotype regarding homosexuality and transgenderism in Indonesia (and Southeast Asia more generally) is that these regions are "tolerant." It is true that there have been—and in some cases, still are—socially recognized roles for male-to-female transgenders, as well as widespread acceptance of secretive homosexual behavior, but transgenderism and homosexuality are hardly valorized in contemporary Indonesian society. Although homosexuality and transgenderism usually escape official comment, religious and state authorities, if asked, swiftly condemn both as sinful and incompatible with "Indonesian tradition." One goal of this essay is to speak to the realities of homosexual and transgendered life without resorting to romanticized views of Indonesian tradition.

"Indonesian tradition" is, in any case, a problematic concept, as Indonesia is primarily the former territorial boundary of the Netherlands East Indies, a Dutch colony from the 1500s until the Second World War (some parts of which did not fall under actual Dutch control until a few decades before the war). Indonesia is in fact made up of approximately 670 ethnological groups (the Javanese, the Balinese, the Bugis, etc.), many of whom had little in common before the colonial encounter and then the beginnings of the nationalist movement in the early twentieth century. However, in the almost sixty years since Indonesia's independence, a national culture has taken root with remarkable swiftness.

Readers unfamiliar with Indonesianist anthropology may be surprised to learn that although scholars of nationalism have convincingly shown how Indonesia is a signal case of an "imagined community,"[12] this national culture is rarely studied ethnographically; Indonesianist anthropology has tended to study what I term "ethnolocal" cultural formations. In Indonesia's current period of crisis, marked by new rhetorics of "ethnic absolutism,"[13] there is an urgent need to understand how national culture is for many Indonesians not a state imposition but intimately authentic and meaningful.

It is with the goal of better understanding this national culture that since 1992 I have conducted fieldwork on three islands: Java, Bali, and Sulawesi. In accordance with my emphasis on translocal culture, I do not see this work as comparative; while interested in similarities and differences among my sites, I view them primarily as elements of one site—Indonesia—in much the same way that an ethnographer studying a single city might portray three different neighborhoods as elements of that one city. I also focus not on ethnolocalized homosexual and transgender professional subject-positions (i.e., so-called traditional or ritual homosexualities and transgenderisms), but on three sexual subject-positions that are national in scope: *gay, lesbi,* and *waria.* As I primarily address *gay* and *lesbi* in this essay, I first briefly situate *waria* in their cultural context.[14]

National Transvestites

The persons are better known to the Indonesian public with the rather derogatory terms *banci* or *béncong,* but themselves tend to prefer *waria,* an amalgam of *wanita* (female) and *pria* (male) coined in the early 1970s.[15] A succinct definition of *waria* is male-to-female transvestites. I use "transvestite" rather than "transgender" because most *waria* see themselves not as becoming female, but as men who have the souls of women from birth, dress as women much of the time, and have sex with men.

In contemporary Indonesia *waria* are truly national (they can be from any ethnicity or religion) and are much more visible than *gay* or *lesbi* Indonesians. Many dress as women twenty-four hours a day, but even those who do not are readily identifiable by most Indonesians due to their effeminate appearance (tweezered eyebrows, long hair, effeminate movements and speech). In any Indonesian city and even in rural areas, you can encounter *waria* on the street or in a park looking for sex work clients. Above all, you will find *waria* working at salons, and you would certainly hope to have a *waria* do the makeup and hairstyling for your daughter on her wedding day. It is this transformative power of *waria* to change the public appearance of others (in line with their ability to change their own public appearance) that is their *ilmu,* their great skill, in Indonesian society, and *waria* cite this as the reason they should be valued (not because of a liberal notion of human rights that argues for validation based on identity alone). *Waria* are part of the recognized social mosaic.

The public position of *waria* extends to mass media and other public fora. You can see them in television comedy shows and Bayer aspirin commercials and performing at amusement parks and Independence Day celebrations. In all of these contexts *waria* are construed as artful and skilled in beauty *and* as silly, worthy targets of disdain. In other words, although *waria* are acknowledged elements of contemporary Indonesian society, they are hardly celebrated. The Western liberal assumption that to be public and visible implies acceptance does not hold here. The parents of *waria* usually accept this fact and release the *waria* from the imperative to marry; some, though, are thrown out of the family forever. *Waria* have been held under water by angry fathers until they have almost drowned, have been tormented, stabbed, and killed by street youths, and have died of AIDS on an island far from home, rejected by their own family. This is not always the case: many *waria* have carefree lives of steady income and relative social acceptance, and in many respects the condition of *waria* is better than that of transgenders, lesbians, or gay men in much of the West. All in all, however, it seems difficult to hold up Indonesia as a transgendered nirvana.

Gay and Lesbi Indonesia

Most Indonesians still confuse *gay* and *waria*, supposing that the former is an English rendition of the latter. *Gay* men and *waria* do not share this confusion, but they do see each other as sharing something: both inhabit alternative masculinities and both are sexually attracted to men.[16] Few *gay* men, however, speak of themselves as having a woman's soul; not all are effeminate, and none dress like women all of the time (though many *gay* men *dédong* or "do drag" for entertainment purposes). Like *waria,* many *gay* men work in salons, but because they are poorly visible to Indonesian society they can also be found in other professions, from the highest levels of government to street sweepers. Indeed, if one common Western misconception about Indonesia (and Asia more generally) is that transgenders are valued members of society, another misconception is that gay men and lesbian women are products of the executive, jet-setting classes. Here the cultural effects of globalization are thought to correlate with class in a linear fashion: the richer you are, the more you are effected by globalization, and

Mobile Cultures

thus the less authentic you are. The proletarian becomes the new indigene. However, as any Nike factory worker in Indonesia could tell you, class is poorly correlated with the degree to which someone is impacted by globalizing forces. And indeed, *gay* men in Indonesia are primarily lower class (90 percent of my informants make less than $60 a month), do not speak English, have never traveled outside Indonesia, and have never met a Westerner before myself, gay or otherwise.

A significant element of *lesbi* subject-positions is the division between persons who see themselves as women who desire sex with other women and typically appear normatively feminine (usually known as *lesbi* or *lines,* which is a *gay* language transformation of *lesbi*), and female-bodied persons who desire sex with women but who can see themselves either as masculine women or as female-to-male transgenders (usually known as *tomboi* or *hunter*).[17] *Tomboi* tend to dress as men twenty-four hours a day; unless they speak, many are mistaken for men on the street.[18] *Tomboi* and *waria* sometimes say that they are "closer" to each other than either are to *gay* men or *lesbi* women, because *tomboi* and *waria* both see themselves as having the soul of one gender but the body of another, and because both are usually visibly nonnormative in gender presentation.

Although the dynamics of *tomboi* and *lesbi* subjectivities might appear to conform to "butch-femme" role playing as understood (and often criticized) in the West, this is not a simple importation. At issue is that the concepts *lesbi* and *gay* have translocated to Indonesia in a context where there is no socially salient female-to-male equivalent to the *waria* subject-position. *Gay,* understood as male homosexuality, is thus clearly differentiated from the preexisting *waria* subject-position (and where *gay* men and *waria* are rarely sexual partners); the categories of female homosexuality and female-to-male transgenderism are more imbricated, and *lesbi* and *tomboi* are ideal sexual partners.[19]

The social bonds among *lesbi* women, *tomboi, waria,* and *gay* men are important to my fieldwork and this analysis. It is true that *gay* men often find themselves spending more social time with *waria* than with *lesbi* women, because *gay* men and *waria* both see themselves as alternative masculinities. Similarly, *tomboi* and *lesbi* women interact more with each other than with *gay* men or *waria,* because they see themselves not only as alternative femininities but as ideal sexual partners. However, there is also much interaction between *gay* men and *lesbi* women. In all three of my field sites, *tomboi, gay* men, *waria,* and *lesbi* women work sometimes side by side in salons and activist organizations or spend time together in everyday interaction.

When I began my fieldwork, I worried that it would be difficult to "access" lesbians. I had been told that it was not possible to study gay men and lesbian women in the same project. As my work progressed, however, I realized that the politics of gender play differently in Indonesia than in the United States. The issue was not one of access as Westerners might think of that term, but simply that the social spaces in which *tomboi* and *lesbi* women move overlap only partially with those of *gay* men and *waria.* Once I was able to familiarize myself with those spaces, I was not only able to interview a large number of *lesbi* women and *tomboi,* but was able to engage in activism with them.

Gay and Lesbi Subjectivities and Mass Media

How do Indonesians come to the idea that they could be *lesbi* or *gay*? This "problem" seems salient to Western observers because, unlike *waria, gay* and *lesbi* are not concepts with significant historical depth; they appear to have first arisen in the 1970s. Additionally, *gay* and *lesbi* remain obscure to most Indonesians. Whether tolerated or condemned, *waria* are well-known members of society. The concepts *gay* and *lesbi,* however, are at present not passed down in either a positive or negative light; they remain unknown, or regarded as English equivalents of *waria.* Even *gay* men and *lesbi* women who went to elementary school in the late 1980s or early 1990s heard in the schoolyard primarily terms for *waria* such as *banci,* but rarely *gay* or *lesbi.* How do these subjectivities take hold in the hearts of so many Indonesians?

There is no single answer. A few Indonesians say that they first learned of the possibility of *gay* and *lesbi* subject-positions when told about the terms by a friend. A few *gay* men say that they first knew of *gay* after wandering into a public area frequented by *gay* men, and a few *gay* men and *lesbi* women say that they became aware of the concepts after being seduced. However, only a small fraction of Indonesians learn of *gay* or *lesbi* subject-positions through all these routes to erotic knowledge combined.

Another possibility is that since the early 1980s, *gay* men and *lesbi* women have been informally publishing small magazines. These zines might play a "conduit" role, importing and transmitting Western concepts of sexuality. However, not a single informant ever cited these zines as the means by which they came to know of *lesbi* or *gay* subject-positions. The primary reason for this is that Indonesians seem to access these zines only after first thinking of themselves as *lesbi* or *gay*.[20] It is also clear that *gay* and *lesbi* subject-positions existed for at least ten years prior to the appearance of the first zine (in 1982). Although impacting the subjectivities of those who read them, these zines do not play a formative role. This may not remain the case in the future, particularly as greater press freedoms and increasing Internet access make these zines more accessible, yet neither they nor the other modes mentioned above explain how Indonesians have come to occupy the subject-positions *lesbi* and *gay*.

The Answer: Mass Media

Recall that *gay* and *lesbi* Indonesians are "problematic" because they are poorly visible to contemporary Indonesian society and absent from all "traditions." How do so many Indonesians come to occupy subject-positions that are not despised so much as ignored?

The answer: nearly 95 percent of my *gay* and *lesbi* informants cite regular mass media as the means by which they first knew they could understand themselves through the concepts *lesbi* or *gay*. This is true whether the persons in question are from Java, Bali, Sulawesi, or other islands; whether they are Muslim, Christian, Hindu, or Buddhist; whether they are wealthy, middle class, or impoverished; whether they live in cities or rural areas; and whether they were born in the 1950s, 1960s, 1970s, or 1980s. Rarely is a cultural variable distributed so widely across such a diverse population. This finding is all the more notable when we compare the life narratives of *lesbi* women and *gay* men with *waria*. I have *never* heard *waria* cite mass media as the means by which they first saw themselves as *waria; waria* learn of the *waria* subject-position from their social environs—schoolkids on the playground, a cousin or neighbor—but not from mass media. Darta's story rehearses a common story of discovery that most *gay* and *lesbi* Indonesians see as a pivotal moment in their life, one they recall without hesitation, as in the case of the following Javanese Christian man in Surabaya:

> In elementary school the only word was *banci* [*waria*]. For instance, a boy who walked or acted like a girl would get teased with the word *banci*. So I didn't know about the word *gay* until junior high. I heard it from books, magazines, television. And I wanted to know! I looked for information; if I

saw that a magazine had an article about *homo*s I'd be sure to read it. I knew then that a *homo* was a man who liked men. But I didn't know that *homo* meant *gay* at that time. So I tried to find out from books and things like that. I learned all of that stuff from the mass media. . . . So having someone come and tell me "It's like this," that never happened. I learned it all through magazines and newspapers. . . . And when I read those things, I knew that I was *gay*.

For this man, *homo* is an impersonalized descriptive category, whereas *gay* is a framework for understanding the self's past motivations, immediate desires, and visions of an unfolding future. Abdul, a Muslim man who grew up in a small town in Sulawesi, tells the following story:

TB: When you were in your teenage years, did you already know the term *gay*?

A: In my environment at that time, most people didn't yet know. But because I read a lot, read a lot of news, I already knew. I already knew that I was *gay*. Through reading I knew about the *gay* world. . . .

TB: What kinds of magazines?

A: Gossip magazines, you know, they always talk about such-and-such a star and the rumors that the person is *gay*. So that broadened my concepts [*wawasan*], made me realize "Oh, there are others like me."

Because *lesbi* and *gay* representations are comingled in these mass media, most *lesbi* women, like the following Balinese woman, also trace their subjectivities to encounters with mass media: "I didn't use the word *lesbi* because I didn't even know the term [when I was young]. I didn't hear about the word *lesbi* until about 1990, when I read it in a magazine. And right away, when I read about *lesbi* and what that meant, I thought to myself, 'That's me!'"

For these Indonesians, the prerevelatory period of sexual subjectivity is experienced locally; the local is the space of the not-*lesbi* or not-*gay*. The moment when "I knew that was me" has a spatial dimension: they enter not only a sexual self-narrative but a metapragmatics of scale for that narrative. The deictic "I knew *that* was me" is profoundly translocal, placing the self in a dialogic relationship with a distant but familiar Other.

The role of mass media is also striking because to this day there is little coverage of Indonesian *gay* men or *lesbi* women. Whereas *waria* see other (Indonesian) *waria* in the mass media, what *gay* and *lesbi* Indonesians usually see is gay and lesbian Westerners. And what they see is not a one-hour special on "Homosexuality in the West." *Gay* and *lesbi* Indonesians speak of a single fifteen-second coverage of Rock Hudson's AIDS diagnosis on one night in the 1980s, an editorial about Al Pacino's role in the movie *Cruising*, a gossip column about Elton John or Melissa Etheridge, or a short review of *The Wedding Banquet* or *My Best Friend's Wedding* (two films that, like *Cruising*, thematize homosexuality).

Some *lesbi* women and *gay* men actually see such films, either because the films make it onto Indonesian screens or, increasingly, are available on video, but over and over again these Indonesians stress the role of print media, particularly newspapers and women's magazines like *Kartini* and *Femina*. In most cases the references to homosexuality are negative: Indonesian psychologists presenting homosexuality as a pathology or disapproving gossip columns. Sporadic coverage of same-sex scandals and arrests dates back to the early twentieth century. The earliest extensive study of contemporary Indonesian homosexuality to my knowledge, sociologist Amen Budiman's 1979 book *Lelaki Perindu Lelaki* (Men who yearn for men), notes:

> In this decade [the 1970s] homosexuality has increasingly become an interesting issue for many segments of Indonesian society. Newspapers, both those published in the capital and in other areas, often present articles and news about homosexuality. In fact, *Berita Buana Minggu* in Jakarta has a special column, "Consultation with a Psychiatrist," which often answers the complaints of those who are homosexual and want to change their sexual orientation. It's the same way with pop magazines, which with increasing diligence produce articles about homosexuality, sometimes even filled with personal stories from homosexual people, complete with their photographs.

Budiman later adds, "It is very interesting to note that homosexuals who originate in the lower classes often try to change their behavior by seeking advice from psychiatric or health columnists in our newspapers and magazines."[21] However, both back in the 1970s and among my present-day informants (a few of whom first became *gay* or *lesbi* in the 1970s or earlier), many *lesbi* and *gay* Indonesians were not changing behavior, but coming to occupy what they saw as legitimate and even in some cases healthy sexualities through these mass media. From their beginnings to the present, these media have "exposed" not a fully articulated discourse of homosexuality, but a series of incomplete and contradictory references, in translation, sometimes openly denigrating and hostile. It is not transmission of identity so much as a fractured set of cultural logics reconfigured within Indonesia. Yet, from "translations" of this reportage (so intermittent that Darta could think he was *lesbi* for years) come subjectivities by which myriad Indonesians live out their lives. There also comes an imagined *gay* and *lesbi* community. As in the case of *waria,* this community is translocal, but unlike *waria,* it does not end at the national border. Although *gay* and *lesbi* individuals do think of themselves as *Indonesians*—to the point that they use nationalist metaphors of the "archipelago concept" (*wawasan nusantara*) to conceptualize their community—they also regard themselves as one "island" in a *global* archipelago of gay and lesbian persons, a constellation including places like Australia and Europe as well as Malaysia and Thailand. They do not regard themselves as a "rerun" of the West; they view themselves as different, but this difference is not seen to create a chasm of incommensurability.[22]

Gay and *lesbi* subject-positions thus lead us to a specific sociological problem. Indonesians learn of the possibility of *gay* or *lesbi* subjectivities through the intermittent reception of messages from mass media. These messages do not intend to convey the possibility of a kind of selfhood. They are often denigrating and dismissive, but above all they are *fragmentary.* In the 1980s an Indonesian might encounter such reportage a few times a year at most if an avid reader; in the 1990s, it became more frequent, but still was quite minimal given the universe of topics appearing in the mass media. The question, then, is how modes of subjectivization become established when the social field in which they arise establishes them neither as discourses nor reverse discourses. Indonesian mass media certainly do not intend to set forth the possibility of Indonesian *gay* and *lesbi* subject-positions, nor do the imported programs they rebroadcast; in fact, they rarely take a negative stance on Indonesian *gay* and *lesbi* subject-positions either. These subject-positions do not appear on the radar screen of these mass media forces as something valorized or condemned; yet it is these forces that, in a very real sense, make *gay* and *lesbi* subjectivities possible.

What is needed is a theoretical framework that can account for a con-

Mobile Cultures

tingent, fractured, intermittent, yet powerfully influential relationship between mass media and subjectivity. Two additional requirements for such a
theory are, first, it must not mistake contingency for the absence of power
but must account for relations of domination; second, it must not render
domination as determination but must account for how *gay* and *lesbi* Indonesians transform their contingent, fractured, intermittent relationship
with mass media.

In the remainder of this essay I set forth a theoretical framework fulfill-
ing these goals. To do so, I first take the reader through a controversy
concerning mass media. It was my encounter with this controversy, one
with no apparent relationship to *gay* and *lesbi* subjectivities, that led, unex-
pectedly, to this framework.

The "Problem" of Dubbing

The relationship between mass media and being Indonesian has a long
history in the archipelago.[23] From the late nineteenth century to the middle
of the twentieth, print media played a central role in the formation of
nationalism among the diverse and far-flung peoples of the Netherlands
East Indies. Print media were also important in the establishment of Indonesian (a dialect of Malay formerly used as a lingua franca of trade) as the
language of this new imagined community, a language that permitted communication among a populace speaking over six hundred languages.[24]

In contrast to some other postcolonial states, such as India,[25] imports
now represent a substantial amount of cinematic and televised fare. Although there is a long tradition of filmmaking in Indonesia dating back to
the early twentieth century and at some points garnering massive nation-
wide audiences, in the late 1990s the Indonesian film industry generally
produced only fifteen to twenty films per year, mostly low-budget erotic
films that went directly to second- or third-run theaters.[26] By the late 1990s
each of Indonesia's five private television stations[27] was importing approximately seven thousand shows per year, many of which originated in the
United States.[28]

It was in the context of this rise in imported television that, in a joint
news conference on April 4, 1996, one year after one of Indonesia's private
television stations went national for the first time, Minister of Information

Harmoko and Minister of Education and Culture Wardiman Joyonegoro announced that television stations would be required to dub (*dubbing, sulih suara*) all foreign shows into the Indonesian language by August 16, in accordance with a soon-to-be-passed broadcasting law, the first set of broadcasting regulations to be issued in eighteen years. This bill, which had been debated in Parliament for several months at that point, was to become one of the most contentious legal documents of the New Order's twilight years (the "New Order" refers to the thirty-year rule of Soeharto, Indonesia's second president, which ended in 1998). The requirement that all programs be dubbed into Indonesian was greeted with little fanfare: as the public relations manager of station TPI noted, many of the programs imported each year by private television stations were already dubbed in response to viewer demand. Acquiescing to the state's long-standing goal of building nationalism through language planning, the public relations manager of station RCTI added that the requirement was "a good policy that will help build Indonesian skills in society."[29]

However, within a month of the announcement, a spokesperson from the House of Representatives suggested, "This problem of dubbing is going to be discussed in more depth."[30] Revealing dissent within the state apparatus, the representative expressed concern that "at present, foreign films on television are not dubbed selectively and show many things that do not fit well with the culture of our people." The influential armed forces faction also weighed in against the measure, but the House forged ahead, incorporating the dubbing requirement in its Draft Broadcast Law of December 6, 1996.

What made the broadcasting bill such a topic of discussion was the way it was debated and revised, extraordinary even for the typically arcane machinations of the New Order bureaucracy. A first draft of the bill was completed by a legislative committee early in 1996 and sent to Parliament for approval. As usual in the New Order, the bill had been essentially crafted by the president and even bore his initials.[31] In December 1996 Parliament duly rubber-stamped the bill, returning it to Soeharto for his signature. However, after seven months Soeharto dropped a bombshell on July 11, 1997: in an official letter he refused to sign the Draft Broadcast Law and returned it to Parliament for revision, claiming that "several articles will be too difficult to implement from a technical standpoint."[32] This unconstitutional act was *the first time in national history* that a president refused to sign a draft law already passed by the House, a refusal made all the more perplexing by his approval of the original bill.[33] House debate on the president's proposed revisions began on September 18, 1997, and was marked by unusual (for the Soeharto era) interruptions from Parliament members and heated argument over executive-legislative relations.

In the wake of the president's refusal, government sources gave conflicting accounts of the issues at stake. However, one issue stood out above the others for its cultural, rather than directly economic, emphasis: the edict on dubbing. This issue was notable for the total reversal that occurred during parliamentary revisions. When the dust cleared in December 1997, Article 25 of the Draft Law, concerning dubbing, had been changed to its opposite: all dubbing of foreign television shows into Indonesian was now forbidden; shows must now keep the original language, usually English, and only use Indonesian subtitles. Why? As one apologist later explained: "Dubbing can create gaps in family communication. It can ruin the self-image of family members as a result of adopting foreign values that are 'Indonesianized' [diindonesiakan]. . . . This can cause feelings of becoming 'another person' to arise in family members, who are in actuality not foreigners. . . . whenever Indonesians view television, films, or other broadcasts where the original language has been changed into our national language, *those Indonesians will think that the performances in those media constitute a part of themselves. As if the culture behind those performances is also the culture of our people.*"[34]

In the end, the final version of the bill indeed forbids dubbing most foreign programs into the Indonesian language. What is of interest, however, is the debate itself. Why, at this prescient moment in 1997, as if foreshadowing the collapse of the New Order regime the following year, did translation become a focal point of political and cultural anxiety? What made the ability of Sharon Stone or Jim Carrey to "speak Indonesian" no longer a welcome opportunity to foster linguistic competency but a sinister force threatening the good citizen's ability to differentiate self from Other?[35] Why would dubbing foreign mass media into Indonesian threaten a national culture so dependent on mass media? Why, even with widespread discontent in many parts of the archipelago, was the state's fear suddenly recentered not on religious, regional, or ethnic affiliation overwhelming national loyalty, but on transnational affiliation superseding nationalism and rendering it secondary?

We now have two problems centering on mass media: How do Indonesians come to see themselves as *gay* or *lesbi* through the fragmentary reception of mass-mediated messages? and Why would the question of dubbing foreign television shows into the Indonesian language provoke a constitutional crisis? Both of these problems raise issues of translation and authenticity in an already globalized, mass-mediated world. I suggest that we might address the first problem through the second. In effect, we can "dub" these two sets of social facts together, and in doing so discover striking convergences and unexpected resonances.[36]

It was long after becoming aware of the link between mass media and *gay/lesbi* subjectivities that I learned of the dubbing controversy. I had been struggling with the question of *gay/lesbi* subjectivities for some time without a clear conclusion, particularly concerning questions of agency. Were *gay* and *lesbi* Indonesians puppets of the West? Were they severed from their traditions once they occupied the subject-positions *lesbi* or *gay*? After all, as I discuss elsewhere, *gay* and *lesbi* Indonesians tend to view themselves in terms of a consumerist life narrative where selfhood is an ongoing project developed through treating one's life as a kind of career.[37] Alternatively, were these Indonesians "queering" global capitalism, subverting its heteronormativity and building a worldwide movement dedicated to human rights? Were they deploying the terms *lesbi* and *gay* tactically, as a veneer over a deeper indigeneity?

A notion of dubbing culture allowed me to move beyond this impasse of "puppets of globalization" versus "veneer over tradition." Through individual encounters with mass media—such as reading one's mother's magazines or an advice column in the local newspaper, or viewing television coverage of a gay pride march in Australia—Indonesians construct subjectivities and communities. "Construct" is the wrong word; it connotes a self who plans and consciously shapes something.[38] Better to say that these Indonesians "come to" *lesbi* and *gay* subjectivity through these entanglements with mass media; their constructive agency is itself constructed through the encounter.

This is not a solely individual process; whereas originary encounters with magazines or newspapers are typically solitary, as soon as the person begins to interact with other *lesbi* or *gay* Indonesians these mass-mediated

Mobile Cultures

understandings of sexuality are reworked in a community setting. They are reworked in ways that could not be predicted from the mass media themselves; romance, for instance, is a crucial element of *lesbi* and *gay* subjectivities but rarely appears in media treatments of homosexuality. Nor could the reworkings be predicted from the norms of Indonesian society, not only because they lead to homosexual subjectivities, but because through this mass media reportage *lesbi* women and *gay* men become linked conceptually and in everyday existence, despite the fact that gender segregation ranges from moderate to pronounced in most of Indonesia. In other words, the idea shared by most *lesbi* women and *gay* men that they are elements of a cogendered community seems rooted in parallel encounters with mass media.

A set of fragmented cultural elements from mass media is transformed in unexpected ways in the Indonesian context, transforming that "context" itself in the process. In other words, *lesbi* and *gay* Indonesians "dub" ostensibly Western sexual subjectivities. Like a dub, the fusion remains a juxtaposition; the seams show. "Speech" and "gesture" never perfectly match; being *lesbi* or *gay* and being Indonesian never perfectly match. For *lesbi* and *gay* Indonesians, as in dubbing more generally, this tension is irresolvable; there is no "real" version underneath, where everything fits. You can close your eyes and hear perfect speech, or mute the sound and see perfect gesture, but no original unites the two in the dubbed production. However, this may not present the self with an unlivable contradiction, because in dubbing one is invested not in the originary, but in the awkward fusion. Disjuncture is at the heart of the dub; there is no prior state of pure synchrony and no simple "conversion" to another way of being. Dubbed culture is a product of localization, and the "message" and sense of "locality" where that message appears are formed at a point that can hardly be called the point of "reception."[39]

It is this dimension of dubbing that transcends the apparent dilemma of "puppets of globalization" versus "veneer over tradition." The idea of dubbing culture indicates that the root of the problem is the notion of authenticity itself, the colonialist depth ontology that layers cultural elements on top of each other and tautologically assigns causal and ontological priority to those already deemed foundational—valorizing the "civilized" colonizer over the "traditional" colonized. In line with the observation that postcolonial nationalisms usually invert, rather than reject entirely, colonial categories of thought,[40] the Indonesian state simply flips the colonial binary, placing tradition over modernity as the ultimate justification for the nation. To the obvious problem of justifying a recently formed nation in terms of tradition, the Indonesian state (like all national states) has worked ever since to inculcate a sense of national culture (*kebudayaan nasional*). This is built on the pillar of the Indonesian language and propagated via mass media. Through mass media, citizens are to come to recognize themselves as authentic Indonesians, carriers of an oxymoronic "national tradition" that will guide the body politic through the travails of modernity. By speaking in one voice—in Indonesian—a hierarchy of tradition over modernity can be sustained and reconciled with statehood.

Dubbing threatens this hierarchy: it is lateral, rhizomatic,[41] "a multiplicity that cannot be understood in terms of the traditional problems . . . of origins and genesis, or of deep structures."[42] The authoritative voice is at odds with the visual presentation. Dubbing sets two elements side by side, blurred yet distinct. The "original" television show may preexist its Indonesian dub temporally, but to the interpreting audience neither voice nor image is prior. They happen together; neither dominates. Agamben, citing Benjamin's concern with the relationship between quotation and the new "transmissibility of culture" made possible by mass media, notes that quotation "alienat[es] by force a fragment of the past . . . mak[ing] it lose its authentic power."[43] But dubbing (in a literal sense as well as the metaphorical sense I develop here) is more than just quotation; it adds a step, first alienating something and then translating it into a new context. The power of the dub comes not by erasing authenticity, but by inaugurating new authenticities not dependent on tradition. It disrupts the apparent seamlessness of the predubbed "original," showing that it too is a dub, that its "traditions" are the product of social contexts with their own assumptions and inequalities.

The Indonesian authorities were keenly aware of these disruptive implications during the dubbing controversy. For decades, Indonesian had been the vehicle allowing Indonesians to speak with one voice. But now the possibility that Sharon Stone could "speak Indonesian" meant that this vehicle was spinning beyond state control—into the control of globalizing forces, but also into an interzone between languages and cultures, a zone with no controlling authority. The sudden shift during the dubbing controversy—from an insistence that *all* foreign television programs be dubbed into the Indonesian language to an insistence that *none* of them could be—reveals a tectonic shift in the position of mass media in Indonesian society. For the first time, fear of this juxtaposition, of Westerners "speaking" the national tongue, tipped the scales against a historically privileged concern with propagating Indonesian as national unifier. Now the ability of dubbing (and of the Indonesian language itself) to explode the national imagined community—to show that one can be Indonesian *and* translate ideas from outside—presented a danger greater than the potential benefit of drawing more sharply the nation's archipelagic edges.

Dubbing culture, then, is about a new kind of cultural translation of the late twentieth and early twenty-first centuries. It questions the relationship between translation and belonging, asserting that the binarisms of import-export and authentic-inauthentic are insufficient to explain how globalizing mass media play a role in constituting subject-positions in Asia but do not determine them outright. More broadly, dubbing culture as a metaphor speaks to the nonteleological, transformative dimensions of globalizing processes. In this metaphorical sense we might say that *lesbi* and *gay* Indonesians dub Western sexual subject-positions: they "overwrite" the deterministic "voice of the West," yet they cannot compose any script they please; their bricolage remains shaped by a discourse originating in the West and filtered through a nationalistic lens. This process of dubbing allows *lesbi* and *gay* individuals to see themselves as part of a global community, but also authentically Indonesian. Unlike *waria*, they never ask Are there people like me outside Indonesia? because it is already obvious—"built into" the dubbed subjectivities—that there are such people. It is by imagining themselves as one national element in a global patchwork of lesbian and gay national subjectivities, not through tradition, that they see *lesbi* and *gay* as *transethnic*—just as the Indonesian nation presents itself as one of a global community of nations.

The notion of dubbing culture is useful for questioning the ability of globalizing mass media to project uniform "ideologies." Although it is true that contemporary mass media have enormous power, it is crucial to emphasize that this power is not absolute; it can lead to unexpected results, like *lesbi* and *gay* subject-positions themselves. The dubbed representation is difficult to interpret as an ideology. In the current climate of interethnic conflict in Indonesia, it bears reflection that *lesbi* and *gay* subjectivities are the New Order's greatest success story, the clearest example of a truly national community, albeit a success story the state never intended.

This metaphorical use of dubbing culture provides a useful fleshing-out of theories linking ideological apparatuses with Althusser's thesis that "ideology interpellates individuals as subjects." By this Althusser meant that ideology forms the subject-positions by which individuals come to represent their conditions of existence to themselves and to others. He terms this function of ideology "interpellation" or "hailing" and illustrates it in terms of a person on the street responding to the hail "Hey, you there!" When the person turns around to respond to the hail, "he becomes a *subject*. Why? Because he has recognized that the hail was 'really' addressed to him."[44] Many social theorists, particularly those interested in mass media, have found this a useful analytical starting point. The question most commonly posed to this framework by these theorists is just the issue of structure versus agency that I noted earlier: "Although there would be no turning around without first having been hailed, neither would there be a turning around without some readiness to turn. But . . . how and why does the subject turn, anticipating the conferral of identity through the self-ascription of guilt? What kind of relation already binds these two such that the subject knows to turn, knows that something is to be gained from such a turn?"[45] Part and parcel of this dilemma of agency is the question How are we to explain the circumstance when people "recognize" something the ideology does not intend?

One way to address this problem might be through the dubbing culture concept, where what is "recognized" in the hail is itself a product of reception, translation, and interpretation, bundled together. This does not entail compliance with state ideology (a necessary caveat because *lesbi* and *gay* Indonesians are not hailed as such by the state). Yet neither does it imply a freewheeling, presocial, liberal self able to assemble any old identity from elements presented by mass media, independent of social context.

Gay and *lesbi* Indonesians often playfully employ the notion of authenticity (*asli*), sometimes even describing themselves as *asli gay*. In doing so, they implicitly challenge the state's monopoly on designating what will count as tradition in Indonesia. This question of authenticity is crucial for mass media studies as well. For Benjamin, the very concept of authenticity is put under erasure by mass media. Because mass media depend on mechanical reproduction (no mass media circulate as a series of hand-crafted

Mobile Cultures

originals) and for Benjamin "the presence of the original is the prerequisite to the concept of authenticity," it follows that "the whole sphere of authenticity is outside technical . . . reproducibility." Benjamin sees the most significant aspect of this reproducibility to be that of movement: "Above all, [technical reproduction] enables the original to meet the beholder halfway . . . the cathedral leaves its locale to be received in the studio of a lover of art; the choral production, performed in an auditorium or in the open air, resounds in the drawing room."[46]

Lesbi and *gay* Indonesians are dubbing culture because they embody subjectivities neither of tradition nor of simple importations from "outside." They are the outside inside, reconfigured. Such Indonesians claim authenticity not in the key of indigeneity but in the key of transformation, much as the Indonesian nation itself is the transformed Netherlands East Indies.

Gay and *lesbi* subjectivities are not moved from one place to another, as Benjamin saw mechanical reproduction, but are the dubbing of cultural logics in new ways. Dubbing culture is thus articulation in both senses of the term:[47] an interaction of elements that remain distinct—like the image of speech and the dubbed voice—and also the "speaking" of a subjectivity. This lets us "queery" globalization without posing an oppositionally authentic "native." After all, *lesbi* and *gay* Indonesians rarely see themselves as "queering" the state-society nexus in an oppositional sense; rather, they see themselves as beating this nexus at its own game, as more national than general society itself.

Dubbing culture also speaks to translation in the age of mechanical production. As Benjamin notes with reference to magazines, "For the first time, captions have become obligatory. And it is clear that they have an altogether different character than the title of a painting."[48] This is because captions are a guide to interpretation, juxtaposed to the work of art yet at a slight remove. They serve as "signposts" that "demand a specific kind of approach." They are a mediation internal to mass media, a translation within.

Dubbing, far more than a subtitle, is a caption fused to the thing being described. It comes from the mouth of imagic characters, yet is never quite in synch. The moving lips never match the speech; the moment of fusion is always deferred as dubbed voice, translation-never-quite-complete, bridging two sets of representations.[49] *Gay* and *lesbi* Indonesians dub culture as they live a subjectivity linked to people and places far away. They are completely Indonesian, but to be "completely Indonesian" requires thinking of one's position in a transnational world.

In speaking of translation, Benjamin wrote: "Unlike a work of literature, translation does not find itself in the center of the language forest but on the outside facing the wooded ridge; it calls into it without entering, aiming at that single spot where the echo is able to give, in its own language, the reverberation of the work in the alien one."[50] *Gay* and *lesbi* Indonesians have made of that echo subject-positions that speak subjectivity and community even under conditions of oppression. They live in the echo, in the mass-mediated margin of incomplete translation, and find there authenticity, meaning, friendship, and love.

In dubbing culture, *lesbi* and *gay* Indonesians show not that "authentic Indonesian tradition" is a lie, but that this authenticity is processual, constructed through active engagement with an unequal world of mass media, nationalism, and the global ecumene. And if tradition and belonging are not given but constructed, they can be contested and transformed. The playing field is certainly not even—*lesbi* and *gay* Indonesians are not about to become fully accepted members of Indonesian society—but it is a playing field nonetheless, and there is space for change. In the interstices of mass media and the contradictions of local experience in a global imaginary, new ways of living, loving, conforming, but also resisting, enter the world.

Notes

Support for research in Indonesia has been provided by the Social Science Research Council, the National Science Foundation, the Department of Social and Cultural Anthropology at Stanford University, the Morrison Institute for Population and Resource Studies, and the Center for the Teaching of Indonesian. Support for the writing of this article was provided by the Luce Foundation and the Department of Anthropology, Research School of Pacific and Asian Studies, Australian National University. Valuable comments and support were provided by Chris Berry, Katherine Gibson, Margaret Jolly, Fran Martin, Bill Maurer, Dede Oetomo, Kathryn Robinson, Louisa Schein, and Audrey Yue.

I follow standard Indonesian orthography except that the front unrounded vowel /é/ (spelled "e" in Indonesian, along with the schwa) is here written "é" for clarity. All informant names are pseudonyms.

Mobile Cultures

1   See David Harvey, *The Condition of Postmodernity: An Inquiry into the Origins of Cultural Change* (Cambridge, England: Basil Blackwell, 1989); Emily Martin, *Flexible Bodies: The Role of Immunity in American Culture from the Days of Polio to the Age of AIDS* (Boston: Beacon Press, 1994); Aihwa Ong, *Flexible Citizenship: The Cultural Logics of Transnationality* (Durham, NC: Duke University Press, 1999).

2   Nikolas Rose, "Identity, Genealogy, History," in *Questions of Cultural Identity*, ed. Stuart Hall and Paul Du Gay (London: Sage Publications, 1996), 129.

3   My thanks to Bill Maurer for drawing the implications of HAM to my attention.

4   Hannah Arendt, *The Origins of Totalitarianism*, 2d ed. (Cleveland, OH: Meridan, 1958), 267–304.

5   See Michel Foucault, *The History of Sexuality*, Vol. 2: *The Use of Pleasure* (New York: Vintage Books, 1985).

6   Ibid., 4–5.

7   This is due to the linkage between *identitas* and state surveillance, not just the fact that it is a loanword. Loanwords can easily become experience-near concepts in Indonesia, as borne out not only by *lesbi* and *gay*, but by words such as *Muslim, Kristen,* and even *Indonesia* (coined by a European in the nineteenth century).

8   J. K. Gibson-Graham, *The End of Capitalism (as We Knew It): A Feminist Critique of Political Economy* (Cambridge, MA: Blackwell, 1996).

9   Ibid., 144.

10 Partha Chatterjee, *Nationalist Thought and the Colonial World: A Derivative Discourse?* (Minneapolis: University of Minnesota Press, 1986).

11 Bill Maurer, "A Fish Story: Rethinking Globalization on Virgin Gorda," *American Ethnologist* 27, no. 3 (2000): 670–701.

12 See Benedict Anderson, *Imagined Communities: Reflections on the Origins and Spread of Nationalism* (London: Verso, 1983).

13 Paul Gilroy, "Nationalism, History, and Ethnic Absolutism," in *Small Acts: Thoughts on the Politics of Black Cultures* (London: Serpent's Tail, 1993), 63–74.

14 For a more detailed analysis of *waria,* see Tom Boellstorff, *The Gay Archipelago: Sexuality, Nation, and Globalization in Indonesia,* unpublished manuscript, chap. 2.

15 *Bencong* is a gay language grammatical transformation of *banci* (see Tom Boellstorff, " 'Authentic, of Course!' *Gay* Indonesians, Language Ideology, and the Metastasis of Hegemony," unpublished manuscript). *Waria* are a rough analog to nationally distributed male-to-female transgendered subject-positions elsewhere in Southeast Asia, such as *kathoey* in Thailand, *bakla* in the Philippines, and *pondan* in Malaysia.

16 By *gay* men and *lesbi* women, I mean Indonesians who refer to themselves as *gay* or *lesbi,* in some contexts of their lives at least.

17   *Tomboi* are also sometimes known as *cowok* (male) in parts of Sumatra, and *sentul* in parts of Java. In parts of Jakarta and north Bali, the *lesbi-tomboi* division is less salient. See Boellstorff, "The Gay Archipelago: Sexuality, Nation, and Globalization in Indonesia." Book manuscript, n.d., for an extensive discussion of *lesbi* women and *tomboi* (*hunter*). See also Evelyn Blackwood, "*Tombois* in West Sumatra: Constructing Masculinity and Erotic Desire," in *Female Desires: Same-Sex Relations and Transgender Practices across Cultures,* ed. Evelyn Blackwood and Saskia E. Wieringa (New York: Columbia University Press, 1999), 181–205; B. J. D. Gayatri, "Indonesian Lesbians Writing Their Own Script: Issues of Feminism and Sexuality," in *From Amazon to Zami: Towards a Global Lesbian Feminism,* ed. Monika Reinfelder (London: Cassell, 1996), 86–97; Alison Murray, "Let Them Take Ecstasy: Class and Jakarta Lesbians," in Blackwood and Wieringa, 139–56; and Saskia E. Wieringa, "Desiring Bodies or Defiant Cultures: Butch-Femme Lesbians in Jakarta and Lima," in Blackwood and Wieringa, 206–29.

18   However, *tomboi* is not universally embodied in a masculine fashion; in southern Sulawesi there are *tomboi* with long hair who wear dresses yet identify as *tomboi.*

19   The use of *tomboi* for butch *lesbi* in Sumatra may lead to confusion, because generally in Indonesia *tomboi* refers to a girl who engages in boy's activities (much like English "tomboy"). For instance, in a television commercial shown nationally in Indonesia in 2000, a mother comments on her favorite brand of laundry detergent as her young daughter of about 8 is shown walking home from school, wearing a school uniform and also a *jilbab* (a veil worn by many Muslim Indonesians that covers the head and hair but not the face). As the little girl runs home from school, getting dirt and later chocolate ice cream on her jilbab, the mother opines, "My girl is a real *tomboi.*" The ambivalence over the term *tomboi* in many regions of Indonesia is also indicated by statements from *lesbi* women in both Bali and Sulawesi that "not all *tomboi* are *lesbi,* and not all *lesbi* are *tomboi.*"

20   Among other factors, this is because these zines have a limited, informal circulation. See Boellstorff, "Zines and Zones of Desire: Mass Mediated Love, National Romance, and Sexual Citizenship in Gay and Lesbian Indonesia." Unpublished manuscript, n.d.

21   Amin Budiman, *Lelaki Perindu Lelaki: Sebuah Tinjauan Sejarah dan Psikologi Tentang Homoseks dan Masyarakat Homoseks di Indonesia* (Men Who Yearn for Men: A Historical and Psychological Overview Concerning Homosexuality and Homosexual Community in Indonesia) (Semarang, Indonesia: Tanjung Sari, 1979), 89–90, 116; my translation.

22   Boellstorff, "The Gay Archipelago: Sexuality, Nation, and Globalization in Indonesia." Book manuscript, n.d.

23 For a more detailed analysis of the dubbing controversy, see Carla Jones, "Watching Women: The Domestic Politics of Middle-class Femininity Formation in Late New Order Indonesia" (Ph.D. diss., University of North Carolina–Chapel Hill, 2001); Jennifer Lindsay, "Speaking the Truth: Speech on Television in Indonesia," in *Media Discourse and Performance in Indonesia and Malaysia,* ed. Ben Arps (Athens: Ohio University Press, forthcoming).

24 See Anderson; H. M. J. Maier, "From Heteroglossia to Polyglossia: The Creation of Malay and Dutch in the Indies," *Indonesia* 56 (1993): 37–65; James T. Siegel, *Fetish, Recognition, Revolution* (Princeton, NJ: Princeton University Press, 1997). For an in-depth analysis of the contemporary relationship between areal languages and Indonesian, see Joseph Errington, *Shifting Languages: Interaction and Identity in Javanese Indonesia* (Cambridge, England: Cambridge University Press, 1998).

25 See Purnima Mankekar, *Screening Culture, Viewing Politics: An Ethnography of Television, Womanhood, and Nation in Postcolonial India* (Durham, NC: Duke University Press, 1999).

26 *Variety* 373, no. 3 (1998): 42. The number of films and television shows produced has varied according to many factors, particularly the general state of the Indonesian economy and political conflict. Detailed historical and contemporary accounts of Indonesian cinema are given in Karl G. Heider, *Indonesian Cinema: National Culture on Screen* (Honolulu: University of Hawai'i Press, 1991), and Krishna Sen, *Indonesian Cinema: Framing the New Order* (London: Zed Press, 1994). Both works were published before the rise of private television in Indonesia. Heider notes that the number of films produced yearly in Indonesia has ranged from zero (in 1946 and 1947, for instance) to over 100 in 1977 and 1989 (Heider, 19). There have been encouraging signs of a renaissance in Indonesian cinema since 1998.

27 RCTI, SCTV, TPI, Anteve, and Indosiar.

28 *Republika* (Jakarta), May 2, 1996. Estimates of the number of shows originating from the United States range from 66 percent (Hermin Indah Wahyuni, *Televisi dan Intervensi Negara: Konteks Politik Kebijakan Publik Industri Penyiaran Televisi* [Television and State Intervention: The Political Context of the Television Broadcasting Industry Public Decrees] [Yogyakarta: Penerbit Media Pressindo, 2000], 116) to 50 percent for the United States and Europe combined; *Variety* 363, no. 11 (1996): 42.

29 *Republika,* May 2, 1996.

30 Aisyah Aminy, quoted in *Suara Pembaruan Daily,* May 3, 1996.

31 *Far Eastern Economic Review* 160, no. 6 (September 4, 1997): 24.

32 Presidential Decree R.09/jo/VII/1997; *Kompas,* July 25, 1997.

33 *Kompas,* July 25, 1997.

34 Novel Ali, "Sulih Suara Dorong Keretakan Komunikasi Keluarga," (Dubbing

Makes a Break in Family Communication) in *Bercinta Dengan Televisi: Ilusi, Impresi, dan Imaji Sebuah Kotak Ajaib* (In Love with Television: Illusions, Impressions, and Images from a Magical Box), ed. Deddy Mulyana and Idi Subandy Ibrahim (Bandung, Indonesia: PT Remaja Rosdakarya, 1997), 341–42; my translation and emphasis. Ilham Bintang and Edward Depari, public relations staff from television station RCTI, claimed that Indonesians would feel they "possessed" the actions of dubbed film stars because the act of dubbing would create a feeling of "closeness," and that it could "facilitate the transfer of foreign values." *Majalah Film* (July 26–August 8, 1997): 24.

35 This phrase draws from a title by Oetomo, "When Sharon Stone Spoke Indonesian." Dede Oetomo, "Ketika Sharon Stone Berbahasa Indonesia," in Mulyana and Ibrahim, 333–37.

36 This seems possible despite the fact that *lesbi* and *gay* Indonesians themselves tended not to take much notice of the dubbing controversy. I have never heard a *gay* or *lesbi* (or *waria*) Indonesian bring up the topic. When I have explicitly asked them about the controversy, *gay* and *lesbi* Indonesians both respond that they prefer subtitles to dubbing for the following reasons: you can learn the original language, "even if it is just 'Buenos Dias' in Spanish," and the dubbing "never follows the actor's lips exactly." A discussion of the more general public reaction to the dubbing controversy is beyond the scope of this essay; see Jones.

37 Tom Boellstorff, "The Perfect Path: Gay Men, Marriage, Indonesia," *GLQ: A Journal of Gay and Lesbian Studies* 5, no. 4 (1999): 474–510.

38 As would "negotiate"; these subjectivities are not negotiated in the sense that Maira speaks of an "identity dub" among South Asian Americans in the New York club scene: Sunaina Maira, "Identity Dub: The Paradoxes of an Indian American Youth Subculture (New York Mix)," *Cultural Anthropology* 14, no. 1 (1999): 29–60. In that case, the institutional context is not mass media but clubbing, and the individuals involved appear to be vastly more wealthy, English-speaking, and mobile than *gay* and *lesbi* Indonesians.

39 Dubbing culture is thus a postcolonial heir to the colonial dynamic between translation and conversion that Rafael explores in the Philippines, "the particular ways by which the boundaries that differentiate the inside from the outside of native societies are historically drawn, expanded, contracted, or obscured." Vicente L. Rafael, *Contracting Colonialism: Translation and Christian Conversion in Tagalog Society under Early Spanish Rule* (Ithaca, NY: Cornell University Press, 1988), 15.

40 Akhil Gupta, *Postcolonial Developments: Agriculture in the Making of Modern India* (Durham, NC: Duke University Press, 1998), 169.

41 Gilles Deleuze and Felix Guattari, *A Thousand Plateaus: Capitalism and*

Schizophrenia, trans. Brian Massumi (Minneapolis: University of Minnesota Press, 1987).

42 Ronald Bogue, *Deleuze and Guattari* (London: Routledge, 1989), 125.

43 Giorgio Agamben, *The Man without Content* (Stanford: Stanford University Press, 1999), 104.

44 Louis Althusser, "Ideology and Ideological State Apparatuses," in *Lenin and Philosophy and Other Essays*, trans. Ben Brewster (London: New Left Books, 1971), 160–62, 163.

45 Judith Butler, *The Psychic Life of Power: Theories in Subjection* (Stanford: Stanford University Press, 1997), 107.

46 Walter Benjamin, "The Task of the Translator," in *Illuminations: Essays and Reflections*, edited and with an introduction by Hannah Arendt; trans. Harry Zohn (New York: Schocken Books, 1955), 220, 220–21.

47 Here I use "articulation" in its English sense. The term originally entered social theory through Marx, but *Gliederung* has only the first of the two meanings noted above. The root word, *Glied*, means "limb" or "joint" but can also mean "penis" (*männliches Glied*). Surely there is great potential in a psychoanalytic treatment that links the moment of speech to erection—the "movement" of the phallus!

48 Benjamin, "Task," 226.

49 As Liu notes in her study of translingual practice in China, in studying how "a word, category, or discourse 'travels from one language to another,' " we must "account for the vehicle of translation" and address "the condition of translation" itself. Lydia H. Liu, *Translingual Practice: Literature, National Culture, and Translated Modernity—China, 1900–1937* (Stanford: Stanford University Press, 1995), 26.

50 Walter Benjamin, "The Work of Art in the Age of Mechanical Reproduction," in *Illuminations*, 76.

MARK MCLELLAND

Japanese Queerscapes:

Global / Local Intersections

on the Internet

Although Japan was slow to reform its telecommunications industry so as to facilitate widespread Internet access, Japanese is now the third most widely used language on the Net after English and Chinese.[1] In 1998 the number of characters used on Japan's 18 million Web sites was already in excess of the total number of printed characters in all Japanese newspapers and magazines published in a year.[2] However, unlike English, Japanese is not an international language[3] and, as Gottlieb points out, the difficulty of learning to read Japanese for non-Japanese means that, "in the case of the Japanese script, geographical location remains very much a predictor of social practice and preference."[4] Despite the potentially "global" reach of the Internet, material written in Japanese is generally accessible only to Japanese people themselves, and so far practically no research exists in English on the ways the Internet is being used in Japan. This essay looks at two "queer" uses of the Internet by two very different Japanese subcultures and suggests ways that the use of the Internet in Japan troubles the rhetoric of globalization that has so far characterized much research on Internet use in Western societies.

I have chosen to focus on two Internet realms, Japanese women's YAOI sites and *nyūhāfu* (newhalf) sites, because of their potential to subvert Western classifications of sexual identity. For instance, YAOI is an acronym made up of the first letters of the phrase *YAma-nashi* (no climax), *Ochi-nashi* (no point), and *Imi-nashi* (no meaning); it describes a genre of Japanese women's fiction/art dedicated to graphic descriptions of "boy love" (sex between boys and young men). There are nearly as many sites featuring boy love created by straight Japanese women as there are sites produced by gay men about homosexuality, and their audience is almost entirely made up of schoolgirls and young women. Nyūhāfu, on the other hand, is a term used to describe transgendered men who work in the sex and entertainment industry. Newhalf are not transsexual, even though some of them do undergo sex-change surgery, but many of them understand themselves to be a distinct "intermediate sex" and seek out and accept their role as entertainers. Newhalf sites are often run by transvestite/transsexual cabarets and bars and serve to promote the bars as well as offer a space for the entertainers working there to discourse about who they are. The political correctness that so often accompanies discussion of homosexuality, transgenderism, and transexualism in English is here largely absent.[5]

These domains are extremely extensive and well organized, with most of the sites being linked together in Web rings that acknowledge a sense of common content and identity. Many site owners are known to each other, and links carry the casual browser from one site to another along pathways established by friendship and common interest. They therefore have some sense of community about them in that they offer a space for like-minded individuals to come together and relax. It is therefore easier to generalize about these sites than about the more diverse sites with "gay" content aimed at gay men.[6] Also, these sites are interesting for being largely "about" sexual interactions between biologically male bodies but not being written or produced by or for gay men. Much queer theory, although gesturing at inclusiveness, tends to become a description of distinctively gay male issues and concerns. In looking at (straight) women's YAOI fiction and the Newhalf Network, the association of male-male sex and gay men can itself be "queer(i)ed." Most important, though, I think that these sites stretch the parameters of the English term queer, which attempts to be as inclusive as possible, and shows its limitations. Queer, it would seem, is not so much about content as about political positioning. It is an attitude;[7] where that attitude is missing, as it is on both the YAOI and newhalf sites, it seems unlikely that any sense of community can be created because neither of these realms sets out to self-consciously "oppose" heteronormative discourse or practices. They offer, not an alternative to the constricting regime of compulsory heterosexuality, but a respite from it. This is the underlying assumption behind Japanese society's often cited "tolerance" of nonnormative sexuality: that it is always circumscribed by heteronormative discourses and institutions.[8]

Japanese women have long been avid consumers of popular entertainers who would seem to disrupt sexual and gender boundaries while at the same time being committed to normative gender performances in their daily lives. In the early modern period, *onnagata* (female-role players) in the kabuki theater were popular role models for many townswomen, who followed the fashions pioneered by men performing as women on stage.[9] Later, in the Taishō period (1912–1927), the *otokoyaku* (male-role performers) in the all-woman Takarazuka Revue became national celebrities to their all-female audience. Both kabuki and the Takarazuka continue to be popular today and gender play on the Japanese screen and stage is still widespread.[10] But perhaps the most intriguing evidence for Japanese women's fascination with transgender/homosexuality occurs in girls' comics (*shōjo manga*) featuring stories of "boy love" (*shōnen'ai*).

Romantic stories about "male love" (*nanshoku*) have a long tradition in Japan, usually focusing on the attraction between a priest or samurai lover (*nenja*) and his acolyte (*chigo*) or page (*wakashū*).[11] However, these early stories were written by men for an anticipated male audience; women *manga* artists and writers did not begin to feature love stories between "beautiful boys" (*bishōnen*) until the early 1970s. These early romances, aptly described as *Bildungsroman* by Midori Matsui, were long and beautifully crafted tales, often set in private boys' schools in the past century.[12] Some manga, however, used figures from Japan's past, such as Yamagishi Ryoko's *Emperor of the Land of the Rising Sun* (1980–1984) about the eighth-century Prince Shōtoku.[13] Schodt describes the manga as "One of the most popular girls' stories of all time [which] depicts a revered founder of Japan as a scheming, cross-dressing homosexual with psychic powers."[14]

In the early 1980s, amateur women manga artists began to create their own boy-love comics and fictions and circulate them at *komiketto* (comic markets) held all over Japan.[15] As well as original works, these women also produced "parodies" (*parodi*) and "fanzines" (*dōjinshi*) based on mainstream boys' manga. Like Western "slash fiction" writers, the authors took heterosexual, heteronormative narratives and "queered" them by imagining sexual relationships between the male characters. These amateur manga tended to focus on the sex and contained less well-crafted stories, leading to the acronym YAOI, as described above. The sexually explicit nature of many of these stories is made clear in another suggested derivation for the acronym YAOI: *YAmete, Oshiri ga Itai!* (Stop, my ass hurts!). Demand for these privately produced texts was such that mainstream publishers began to sign up the most talented of their creators and make them commercially available. The YAOI manga are now big business and hundreds of new titles are released each year. One of the earliest boy-love monthly magazines was *June* (pronounced ju-neh), first published in 1978. In 1995, *June* was still being published, now in a three-hundred-page bimonthly format and with a circulation of between 80,000 and 100,000.[16] *June* was so successful in pioneering a new style in boy-love stories that the term *June-mono* (June things) now refers to boy-love stories in general. Many other boy-love manga followed *June*'s lead, and there are now so many YAOI titles, and such is Japanese women's interest in them, that special editions of general manga and animation magazines often bring out boy-love specials. For instance, the February 1999 issue of *Pafu*, describing itself as a "Boy's Love Special," contained synopses and illustrations from a wide variety of boy-love comics organized according to genre, including sexual love.

As with Western slash fiction writers, the advent of the Internet provided a new forum for women writers and artists to distribute and popularize their work, and the Japanese Net contains several thousand sites created by women celebrating the love between "beautiful boys." The strict division of labor in many Japanese companies between the male career-track regular employees and the noncareer female "office ladies" has resulted in word processing and data input being gendered as women's work; many women thus develop computing skills superior to their male colleagues'. Furthermore, the fact that much routine computing work is contracted out to women in the home is indirectly facilitating women's access to the Internet.[17] Recent statistics indicate that women are the majority of new Internet users and that they access the Net primarily for entertainment and not business.[18] The various structural features of Japan's employment system that disenfranchise women may in fact be supporting their access to the Internet, and, because most women work in noncareer positions, they have greater time to devote to their hobbies than do men.

A search for YAOI on Yahoo Japan (June 2000) produced 557 individual Web pages as well as two links sites: *Creative Girls' Home* and *Yaoi Intelligence Agency*.[19] *Creative Girls'* had 801 sites listed, all connected in some way with "YAOI, boys' love (*bōizurabu*), and *June*," whereas *Yaoi Intelligence* provided a choice of 43 different categories of "*June* and boys' love" pages. These included 543 "original," 400 "same-character," 225 "games" (where players role-play as boys), 140 "parody," 98 "novels," 90 "adult," and 81 "sm." Despite the fact that all the sites on *Creative Girls'* are in Japanese (sites in English and are not allowed to join), T'Mei, the Ringmaster, provides a brief English introduction. She stresses that the illustrations must not be stolen for reproduction on other pages, commenting, "Do not presume that we will never notice your sneaking in and stealing our works, for there are many ways to detect your shameful acts." To stop "foreigners" from accessing and taking images for use on their own sites, a few Japanese sites have introduced password protection. In these instances, the Web page owner simply posts a message on the site's entrance page stating, "In order to stop foreigners entering and stealing our illustrations, we have introduced a password," which is usually followed by an explanation of what the password is. Here the use of the Japanese language itself is a kind of code that is expected to keep foreigners out. There seem to be two reasons behind this precaution: as mentioned above, some foreign site owners have been stealing images and reproducing them on their own sites without due recognition; however, other Japanese site owners have complained that their sites are being linked to "unpleasant" (*iyarashii*) foreign sites that, in this instance, probably refers to child pornography.

The number of boy-love sites is so large that it is difficult to make generalizations about them. Some consist only of illustrations, either created by the site owner herself or by her guest, friends, or members of the "circle" to which she belongs; other sites are exclusively text-based, consisting of *shōsetsu* (short stories). Most sites, however, contain a mixture of the two and other material, often including a profile of the site owner; her diary, where she details what she has been reading or doing; a guest slot, where she features the work of a friend; and a BBS where browsers can comment on the site or offer news or information relating to new publications. A brief description of the sites' contents is listed on their Web links entry. For instance, *Yaoi a laboratory* describes itself as dedicated to commercial YAOI stories, containing criticism and ranking of the work of YAOI writers; *I'm on your side* (subtitled BOYS OR GUYS LOVE OK) is an interactive game based on the male students of a fictional university and high school that share the same campus; *Catnap* is dedicated to love stories centering on the members of boy band L'Arc en Ciel and also features illustrations and manga; and *Sadistic* contains original stories about men in their twenties with an emphasis on SM and hard sex.[20]

That an exclusively female audience is anticipated for this material is made clear on the entrance page to most sites. The creator of *Sadistic*, for instance, states, "I recommend that men and people who do not understand YAOI should proceed no further; I welcome women over the age of 18" (but no age check is given). *Catnap*'s author writes that her site is "basically for women," continuing, "If you don't like YAOI or don't know what it is, please leave quickly." Despite the common assumption that women are more interested in romance and relationships than sex, many of the illustrations and stories contain graphic sexual scenarios. One story on *Sadistic* involves a 15-year-old boy who seduces his 22-year-old neighbor. Although his family moves away from the area soon after, the boy has been so deeply impressed by his first sexual experience that he is unable to forget the older man, and the writer describes a number of scenes in which the boy masturbates while day dreaming about the touch of his first lover's lips and hands: "As I lay in bed I began to think of Toshiaki and my hand naturally stretched down to my groin. Oh, oh . . . I can imagine that big, firm hand on my body . . . imagine him looking at me. Oh, oh, Toshiaki! To be clasped to that breast . . . to be kissed by those lips is a dream. I love you Toshiaki. To be together with him is to dream. I . . . love . . . you. Oh! My sperm should flow along with his . . . he should hear my cries . . . With sticky white liquid on my fingers, I stare into space . . . "

As he grows older he begins to sleep with women in a vain attempt to recreate the intensity of his first sexual encounter. These graphically described sex scenes become increasingly bizarre. At one stage, he is asked by a female partner whether he has ever experienced anal sex (i.e., anally penetrated a woman), in response to which he muses, "Is it a lie to say this is my first time when last time it was with a man?" And although he penetrates the woman and "his body convulsing . . . spat sperm out into a condom," his thoughts are once more with his first love. Afterward he thinks to himself, "Today, as always, it wasn't especially pleasant. It feels like all I have done is ejaculated. [I feel] more or less empty . . . let's face it, it's impossible with anyone but him . . . " This story line, mixing heterosexual and homosexual encounters and focusing on sexual acts unusual for women such as anal intercourse, has parallels in "ladies comics," again written by and for women, that emphasize sex. As Schodt says of these comics, they "would make American and European feminists wince" because they depict "a woman seducing a son's very young friend, a woman becoming a molester of men on a subway, and women characters who apparently enjoy gang rapes [and] sodomy."[21] However, although sexually graphic, the sex in many YAOI stories does not itself seem to be the "point" but is used to underline the centrality of the characters' feelings. As I have argued elsewhere, this differentiates Japanese women's "homosexual" narratives from those characteristic of Japan's gay press.[22]

Because YAOI is primarily about sex between "beautiful boys" (*bishōnen*) and "beautiful men" (*biseinen*) it confounds Western conventions that stigmatize the sexual representation of children.[23] These stories and illustrations that imagine sexual interaction between men and young boys are known as *shōtakon* (Shōtaro Complex, Shōtaro being the boy hero, always dressed in short pants, of a popular 1960s animation show entitled *Tetsujin 28-go* in Japan and released in the U.S. as *Gigantor,* a term created by YAOI writers and modeled on the loanword *rorikon* (the well-known Lolita Complex). In Western societies it is hard to imagine sexual scenarios more transgressive than transgenerational homosexual acts between adult men and pubescent boys, and yet this is a central trope in women's YAOI. This differentiates YAOI from Western slash fiction that imagines sexual interaction between the *adult* male stars of TV shows such as *Star Trek* or the *X Files* and is a clear example of the cultural relativity of sexual values.[24] Despite the fact that women and children are often assumed to be the primary "victims" of pornography, YAOI is a pornographic genre created by women about (male) children and is considered innocuous enough that it appears in comics commercially produced for an audience of schoolgirls, young women, and housewives. Schoolgirls and housewives are not normally considered a "queer" constituency, and yet their interest in graphic homosexual love stories involving boys troubles Anglo-American assumptions about the synchronicity of "sexual identity" and sexual fantasy.

Japan's Newhalf Net

Japan has a long tradition of transgendered men offering sexual services to gender-normative men. In the Tokugawa period (1600–1867), transgendered prostitutes (*kagema*), who were often affiliated with kabuki theaters,

Mobile Cultures

would offer their services to male members of the audience.[25] In the Taishō (1912–1927) and early Shōwa (1927–1989) periods this role seems to have been taken over by *okama,* a slang term for the buttocks that, when applied to male homosexuals, means something like the English "queen." In the 1960s and 1970s, the term *geiboi* (gay boy) referred to cross-dressing male hustlers, and *gei* (gay) still carries transgender connotations today.[26] Giving fixed content to any Japanese terminology dealing with sexual- or gender-nonconformist individuals is problematic and producing English-language equivalents almost impossible.[27]

Nyūhāfu is particularly difficult to translate, partly because its meaning in Japanese is ambiguous. The term was first popularized in Japan in the early 1980s due to the success of Matsubara Rumiko, a male-to-female transgendered model and singer. In 1981 she issued an album of songs entitled *Newhalf* and the next year published a photo collection.[28] Newhalf, along with gay boy and Mr Lady (*Mr redi*), became one of the many terms used in the media to refer to transgendered men working in the entertainment industry. Since the legalization of sex-change operations in Japan in 1998 and the resulting resurgence of media interest in transgender identities, newhalf has established itself as the most popular term for male-to-female transgenders. Several books, such as *Deciding to Be a Newhalf and Living Like "Myself,"* have been published since 1998, but the variety of identities expressed by individuals using the newhalf label is such that it is impossible to fix its meaning.[29]

On the surface, it would seem that newhalf refers to individuals who, in English, would probably be described as transsexual, but definitions of newhalf in the Japanese media contradict this. For instance, one definition in a sex industry guidebook defines newhalf as "male homosexuals who have had a sex-change operation."[30] The commonsense assumption that newhalf are male homosexuals (*dansei dōseiaisha*) is also clear from an article in the popular magazine *Da Vinchi,* which describes them as "male homosexuals who have 'come out,' undergone a sex change and work in the sex industry."[31] This definition is problematic, as most newhalf who introduce themselves on the Internet would not see themselves as male homosexuals but a distinct "intermediate sex" (*chūsei*); some newhalf take hormones, some have silicon implants, and some have their male genitalia removed, but by no means all undergo sex-change operations. Newhalf do, however, tend to work in the entertainment industry in some capacity or other; therefore, newhalf is better understood as an occupational category rather than a sexual orientation.[32] The interviews in *Deciding to Be a Newhalf* support this; several of the newhalf sex workers interviewed cite commercial concerns as reasons for undertaking specific transgender practices. For instance, Cherry expresses affection for her "nicely shaped penis" because her clients often request that she penetrate them.[33] However, other newhalf in the collection say that they decided to have their penis removed and an artificial vagina created so that they could avoid being asked to provide either active or passive anal sex. For some newhalf, then, decisions about how to transgender their body are taken with their livelihood in mind and not out of any desire to make their exterior body correspond to an interior sense of gender identity. Newhalf therefore share many similarities with transgendered men in other societies who also seek out work in the prostitution world, such as the *travesti* of South America, who Cornwall points out are "neither . . . 'transvestite[s]' nor . . . 'transsexual[s],' as defined in Western terms."[34] Newhalf also share similarities with the *bakla* of the Philippines, and some Philippine male-to-female transgendered prostitutes enter Japan on "entertainer" visas to seek out jobs in the sex trade.[35]

Newhalf can be understood as a site of identity. However, it is an identity based on occupation, because being a newhalf in Japan is not seen as a part-time activity, whereas simply cross-dressing as a woman is.[36] The newhalf in *Deciding to Be a Newhalf* speak of themselves as "professionals." It is true that newhalf have "come out" in that they transgender the body in very obvious ways, often taking hormones or obtaining breasts through silicon implants. A newhalf is therefore very different from a man who simply likes to cross-dress (*josō*), (although the Internet also provides easy access to information on clubs and bars that offer professional stylists who help their male guests create the most attractive female persona). However, the association of newhalf with the sex and entertainment industry makes the conceptualization of newhalf as a political identity problematic, as newhalf often present themselves as offering a service for men either as "hostesses" in clubs, cabarets, or bars, or as "escorts" and "companions." They very much locate themselves in the entertainment sphere. When offering sexual services, newhalf tend to stress their *intersexual* status by pointing out their firsthand knowledge of male anatomy and their ability to offer increased sexual pleasure to straight men. Unlike biological women, newhalf "understand" straight men's desires because they are believed to share them.[37]

Many newhalf sites are hosted by clubs, bars, cabarets, and escort agencies and provide both information about the venue and the services on offer as well as an opportunity for the newhalf employees to introduce themselves and discourse about what being a newhalf means. Many sites also include BBS and chat rooms where a variety of individuals can write in with their questions and remarks. Like Japanese media in general, these sites contain a wide variety of levels and genres, from graphic sex talk and pornographic pictures to more sophisticated reflections on "how to sex," personal biographies and experiences of newhalf employees and visitors, and more general news. They are not simply business sites but "realms" offering a great deal of information, entertainment, and sexual titillation. Two typical sites are *Newhalf Health Aventure* and *Virtual Gaybar Elizabeth*.[38] The latter is an information-based site, although the emphasis is very much on entertainment. It is a very colorful, well-designed, and interactive site; as visitors browse through the many pages on offer, they are treated to a synthesized rendition of *Phantom of the Opera*. Misaki, the Web mistress, greets the visitor with the phrase "On a cold day get warm by imagining Misaki's naked body. What? You've got an erection . . . Well, there's nothing I can do about that." But the intended audience of the site is not exclusively male. For instance, one page is for women who like to have newhalf friends; as Misaki points out, "Some women seem to like men who are like women [*onna ni chikai otoko*]." This includes sexual interest too, for many of the women writing in to the page inquire about whether newhalf are interested in having sex with women—Misaki says some are—and how they might go about doing this. As Misaki, who is sexually interested in both men and women, writes, "Basically I have a woman's heart but there still remains about 10 percent inside me which could be called 'male.'" Although not confrontational in an Anglo-American sense, Misaki does discuss "identity politics" when s/he argues that "some people might think I want to live as a woman; I don't, I want to live as myself [*watshi toshite ikitai*]."

Newhalf Health Aventure (*Nyūhāfu herusu abanchūru*) is basically a salon offering sex. "Health" (*herusu*) in Japanese is short for "health massage," just one of the euphemisms developed in the 1980s to disguise the real business of prostitution taking place in massage parlors.[39] *Health Aventure* is upfront about the services offered by its newhalf employees, stating, "We, the newhalf at *Aventure,* try to ensure that all our customers feel satisfied and secure so that [they can experience] enjoyable sex by using our hearts, bodies, skills and magic. We respectfully wait for your visit from the bottom of our hearts. Credit cards accepted." Immediately below are the club's telephone number and a chart detailing the "courses" (*kōsu*) on offer, their duration, and price. These include the basic "health" course, which lasts 30 minutes and involves "kissing, fellatio, etc., but anal fuck (AF) and reverse anal fuck (*gyaku* AF) are not included." This is followed by the 60-minute "regular," which can include AF. The "long regular" is the same as the above but lasts for 90 minutes. The "optional course" includes "soft SM, dressing up as a woman [*josō*] and lesbian play [*rezupurei*]."[40] The "king course" involves two newhalf playmates, and the "Cindarella course" enables a customer to cross-dress in the club's clothes and then go out on a date with one of the newhalf hostesses. For busy businessmen, lunchtime courses are offered Monday to Friday between 12:00 P.M. and 4:00 P.M. at a reduced rate.

The main purpose of *Aventure*'s home page is to advertise its services, and each of the newhalf "companions" working for the club is profiled.[41] This information includes pictures, age, blood group, star sign, anatomical details such as whether they have breasts and if so whether silicon or the result of hormones, and the current state of their genitalia. Also detailed are the sexual acts the newhalf will or can perform. This kind of description sounds extremely clinical, but the Web page manages to offer this information, to borrow a phrase, "in the best possible taste," employing the exquisitely polite Japanese that is characteristic of highly trained professionals working in the service industry. Being offered a "reverse anal fuck" in the same language a five-star hotel waiter might offer a napkin makes for disorienting reading to my English mind, but because the sex industry is a relatively expensive service industry, the same linguistic rules apply. As Kondo comments, "Awareness of complex social positioning is an *inescapable* element of any utterance in Japanese, for it is *utterly impossible* to form a sentence without *also* commenting on the relationship between oneself and one's interlocutor."[42] This applies equally to the relationship between the purveyors of sexual fantasy and their clients.

There are several hundred newhalf sites from all over Japan, most of which offer, to some degree or other, sexual services. Not all are hosted by large institutions such as *Aventure;* for instance, *Home Delivery Newhalf System* is the home page of Momo and Sakura, who provide the following sexual services either at a client's home or hotel room: kissing, fellatio, vibrator, anal sex, reverse anal sex, and SM play.[43] Momo and Sakura are clearly in partnership together (they offer "double play"), and their Web site, like that of *Aventure,* is very clear about what services are on offer and how much they cost. Other sites are more circumspect and offer newhalf the chance to post their pictures and describe the kind of acts they will perform but without detailing fees. *Newhalf Net* has a short, text-based iMode feature for those using a mobile phone to surf the Net. This contains brief five-line biographies of newhalf, their preferred sexual acts, telephone numbers, and email addresses.

Other sites listed on the Newhalf Net, such as TV'S FORUM JAPAN, that at first glance might seem to be more information-oriented, on further inspection also primarily deliver "entertainment" of a sexual nature.[44] For instance, TV'S FORUM describes itself as "a place where people who love women's underwear can get together" and features pictures of men posing in a variety of women's underwear as well as stories detailing their sexual exploits involving partners of both sexes. As with most newhalf sites, email addresses are given and viewers are encouraged to write and make dates to "play."

As frequently occurs in Japanese sex industry discourse, identities, terminologies, and practices blur and become confused. The ruling paradigm for sex industry participation is "play" (*asobi/purei*), and, as with any game, the rules can be bent or broken, especially if the client is prepared to pay more. Japan's noninterventionist legislation regarding private sexual practice has enabled the Internet to offer a cornucopia of erotic entertainment where there is surely something on offer for people of all persuasions. None of the sites I have discussed are password-protected, and none I attempted to enter required proof of age; although sometimes the question "Are you over 18?" was posted on the first page, the browser had only to click in the affirmative to enter.

Conclusion

The two Internet realms discussed, women's YAOI sites and the Newhalf Net, trouble the parameters of even a term like queer, which seeks to be inclusive of all sexualities that fall outside "mainstream" heterosexuality and the discourse attempting to tie sex to reproduction within the family.

Schoolgirls as a constituency are not generally considered queer, yet their interest in homosexual love stories between young boys clearly falls outside the parameters of what would be considered acceptable in Anglophone societies. Newhalf, too, in their acceptance of the space made available to them in Japan's sex industry and their self-promotion as an "intermediate sex" better able to satisfy the sexual demands of (straight) men because of their privileged understanding of male anatomy, trouble the political associations of queer and make it seem unlikely that newhalf could be included in an umbrella category of groups as diverse in their interests as gay men, lesbians, and those Japanese individuals who understand themselves to be transsexual in the English connotation of this term.

As outlined above, neither YAOI nor the newhalf phenomenon represents a radically new departure in Japan's sexual culture. The Internet has not enabled the emergence of a new type of sexual discourse but simply allowed greater access to sexual images, narratives, and practices; it has made them more popular and more readily available. Whereas previously a schoolgirl would have had to attend a komiketto to purchase her favorite YAOI manga, paying large sums of money on transport, entrance fees, and hard copies of the comics, she can now access her favorites sites from the privacy of her bedroom, download images to keep, and even upload her own art and stories. Similarly, a man (or woman) with an interest in transgendered men who previously would have had to journey to the red light districts of Japan's major cities to meet and converse with newhalf is now able to enter this realm through the Internet. It is possible to download images of one's favorite newhalf, read about her doings in her diary, send her email, or chat with her live. It is possible to make sexual assignations or simply organize a date while saving money by cutting out the expensive fees charged by clubs and cabarets for making introductions. A man can even download information about several different newhalf on his mobile phone and then make a date to meet one of them during his lunch hour or stop off before his long commute home at one of the love hotels built near many train interchange stations.

In making more easily accessible the variety of sexual discourses, representations, and practices that have long been a part of Japan's popular culture, it is unlikely that the Internet is, by itself, going to encourage the increasing politicization of sexuality so long as Internet use is understood as a form of entertainment. Just as the video recorder and cable TV have brought pornography into the domestic sphere, the Internet,[45] too, is further blurring the boundaries between the private home and the commercial sex scene, or indeed the office and the world of sexual entertainment.[46]

So far, the Japanese government's reluctance to regulate sexual expression on the Internet has meant that it is in Japanese, not English, that the widest range of sexual representations and services are freely available. These diverse realms that confound Anglo-American understandings of pornography, sexual identity, and the correspondence between sexual identity and sexual fantasy have been protected from the disapproving Western gaze by the inaccessibility of the Japanese language. There are signs, however, that especially with regard to child pornography (four-fifths of which is said to originate in Japan) Western nations are putting pressure on Japan through international conventions to begin the process of Internet regulation.[47] Thus, although sexual sites on the Japanese Internet, so long as they are inscribed in the discourse of "entertainment," are unlikely to become politicized, the availability of material disapproved of in more censorious Western nations is itself likely to become a political issue.

Notes

Translations are my own unless otherwise noted.

1 According to *Global Internet Statistics* ⟨http://www.glreach.com/globstats/index.php3⟩ (June 2002), 40.2 percent of the Net's online population was using English, whereas 9.8 percent was using Chinese, 9.2 percent Japanese, 7.2 percent Spanish, and 6.8 percent German; other languages were all less than 5 percent.

2 Nanette Gottlieb, *Word Processing Technology in Japan: Kanji and the Keyboard* (Richmond, U.K.: Curzon Press, 2000), 182.

3 According to *Global Internet Statistics*, 430,000 Japanese live in the United States and 2 million live in Brazil. Even if the majority of these were online, this is only a small proportion of the estimated 70 million Internet users in Japan. However, the majority of these users access the Net via cell phones and not PCs, limiting use to texting and downloading ringer melodies and animated screen graphics.

4 Gottlieb, 200.

5 "Political correctness" has yet to make it to Japan. For instance, the "lesbian and bi women's forum" *Bibian*, 7 June 2000, ⟨http://www.silkroad.ne.jp/bibian⟩ (7 June 2000), which contains sexuality information and chat rooms

for women, opens with a bare-breasted and provocatively clad blonde woman, seemingly scanned in from the pages of *Playboy*. Interestingly, this site is pioneering the adoption of the term *bian* (from *rezubian*) as an alternative to *rezu*, which is associated with women performers in male pornography, and is a further example of how Western borrowings like "newhalf" are invested with specifically Japanese meanings.

6 For a discussion of how gay men use the Internet in Japan, see Mark McLelland, "Out and About on Japan's Gay Net," *Convergence* 6, no. 3 (2000): 16–33.

7 "Queer" developed in the late 1980s as a new adversarial site of identity for individuals who felt "lesbian" and "gay" to be too limiting and exclusionary of other sexual minorities such as bisexuals, transsexuals, and sex workers. It is used in this sense in Michelangelo Signorile's *Queer in America: Sex, the Media and the Closets of Power* (New York: Anchor, 1994). However, with the integration of queer theory into the academy and the increasing commodification of queer cultures, much of its confrontational force has been lost. As Morton comments, queer is now often used to mean "the embracing of the latest fashion over an older, square style by the hip youth generation." Donald Morton, "Birth of the Cyberqueer," in *Cybersexualities: A Reader on Feminist Theory, Cyborgs and Cyberspace*, ed. Jenny Wolmark (Edinburgh: Edinburgh University Press, 1999), 295. Neither the schoolgirl readers of YAOI nor newhalf sex workers are queer in either of the above senses. However, queer in the lifestyle sense has now entered Japanese through the magazine *Queer Japan* (first published 2000). Volume 2 (June 2000) is dedicated to "salarymen doing queer" and focuses on lifestyle and culture. It is too soon to judge whether this new departure in Japanese gay media will be successful.

8 Sharon Chalmers, "Lesbian (In)visibility and Social Policy in Japanese Society," in *Gender and Public Policy in Japan,* ed. Vera Mackie (London: Routledge, forthcoming).

9 Liza Dalby, *Kimono: Fashioning Culture* (New Haven: Yale University Press, 1993), 275.

10 Mark McLelland, *Male Homosexuality in Modern Japan: Cultural Myths and Social Realities* (Richmond, U.K.: Curzon Press, 2000), chap. 3, 43–60.

11 Tsuneo Watanabe and Jun'ichi Iwata, *The Love of the Samurai: A Thousand Years of Japanese Homosexuality* (London: Gay Men's Press, 1989); Gary Leupp, *Male Colors: The Construction of Homosexuality in Tokugawa Japan* (Berkeley: University of California Press, 1995).

12 Midori Matsui, "Little Girls Were Little Boys: Displaced Femininity in the Representation of Homosexuality in Japanese Girls' Comics," in *Feminism and the Politics of Difference,* ed. S. Gunew and A. Yeatman (Boulder, CO: Westview Press, 1993), 178.

13 Shōtoku Taishi (574–622) was never an emperor in his own right but served

as regent for his aunt, the Empress Suiko. He is famous for introducing the Chinese calender and drafting Japan's first constitution. He was also a great sponsor of Buddhism and is revered today as an incarnate bodhisattva and a major architect of the Japanese state.

14 Frederik Schodt, *Dreamland Japan: Writings on Modern Manga* (Berkeley: Stone Bridge Press, 1996), 182.

15 Sharon Kinsella, "Japanese Subcultures in the 1990s: Otaku and the Amateur Manga Movement," *Journal of Japanese Studies* 24, no. 2 (1998): 289–316.

16 Schodt, 120.

17 *Wall Street Journal*, "Your Career Matters: Net Lets Japanese Women Join Work Force at Home," February 29, 2000, B1.

18 Gottlieb, 181.

19 *Creative Girls' Home*, 15 September 1998, ⟨http://www.lunatique.org/yaoi⟩ (5 June 2000); *Yaoi Intelligence Agency*, 2000, ⟨http://www.may.sakura.ne.jp/~yia/se/⟩ (5 June 2000).

20 *Yaoi a laboratory*, 16 June 2000, ⟨http://www.lilac.cc/~maco/⟩ (16 June 2000); *I'm on Your Side*, 1 March 2000, ⟨http://www.bridge.ne.jp/~pbem/DEMO/SIDE.html⟩ (16 June 2000); *Catnap*, 14 June 2000, ⟨http://www.people.or.jp/~asagi/catnap/⟩ (14 June 2000); *Sadistic*, 14 June 2000, ⟨http://www.2.networks.ne.jp/~foo/ SDSTC/⟩ (14 June 2000).

21 Schodt, 125.

22 Mark McLelland, "No Climax, No Point, No Meaning? Japanese Women's Boy-Love Sites on the Internet," *Journal of Communication Inquiry* 24, no. 3 (2000): 274–94.

23 Despite the fact that 15 percent of the 150 pornographic Internet sites sampled by Mehta and Plaza contained images of children, they report, "We never came across an image depicting a sexual act between an adult and a child/adolescent, or acts between children," which suggests that these images are very rare on the American USENET system. But, such images are, of course, ubiquitous on Japanese YAOI sites. Michael Mehta and Dwayne Plaza, "Pornography in Cyberspace: An Exploration of What's in USENET," in *Culture of the Internet*, ed. Sara Kiesler (Mahwah, NJ: Erlbaum, 1997), 64.

24 For a discussion of slash fiction, see Mirna Cicioni, "Male Pair-Bonds and Female Desire in Fan Slash Writing," in *Theorizing Fandom: Fans, Subculture and Identity*, ed. C. Harris and A. Alexander (Cresskill, NJ: Hampton, 1998), 153–78; Constance Penley, "Feminism, Psychoanalysis and the Study of Popular Culture," in *Cultural Studies*, ed. Lawrence Grossberg, Cary Nelson, and Paula A. Treichler (New York: Routledge, 1992), 479–500; Henry Jenkins III, *Textual Poachers: Television Fans and Participatory Culture* (New York: Routledge, 1992).

25 Leupp, 72.

26 *Geiboi* is used in this sense in Matsumoto Toshio's movie *Bara no sōretsu* (Funeral procession of roses, 1969). Shot in a semidocumentary style, the film documents Tokyo's late 1960s gay bar (*geibā*) scene and stars the famous transvestite actor Peter, who is now one of Japanese television's top hostesses.

27 For a discussion of terms relating to gender nonconformist individuals in Japan, see McLelland, *Male Homosexuality in Modern Japan*, 7–12.

28 Rumiko Miyazaki, *Watashi wa toransujendā* [I am transgendered], (Tokyo: Neoraifu, 2000), 202.

29 Anri Komatsu, *Nyūhāfu ga kimeta "watashi" rashii ikikata* [Deciding to be a newhalf and live like myself], (Tokyo: KK Ronguserāzu, 2000).

30 Altbooks, *SEX no arukikata: Tōkyō fūzoku kanzen gaido* [How to find your way around Tokyo's sex scene: A complete guide], (Tokyo: Mediawākusu, 1998), 167.

31 *Da Vinchi,* "Sei wo koeta hito bito wo rikai suru hito koto yōgo kaisetsu" (An explanation of terms for people who have gone beyond their sex), March 1999.

32 As described later, some newhalf offer services for men, women, and men dressed as women.

33 Komatsu, 128.

34 Andrea Cornwall, "Gendered Identities and Gender Ambiguity among *Travestis* in Salvador, Brazil," in *Dislocating Masculinity: Comparative Ethnographies,* ed. A. Cornwall and N. Lindisfarne (London: Routledge, 1994), 114.

35 *The Sex Warriors and the Samurai,* prod. Parminder Vir, dir. Nick Deocampo, 25 min., Formation Films Production for Channel Four, 1995, videocassette.

36 Being an *okama* or effeminate homosexual (rather like the English term "drag queen") can also be seen as a part-time activity. See my discussion of the okama farmer who works on his farm during the day and at night serves as a hostess in a bar (McLelland, *Male Homosexuality in Modern Japan,* 48).

37 Despite the fact that some newhalf can pass as women, in popular representations they are shown acting more like men. For instance, I saw a reconstructed scenario on Japanese TV, supposedly of an actual event, in which two "women" in bikinis entered a pachinko parlor full of men playing the machines. While one distracted the customers with a lewd display, the other stole their buckets of pinballs, which can be redeemed for cash. When apprehended by the staff, they started a fistfight and on the arrival of the police, it turned out that the women were newhalf.

38 *Aventure,* 14 February 2000, ⟨http://www.newhalf.co.jp/⟩ (1 July 2000); *Virtual Gaybar Elizabeth,* 27 January 1999, ⟨http://homepage1.nifty.com/Newhalf/index.html⟩ (5 July 2000).

39 For a discussion of Japan's sex trade, see Peter Constantine, *Japan's Sex Trade:*

A Journey through Japan's Erotic Subcultures (Tokyo: Tuttle, 1993); and Altbooks.

40 In this context, *rezupurei* refers to a cross-dressed male client pretending to be a lesbian.

41 Although counters advertising the number of hits can be unreliable, it would seem that *Aventure* is popular, having attracted 82,002 hits between 14 February and 30 May 2000. On 29 May alone, it attracted 1,145 visitors.

42 Dorinne Kondo, *Crafting Selves: Power, Gender, and Discourses of Identity in a Japanese Workplace* (Chicago: University of Chicago Press, 1990), 31.

43 *Home Delivery Newhalf* System, September 1998, ⟨http://members.xoom.com/_XMCM/newhalf/eigyou.html⟩ (15 July 2000).

44 *TV's FORUM JAPAN,* 17 July 2000. ⟨http://www.geocities.com/WestHollywood/Village/9111⟩ (17 July 2000).

45 The mobile phone is another technology disrupting the traditional distinction between the desexualized domestic sphere and the world of commercial sex. It is used by gay men who live with their parents (or wives or partners) to negotiate their sexual relationships (see McLelland, *Male Homosexuality in Modern Japan,* 212–14) and by schoolgirl prostitutes who call into "telephone clubs" where potential clients wait to receive their calls. See Takarajima, *Ura Tōkyō kankō* [Backstreet Tokyo sightseeing] (Tokyo: Takarajimasha, 1998), 54–55; "Clueless in Tokyo: Schoolgirls Exchange Sexual Talk for Money to Buy Designer Clothes," *The Economist* 339, no. 7969 (June 8, 1996): 66.

46 I had to obtain a letter from the University of Queensland explicitly granting me exemption from a university statute forbidding the use of office computers for the viewing of pornographic images in order to complete the research for this chapter.

47 "Japan's Shame: Lawmakers are finally pushing legislation to help end the country's dubious distinction as the world's main source of child pornography," *Time International* 153, no. 5 (April 19, 1999): 34.

VERUSKA SABUCCO

Guided Fan Fiction:

Western "Readings" of Japanese

Homosexual-Themed Texts

My intention in this essay is to deal with the growing Western fandom centered on Japanese "queer" pop culture texts, such as *shōnen ai* ("boys love"), *manga* (comics), and *anime* (cartoons), as well as YAOI, which are mainstream popular texts rewritten by fans as homosexual manga.[1] I refer to these texts as *june* or "boys love" stories, as their readers also call them that. These cultural products focus on male homosexuality. However, they are created by and almost exclusively for women. They belong to a well-known subgenre, flourishing both in the Japanese official publishing world and on the *dōjinshi* (fanzine) scene. First, I sketch the history of the manga and anime world. Following Sharon Kinsella, I point out that television and publishing industries "developed a symbiotic relationship" that allowed both manga and anime to thrive.[2] The most recent expansion of the Internet is seen, together with the earlier spread of the computer games industry, as one of the possible causes of the shrinkage both of the anime audience and of manga sales, but it is also one of the means allowing Japanese popular texts to gather a growing audience in Western countries. Accordingly, it is probably the most common means by which shōnen ai and YAOI texts have become known to Western manga, anime, and slash fans in the past few years.[3]

The main focus of this essay is the analysis of the peculiar decoding of shōnen ai and YAOI done by their Western fans.[4] I define this peculiar fans' reading procedure as "guided fan fiction": the process of making up the story of a manga from the sequence of pictures and pages and from the few words and sentences each fan is able to understand. What each fan does can be seen as creative reading, as a variation on a theme; each fan, each reading, is a variation. In my opinion, Western readers' reception of shōnen ai and YAOI texts is often different from the average Japanese reception. This is not only because, as I observed, Western fans often know little or no Japanese, limiting their reading to "watching pictures," but also because the meaning encoded in those pictures is decoded by Western readers. My working conclusion is that the Japanese "queer" culture represented by shōnen ai and YAOI is not the same queer culture recreated by their Western fans; it is a partially different culture, born from the process of "interpretation, appropriation and reconstruction" that those manga and anime undergo.[5]

The actual origins of modern manga can be dated back to the satirical comic strips that first appeared in Japanese newspapers and magazines during the 1920s. However, it was the postwar period that witnessed the rise of the most famous manga author, Tezuka Osamu. The first black-and-white (1963) and color (1965) animation series released in Japan were drawn from his *Tetsuwan Atom* (*Astro Boy*) and *Jungle Taitei* (*Kimba, the White Lion*) manga, respectively. The manga-anime connection was born, and soon the merchandising industry joined this dyadic relationship. *Kimba* and *Astro Boy* hold another record, being the first Japanese animation series shown in the United States (in the 1960s) and being among the first shown in Western European countries. Those series, followed in time by other popular adventure, science fiction, and shōjo (girls') series, were watched by children who grew up to become the vanguard of a now huge Western anime fan base. Western producers sensed a new market and since the mid-1980s quite a few have started to issue translated anime and manga or manga-style comics created by Western authors. Frederick L. Schodt makes a point that applies to the whole Western manga and anime fan world: "Publishers issue *manga*, but the real driving force behind the spread of *manga* and *anime* in the English world is the fans."[6]

In Japan in the early 1970s, finally affordable offset printing and photocopying facilities made producing a dōjinshi (a fanzine or amateur publication) a cheap process, so that an increasing number of authors could produce and sell their own comics. Dōjinshi can be classified into two main categories: the "original" and the *aniparo*. Characters and events in original stories are created by amateur authors themselves; aniparo can be defined as apocryphal fiction based on famous anime and manga series.

The 1970s witnessed another revolution in the manga world, when the first *shōnen ai manga* made their appearance. Following the track of the first shōnen ai artists, in October 1978 *June* magazine was founded. It was the first and continues to be the foremost shōnen ai magazine, to the point that its name is now used as an umbrella term for the whole boys-love genre. However, it was not until the mid-1980s that YAOI, a subgenre of aniparo in the form of manga or *shōsetsu* (novels), became diffused. The YAOI tell stories of romantic and sexual involvement between male fictional characters extrapolated mostly from manga and anime action-adventure, sport, or speculative fiction series, such as the soccer players of *Captain Tsubasa* or the young warriors of *Saint Seiya*. Since then, the boys-love genre has boomed, both in the professional and the amateur world. At the turn of the century, more than fifteen years after its revamp, the boys-love subgenre is thriving in both the official and dōjinshi worlds.

In Japan, computer games have been popular since the late 1970s. Since 1979, when Taitō marketed the famous *Space Invader,* the number of computer game players has increased dramatically.[7] Kinsella points out that this, together with the spread of the Internet starting around the late 1990s, can be directly related to the shrinkage of manga readers and anime audiences from 1995: "A slight dip in manga circulation figures in 1986 following the introduction of home computer games (*famikon*) and *Nintendo,* another slight dip in early 1995 following the launch of Sony *Playstation* in December 1994, and another dip following the introduction of Microsoft *Windows 95* in November 1995. . . . Rather than watching animation on television, fueling the purchase of more manga books, Japanese children were spending more time playing interactive animated computer games."[8]

Anime based on computer games, such as the *Pokemon* anime series, are probably meant to bring the younger audience back to the TV, and eventually to manga. Curiously enough, the dōjinshi world survived the advent of computer games quite easily. Because most aniparo authors are themselves players of computer games, they began to create computer game–based dōjinshi, where computer game heroes lived new adventures, sometimes erotic ones.

Paradoxically, what appears to be one of the causes of the manga and anime industries crisis in Japan is one of the causes of the rapid development of a huge Western fan base for those same cultural products. Schodt states, "From early on, one of the most important tools in holding the *manga-anime* fan community together has been computer networks." I must add, however, that it has been only since the mid-1990s that mailing lists, message boards, and Web pages created and maintained by manga and anime fans can be counted in the hundreds. They appear in Japanese, Chinese, French, Italian, and Spanish, but mostly in English (a language that has become the Esperanto of fandom). Nowadays, "The most popular gathering spot for *manga* fans in the U.S. [is] the global Internet—and its offspring, the interactive, graphic intensive World Wide Web."[9] This statement by Schodt might be modified if we note that at the moment the Internet is probably the most popular international gathering spot and archive of fans' creative output such as fan fiction stories, fan art, reviews of articles, source of (mis)information, fan translations of manga, and fan-subtitled anime, not only for U.S. fans but for fans all over the world.[10] People overseas can "meet" each other on this virtual common ground, thus becoming part of a truly international fandom. I share Schodt's optimistic conclusion: "The fan communities are increasingly intertwined, and friendships continue to grow across oceans and language barriers."[11] Because the Internet is fast, comparatively inexpensive, and worldwide—or at least within the reach of an ever increasing number of people—it is no surprise that it is becoming a fan heaven.

The vast majority of Western shōnen ai and YAOI fan Web pages and mailing lists appeared some years later than pages and lists devoted to mainstream anime and manga. In 1995 there were still very few fan pages focusing on june texts, and they all revolved around the most famous series, such as *Zetsu ai*.[12] However, by the late 1990s, URLs devoted to Japanese boys-love products, original or YAOI, reached the hundreds. To give just a few examples, there are more than 450 pages for *Ai no kusabi*, 64 for *Kizuna*, about 70 for *Zetsu ai/Bronze*, and several of the more recent pages are even devoted to the promotion of comparatively obscure series.[13] This trend can be partly explained by the recent official release of some original boys-love dubbed anime and translated manga, chosen by Western publishers from among the most successful ones in Japan.[14] *Kizuna* was released in the United States in 1998, and *Fake* in 1999. *Kusatta Kyōshi no Hōteshiki* was recently officially dubbed in Spain, and in Italy six boys-love anime and one manga (*New York New York*) have been officially released since 1994. *Zetsu ai manga* is being translated in France. Distributed in comic shops, those texts gathered new june fans from the hitherto untapped manga and anime fans outside the original language and Internet-based fan scenes. If some june fans simply enjoy the available translated text, others may start looking for more: for boys-love manga by a specific author, or revolving around a certain theme, or belonging to a peculiar subgenre that best matches their taste. Yet, to get accurate information about those cultural products, Western fans must rely almost exclusively on online synopses and recommendations from other fans. However, Internet fandom is not only a source of information about manga and anime; it is also a source of information about how and where to get those texts as well as, sometimes, of the texts themselves. Because it is becoming easier for fans to get professional equipment that was once prohibitively expensive, some groups of fans have created fan subtitling cooperatives. The aim of these cooperatives is to subtitle and release those anime that will never easily reach the official market, such as *Ai no kusabi, Kaze to ki no uta,* and the three anime made from *Zetsu ai/Bronze.* Fan translation of *Kizuna manga* is now in progress and can be downloaded from the Web. Fan translations of the first eleven *tankōbon* (manga volumes) of the *Zetsu ai/Bronze* manga series are also available to fans. And there are translations and detailed summaries of lesser known manga. However, there are almost certainly no fan translations of *shōsetsu june* (june novels) because of the difficulty involved, especially for a Western reader semiliterate in Japanese.

It can be safely said that Western june fandom is basically a Net fandom. Paper fanzines are exceptional, to the point that even the most famous, if not only, boys-love Western online magazine, *Aestheticism,* discontinued its paper edition after just a couple of years.

Having outlined the role of the Internet in shaping a Western shōnen ai and YAOI fandom, I now deal directly with the complex connections binding Western fans to original boys-love manga and anime.

I decided to leave aside YAOI fan pages and limit my research to Western fan pages devoted to original boys-love series for two reasons. First, Japanese YAOI dōjinshi are largely unknown in the West, given the inherent difficulty in locating a specific title once the few copies in a dōjinshi's print run have been sold in Japan.[15] This makes it impossible for the vast majority of YAOI dōjinshi to form a common reference point.[16] Because of that, I excluded from my research Western fan pages devoted to dōjinshi manga. Second, there is a basic difference between Western Web pages presenting YAOI fan fiction written by Western fans and those devoted to original june manga and anime. In fan pages devoted to original june, fans try to rebuild,

Mobile Cultures

from sparse knowledge, the original meaning of the text the page is devoted to. In contrast, only those Western-produced YAOI fan fictions based on good knowledge of the original text can be useful tools to analyze the writer's interpretations of the characters and their relations.

I also focus on boys-love manga, leaving aside anime, because the manga to anime ratio is heavily in favor of manga, and most june anime have been subtitled or dubbed officially or by fans, whereas just a few manga are in the process of being translated. Therefore, it is in trying to read a manga that fans face the greatest cross-cultural problems.

The material foreigners prefer . . . may not be what is preferred

in Japan, and it may be interpreted differently.

—FREDERIK L. SCHODT, *Dreamland Japan:*

Writings on Modern Manga

As comics, manga are texts that use two codes, words and art, combined in sequential panels that tell a story. There are at least three elements a Western fan must face when approaching a manga: language, manga visual conventions, and Japanese cultural conventions. The degree to which a fan is accustomed to these may vary, influencing the reading procedure or interpretation of a manga. Reader-oriented theorists state that every reading of a text is somewhat a recreation of it, that the meaning of a text depends at least partially on what the readers put into it.[17] In this case, the active and creative element of reading must be stronger as the knowledge of Japanese language, manga, and cultural conventions is weaker.

What happens when a Western fan buys a manga that has not been translated into a language he or she knows? My hypothesis was that in the vast majority of cases a fan knows little Japanese. This hypothesis is supported by the data gathered from my experience in online Western june fandom and from two june mailing list polls asking members about their knowledge of Japanese language. The "How much Japanese can you read in a *manga?*" poll ran first on the AMLA mailing list founded by the staff of the *Aestheticism* online magazine. I then reformulated and reproposed this question to the YSAL, the only Italian june mailing list, and to thirty-four Italian offline buyers of june manga. Thirty-seven people out of 331 mailing list members responded to the AMLA poll.[18] Of the Westerners who answered, 11.76 percent don't know Japanese at all, 41.17 percent grasp the gist of a manga, and 23.52 percent can understand most of the text. Fourteen of the seventy-four members of the Italian YSAL mailing list responded. Of the thirty-four offline june readers contacted, ten responded. I decided to combine the two samples, with these results: 29.16 percent stated that they knew no Japanese at all, 70.83 percent could understand no more than a few words in a manga, and none knew Japanese fluently.

I asked another question of YSAL members and the offline june readers: "Did it ever happen that what you thought was happening in an untranslated *manga* turned out to be wrong when you read a translation of it?" Nine (37.5 percent) answered that it had, or that it probably had, but they could not know for sure because they did not know Japanese and did not have a translation of the manga. Deborah L. Reed gives us an example of her misreading of a manga story that she was able to correct afterwards, thanks to an explanation from another june fan: "When I first read *Love Mode* . . . I believed that Aoe was somehow indifferent to Izumi-the-prostitute's traumatic past when he hired him to work at the Blue Boy (Aoe's escort club). . . . Aoe was rescued from the doghouse when Grace revealed that Izumi was actually working for the Blue Boy because Kiichi-sensei decided that job would be the best way for the boy to recover from the traumatic aftereffects of a gang rape. (I'm trusting that Grace got this from the texts and isn't making up *Love Mode* more than I do. Otherwise, this is just another example of the jungle telegraph in action.)"[19]

Fans are conscious that similar accidents are likely to happen. For this reason, it is not uncommon to find disclaimers on fan Web pages regarding the level of knowledge of the fan who owns it and thus of the accuracy of his or her assertions regarding the manga or anime the page is about. The following disclaimers also constitute evidence that summaries can be done by fans who know little or no Japanese:

> I cannot read Japanese, so I will be unable to comment on the plots as a whole. However, I will summarise the main content of the short story and attempt to do a short review.

> I'm currently trying to learn Japanese by summerizing [*sic*] a number of selective chapters from the series (from *Bronze* right now), but because of my lack of Japanese, I can only attempt a somewhat accurate summary (at least I'm trying).[20]

Mobile Cultures

Those translating from another non-Japanese language they know are also aware that they are producing a second-generation translation that, by its very nature, can only be inaccurate: "Here I trace my way through Minami Ozaki's *Bronze* . . . this is a somewhat piecemeal and incomplete treatment, not a synopsis or even a review. These are my own comments on *Bronze*, personal and biased as they are, along with fragments of translation, which may be sporadic and not necessarily accurate. *It's also the English translation of a Chinese translation of the Japanese original.* . . . A fragmentary script began to develop, with the gaps in my understanding being filled by my own guesses as to what was going on."[21]

Surely, fans who do not know Japanese constitute a category more prone to huge misreadings of those texts or situations that need a knowledge of the written code to be understood. Instead, those fans have to rely heavily on only a visual code, which, though simple at first, can be tricky.

Readers face many manga conventions and some pictures hold cultural references they will not know. The flower background is a common example of a typical shōjo and june manga visual convention used by the artist to enhance the beauty of a character in the foreground or to emphasize a romantic scene. But how many fans know the exact meaning of the funny crow that often flies in the background when a character is perplexed and surprised? Sometimes, a fan does not have the cultural tools to decode some symbolic pictures or sequences referring to Japanese culture and institutions. For example, in the third issue of Kodaka Kazuma's manga *Kizuna* we see the sun glint off the lapel pin of a *yakuza* man.[22] Most fans will read it as an effect, but the minority who know more about yakuza customs will understand that the pin is the badge of a yakuza family. Scooter X, a june fan, experienced the consequences of the cultural gap once the manga he used to picture-watch was translated in a language he knew:

> I've been reading the *Gundam Wing* comics that are being released in the United States. I've learned a few things. I used to think I was missing a lot by not being able to read Japanese . . . now I am not so sure. . . . The little four-panel funny comic strip at the back (sorry, don't know the word for these) are as incomprehensible to me in English as they are in Japanese. I used to ponder them in doujinshi, without a clue ("do they read vertically or horizontally? Are they related, or is each panel different . . ."). Now I realize they must relate on a series of cultural norms I can't follow. English doesn't make them any less opaque.[23]

To make things more complex, some june manga artists portray their characters as crucified, as angels, dressed up as cardinals, or beside a Christmas tree. These are all images taken from Christian mythology. Furthermore, Ozaki Minami often draws characters from her manga series dressed as Nazi soldiers or wearing swastika-shaped earrings.[24] However, those decontextualized Western elements do not have the same cultural meaning a Western reader might attribute to them. They are there for completely different reasons: because angels can represent innocence, because the Christmas atmosphere is evocative, or sometimes just for decorative reasons.[25] Anne Allison notes: "To what extent late capitalism breeds an economy of images and gazes that is transcultural must be investigated, but it cannot yet be assumed that such an economy is always embedded with the same . . . constructions as in a western context."[26]

In some cases, we can witness a circularity in the process that Tobin calls "domestication."[27] As I noted above, it is not uncommon for manga artists to make use of Western cultural elements or literary genres, which are interpreted by Japanese and recontextualized in Japanese popular culture products. During this process, these Western cultural items lose part of their original meaning and acquire new meanings from the authors' culture. The resulting cultural element is then decoded again by a Western reader, who, seeing the presence of Western characters, setting, words, or genres, either is puzzled about how exactly he or she is supposed to interpret them or simply attributes their original Western meaning to them.

There are at least two other elements outside the text that can influence a reader's perception of what is happening in a manga. One includes critics, summaries, and reviews by fans; the other consists of fan fiction stories. Both are common on the Web.

As noted above, reviews and synopses of boys-love series are often published on the Web by Western fans who either have a grasp of Japanese or who put together information gathered from friends, mailing lists, and other sources, such as Web pages devoted to the same series. In fandom communities on the Internet it is not uncommon that information already fragmented and often not completely correct is passed on as in a telephone game, sometimes to the point that caution is forgotten and the misinformation is sometimes seen and spread as the truth about a certain manga.

As an interpretation of the original text presented in a fictional form,

Mobile Cultures

Western YAOI fan fiction is based on the reader/writer's decoding of events, relationships, and characters in a manga. Sometimes, the same element is present in a relevant number of YAOI stories; originally a single fan's idea, for various reasons it has been adopted by other fan authors too. This can mislead a fan who, seeing the recurring element in YAOI fiction, may start to believe that this element comes from the original manga and start spreading this information. The following post by Maygra, a member of the AMLA mailing list, is a good summary of the position in which fans often find themselves:

> I have four volumes of *West End* and I could no more guarantee an accurate portrayal of those two than I could of Hiiro Yuy . . . because I can't read the source, I can only look at it. Can I get the basics of their relationship? Maybe, but not without reading the summary/review at *Aestheticism,* which is based on someone else's translation so I am still getting source second hand. . . . I don't read *Gundam Wing* [fan fiction] and I think I've seen maybe five of the *anime* releases. . . . Could I write any of them? . . . I might then be prompted to re-watch and write—or I might base my interpretations on those made by the fiction writer I just read.[28]

Aestheticism columnist MJ Johnson points out, "One approach views the character in terms that are familiar to you and hence makes him comprehensible to the thinking of your own culture."[29] The "guided fan fiction" is a creative (mis)reading produced by Western readers of a text, in this case a manga. I argue that this new reader-produced manga recreated by Western eyes and minds is more a Western than a Japanese text. This recreated manga probably resonates with the reader at a social, cultural, and personal level more than the manga that the fan would encounter if he or she knew how to read all its codes and cultural conventions. The decisions the characters take, their motivations, their inner thoughts, and the nature of their relationships are more Western than Japanese because they are ascribed to the characters by their Western readers.

To support my hypothesis, let me describe my picture-reading with another june fan of *Fly Me to the Heaven,* a side story of Shimizu Yuki's manga series *Love Mode.*[30] The series revolves around a male escort service manager named Aoe Reiji, his family, and his employees. (Employees can choose whether to have paid sex with their customers.) I first summarize

Fly Me to the Heaven, then report the plot as we understood it from our picture-reading, comparing it with a more accurate depiction of the events done by another fan.

In the opening sequence we see a young man called Seiichi talking to someone in an elevator.[31] The words "VIP" and "No.1" recur in the balloons. They talk about "B&B"; a picture-reader familiar with the series knows it is the escort service agency name. In accordance with our expectations, Seiichi enters a luxurious hotel room. There he finds a young boy called Tomoki waiting for him. Seiichi is perplexed and makes a telephone call. Readers familiar with this series can deduce that he is calling an escort service manager (a similar situation can be found in the first volume of *Love Mode*). Again, the word VIP is present in the conversation. When Seiichi finishes talking on the telephone he notices that Tomoki is taking some pills. He looks at him disapprovingly while saying something. Tomoki seems very scared at the idea of Seiichi's going away and tries to stop him. Seiichi gives up and in the next panels we see them having sex. Tomoki seems to be suffering. In the following pages it seems that Seiichi has decided he wants to have a relationship with Tomoki. The boys' expressions waver from perplexed to a melancholic happiness. Their sexual life improves. In a flashback, we see Seiichi finding an empty blister pack for a pill in the wastepaper basket. He says something, presumably about the pill, and Tomoki gives him the pills he has on him. Then we see panels of them happy together. One night, Tomoki collapses. On the next pages, Seiichi is talking to Reiji, who is carrying patients' notes and says something that shocks Seiichi, who goes to the hospital where Tomoki is. They have a confrontation. Tomoki seems resigned, even if his doctor—Reiji's brother, Kiichi—says something about B&B that makes him smile. On the next page, Seiichi has sex with a rich man while thinking about Tomoki. On the next two pages, we see him in the same elevator as before in the company of the same man; again, we read the word VIP. Seiichi is surprised by something the man says. On the next page, we see a small panel of Reiji's office building and a small traditional Japanese home, where Tomoki is hanging out the washing. Seiichi appears in the courtyard, and they share an embrace. It seems they will be partners again. Tomoki talks to Seiichi, and they remember Tomoki losing his senses. We do not understand a flashback sequence of Tomoki in the hospital seeing Seiichi taking flowers to another boy. Seiichi leaves, presumably to perform an errand. Tomoki falls asleep watching the sky.

We interpreted the story as follows. Seiichi is a VIP B&B customer who does not want Tomoki as a host because he is too young and he thinks Tomoki is on drugs. Tomoki is scared, thinking Seiichi is going to tell this to his employer and he will be fired, so he begs him to stay. We think that Seiichi falls in love with Tomoki and helps him quit drugs. After Tomoki collapses, Seiichi decides that Tomoki is not worthwhile, and so he unsuccessfully tries to forget him by dating other men. Tomoki retires from service and lives a simple life while detoxing from drugs. Seiichi finds him through B&B and their love story ends happily.

This is the real story, or at least the story according to Sirin Sirimontri, a fan who has some understanding of Japanese.

> The secret child of a famous actress . . . Tomoki enters the hospital since he was a kid because of his mental sickness. He met Seiichi when he came to visit Izumi (the ex. No. 1 of B&B) and was taken by him so much that he wanted to become his lover. Fortunately his doctor was Kiichi, so he granted Tomoki's wish to come to reality. Tomoki hired Seiichi to be his lover for 2 weeks, but the contract ended earlier than the dateline because Tomoki got sick. He finally decided to come back to stay home instead of going to the hospice, and lived his last chapter of life with Seiichi who . . . after one word from Jin-san [the man in the elevator, whom he knows] retired from B&B and go stay with Tomoki.[32]

Of course, generalizations cannot be made on the basis of a two-person experience and it would be advisable to repeat this experiment with a broader sample to obtain quantitatively significant data.[33] Nevertheless, our experience can help pinpoint some implicit cultural assumptions we made about how the characters were behaving like Western genre fiction characters and according to Western parameters. Where, except in a most controversial Western text, would we see a doctor suggesting that a minor pay for sex with the hustler of his dreams? Keeping in mind that june are mass-produced fantasies, we recreated a stereotypical Western plot where a golden-hearted damsel in distress (in our case, an innocent boy forced into prostitution) waits for a Prince Charming to rescue and marry her (or him). Interpreting this manga as being about the prostitution of minors also seemed natural to us; in Western mainstream mass products, minors in their early teens are often represented as either innocents forced to have sex or as mischievous Lolitas when an older party is involved. Tomoki's wide-eyed appearance made it impossible for us to contemplate the latter. Our attention focused on the single frame showing his suffering face during the sex act, even though this is not an unusual expression for willing anal intercourse bottoms in june. Accordingly, we ignored or misinterpreted all clues pointing to other possible readings of the situation. For example, Tomoki's shyness and hesitancy could have been due to inexperience rather than reluctance. We attributed his happiness at being with Seiichi to an almost childish joy at being taken care of. When we produced the trite drug abuse theme we discarded all the hints, which were actually evident, of his deadly illness, a plot device as typical here as it is in Japanese shōjo manga. In our minds, Tomoki was already the unwilling-underage-prostitute, a stereotypical good boy with a trusting nature that made him the perfect victim of drug dealers and of a sleazy escort service recruiting workers from what we presumed to be his disadvantaged background. We completely forgot that Aoe Reiji, the escort service manager, and his brother Kiichi are the protagonists of *Love Mode* and have usually been represented as good and helpful characters. We forgot that senior high school teacher Masayoshi, one of the main characters of the famous lighthearted comedy *Kusatta Kyōshi no Hōteshiki* (*The Pervert Teacher's Equation*), also runs the transvestite host club owned by his father. In a word, yakuza and people dealing in the prostitution trade or practicing other professions usually considered less than respectable are not necessarily negative characters in june, and their Japanese readers apparently do not feel compelled to pass moral judgment on them. In manga, fantasy elements mix easily with a realistic setting. According to many june, this is a happy gay world. It is also a world where Aoe Reiji can be the B&B escort service manager and still be our hero, and where a minor can be a willing and active participant in the sexual act with an older partner without causing controversy. The peaceful closing sequence suggested to us a happy ending, and for us a happy ending could not be a beautiful death, even though this is a common plot resolution in dramatic shōjo manga. We looked for a typical Western genre fiction plot and that was what we produced in the end, forgetting that this was a cross-cultural picture-reading of a Japanese genre text meant to be read by Japanese readers. During the guided fan fiction process, the new meaning is superimposed on the original, creating Western stories drawn in a Japanese style.

The "Westernization" of the text can reach a point where readers are upset by the real text once they read a translation of it. As Johnson concludes, "The square peg of Western assumptions takes a little bashing before it'll go into the round hole of Japanese culture."[34]

Notes

I wish to thank Deborah L. Reed for her insightful advice. The basic definition of "guided fan fiction" is her concept and I am borrowing it with her permission. Thanks to Mirna Cicioni for helping me with a first outline of this essay and for her editing. Thanks also to Mary Ellen Curtins, MJ Johnson, and the other members of the AMLA who kindly gave me permission to quote them here. Their observations and ideas have helped me form my own.

1   A caveat regarding the application of theoretical paradigms crafted in a Western culture to non-Western cultures can be found in Anne Allison's *Permitted and Prohibited Desires: Mothers, Comics and Censorship in Japan* (Berkeley: University of California Press, 2000), 31–40. Here, the author describes the difficulties she faced in applying the Western "male gaze" theory to Japanese manga and expresses her legitimate perplexities, wondering "how useful western-based theory is to those of us who study non-western cultures" (33). In my case, I decided to put the word "queer" in quotes when referring to Japanese cultural products to emphasize that queer culture developed in a Western context, where sex and gender conventions are not the same as in Japan. Consequentially, "queer" must be used keeping in mind that in Japan there is no queer culture as we think of it. See also Barbara Summerhawk, Cheiron McMahill, and Darren McDonald, eds., *Queer Japan: Personal Stories of Japanese Lesbians, Gays, Bisexuals and Transsexuals* (Norwich, VT: New Victoria Press, 1998), and Mark McLelland's critique, "Essay Review of *Queer Japan*," *Sexualities* 3, no. 1 (spring 2000): 150–53.

2   Sharon Kinsella, *Adult Manga: Culture and Power in Contemporary Japanese Society* (Richmond, U.K.: Curzon Press, 2000), 31.

3   Slash is a subgenre of Anglo-American media fandom that depicts homosexual relationships between male media characters, such as Captain Kirk and Mr. Spock from the *Star Trek* TV series. This rewriting may range from extremely sentimental to explicit eroticism.

4   Although my sources have been mainly English-language fan Web pages and mailing lists, I am writing about Western fandom instead of English-speaking fandom. I came to this decision because a significant number of active members of shōnen ai and YAOI mailing lists are people whose first language is not English. I took care to search for the admittedly few non-English june fan Web sites, too.

5 Henry Jenkins III, *Textual Poachers: Television Fans and Participatory Culture* (New York: Routledge, 1992), 162.

6 Frederik L. Schodt, *Dreamland Japan: Writings on Modern Manga* (Berkeley: Stone Bridge Press, 1996), 328.

7 Massimiliano Griner and Rosa Isabella Furnari, *Otaku: I giovani perduti del Sol Levante* (Otaku: The Lost Youths of the Rising Sun) (Rome: Castelvecchi, 1999).

8 Kinsella, 44.

9 Schodt, 332–33.

10 Fan fiction consists of narrative fiction produced by a fan out of a certain text and revolving around characters and events extrapolated from that text. Fan art, usually illustrations, represents characters and events inspired by a certain text.

11 Schodt, 332.

12 *Zetsu ai* [*Desperate Love*]/*Bronze* by Ozaki Minami is an ongoing manga series dating back to 1989. It revolves around the obsessive love that idol pop singer Nanjo Kōji feels for reserved soccer player Izumi Takuto. From this series three anime have been released: *Zetsu ai, Bronze,* and *Catexis.* In the 1980s Ozaki played a strong role in revamping the boys-love genre with her YAOI dōjinshi series based on the *Captain Tsubasa* series. Ioshihara Rieko's *Ai no kusabi* (*Love's Wedge*) is a novel that was first serialized in *June* magazine in 1986 and then turned into an anime. It is set on an alien planet ruled by a humanoid, genetically engineered race whose voyeuristic pastime consists of watching slaves have sex with each other. The anime plot revolves around the love that a member of the elite feels for one of his slaves. *Kizuna* (*Bonds*) by Kodaka Kazuma is a manga series started in 1992 and still running. This series has also been turned into an anime. It can be defined as a yakuza soap opera. *Kizuna* revolves around the life of two sons of a *yakuza don* (boss): Kei, the boyfriend of Ranmaru, and Kai, who is infatuated with Ranmaru but actually in love with Masa, the man who took care of him after he lost his mother when he was a child. These series can be seen as the basic june bibliography together with the tragic Takemiya Keiko's *Kaze to ki no uta* (*The Song of Wind and Trees*), a manga dating back to 1976. It was one of the first shōnen ai published and made into an anime in 1987. Other manga that have been translated or turned into anime, including *Fake* by Matoh Sanami, *Kusatta Kyōshi no Hōteshiki* (*The Pervert Teacher's Equation*) by Kodaka Kazuma, and *New York New York* by Ragawa Marimo, are popular but cannot be seen as "classics" on a par with those mentioned earlier.

13 These data come from a search carried out with Altavista. These values must be read with a degree of caution, partly because most of the *Ai no kusabi* and *Kizuna* listed links are just anime reviews. Even more important, a certain

proportion of boys-love fan pages are devoted to more than one manga, shōsetsu, or anime; for example, the same page may turn up in a Web search under the headings *Kizuna, Ai no kusabi,* or *Zetsu ai.*

14 Because YAOI are apocryphal texts, they cannot be officially released; that would be copyright infringement. Thus, YAOI is confined to the dōjinshi (fanzine) scene.

15 The print run of a dōjinshi may range from 100 to 6,000 copies. See Schodt, 38. Because dōjinshi are produced and sold by authors at conventions, by word of mouth, and at a few manga shops, they are difficult to find and purchase in the West.

16 There are some exceptions; YAOI dōjinshi by famous authors like Kodaka Kazuma or Ozaki Minami are difficult to find but widely known.

17 For a brief synopsis of the debate those theories fit into, see Stefan Collini, introduction to *Interpretation and Overinterpretation,* by Umberto Eco (Cambridge, England: Cambridge University Press, 1992), 5–29.

18 The *Aestheticism* mailing list (AMLA) is mostly a list devoted to critical appraisal of manga, anime, and shōsetsu stories; thus, it must be kept in mind that its members are probably better educated than members of other boys-love mailing lists and more willing to make the effort to study Japanese. Consequently, the number of people knowing or having an inkling of Japanese on this mailing list might be slightly higher than on the average mailing list.

19 Deborah L. Reed, "Re: [*AMLA*] just the facts (was Re: Definitions of beauty (was: images in statements)," 23 May 2000, ⟨groups.yahoo.com/group/AMLA⟩ (message deleted from the *Aestheticism* mailing list archive).

20 Miyuki, "*Zetsu ai/Bronze* fan page," ⟨www.geocities.com/Tokyo/Shrine/3303/z-index.html⟩ (4 January 2001); Kamui K., "*Bronze* fan page," 1996, ⟨kamui_kun.tripod.com/Zetsuai/zindex.html⟩ (4 January 2001).

21 Wild Angels' Gate, "Bronze Zetsu Ai since 1989 fan page," 11 September 2000, ⟨members.nbci.com/fireflower/bronze⟩ (4 January 2001).

22 Kazuma Kodaka, *Kizuna,* vol. III, (Tokyo: Biblos, 1996), 140.

23 Scooter X, "[amla] Re: read any good manga? (translated comics)," 17 July 2000, ⟨http://groups.yahoo.com/group/amla/message/6327⟩ (4 March 2001).

24 Some of these pictures can be found on the cover of Ozaki Minami's *Bad Blood* manga and *God* artbook.

25 A side story, featuring very sensual gay look-alike angels from the *Kizuna* manga main characters' story, has been published in Kodaka Kazuma, *Kizuna* (Tokyo: Biblos, 1999), 5:171–90.

26 Allison, 38.

27 Joseph J. Tobin, *Re-Made in Japan: Everyday Life and Consumer Taste in a Changing Society* (New Haven: Yale University Press, 1992), 4.

28 Maygra, "Re: [*AMLA*] Mainstreaming slash (was looking for perspective)," 16 April 2000, ⟨http://groups.yahoo.com/group/amla/message/3283⟩ (4 March 2001).

29 MJ Johnson, "Re: [amla] Genders: Back to Nuriko (FY spoilers, sortof)," 12 July 2000, ⟨http://groups.yahoo.com/group/amla/message/6228⟩ (4 March 2001).

30 Shimizu Yuki, "Fly Me to the Heaven," in *Love Mode* (Tokyo: Biblos, 1999), 103–66.

31 A fan who picture-reads the story cannot know the names of the characters. I give them here for easier understanding. Because I am familiar with the series, I know the names of the characters. Furthermore, the plot of *Love Mode* is summarized on some fan Web sites. However, please note that I picture-read "Fly Me to the Heaven" before reading the summary done by a Japanese-literate fan. I chose "Fly Me to the Heaven" because its main characters had never appeared before in a manga series and the story itself has only bare connections with the main plot; this meant that I was not carrying any prior knowledge enabling me to understand it better than any other non-Japanese-speaking Western fan of *Love Mode*.

32 Bellbomb, "*Love Mode* fan page," 25 December 2000, ⟨www.geocities.com/Tokyo/Lights/7363/lovemode.html⟩ (4 January 2001).

33 An interesting quantitative approach to reading strategies and interpretation can be found in Elaine F. Nardocchio, ed., *Reader Response to Literature: The Empirical Dimension* (Berlin: Mouton de Gruyter, 1992).

34 MJ Johnson, "Re: [amla] Seme behavior," 4 May 2000, ⟨http://groups.yahoo.com/group/amla/message/4278⟩ (4 March 2001).

CHRIS BERRY AND FRAN MARTIN

Syncretism and Synchronicity:

Queer'n'Asian Cyberspace in 1990s

Taiwan and Korea

The observation that public lesbian/gay/queer (hereafter l/g/q) cultures emerge most frequently along with late capitalism, the rise of the middle class, consumer culture, urbanization, and mobility appears equally applicable to Asian contexts. Yet, in some cases—notably, those of many of the four "Asian tigers" or Newly Industrialized Economies (Taiwan, Hong Kong, South Korea, and Singapore)—these preconditions prevailed well before the rapid growth and emergence of l/g/q cultures at various points in the 1990s. Here, it seems plausible that an additional factor has been at play: computers and computer-mediated communication (CMC). This study reports on and analyzes data gathered in the late 1990s to examine this hypothesis in Korea and Taiwan.[1]

To examine the nexus between CMC and l/g/q cultures in Taiwan and Korea is to enter into at least two larger debates. One concerns how best to conceptualize the process that has been called "global queering," an increasingly pressing issue for people involved in research on sexual cultures outside the Anglo-American contexts in which terms such as "queer" have been invented.[2] In a number of essays, Dennis Altman and Donald Morton have each argued that the adoption in "other" parts of the world of cultural forms associated with a largely "American" version of gayness proceeds as a consequence of "capitalist imperialism" and imperils the survival of local forms of sexual expression.[3]

Although Morton and Altman are at odds on certain issues, they share a homogenizing view of cultural globalization. One potential counter to this view lies in the work of Peter Jackson on the appropriation of Western gay culture and terminology into a Thai context. He finds that "contemporary attitudes to homosexuality and transgression derive from an ancient and distinctively Thai cultural source . . . these indigenous attitudes have led to a specifically Thai formulation of the new sexual identity of gay."[4]

A different alternative can be developed from the work of Arjun Appadurai. Altman, Morton, and Jackson share a tendency to figure both global (American) culture and the traditional "local" cultures it encounters outside the "West" as fixed and conceptually oppositional entities, one either taking over or successfully absorbing the other. In contrast to this, Appadurai suggests the possibility of a "heterogenizing" view of cultural globalization. According to this view, far from being witness to the shoring-up of "Western" economic and cultural domination, the moment of cultural globalization is characterized precisely by challenges to the authority of the West from forces of cultural difference unleashed by decolonizations and the ensuing complex global economic and cultural shifts. This process in turn transforms all forces involved in the interaction.[5]

In relation to this first debate, then, the pertinent questions are: Does the appearance of l/g/q cultures and identifications in "Asia" represent one more step along the road toward global cultural homogeneity? Will local traditions concerning sexuality and gender successfully absorb the encroaching Western l/g/q cultures and identifications? Or will the different histories that condition the production of these identifications outside the West produce forms of difference irreducible to the banal familiarity of Anglo-American "lesbian/gay," while at the same time transforming and diversifying both local and global l/g/q cultures?

The second major debate concerns the role of CMC in the process. Most current writing assumes that CMC is not simply a vehicle speeding up the transfer of information, but that the material conditions of CMC practices have determining effects on the online subjectivities of those involved in them. Such work focuses on the kinds of identities individuals construct using CMC, with a strong focus on radical differences between on- and off-line identities.[6] Here, our interest is focused more on collective formations such as cultures and political movements, and we are interested in online identities and subjectivities insofar as they enable or obstruct such collective formations.[7]

Our analysis of the data we collected between August 1997 and January 1998 in South Korea and Taiwan on the uses of CMC in l/g/q communities inevitably finds itself already entangled in both these areas of debate. First, although the Internet is often linked explicitly with strongly homogenizing arguments about cultural globalization, the information we have gathered to date suggests a view more akin to Appadurai's heterogenizing one, for reasons we hope will become clear in the following discussion of the project itself.[8] Second, it is clear not only that the Net provides a space in which heterogeneity is produced, but also that the anonymity of cyberspace has been a crucial precondition for the development of l/g/q communities in societies where it is socially (but not legally) difficult to have an l/g/q identity in the offline world.

Much of the recent debate outlined above has proceeded on a rather general level and, significantly, has often taken the form of "internal" disagreements among English-speaking scholars. Indeed, it could be argued that these arguments generally, presenting as they tend to do pictures painted in broad brushstrokes of scenes such as "the Disneyfication of the globe" and "escaping the body," may be criticized most effectively for their failure to account for the specific, material processes through which cultural products and practices travel the globe and are altered and assimilated "elsewhere" in specific local contexts, often through indigenization with less recognizably "global" forms.[9] Our research follows the trend of recent years in cultural globalization studies in indicating the inadequacy of the "*either* Global McGay *or* pristine local tradition" approach to cultural globalization, and we suggest Marcos Becquer and Jose Gatti's term "syncretization" as an alternative approach. We use the term in the sense suggested by Becquer and Gatti to refer to "the tactical articulation of different elements," a paradigm in which these form "a heterogeneous front of distinct [elements] in altered relations to each other."[10] Like Becquer and Gatti, we find syncretism a more productive concept than hybridity, which invokes a reproductive rather than a political metaphor and risks assuming the pure origins of the hybridized elements.[11] The data we present below are far from complete, but we would argue that understandings of the processes we have all been attempting to describe can only be aided by more practical research on specific cultural forms, such as the development of l/g/q Nets in Taiwan and South Korea, which is our subject here.

Specifically, our project aims to consider the effects of the general availability of CMC on the emergent l/g/q communities of Taiwan and South Korea, which have functioned as such since the early 1990s—the same moment at which CMC began to become generally available.[12] In contrast, when lesbian and gay communities began to identify themselves as such in the early post-Stonewall era in the United States and Europe, they did so well before the general availability of these technologies. We want to ask what sort of effects this availability of Internet technology have had on the kinds of individual and collective l/g/q subjects constructed in Taiwan and South Korea. Are these emerging subjectivities and communities differing from existing Anglo-American models of the l/g/q because of the role of CMC in their constitution, or has the technology been reinforcing familiar models?

The Context

Taiwan and South Korea have enough in common to provide a suitable comparative context for studies of sexuality. Similarities can be found with regard to the legal regulation of sexuality, ethical conventions informing kinship structures and obligations, political and economic history, and the circumstances of same-sex subcultures prior to the emergence of publicly visible l/g/q culture. Despite these similarities, there are also significant differences in the history of this emergence that need to be accounted for.

There are no legal strictures or prohibitions specifically directed against homosexual behavior, nor do there seem ever to have been any such regulations, in either Taiwan or South Korea.[13] In part, this may be because both places were colonized and occupied by Japan, which did not have any specific laws regarding homosexuality to impose on its colonies, rather than by European powers, which often imposed such laws on territories they took over, for example, Hong Kong.[14] This absence of specific laws should not be taken as evidence of equal status before the law, however. Same-sex sexual behavior has had little public recognition in either place, making those who wish to engage in it liable to prosecution under laws regulating "public obscenity," loitering, hooliganism, and so forth.[15]

Furthermore, ethical conventions informing kinship structures and obligations place a strong emphasis on heterosexual reproduction in both Taiwan and South Korea. In both states, these ethical conventions are heavily informed by Confucianism, which regards the production of offspring, particularly male offspring, as a filial obligation in order that chil-

Mobile Cultures

dren continue the paternal family line. Other sexual behaviors may be tolerated, but often as an additional indulgence, provided this obligation is fulfilled, rather than as an alternative to it.[16]

Politically, following the end of Japanese colonization in 1945, Taiwan and South Korea were caught up in the Chinese and Korean civil wars. As a result of ensuing events, both places were ruled by repressive, right-wing regimes that imposed martial law for many years but also pursued strong economic growth policies. During these times, the populations were strongly disciplined from above and the development of alternative, popular initiatives of any sort was harshly restrained.[17]

In these legal, cultural, and political circumstances, l/g/q subcultures did exist in both Taiwan and South Korea prior to the developments of the 1990s. However, they existed only as discrete subcultures largely invisible to the general public, focused mainly on bars and public cruising and meeting places such as parks and hotels in major urban centers. As far as is known at the moment, these subcultures do not seem to have included a substantial lesbian subculture in Korea, unlike in Taiwan.[18]

In the past two decades the right-wing regimes in Taiwan and South Korea have been dismantled and replaced by democratic regimes and much more open and pluralist cultures and policies. Combined with economic growth, which has given young people the option of greater independence from their families should they need to take it, this produced preconditions conducive to the emergence of publicly visible l/g/q cultures by the 1990s, if not earlier. However, as the time line in Table 1 indicates, a publicly visible culture emerged earlier in Taiwan than in South Korea. Various differences may be considered to account for this.

First, whereas local Taiwanese l/g/q activists could draw on a long, rich, and varied history of same-sex cultural activities and traditions in Chinese and Taiwanese culture, this was not the case in South Korea. There has been much discussion and speculation about historical precedents in the Korean context, however. For example, it has been alleged that the second daughter-in-law of Korea's most famous king, King Sejong (1397–1450), was a lesbian, and this became a major topic of conversation. However, so far, there is comparatively little research evidence to support such speculation.[19] Second, although many different religions claim followers in both places, including Buddhism and folk forms of syncretic religious practice, Christianity is much more important in South Korea than in Taiwan, mak-

Table 1. The Emergence of L/g/q Communities in Taiwan and South Korea.

	TAIWAN	SOUTH KOREA
1984	First major gay novel (*Crystal Boys*) by Pai Hsien-Yung	
1986	First application for same-sex marriage	
1990	First openly homosexual social group (*Women Zhijian,* a lesbian group, whose name is derived from the French lesbian-themed film, *Entre Nous*)	
1993	First publicly available magazine (*Aibao,* a lesbian magazine)	First gay and lesbian community group, *Chodonghoe,* established
1994	Steady output of films and novels well established	First gay activist comes out in the media
1995		Student groups established
1996	Taipei gay marriage of prominent author attended by mayor's representative	First lesbian activist comes out in the media.
		Community groups multiply
	G&L, first gay glossy magazine	Nonprofit magazines available
	Research groups established in many universities	
1997		First Seoul Queer Film & Video Festival banned, but censorship regulations changed from blanket ban on l/g/q representation to ban on "excessive homosexuality"
1998	Second glossy magazine, *Together*	First glossy magazine, *Buddy*

ing it the second most important Christian country in Asia after the Philippines. Furthermore, whereas Catholicism is the dominant Christian denomination in the Philippines, it is right-wing U.S. Protestant fundamentalist groups that dominate in South Korea.[20]

Also, whereas the slow dismantling of military rule and the culture surrounding it began in Taiwan in the early 1980s, this period was still a time of the most severe repression in South Korea. In Taiwan, this dismantling may be attributed to the combination of internal pressures and a desire to demonstrate the political credentials of the regime in contrast to the People's Republic of China, which had recently been recognized by the United States and the United Nations. This desire to win international respect as a democratic society has extended to a desire to appear more liberal and tolerant in various regards, including toward sexual nonconformists.[21] In contrast, 1979 in South Korea saw the assassination of a president and 1980 the Kwangju massacre of protestors against the repressive regime, and the severity of the regime only began to abate with the prospect that the 1988 Seoul Olympics would focus international media on the country's political and human rights record.[22] To date, possibly for the broader cultural reasons advanced above, that political change has not extended to the culture surrounding sexuality and kinship, where conservative and traditional family values continue to be touted widely as evidence of South Korean social and political success.

Information Retrieval

Unsurprisingly, in light of the different historical and cultural contexts outlined above, we had significantly different experiences in carrying out our research in the two states. These differing experiences can themselves be considered findings highlighting some of the differences between the Taiwanese and South Korean situations.

The translation, distribution, and retrieval of our questionnaire addressed to l/g/q Net users went smoothly in Korea, where it was apparently the first such study to be conducted. Questionnaires were distributed in two sets.[23] One set went out to various community and activist groups; these respondents are referred to hereafter as activists. The second set went out to various bars in the Itaewon district south of central Seoul, which attract younger patrons than the older bar district located around Tapkol Park to the north; these respondents are referred to hereafter as bargoers. A total of one thousand forms was distributed, divided into two more or less equal sets; 109 forms were returned by activists, and 86 by bargoers, making a total of 195 or an overall response rate of approximately 20 percent.

This distribution method was chosen to focus the survey on those sectors of the broad l/g/q communities considered to be most closely associated with the emergent public l/g/q culture. Two reservations should be borne in mind, however. In the absence of any general data about the l/g/q population of South Korea, no claims about general representativeness can be made.[24] Second, although the survey was anonymous, we estimate that at least 70 percent of forms were completed in group situations, either in bars or group meetings. This may mean we need to be cautious about results such as those indicating that relatively few respondents participated in l/g/q culture to find sexual partners.

The experience with the questionnaire method in Taiwan was significantly different and more difficult. Having been warned of the very low return rates encountered by previous researchers after distributing questionnaires in bars, we thought posting the questionnaire at local l/g/q bulletin board (BBS) sites seemed a logical alternative, but after the translated questionnaire was posted at several of these, we were advised by an interviewee to remove it due to some hostility it was attracting online. The hostile response to the questionnaire was partly the result of a recent incident in which a scholar had quoted at length from conversations from BBS sites in an academic paper, which had made the contributors to these "personal discussions" feel a sense of invasion by this unauthorized "outsider," who was, like us, speaking from a position outside the local scene in Taiwan, conducting his research from Stanford University.[25]

The interviewee explained that the resistance to the questionnaire posted by two anonymous "Australian researchers" was also due to the character of Taiwan's l/g/q BBS sites. Due partly to the fact that participants in discussions at BBS sites must be registered members, the sites are characterized by their small size, local constituency, intimate atmosphere, and consequently high level of suspicion of outsiders. Other factors, too, probably contributed to the failure of the questionnaire method in Taiwan. First, the explosion in local academic discussion of the l/g/q Internet in Taiwan prior to the time of our research may have led to a kind of research fatigue on the part of its users.[26] Second, the relatively more developed state of both the l/g/q Internet and l/g/q cultures generally in Taiwan as opposed to Korea at this time may have meant that l/g/q subjects felt a degree of security in their own position and were therefore less keen for academic acknowledgment.

The difficulty in obtaining responses to the questionnaire online means that the data concerning Taiwan come from other sources, including extensive formal and informal interviews with twelve frequent BBS users and site managers.[27] The Korean survey was also supplemented with interviews.

Patterns of Computer and Internet Use

Here we present the results of the survey together with additional data drawn from the other Korean and Taiwan sources to give a picture of computer and Internet use among l/g/q communities in Taiwan and South Korea. The results are broken down into four categories: general demographic information, data on general computer use, data on participation in l/g/q culture, and information on computer use for l/g/q activities.

In regard to the first category, demographics, the participants in the publicly visible l/g/q cultures of Taiwan and South Korea as of late 1997 were young, highly educated, and, in many cases, still students (see Figure 1). Most of the responses to the survey were from men (see Figures 2a–c), and this was especially pronounced among the activists. Although this is certainly connected to who was distributing the questionnaires and the venues in which they were distributed, it is also the case that the lesbian scene is smaller than the gay male scene in both South Korea and Taiwan. In both places, particularly in South Korea, the transgender scene is relatively separate from the l/g/q scene, helping to explain the low number of transgender respondents to the survey.

The Korean survey produced a wide variety of nominations for sexual identity. Although the majority chose either lesbian (*le-su-bi-an*) or gay (*ge-i*), about 15 percent of respondents chose to identify as bisexual (*yang-song-ae-ja*), and 10 percent of activists but almost no bargoers chose to identify as queer (*kkui-o*); 5 percent of activist respondents but no bargoers chose the local neologism *iban*, which is similar to queer in meaning and connotation.[28] Interviewees in Taiwan, similarly, identified with the English terms lesbian and gay as well as queer (*ku'er*) and the Mandarin categories of *nantongzhi* (male-gay) and *nütongzhi* (lesbian). Although the precise local significances of these terms were not explored through the questionnaire, the responses gathered in both places to the question of sexual identi-

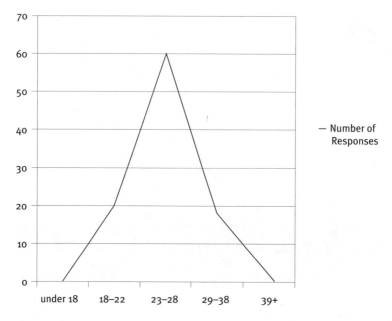

Figure 1. Age Distribution.

fication confirms that the majority of respondents identified with more or less syncretic, modern sexuality categories.[29]

The most significant general demographic difference between Taiwan and South Korean l/g/q community members concerned their domestic situation. The majority of the respondents to the Korean survey were living with their parents. This is quite different from Taiwan, where interview responses indicated that a much higher proportion of l/g/q-identified people were living away from their family. This is because it is more common for Taiwan's tertiary students to live in student dormitories and also because it is much easier to rent an apartment in Taiwan than in South Korea, where the standard requirement of a very high deposit makes it more difficult for young singles to rent.

The information gathered in the second category, on general computer use, indicated a very high level of access and high frequency of use among the l/g/q population in both South Korea and Taiwan.[30] There was a notable gender difference around computer usage rates in the Korean survey, with 40 percent of total female respondents indicating they never used the computer although 90 percent had access. In Taiwan, interview responses

Mobile Cultures

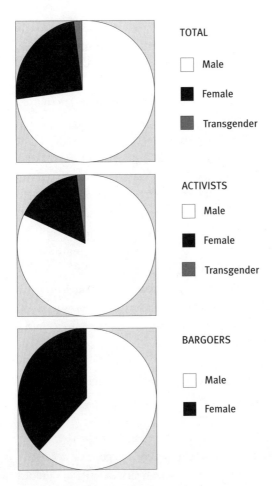

TOTAL

☐ Male

■ Female

▪ Transgender

ACTIVISTS

☐ Male

■ Female

▪ Transgender

BARGOERS

☐ Male

■ Female

Figure 2. Gender Distribution.

indicated that computers were also very much a male activity there, and a 1997 government survey of 38,645 of Taiwan's Internet users indicated that 68 percent of those users were male.[31] As far as we know, there were no lesbian Web site managers in South Korea at the time the survey was carried out, although each of the three major multifunction sites discussed below had separate lesbian-run spaces, such as *Sappho's Daughters* in Nownuri's *Rainbow* site. Interviewees in Taiwan indicated that there was only one really popular all-lesbian BBS site at the time, situated on the server at Tamkang University (Danjiang Daxue), as well as a reasonably sized and rapidly growing network of lesbian-run and targeted www sites.

Perhaps unsurprisingly, given that one of the sets of questionnaires in South Korea was distributed in bars, data in the third category about participation in l/g/q culture indicated that bargoing and socializing were the most popular activities. A number of people also indicated an interest in other activities, ranging from activism to reading l/g/q books and novels. The most unexpected result in the Korean survey was in response to a question asking whether respondents were worried about anyone else knowing of their sexuality. We had expected a great majority of respondents to say they were worried, as the Korean scene remained highly closeted at the time in comparison to the Taiwan scene, which had become very publicly visible within only a few years. And indeed, some respondents angrily added "of course!" to their tick in the yes box or another comment indicating that they felt we did not need to ask this question. However, fully half the respondents said they were not worried.[32]

The fourth category of data concerned the use of the computer for l/g/q activities. Given the gender differences around general computer use, it was clear that these activities were more common among gay men than among lesbians in both South Korea and Taiwan. Overall, however, we estimate that for both men and women, this probably indicates a much higher level of l/g/q computer use in Taiwan and South Korea than would have been the case in, say, Australia at the same time.

Figure 3 shows the different responses in the Korean survey to our questions about the kind of l/g/q computer activities people were engaging in. Interviews indicate that all of these activities were also popular in Taiwan. Most significant here is the relatively low use of overseas sites, despite the fact that the Web has many l/g/q sites from all over the world and that educated young Taiwan and Korean citizens have a high level of foreign-language proficiency. In Taiwan's case, interviews and discussions indicated relatively low use even of those overseas l/g/q sites that are in Chinese. This low use also correlates to the kinds of activity that are most popular, namely, extensions of the kind of chatting, socializing, and cruising activities you might find in bars, followed by information seeking. Interview responses in Korea indicated that people often wanted to meet others on the Net as a possible prelude to meeting them elsewhere in real space, or at least that they wanted a situation where that possibility would be open to them. Clearly, it is easier to meet someone who is living in the same town or country than someone living overseas. This result clearly runs counter to some of the

Mobile Cultures

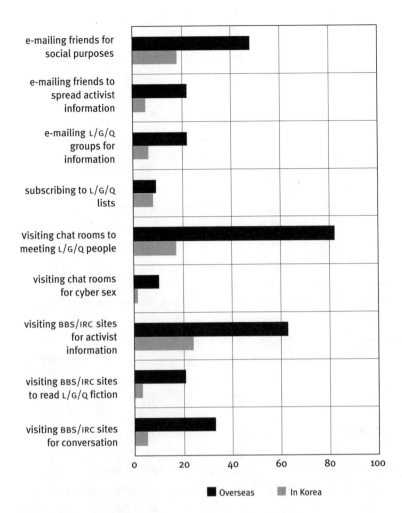

Figure 3. Which Computer Activities Do You Engage In?

common utopian and alarmist rhetorics about the Net as radically alienated from everyday life and global rather than local and integrated.

Finally, a note of caution about the low reported use of overseas sites. In the Korean survey, many of those who acknowledged going to overseas sites claimed to be seeking out "activist information." However, about 60 percent of the overseas sites named as popular by respondents were pornography sites. Although this use of overseas sites might conform to a broad interpretation of activist information, it also indicates a certain inclination to underreport overseas site use. As one of our interviewees pointed out, if so few Koreans are going to overseas sites, and given that no gay pornography is available in Korea, why does every Korean gay man know the names of the major American gay porn stars?

Taiwan and Korea's L/g/q Net Sites

L/g/q Net use in Taiwan and in South Korea were quite distinct in terms of the most popular technologies used for Net activities and in terms of the character of sites themselves, although there were many common points in activities undertaken at sites in both places.

In Taiwan, there are several such technologies available, and interactions using them are primarily Chinese character-text-based. The oldest form of interactive Internet communication in Taiwan is Internet Relay Chat (IRC). Second, there are the popular sites on BBS known as MOTSS boards (member of the same sex), and which allow for group "chat," one-on-one "talk," and the publication of documents or "posts." Finally, there are the newer World Wide Web sites. Before 1994, there was no local Net system in Taiwan, and people looking for lesbian or gay information or chat had to search out overseas-based, predominantly English-language gay or lesbian IRC sites or Web pages. But 1994 saw the establishment of Taiwan's first gay BBS board (or MOTSS), which was quickly followed by others, making MOTSS boards by far the most popular form of l/g/q Net use. Estimates of the total number of MOTSS boards at the time of our survey put the figure at around eighty. In 1997, local l/g/q WWW pages began to be established; these still numbered somewhere under fifty at the time of our survey and were less popular than MOTSS boards due to their generally less interactive character.[33]

As in Taiwan, individual Web pages are less popular in Korea than sites that facilitate a high degree of interaction, and the Korean sites that do this also use predominantly Korean script (*hangul*). However, where the most popular Taiwan sites at the time of our survey were MOTSS BBS boards, the most popular Korean sites were and are located on the World Wide Web. The primary reason for this difference is related to issues of server access. Taiwan's MOTSS boards are established almost exclusively on institutional BBS at universities. In Korea, it seems that access to university servers is less straightforward and that they often are not particularly reliable, making

Mobile Cultures

them less attractive to students. Furthermore, most Korean users of BBS and Web sites are likely to have been using them before entering university, meaning they are already subscribers before becoming students. Because of all these circumstances, when university students do set up groups, it seems they do so on commercial servers rather than on their own university server. Hence, the most popular Korean sites are generally www sites established on the three major, commercial, user-pays servers: Chollian's *Queer-net*, Nownuri's *Rainbow* site, and Hitel's *Dosamo*. These are huge text-based sites incorporating multiple chat rooms, message boards, and other subgroups; one interviewee estimated that one of the sites was getting up to five thousand hits per day. The general nonregulation by Taiwan university administrations of students' homosexual behaviors, on the other hand, becomes extremely significant with regard to the flourishing l/g/q Net cultures there, given that the vast majority of "l/g/q space" on Taiwan's Net at the time of our research was actually based on university, rather than commercial, servers. Once a site was established by a group of interested students who applied to the university's central BBS administration, students could access the site from their free university Internet account, paying only the cost of the call from their modem, or nothing at all if they accessed the site from university computer labs, as was often the case. In Korea, access to l/g/q Internet sites was far more expensive, as one had to be a paid-up subscriber to one of the commercial systems to fully access the sites there, although the questionnaire results indicated that this did not deter people, as many respondents indicated that they subscribed to all three servers to access all three sites. The reliance of Taiwan's l/g/q sites on the institutional BBS also meant that the majority of the users of the MOTSS boards were university students, with some older nonstudents and also high school students included, whereas Korea's l/g/q Internet culture was more mixed.

Several interviewees made the point that many BBS users had no access to other aspects of l/g/q culture, the MOTSS board or Korean www site becoming their entire "l/g/q life." Users may have been too young to attend bars, unable to afford the fees there if they were students, or, even more likely, they may have lived on campus or with a family remote from the l/g/q cultures of Taipei or Seoul or the other large cities. Given this, it is not surprising that for many users, Taiwan's *tongzhi wanglu* (l/g/q Net) or its Korean equivalent was a form of alternative social space offering new ways in which to identify as an l/g/q subject: one need not ever have gone to an l/g/q bar, nor had a sexual experience with someone of one's own sex, nor even known any other l/g/q people offline. In the following section, we describe some ways in which the Taiwan and Korean l/g/q Nets function as what we call "online discursive communities."

That online communities function as social units is suggested by the fact that users of a particular site may know each other's identity and become friends offline, the site taking on the function of a "club." One interviewee in Taiwan mentioned instances in which a MOTSS member would hold a birthday party or other celebration to which the condition of entry was membership in a particular MOTSS. Similarly, a Korean interviewee explained that he had posted a message when he was living in a small college town asking if there was anyone else online from the same town. After various exchanges on the Net, the group met to see a movie and then began more regular social activities.

Nevertheless, the major function of the l/g/q Net remained the communications established online among l/g/q subjects. When questioned about the most frequent forms of communication at the sites, interviewees suggested that discussions of personal and emotional issues were most popular. One Taipei woman, about 24 years old, told how she saw young university and high school students posting accounts of difficult breakups with lovers and getting instant support and advice from other MOTSS users. She compared this to when she was "that age," when "we had to keep it to ourselves; we had no one to tell—you'd just go and shoot baskets or whatever till you felt better. These kids today have it so good." Taiwan's MOTSS sites and Korean WWW sites clearly serve an important function in the emotional support of their users, particularly in helping members negotiate ways to imagine themselves as l/g/q subjects through communication with others like themselves.

One feature that distinguishes both Taiwan MOTSS sites and Korea WWW sites from other specialized sites—for example, sports or movie sites—is that at these sites, anything and everything gets discussed, regardless of whether it bears a direct or obvious relation to sexuality as such. Discussions at other specialized sites, on the other hand, tend to stick closely to the designated topic or risk being criticized as "irrelevant." One interviewee in Taiwan explained the broad-ranging discussions on MOTSS boards as the result of users looking for a place where they could feel comfortable speak-

Mobile Cultures

ing about anything without having to exercise internal censorship: the participants could feel freer in the knowledge that the people they were chatting with were also l/g/q subjects.

Other popular topics include searches for sexual or emotional partners, although these were less up-front at the time of our survey in Korea, where print media did not accept personal classifieds and many people would have found frankly sexual classifieds socially unacceptable in any public form. Searchers in both places might have been looking for someone to "talk" to one-on-one online; some speak on the phone after meeting online but never go beyond that; and some meet offline. L/g/q sites also hosted discussions on local l/g/q politics and culture; for example, debates about movement strategy, responses to homophobia, debates over current developments in local feminism, and issues related to gender and sexuality in local culture were all frequently addressed. *Tongzhi* activists in Taiwan distributed information about current issues and activities in this way, and the sites were also used to collect signatures on petitions to the government on issues relating to sexuality. For example, a petition was widely posted in 1997 protesting the Taipei city government's decision to outlaw prostitution in the municipality; this in turn sparked debate about the gender politics of sex work, feminist arguments about "the exploitation of women" clashing with other feminist discourses on the rights of sex workers to autonomy over their body and income. And around the time of the banning of the First Seoul Queer Film and Video Festival in September 1997, news and petitions were circulated and gathered simultaneously in Korean and English by fax, email, snail mail, and by hand.

Finally, Taiwan and Korean sites were also used for the publication of l/g/q cyberfiction. Although this happened less in Korea, there had been a recent boom in cyberfiction, much of it quite sexually explicit. No star writers had emerged in Korea. In Taiwan, on the other hand, there were already two books, both by male Taiwan writers and published by tongzhi publisher Huasheng (Worldson) in Hong Kong, which were marketed as "queer Internet literature"; that is, their contents appeared first on the Net and only later in book form.[34]

In summary, then, our data showed that Taiwan MOTSS boards and Korean www sites in the late 1990s were extremely highly used, extremely lively spaces of l/g/q emotional support, political debate, and sexual and creative expression. Their existence meant that massive numbers of people with otherwise limited access to any sort of l/g/q culture could imagine themselves as a community and participate, at little or no cost, in "community events" online twenty-four hours a day. In Taiwan, MOTSS users were recognized by non-Net users as a group referred to as *tongzhi wangyou* ("l/g/q Net users"),[35] which produced its own literature; they participated in academic discourse on queer theory and made its presence felt in the political struggles of the tongzhi movement.[36] The managers of the Korean WWW sites and those most involved in their activities also had a distinct identity within the more active elements of the l/g/q community. Without the need ever to coalesce as an offline community, Net users function primarily as a "discursive community," that is, a community—organized around sexual identification—whose interactions are primarily mediated through Chinese-character text on Taiwan's local MOTSS boards or through Korean hangul text on local Korean WWW sites.

Some Preliminary Conclusions: The Net in Taiwan and
Korea and "Global Queering"

What does the information we have gathered tell us about the relationship between the late 1990s emergence of Taiwan and South Korean l/g/q Net space, Net communities, and Net identities on the one hand, and global queering on the other? In light of the debates on the globalization of queer cultures and the character of the Internet in which this piece finds itself implicated, it is interesting to note that Taiwan's MOTSS boards are seen by users as intensely "local" Taiwan spaces and that the Korean questionnaire results also indicate a predominantly local focus of activities. One interviewee in Taiwan reported that if you asked a tongzhi whether he or she had been on the wanglu (Net), you would be understood to be asking if the person used the island's local BBS network rather than the transnational Internet, which is designated by a separate term (*wangji wanglu*). It is the case that Internet technology can be—and undoubtedly is—used in both South Korea and Taiwan to access information about overseas l/g/q cultures. But it should be remembered that the process of searching out English-language overseas Web pages on a browser like Netscape requires the use of English, not only to read the pages found but also to operate search engines in the first place; is far slower and more complicated than accessing local BBS sites; and requires quite different and more sophisticated software. Furthermore, it is difficult for those outside Taiwan and South Korea to access the Taiwan and Korean l/g/q sites. Taiwan's BBS boards are accessible with difficulty from overseas, but the process becomes very slow and cumbersome, and one needs the requisite Chinese software. And although it may be easier to arrive at the Korean WWW sites from overseas, one needs to be a subscriber to participate fully, as well as have Korean-language software to read the material on the sites.

In these circumstances, we believe that Taiwan and Korean l/g/q Net spaces are characterized by processes of syncretization like those discussed earlier, rather than simply acting as helpmate to cultural homogenization or as spaces where the local same-sex culture absorbs and assimilates the foreign. Given that the overwhelming majority of l/g/q Net activity in Taiwan and Korea happens on local, interactive Chinese- and Korean-language systems, it is not surprising to find that signifiers that are readable in English as representatives of Anglo-American l/g/q culture—indeed, such terms as lesbian, gay, and queer themselves—take on, in these "other" cyberspaces, the character not so much of emissaries of an invasion by the "globally gay" as that of rapidly multiplying syncretized signs perhaps unrecognizable outside their local contexts. To take the example of the term *la-zi,* one of the commonest terms for lesbian on Taiwan's WWW sites and MOTSS boards: on the one hand, this term phonetically cites the English word lesbian, but at the same time it is also a reference to the nickname of the protagonist in Taiwan's famous lesbian novel of the early 1990s, Qiu Miaojin's *Crocodile Journal.*[37] The term, then, is reducible to neither of the citations it performs: neither the location of local subjection to the "imperialism" of English language–based sexual categorization, nor a form of "purely local" sexual understanding.

Both as separate spaces within the range of spaces occupied by the emergent l/g/q communities and through their articulation with other spaces and activities engaged in by those communities, the l/g/q Nets in South Korea and Taiwan in the late 1990s were structurally distinctive elements of the contemporary l/g/q movements, with material effects on the ways those communities understood and represented themselves. Sometimes, there is a tendency to see the Net and real space in oppositional terms, to worry that virtual reality draws people away from spaces outside the Net, reducing their capacity for activism and involvement in publicly visible l/g/q communities. This perhaps would be an l/g/q variant on the common general media stories about the Net's eating up people's lives and so forth. Indeed, in both Taiwan and South Korea some activist respondents raised concerns about this issue, in particular in relation to the issue of coming out. At a time when some parts of the l/g/q movements in both places were calling for public self-naming as an activist strategy, the Net offered a space in which anonymity could be assured as identity became fluid and untraceable, which was a concern for some.

However, this research indicates that virtual and real space are fully articulated and integrated, making the availability of the Net a crucial element in the rapid development of visible l/g/q cultures. As demonstrated in the examples given, our interview respondents indicated that activists and other community organizers do not choose between the Net and real space, but work actively in and out of both. Although neither homosexual behavior nor activism and organizing are illegal in either Taiwan or South Korea, Taiwan and South Korean l/g/q citizens are not afforded any specific rights protections, and the very high cost of living in both states can make people economically dependent on parents. This can make it very difficult to find a place in real space to hold a meeting and can make individuals initially apprehensive about meeting in real space, particularly in South Korea, where l/g/q cultures have achieved less general visibility than is the case in Taiwan.[38] The special combination of anonymity and accessibility characterizing the Net becomes important here, enabling rapid and safe initial connections and communications so that people may quickly establish levels of mutual confidence and understanding, and then either move into less user-friendly offline space or continue to operate effectively in the localized Net spaces they have created to fit their particular needs.

Given this, our argument is that the distinctive l/g/q content and uses of the Net in Taiwan and Korea bespeak a complex process of cultural syncretization rather than an unproblematic "reflection" in Taiwan's or South Korea's l/g/q cultures of the globally queer. The argument to which our research leads us is that Internet technology becomes, in these "other" places, a particularly efficacious catalyst for the negotiation of new and culturally syncretic formations of nonnormative sexual identification and community, which can be read as foregrounding the historical specificities and limits of the Anglo-American sexual cultures rather than simply as "spreading" or reproducing those cultures. Further, the research also indicates different directions in thinking about the impact of Internet technology in relation to cultural globalization. Net technology is used in Taiwan and South Korea for the imagining of l/g/q discursive communities that are as locally particular as they are articulated in complex ways to globalizing narratives of "lesbian and gay identity." The technology shows itself, then, to be at least as enabling in the imagining of new local and syncretic forms of l/g/q subjects and community as it has been argued elsewhere to be in the global advance of homogenized Western gayness.

Notes

1   This is a revised version of an article that originally appeared as "Queer'n'Asian on the Net: Syncretic Sexualities in Taiwan and Korean Cyberspaces," in *Critical InQueeries* 2, no. 1 (1998): 67–94.

2   The term "global queering" was used as a title for Dennis Altman, "Global Queering," *Australian Humanities Review,* no. 2 (1996), ⟨http://www.lib.latrobe.edu.au/AHR/⟩ (21 March 2001). For a set of recent interventions into these debates, see, for example, *GLQ* 5, no. 4 (1999), special issue on *Thinking Sexuality Transnationally,* ed. Elizabeth A. Povinelli and George Chauncey. In that volume, see particularly Lisa Rofel, "Qualities of Desire: Imagining Gay Identities in China," 451–74.

3   Dennis Altman, "The World of 'Gay Asia,'" in *Asian and Pacific Inscriptions,* ed. Suvendrini Pereira, a special book issue of *Meridian* 14, no. 2 (1995): 121–138; Altman, "Global Queering," and responses. Following responses to his *AHR* piece, Altman's later article, "Rupture or Continuity? The Internationalization of Gay Identities," begins to show a more nuanced argument on these issues: *Social Text,* no. 48 (1996): 77–94. Donald Morton, "Global (Sexual) Politics, Class Struggle, and the Queer Left," *Critical InQueeries* 1, no. 3 (May 1997): 1–30; see also Altman's response, 31–34. See also Morton's "Birth of the Cyberqueer," in *Cybersexualities: A Reader on Feminist Theory, Cyborgs and Cyberspace,* ed. Jenny Wolmark (Edinburgh: University of Edinburgh Press, 1999), 295–313.

4   Peter A. Jackson, "The Persistence of Gender," in *Australia Queer,* ed. Chris Berry and Annamarie Jagose, a special issue of *Meanjin* 55, no. 1 (1996): 111.

5   Arjun Appadurai, "Disjuncture and Difference in the Global Cultural Economy," in *Global Culture: Nationalism, Globalisation and Modernity,* ed. Mike Featherstone (London: Sage, 1990), 295–310, and reprinted with other pertinent essays in Arjun Appadurai, *Modernity at Large: Cultural Dimensions of Globalization* (Minneapolis: University of Minnesota Press, 1996), 27–47.

6 These ways of considering the sort of subject enabled by this technological form bear traces of certain postmodern rethinkings of the monadic individualist subject, which read technologies not as external to but as constitutive of contemporary bodies and selves. For example, see Donna Haraway's "Manifesto for Cyborgs," *Socialist Review,* no. 80 (1985): 65–107, and Peter Ludlow's introduction to the section "Self and Community Online," in *High Noon on the Electronic Frontier: Conceptual Issues in Cyberspace,* ed. Peter Ludlow (Cambridge, MA: MIT Press, 1996), 311–316.

7 However, we have given more extensive consideration to the implications of these data for debates about Net subjectivities and identities elsewhere: Chris Berry and Fran Martin, "Queer'n'Asian on—and off—the Net: The Role of Cyberspace in Queer Taiwan and Korea," in *Web Studies: Rewiring Media Studies for the Digital Age,* ed. David Gauntlett (London: Arnold, 2000), 74–81.

8 The Internet is one of the three factors identified by an influential 1996 *Economist* article as bringing about the encroachment of the global "McGay." "It's Normal to Be Queer," *The Economist* (6 January 1996): 68–70. The other two factors are identified as the spread of the AIDS virus and economic globalization. The Internet is persistently linked with the spread of economic and cultural imperialism as well as the breakdown of local sovereignties. See, for example, Heather Bromberg, "Are MUDs Communities? Identity, Belonging and Consciousness in Virtual Worlds," in *Cultures of Internet,* ed. Rob Shields (London: Sage, 1996), 143, for further discussion and references; also Dan Thu Nguyen and Jon Alexander, "The Coming of Cyberspacetime and the End of Polity," in Shields, 99–124.

9 *The Economist* claims, for example, that "what McDonald's has done for food and Disney has done for entertainment, the global emergence of ordinary gayness is doing for sexual culture" ("It's Normal," 70).

10 Marcos Becquer and Jose Gatti, "Elements of Vogue," *Third Text,* nos. 16–17 (1991): 69–70.

11 Ibid., 68.

12 In speaking of l/g/q subjects and communities in the Taiwan and South Korean situations, we refer to recent forms of "homosexual identification" that occur alongside and as a result of a general visibility of sexually nonnormative subjects within culture, that is, the appearance of recognizable, public identities such as lesbian, gay, queer, or homosexual, as distinct from older, subcultural, and less generally visible traditions around sexually nonnormative behavior.

13 Historically, the exception to this has been the military, where homosexual behavior has been a reason for discharge and exclusion in both South Korea and Taiwan. However, in the early 1990s, those grounds were dropped in

Taiwan. When gay men objected, arguing that they were recognized by the state only as cannon fodder, they were berated for not following the example of American gay men who wanted to serve in the military. Cindy Patton, "Yuwang yinxing hongzhaji: xinxing guojiazhong 'yiji' quanqiuhuazhi xianxiang" ("Stealth Bombers of Desire: The Globalization of 'Alterity' in Emerging Democracies"), trans. Zhuang Ruilin, *Working Papers in Gender/Sexuality Studies,* ed. Center for the Study of Sexualities, National Central University, Chungli, nos. 3–4 (1998): 303. Furthermore, although homosexual behavior itself may not be prosecuted in either state, the representation of homosexuality in public spaces has been a problem. Since the research for this paper was done, it seems the South Korean government has picked up on what is happening on the Net, is treating it as a public space, and is attempting to ban homosexual content under the guise of protecting minors. International Gay and Lesbian Rights Commission (IGLHRC), "Action Alert: Bigotry and Censorship Masquerade as Protection of Youth," International Gay and Lesbian Human Rights Commission, 23 August 2001, ⟨http://www.iglhrc.org/world/ne_asia/Korea2001Aug.html⟩ (3 October 2001).

14 In the case of Taiwan, the history of the period between 1911 and 1945 with regard to family law, in which regulations governing sexual behavior might have appeared, remains difficult to document. Japanese civil law was enforced in Taiwan from 1898, meaning that the island had a Family Law Code before the Chinese Mainland, whose first pure family law was drafted in 1911. In that year the Japanese occupiers revoked all Japanese family and inheritance law over Taiwan, on the grounds that it encountered there significant cultural differences that made it difficult to implement, but it was not until the Recovery of Taiwan by China in 1945 that the Republican family law, drafted in 1911, came into effect. However, it is likely that questions of homosexuality or sodomy may have fallen under not family but criminal law codes. It was Japanese criminal law, which makes no direct references to either homosexuality or sodomy, that was enforced in Taiwan during this period (1898–1945). See Deng Xue-ren, *Qinshufa zhi Biange yu Zhanwang* [Family law's transformation and future prospects], (Taipei: Yuedan, 1997). This indicates that Taiwan's legal code between 1898 and at least 1911 may have been less concerned with acts of male-male sex than was the Qing code enforced at that time on the Chinese Mainland, in which a substatute governing homosexual rape had been in place since 1740. See Bret Hinsch, *Passions of the Cut Sleeve: The Male Homosexual Tradition in China* (Berkeley: University of California Press, 1992), 142–43.

15 In contemporary Taiwan, for example, the laws most often used to prosecute those showing homosexual behavior in public are those that criminalize *fanghai shanliang fengsu* ("the endangering of fine customs and traditions")—

Article 2, clauses 80–84, "Laws for the Protection of Social Order," in *Zui Xin Liufa Quanshu* [The latest edition of the six legal categories], ed. Zhang Zhiben and Lin Jidong (Taipei: Da Zhongguo, 1996), 555—and those that specify *fanghai fenghua zui* ("the crime of endangering cultural decency"): Criminal Law Article 16, clauses 224, 225, 227, 233, in Zhang and Lin, 390. In Article 16, all clauses that cover the possibility of sexual behavior toward men classify it as *weixie xingwei* (obscene conduct), a fact that has been protested in recent years by antihomophobia lawyers. See Wang Ru-xuan, introduction to *Fan Qishi zhi Yue* [A date on which to oppose discrimination], (Taipei: Tongzhi Gongzuo Fang, 1993), 2, 6–7.

16 David Hall and Roger Ames, in *Anticipating China: Thinking through the Narratives of Chinese and Western Culture* (New York: State University of New York Press, 1995) and *Thinking through Confucius* (New York: State University of New York Press, 1987), offer detailed discussion of the ways traditional forms of Confucian ideology specify the production of descendents by the son as a primary filial duty. In a contemporary Taiwan context, Chen Mei-Ling explains in the Taiwan civil law textbook that the concept of marriage is legally defined with explicit prescription of the sex of the parties entering into it (one male, one female) and that therefore those of the same sex cannot marry, as this would constitute an "endangerment of social order and fine traditions." Chen Meiling et al., eds., *Minfa Rumen* [An introduction to civil law], (Taipei: Yuedan, 1993), 527. The traditional-familialist bias of Taiwan family law has been roundly critiqued in recent years by lesbian and gay activists and feminists alike; see, for example, all issues of the *Awakenings* magazine since 1994 (*Funü Xinzhi*, Taipei), which contain abundant articles detailing the efforts of feminists to reform this area of ROC law with its emphasis on the continuation of the paternal family line through the production of heirs who "belong" (in cases of divorce) to the father. See especially Huang Yu-Xiu, "Sexual Equality before the Law" *Funü Xinzhi*, no. 146 (1994): 4–6. Taiwan's family law is at present in the process of revision by the government in consultation with feminist groups. Korean feminist scholars have also engaged in an extensive critique of patrilineal laws. For example, see Yang Hyon-Ah, "Hankuk Kajokpop-eso Omoni-nun Odi-e Iss(Oss)-na?" [Where is (not) the mother in Korean family law], in *Discourses and Realities of Motherhood: Mothers' Gender, Livelihood, and Sexual Identity* [*Mosong-ui Damron-gwa Hyonshil: Omoni-ui Song, Sarm, Jongchesong*], ed. Kim Yong-Hee, Jong Jin-Song, and Yun Jong-ro (Seoul: Hanam, 1999), 117–36.

17 Alan M. Wachman, *Taiwan: National Identity and Democratization* (Armonk, NY: M.E. Sharpe, 1994); Bruce Cumings, *Korea's Place in the Sun: A Modern History* (New York: Norton, 1997).

18 Chris Berry, "Seoul Man: A Night on the Town with Korea's First Gay Activ-

ist," *Outrage,* no. 159 (1996): 38–40. On Taiwan's lesbian culture in the "pre-bar" times of the 1960s–1970s, see Antonia Chao, "Embodying the Invisible: Body Politics in Constructing Contemporary Taiwanese Lesbian Identities" (Ph.D. diss., Cornell University, 1996), especially chap. 2.

19 On Chinese culture, see Hinsch; Giovanni Vitiello, "The Fantastic Journey of an Ugly Boy: Homosexuality and Salvation in Late Ming Pornography," *Positions: East Asia Cultures Critique* 4, no. 2 (1996): 291–320. For a novelistic representation of male-male sexual subcultures in Taipei in the 1970s, see Pai Hsien-Yung, *Crystal Boys [Niezi]*, trans. Howard Goldblatt (San Francisco: Gay Sunshine Press, 1995). The traditional Taiwanese opera *Gezai Xi* or (in Min'Nan language) *Goa'A Hi,* in which female actors play both male and female roles, is sometimes recognized as a location of an "indigenous" traditional female-female erotic, as indicated by the deployment of an all-female opera troupe as the setting for a lesbian romance in Cheng Sheng-fu's 1991 film, *Shisheng Huamei (The Silent Thrush)*. See also Teri Silvio, "Drag Melodrama/Feminine Public Sphere/Folk Television: 'Local Opera' and Identity in Taiwan" (Ph.D. diss., University of Chicago, 1998), and Teri Silvio, "Reflexivity, Bodily Praxis, and Identity in Taiwanese Opera," *GLQ* 5, no. 4 (1999): 585–603. On Korea, Richard Rutt, "The Flower Boys of Silla (Hwarang): Notes on the Sources," *Transactions of the Korea Branch of the Royal Asiatic Society* 38 (1961): 1–66, is known to Korean l/g/q activists, but those interviewed for this study indicated no knowledge of local writings.

20 Byung-Nak Song, *The Rise of the Korean Economy* (Hong Kong: Oxford University Press, 1990), 47–50; Spencer J. Palmer, *Korea and Christianity* (Seoul: Seoul Computer Press, 1986); and David K. Jordan: "Changes in Postwar Taiwan and Their Impact on the Popular Practice of Religion," in *Cultural Change in Postwar Taiwan,* ed. Steven Harrell and Huang Chün-chieh, (Taipei: SMC Publishing, 1994), 137–60.

21 Patton; Chao.

22 Wachman; Cumings.

23 We would like to thank Lee Chung-Woo, Seo Dong-Jin, and the staff of the Seoul Queer Film and Video Festival for distributing and collecting the survey forms. They also helped to translate the questionnaires, together with Kim Hyun-Sook, who also helped with the design of the questionnaires. Yi Huso read the essay and offered helpful comments and explanations from New York. We would also like to thank the people who took the trouble to fill out the questionnaires, both those in Korea and those who did fill them out in Taiwan. Thanks also to National Taiwan Central University's Centre for the Study of Sexualities, as well as Grace, Bruce Chen, Tawei Chi, and Josette Thong in Taiwan, all of whom were immensely helpful in the organization of the Taiwan research.

24 Although some researchers have attempted to survey gays and lesbians in Korea, most have been public health organization representatives concerned primarily with sexual behavior alone and not with establishing baseline data about gays and lesbians in Korea. Furthermore, according to local activists, many members of the community assumed that these researchers were homophobic and therefore did not attempt to answer their questions accurately. Other unpublished research has been attempted by some university students.

25 This was Chen Cong-Qi's paper "Are You a Gay, Kuer or Tongzhi? Notes on the Politics of Hybrid Sexual Identity," presented at the second International Conference on Sexuality Education, Sexology, Gender Studies and LesBiGay Studies, National Central University, Taiwan, 31 May—1 June 1997. Interestingly, a near-identical debate was sparked at the 1998 International Conference on Sexuality Education, Sexology, Gender Studies and LesBiGay Studies, in which this time a feminist scholar was berated for quoting from "private" conversations on a feminist BBS site.

26 See Chen's paper cited above as well as those of Linda Yang and Lucifer Hung, presented at the same conference. National Central University also organized a miniconference on "Queer Internet Activism" in December 1997; authors Tawei Chi, Lucifer Hung, and WAITER frequently publish fiction, poetry, and theoretical material in mainstream and l/g/q media, centering on Internet spaces and cultures in Taiwan.

27 The Taiwan information comes also from a regular column on lesbian Net culture published each month in the local lesbian magazine *Nü Pengyou* (*Girlfriend*); attendance of a miniconference on queer Internet activism (December 21, 1997, organized by National Central University); three academic conference papers on queer Internet use from the second Conference on Sexuality and Gender Studies, 1997, National Central University (Linda Yang's "Virtual Space and the Flow of Sexual Discourse," Lucifer Hung's "Identity Politics Ends/And Its Own Lack: From the Interaction within Taiwanese Cyberspace to the Dynamics/Visibility of Queer Politics/Discourse," and Chen Cong-Qi's "Are You a Gay, Kuer or Tongzhi?"); selected mainstream media articles gathered on Internet regulation; personal visits to l/g/q sites; readings of local cyberfiction; and the fifteen or so responses we did get to the questionnaire, although these last are clearly too few to be statistically meaningful.

28 Accounts of the derivation of the term vary according to which Chinese character "i" it is believed to refer to. Some hold the literal meaning to be "second rank" or "second level," carrying connotations of both abnormality and nonconformity. Others hold that it means "ordinary people," and is used on signs telling the public to stay out of staff-only areas; hence it implies a

special category of persons. Consultations were held with local activists about what the most common local terms for sexual identity were, before the questionnaires were finalized and distributed.

29 We take terms such as *le-su-bi-an* and *nantongzhi* to be syncretic and specific to the modern period in that they reference both local language and culture and a globalizing understanding of public sexual communities and identities. Such understandings are taken to be "modern" in contrast with earlier, local forms of sexuality categorization not similarly undergirded by these notions of public sexual identity and community and less clearly articulated with globalizing models of "lesbian and gay identity." The term *tongzhi* has been appropriated in recent years in both Taiwan and Hong Kong to refer to a coalitionist view of something like lesbian/gay/bisexual, and sometimes as a translation of queer. Etymologically meaning "same-will," the term literally means "comrade" in the political sense deployed by both the KMT Nationalists and the Communist Party of China, while also referencing in its first component (*tong*) the term *tongxinglian* (homosexual/ity).

30 Of course, frequent computer users might have been more inclined to complete the survey than nonusers, but this still indicates a very high level of use indeed.

31 Kai Tuo, Fan Shuteng Workshop (Gongzuo Xiaozu), "Taiwan 1997 Wanglu Shiyong Diaocha Huodong" [The 1997 Taiwan Internet Use Survey], Fan Shuteng Wanglu Diaocha Gang [Yam Online Survey Net], July 1997, ⟨http://taiwan.yam.org.tw/survey⟩ (20 March 2001).

32 Although the economic crisis of the late 1990s raised expectations about greater conservativeness in Korean society in general, the successful launch of the first gay and lesbian glossy magazine, *Buddy*, despite predictions that no one would dare be seen buying it publicly, was among the earliest evidence that this was not so. Nonetheless, an unexpected result like this would of course require further research before any conclusions could be drawn from it. Perhaps unsurprisingly, given the results of this research, *Buddy* has a regular column on the World Wide Web as well as its own Web site. Buddy, *Buddy Digital Queer Society,* 1998–2001, ⟨http://www.buddy79.com⟩ (20 March 2001).

33 Nevertheless, Taiwan www sites become more sophisticated and interactive all the time; see, for example, Dingo's series of lesbian pages and "cyber-pub," online since 1996: *To-Get-Her Lez Cyberpub,* 24 November 1996, ⟨http://www.to-get-her.org/⟩ (20 March 2001). For a Taiwan lesbian BBS and www resource list with discussion of lesbian Internet culture in and history of Taiwan and links, see Chang Zhong's pages at *Chang Zhong de Jia* (*Chang Zhong's Home*), 21 February 1997, ⟨http://www.geocities.com/WestHollywood/Heights/1777⟩ (20 March 2001). For a Taiwan tongzhi www resource list with links, see Gin

Gin (Jing Jing), *Gin Gin Wanglu Ziyuan* [Gin Gin's Internet Resources], *Club 1069*, 2000, ⟨http://club1069.com/gingins/4[1].htm⟩ (20 March 2001).

34 These are *Xiao Mo*, by "ask," (Hong Kong: Huasheng Shudian, 1996) and *Meimei Wan'An* by "garrido" (Hong Kong: Huasheng Shudian, 1996).

35 See note 27 on the term tongzhi.

36 The *tongzhi wangyou* were the group addressed in the papers mentioned above at the 1997 second International Conference on Sexuality Education, Sexology, Gender Studies and LesBiGay Studies, National Central University.

37 Qiu Miaojin, *Eyu Shouji* [The crocodile's journal], (Taipei: Shibao, 1994). Words that may mean something like lesbian on Taiwan's MOTSS pages include *tongzhi, nütongxinglian, nütongzhi,* lesbian, lez, *la-zi, la-la, ku'er,* queer, *guaitai,* dyke, *dai-ke,* T, Tomboy, *po,* butch, *laogong,* femme.

38 For further discussion of this phenomenon in Korea, see Chris Berry, "My Queer Korea: Identity, Space and the 1998 Seoul Queer Film and Video Festival," *Intersections,* no. 2 (May 1999), ⟨http://wwwshe.murdoch.edu.au/intersections⟩ (20 March 2001).

DAVID MULLALY

Queerly Embodying the Good

and the Normal

Who would want to be *homosexual,*
a person who is *repulsed* by society,
an individual who is *revolting,*
an act that is *immoral*?
Being gay is *emotionally devastating.*

How many people know that being "gay" is not a *choice,*
but it is a disease that is passed on genetically, hidden on the
x chromosome like color blindness and *hemophilia* etc.?

Click **HERE** to **ENTER**

—http://xq28.hypermart.net
(italicized words in English with Thai glosses)

So reads the welcome mat to the multilayered and ever-evolving Thai Web site, *xq28.*[1] It began with an anomalous Thai queer, "James."[2] Our protagonist was unsatisfied by the answers in his world that solve the queer questions of the self, "How and why am I different?"[3] He was somehow queer without having been forced to wear a skirt in childhood (*jap hai nung krapong*), the most often ventriloquized etiological explanation for queer bodies sexed as male. But while traveling the Web, James found an alternative answer when he met American folk theory writ scientific: the gay gene. The gene was iconic proof of the popular Anglophone gay folk theory "I was born gay." This young university student in Bangkok decided to anonymously disseminate this way of knowing queer causality among Thai subjects by translating it into Thai and creating his own Web site, christened *xq28* after the gay gene, in 1998. The electronic entry of *xq28* onto the Thai mediascape does not represent the first emergence of a Thai queer media voice: Thailand, like Japan but unlike many of the other contexts discussed in this volume, had a well-developed lesbian and gay media culture in the form of magazines and newsletters prior to the advent of electronic media. But the emergence of queer Internet cultures like that seen at *xq28* does mark the appearance of a new medium for queer collaborations. This medium differs significantly from old queer media in that it is not home to queers alone (straight subjects also participated in the discussions at *xq28;* see below) and it allows for more immediate communication than did old media technologies.

Thailand, too, is a place where much effort goes into assuring that children recognize and embody the wholesome goodness of heteronormality. However, Thai heterosupremacy is not evidenced in blatant displays of "hostility and aggression" that Anglophones label "homophobia."[4] The conclusion often made by foreign observers that Thai subjects are somehow "tolerant" of queers based on this visible "lack" has by now been widely critiqued.[5] Critics of this view argue that Thai indifference is not tolerance, but an effect of cultural injunctions aimed at curbing open acts of hostility, aggression, and dislike.[6] The will to subordinate queers by monopolizing the status of the good and normal is thus somewhat masked in the Thai context. In light of Rattachumpoth's acknowledgment that Thai queers survive cultural, not physical, violence, I look in this essay at attempts to make sense of queer within a heterosupremacist language and culture, attempts that counteract colonization by "common knowledge."[7] I have used 358 comments left behind by some of the site's consumers to identify recurring strategies that refigure dominant meanings of queer.[8] In these visitors' comments there is little proof that many of the site's consumers actually read the gay gene theory, supporting Sproull and Faraj's contention that people travel the Web not simply to find information but to find "affiliation, support and affirmation."[9] Myself a white male Australian interpreter with experience of living in northeast Thailand as a high school exchange student in 1997, I have looked mainly at the recurring discourses circulating through this new medium aimed at queer "affiliation, support and affirmation."

One place that James outwardly expresses his queerness, he tells us, is the Web. The Web allows subjects branded by stigmatizing meanings and discourses the autonomy to define selfhood according to their own interests.[10] Nevertheless, it is important to note that this refiguration is effected through words alone, without the body and its potential to contradict the speaker. The Web thus enables intervention in the power struggles over queerness at the level of *written* meanings. Hall has pointed out that meaning production often depends on larger units of speech: narratives, groups of images, whole discourses.[11] This insight, along with a social constructivist approach to meaning, grounds this essay. It is also used to militate against ethnocentric readings of the subjects who appear in this text. Thai, with its own particular history and myths of heteronormality, is marked by several points of difference from English positionings of queerness and queer subjects. To interpret my English words with an unreflective obedience to larger Anglophone conceptualizations would be to misrepresent my informants, who "make sense" specifically within Thai, and additionally would bespeak the naïve belief that English and Thai words with apparently the same referent are simply different voicings of the same thing. For instance, to decode the hegemonic representation of male queer in Thailand that features throughout this essay (the *kathoey*) based on the English concept of "transgender" (distinct as it is from the concept of a [gender-neutral] "homosexual") would be misleading. There is little benefit in trying to understand Thai queers by unreflectively squeezing them into complex Anglo concepts and post-Stonewall gay-affirmative discourses.

This essay follows Miller and Slater's timely contention that we need to pay more attention to "the Internet" as a technology embedded in social spaces.[12] *Xq28.hypermart.net* is an address that anchors shifting data on an essentially transnational network, but unduly accentuating this fact risks the erasure of the sociocultural specificities of the site's producers and consumers. For the voices crystallized on the Web are not traces of a "virtual life," somehow radically separate from offline "real life."[13] They are merely voices in a new context created through current media technology. Furthermore, I take an antithetical view to the claim that the Internet has reduced physical location to a mere "accident of proximity."[14] Access, Wakefield has reminded us, is a critical factor that highlights that the Web is embedded not only in social spaces but in a physical locality as well.[15] The material requirements needed to access the Web (not to mention the computer literacy, the time, and the desire) restrict access for a majority of Thais in what is predominantly an agricultural society. The limited access to the medium and the mobile and transitory character of its users, both within

Thailand and outside, mean that this micronumber of normative subjects and (predominantly male) queer subjects cannot be assumed to be an exhaustive sample of Thai subjects.

The following "real-life" conversation evidences the context of Thai common sense and the sociocultural space of (male) queer in which *xq28* is firmly embedded. The conversation appeared in an English-language newspaper and takes place between a heteronormal male taxi driver and a queer male journalist in Bangkok. Rattachumpoth recounts it, with the taxi driver beginning by asking:

> Are you married?
> No.
> Ah, do you have a *faen* [boyfriend or girlfriend] then?
> Yes.
> Is your *faen* beautiful [*suay*]?
> No he's* not beautiful; he's very handsome [*roop lor*] [*the third-person singular, *kaw,* is used for both "he" or "she"].

This last was greeted by confused silence. Then, almost half a full minute later:

> So you're a *kathoey* then?
> No, I don't dress in women's clothes. I've never wanted to be a woman: I'm gay.
> But aren't gay and *kathoey* the same thing?
> No.
> But you can't be! You look like a man, you're not effeminate. You're pulling my leg, aren't you?
> (Laughs without waiting for response).[16]

On several occasions in the above exchange, Rattachumpoth "suffers from the imposition of meaning."[17] Broadly speaking, this was owing to the driver's obedience to the dominant Thai way of seeing queer bodies. The taxi driver's interpretation of the adopted lexical signifier *gay* to refer to the (obviously) transgendered/transsexed subject, the proto-kathoey, is one instance. *Gay,* we are sometimes told, is a label signifying a "gender-normative" queer male and, albeit a slippery term, it is nevertheless meaningfully distinct from kathoey. Originally signifying a non-kathoey (i.e., "masculine") male prostitute, it has since shifted to be positioned by queers in broad opposition to kathoey (not in opposition to "straight," as the English "gay" implies today).[18] However, all this is derailed when hetero-supremacists assume monoglossic authority by understanding the lexeme *gay* to be a univocal signifier of kathoey.[19] Gays, I was told by kathoey and "normal" friends, are simply kathoeys who do not dare show it. Contention around the slippery extensional range of the word gay, if nothing else, indicates that male queer in Thailand is a much contested domain in a busy marketplace of meanings and discourses. This further emphasizes the necessity of acknowledging the "plasticity and heterogeneity" inherent in a cultural space where a queer subject's own interpretation of self may be interpreted differently by others.[20]

Problematizing the labels gay and kathoey by highlighting their fluid extensional range (rather than their distinction based on the Anglophone split between homosexual and transgender) not only acknowledges the differences and contradictions that can arise within a subject deceptively stabilized by an identity label, but ratifies van Esterik's argument that gendering "actions and practices" are higher in significance for Thai subjects than gender categories in themselves.[21] Morris might concur, having noted that Thai subjects invest the sense of sight with the ability to discern the truth and make "the real become . . . synonymous with the visible, and performance . . . purely symptomatic of identity."[22] "Seeing," as Gatens has pointed out, involves more creative work than a simple perceptual exercise in extracting meaning intrinsically stored in the visualized object.[23] The observation of a subject's gendering actions and practices is primary in "knowing" his or her erotic proclivities. This is notable for two reasons: first, because, unlike Rattachumpoth, few would actually voice their non-normative erotic proclivities; second, because the notion of a homosexual orientation not attached to gender disloyalty is little known in this cultural setting. Yensabai points out the obvious: the way to know who can be colonized by interpretation as a queer traitor is to see which subject's performance of gender is misaligned with his or her sexed body.[24] Under this ideology of transparency, then, the anomaly of the masculine-signifying subject sexed as male attracted to men was interpreted by the taxi driver as a joke.

The cultural tendency of gender practices to signify erotic orientation, normative or otherwise, places the masculine male subject in a superior position. Heterosupremacist culture creates its own coup by believing that queer treachery is always self-evident. Male queers, like women, are fantasized as obviously different; thus, the physiologically similar subject who could otherwise infiltrate the homosocial order is corporeally marked. Following this, the verb *sadaeng ork* is pivotal in discourse on queers. A literal translation of this term is *acting out,* but it is variously glossed in English by lexicographers as "express; display; manifest; show."[25] This term can be loosely compared to the Euro-American idea of being "out," in that acting out, like being out, is located "inside the realm of the visible, the speakable, the culturally intelligible."[26]

Morris has provocatively stated that the acting out of kathoeys "might well be understood as the compulsive acts of those whose very condition of being is that of eternal and violent exposure. From within dominant ideology [of face], *kathoeys* have always already lost [it] and they must therefore make of this loss a spectacle."[27] According to this view, kathoeys can be seen as spectacular objects positioned to reflect a list of "do nots" for those aspiring to be counted as good and normal men. They are visible proof of a host of speakable discourses and intelligible meanings that naturalize and glorify masculine male subjects. This spectacularity also provides humorous entertainment.[28] Whereas the kathoey and her actions signify humor (as opposed to, for example, disgust or transgression) under the hegemonically shared rules prescribing the production and reception of meanings, queer males are effectively contained to the position of the laughable fools who perform for the cruel amusement of their audience.[29] Furthermore, the humor of the kathoey is seen to reside in the kathoey herself, not in the collective minds of her heterosupremacist colonizers.

The voices gathered at *xq28,* though, expose as an optical delusion the fantasy that queers are obviously different or "violently exposed." Not all male queers "speak" their treachery offline through a visible nonmasculine gender performance, and even fewer voice it in words. A fear of destroying social cohesion and the best avoided risk of sanctions that work by tarnishing one's image are two reasons that have been given to account for the tendency of Thai queers to avoid the ritual of coming out.[30] Comments on *xq28* evidence that this tendency can even be extended to friends of queers considered by others to be queer by association. However, although admitting to treason of the heteronormal order does attract sanctions, I do not believe this can be extended to argue that there is a "silence around homosexuality."[31] Thailand hears, indeed, a wide range of discourses on queerness. But it is crucial to note that these discourses are authored by a source with a heavy investment in the maintenance of heterosupremacy.

Mobile Cultures

The opening page shown above hails the potential consumers of *xq28*. For the rightly gendered queer subject who does not make a habit of admitting "the secret" and has no access to any supportive networks to contest the violence of being (made) queer, the ability to express his frustration openly on the Web is an accomplishment that should not be overlooked. Party poopers who would contend that the "Who'd want to be gay?" self-defense dominating the opening page perpetuates the understanding that gay = bad are in one sense correct. However, this objection silences the expressive commitment of the claim, in this case, an emotional statement of a young man's frustrations in the face of heteronormality's will to silence dissenters.[32] Being queer, James tells us, is not a laughing matter. When one (mis)recognizes shades of the traitorous *tut* (faggot) in oneself, blaming the genes may shift the guilt. Interestingly, many nonqueer consumers, particularly "real men," expressed their sympathy and pledges to be kinder to queers who, they realized at *xq28*, do not want to be that way. It would be cruel, after all, to punish those who cannot help being what they are. The paradox, however, is that by being subject to the position that hetero-supremacist culture already "knows" is constituted by treachery, the queer subject's crime will always be, simply, to be. Unless these discourses are challenged, every queer subject will continue to be (made) self-evident proof of this treachery.

Not surprisingly, along with the voicing of pain silenced in offline life, direct attempts are made at *xq28* to challenge the stigma of being (made) queer in the heterosupremacist culture. Discourses collectively figured to sanitize the negative associations of queerness are voiced. One such voice can be heard in the following statement by a gay *xq28* consumer: "I do not accept that I am *gay* because it is a word that people who don't understand call people who happen to be born different from people in general. I am a person who wants to spend my life as it is and cause no trouble for anyone. I want to try and do goodness on every occasion to make society better."[33] Here, an outright disavowal of the stigmatizing verdict and sentence of gay occurs. Abnormal erotic leaning is made insignificant with the recurring message that the real worth of persons is in the things that they do, not in the things they are said to be. "A good and simple life that causes no trouble for others is a way of life that no one can fault" (*mai sarng kwarm duad ron hai khrai koh por*), so the mantra goes. This discourse has a history that stretches well beyond *xq28*, being evoked by authority figures near and far from the time of childhood. *Xq28* is surrounded with this sentiment of Buddhist origins, as well as its related knowledge that "while you cannot choose your birth, you can choose how you lead your life." Subjects from all four categories ("real men," "real women," gay, and lesbian) relied on this discourse to support queerness. In other words, according to this line of reasoning, one cannot choose one's queer birth, but one can choose a life that signifies goodness.

The "good person" (*khon dee*) is a subject position closely linked to this ideal that also feeds nationalistic discourses on good citizenship found in primary school textbooks. The citing of this all-genders-welcome category was another method of absolving oneself from the stigma of being (made) queer. This cleverly opens up a space in which subjects can continue defying the heteronormal order in a morally legitimate and meritorious way. Other speeches affirming queers by allowing them access to "the good" were differently nuanced; for example, as long as you have good habits, it does not matter what (kind of treacherous subject) you are. This was frequently voiced by "real men," along the lines that you should be friends with someone for reasons other than his or her erotic (or gender) orientation. For the well-behaved, queer status would be overlooked. In disavowing gayness and embodying the khon dee, resistance is enacted through rejecting the stigmatized category while replacing it with a culturally valorized label.[34] In judging the queer subject, these discourses give way of life the most significatory power, rather than status in the heterohierarchy.

When legitimacy is figured to be given to those who exemplify "a parent's highest wishes" (*kwam wang an yai thi sud khong pho mae*), ultimately embodying the ideal of the good person, some subjects will be judged to have strayed from the middle path. Once off, the spoils of the category of the good, for instance the real man's friendship, are lost. Most often guilty of not making the grade are those loud-mouthed kathoeys. The kathoey is faulted for shunning modesty and restraint by acting out beyond levels deemed acceptable by the jury of the good and normal. This, several heteronormal consumers enlightened us, gave queers their bad reputation. Interestingly, although gays joined in, real women were the predominant authors of this explicitly anti-kathoey discourse: "Usually I am a person indifferent to gays. But as far as I've met gays, or *kathoeys*, they have really bad habits like bullshitting, gossiping and they like to act out beyond decency. OK, I understand that you're gay, but you should act out as little as you can, be conscious whether you're prim and proper."[35] This clash between valorized feminine gender propriety and the entertaining, outrageous kathoey public performances provided a thematic conflict in *Satree Lek* (*The Iron Ladies,* 2000), a movie based on the kathoey volleyball team from Lampang who won the national championships in 1996.[36] Authority figures, such as a district chief officer and the director of the national volleyball competition, avoid being labeled intolerant by explaining to the team's coach that a queer team in the national championships was not inappropriate in itself, but their acting out was. Due to this pressure, the team toned down their act by playing without the corporeal inscriptions of kathoeyness, particularly makeup. They were then caught in a catch-22: without makeup they lost their form and could not win, but with it they were too *rat* (outrageous) for the normality police. The conflict is resolved at the end of the movie, however, when order is restored with the coach's pointing out that the kathoeys, although they act out, do not slander like those who are outspokenly anti-kathoey. The kathoey who cares for the views of her watching audience must walk a tightrope between acting decently in the restrictive way proposed for females and acting out too much.

Another recurrent discourse that was raised by gay-identifying consumers of *xq28* is less concerned with gender propriety than with gender itself: "I don't think that I'm inferior and I don't think that I am gay. I always think that I am a man, but a man who loves men."[37] This presentation of self is marked by an avoidance of all categories other than "man," a trend also found in personals columns and noted by Storer.[38] This petition to embody manhood is made by non-kathoey queers troubled that they have not been afforded the masculine (and its benefits) by virtue of their gendered body. This struggle for the masculine recognition denied them by the common sense that queers are psychological hermaphrodites led to the creation of a new way of referring to themselves. These non-kathoey queer males are without lexical space, reflecting their lack of cultural and semantic space, for even the lexeme gay can signify effeminacy (as with the taxi driver's comments). This new form of self-naming arose when many *xq28* users expressed criticism of the idea that queers are abnormal implicit in the term *phuchai pokati* ([hetero] normal man) posted on an *xq28* message board.[39] It was decided that the terms "nongay man" (*phu chai mai gay*) and "gay man" (*phu chai gay*) better reflected their self-conceptualization.[40] Gay is shifted from the status of a noun to the less weighty adjective coupled with the word "man." This is noteworthy first because gay is already semantically encoded as male and second, "man" typically denotes heteronormalcy. On a strict heterosupremacist reading it is, ironically, both semantically redundant and a contradiction in terms. But for the queers on *xq28*, it marks a new way to understand the non-kathoey queer male in relation to his heteronormal brother: namely, that he differs not in maleness but in the domain of erotic orientation alone.

In making this argument, these queers prize open the gates to normality, the stamping ground of heteronormals. The tenet naturalized into common sense throughout is that on a body sexed as male, masculinity alone signifies normalcy, and normalcy is the key to (gendered) social prestige. The fantasy that all queers are visibly exposed and transsexed is dispelled. These queers reverse the negative associations of queerness; that which is deemed repulsive, revolting, immoral and/or emotionally devasting about being made queer is exterminated. The kathoey, with its no-through-route to "the good" and "the normal," is rejected, and the border keeping her out is (sometimes abusively) manned. In other words, these queers recycle the heteronormal male's appropriation of masculinity, along with his misogynist compulsion to expel the feminine. Paradoxically, this compulsion, founded as it is on the sexist masculine/feminine split and its correlative good/bad, is the same one originally used to subordinate queers. The hegemonic representation of male queer, the kathoey, is misconstrued as having the capacity, or perlocutionary power, to degrade queerness in itself.[41] Attention to the broader cultural and economic conditions, desires, and processes that reproduce the supremacy of male heteronormality, and the consequences of these for those who do not embody heteronormality, is thereby stalled.

The irony of the Internet is that while it is geographically "borderless" it is concurrently English-based and dominated by Euro-American ideas. This is largely because half of the world's Internet users are American. Although the Internet is potentially a site where people can reach out beyond their own culture, Berry and Martin highlight, for example, that overseas sites have been frequented less than local sites by queers in Taiwan and Korea.[42] Although the Internet habits of queer consumers cannot be extrapolated from this microstudy, it does suggest that American queer info sites like those given in the U.S. magazine *The Nation*, with an emphasis on coming out and the dispelling of American homophobic myths, for example, would hold little cultural relevance.[43] Thai queers, as evident on *xq28*, evoke different discourses to deal with the emotional distress caused by their culture's stigmatizing of gender/erotic-disloyal subjects. In the messages left by *xq28* users, the gay gene itself is read as a "scientific" signifier of the Buddhist common sense that assists in accepting the (dissatisfying) way things are, namely, that one's birth (incarnation) cannot be chosen (*luak kerd mai dai*). So, although the gay gene may have been adopted from the "placeless space" that Americans have created on the Net, it is nevertheless largely rendered meaningful within a specific realm of Thai Buddhist discourses, notably unlike its English interpretations.

One commiserating male heteronormal visitor, after learning about this "cause" of queerness, stated, "Society should accept and understand that it's a matter of not being able to choose one's birth. When society understands this, gays can live openly. You won't have to force yourself to marry the opposite sex to hide your secret and that way you won't spread the faulty gene."[44] The continuing hegemony of heteronormality is witnessed in the final line of this quote. *Xq28* may provide the space for queers (and "normals") to come together to deal with queerness, but it hardly challenges the conditions that reproduced queerness as a lot that has to be "dealt with" in the first place. We have seen the possibility for autonomy given in cyberspace to male queers to be counted as good and normal, to be "seen" as men. This is perhaps both a challenge to the hegemonic understandings of the queer self and the cultural common sense that queer males are less than men and less than the idealized normal; it is a grab for authority made in the terms of hegemonic gender ideology. As Rattachumpoth showed, the space to embody this position—so radically opposed to the common sense sponsored in the interests of heterosupremacy—is not often allowed. What is highlighted by this observation is the impact of having the space one thinks one inhabits erased by the different understandings of others. A new outfit, made from Buddhist discourse on the simple life and masculinity, clearly signifies the good and the normal. However, it is also shaped by knowledge that subordinates the kathoey and fixed by installing a distance between the gay man and the kathoey's effeminacy. A voicing of pain and a sense of shared identity among isolated queers, common in its rejection of the kathoey, can be read from *xq28*. However, these male queers are affiliated in the relief gained through embodying the good and the normal, a cliché that is rooted deep in heteronormal culture. What we are witnessing, then, is hardly a radical reformulation of cyber-queer identity. The Net, it seems, is thoroughly saturated with the forms of power that also structure the offline world.

Notes

1 After writing this text, *xq28* changed its address and format, including the opening page, to *xq28.net*. The site now has a small English version.

2 I have used the term queer in this text by reason that, of all available terms, it has the least stabilized referent. As noted by Warner, it is also centrally distinguished by the notion of normality rather than heterosexuality, and is thus not far removed from Thai configurations of gender/sexuality. Michael Warner, introduction to *Fear of a Queer Planet: Queer Politics and Social Theory* (Minneapolis: University of Minnesota Press, 1993), vii–xxxi.

3 Jennifer Terry, "The Seductive Power of Science in the Making of Deviant Subjectivity," in *Posthuman Bodies,* ed. Judith Halberstam and Ira Livingston (Bloomington: Indiana University Press, 1995), 135–61.

4 David Buchbinder, *Performance Anxieties: Re-producing Masculinity* (St. Leonards, Australia: Allen and Unwin, 1998).

5 See, for example, Andrew Matzner, "Thailand: Paradise Not (On Human Rights and Homophobia)," 1998 ⟨http://home.att.net/~leela2/paradisenot. htm⟩, in Matzner, *Transgender in Thailand,* ⟨http://home.att.net/~leela2⟩ (3 May 2000); Rakkit Rattachumpoth, foreword to *Lady Boys, Tom Boys, Rent Boys: Male and Female Homosexualities in Contemporary Thailand,* ed. Peter A. Jackson and Gerard Sullivan (New York: Haworth, 1999), xiii–xx; Graeme Storer, "Performing Sexual Identity: Naming and Resisting 'Gayness' in Modern Thailand," *Intersections: Gender, History and Culture in the Asian Context,* no. 2 (1999), ⟨http://wwwsshe.murdoch.edu.eu/intersections/issue2/Storer. html⟩ (7 July 2000); and Peter A. Jackson, "Tolerant but Unaccepting: The Myth of a Thai 'Gay Paradise,'" in *Genders and Sexualities in Modern Thailand,* ed. Peter A. Jackson and Nerida M. Cook (Chiang Mai, Thailand: Silkworm Books, 1999), 226–42.

6 Podhisita Chai, "Buddhism and Thai World View," in *Traditional and Changing Thai World View* (Bangkok: Chularlongkorn University, 1985), 25–53.

7 Rattachumpoth.

8 In the space provided for self-identification in the messages, 53 percent (191) identified as gay, 23 percent (81) as real women, 13 percent (47) as real men, and 10 percent as lesbian. Among these four categories, 68 percent left email addresses; presumably, networks could then be established.

9   Lee Sproull and Semer Faraj, "Atheism, Sex, and Databases: The Net as a Social Technology," in *Culture of the Internet*, ed. Sara Kieser (Mahwah, NJ: Erlbaum, 1997), 38.

10 Elizabeth Grosz, "A Note on Essentialism and Difference," in *Feminist Knowledge: Critique and Construct*, ed. Sneja Gunew (London: Routledge, 1990), 332–34.

11 Stuart Hall, *Representation: Cultural Representations and Signifying Practices* (London: Sage, 1997).

12 Daniel Miller and Don Slater, *The Internet: An Ethnographic Approach* (New York: Berg, 2000).

13 See Robins and Blackman for a critique of the split between "real life" and "virtual life" that has plagued many cyberstudies. Kevin Robins, "Cyberspace and the World We Live In," in *The Cybercultures Reader*, ed. David Bell and Barbara M. Kennedy (London: Routledge, 2000), 77–95; Lisa M. Blackman, "Culture, Technology and Subjectivity: An 'Ethical' Analysis," in *The Virtual Embodied: Presence/Practice/Technology*, ed. John Wood (London: Routledge, 1998), 132–46.

14 Barbara Kirshenblatt-Gimblett, "The Electronic Vernacular," in *Connected: Engagements with Media*, ed. George E. Marcus (Chicago: University of Chicago Press, 1996), 28.

15 Nina Wakefield, "Cyberqueer," in *The Cybercultures Reader*, ed. David Bell and Barbara M. Kennedy (London: Routledge, 2000), 403–15.

16 Rakkit Rattachumpoth, "Dispelling Myths/Myth vs. Reality," *The Nation* (15 January 1998), ⟨http://202.44.251.4/nationnews/1998/199801/19980115/21062.html⟩ (15 June 2000).

17 Martin Krampen, "Phytosemiotics," in *Frontiers in Semiotics*, ed. John Deely, Brooke Williams, and Felicia E. Kruse (Bloomington: Indiana University Press, 1986), 83–95.

18 Jackson, "Tolerant," and "An American Death in Bangkok: The Murder of Darrell Berrigan and the Hybrid Origins of Gay Identity in 1960s Thailand," *GLQ* 5, no. 3 (1999): 361–411; Storer.

19 Mikhail Bakhtin noted that although discourses and meaning are multivocal, attempts are often made to "reduce meaning to a univocal, unproblematic, authorized, single ['monoglossic'] signification" (quoted in Buchbinder, 141).

20 Rosalind C. Morris, "Three Sexes and Four Sexualities: Redressing the Discourses on Gender and Sexuality in Contemporary Thailand," *Positions* 2, no. 1 (1994): 15–43.

21 Jillana Enteen, " 'Whiskey Is Whiskey: You Can't Make a Cocktail from That!' Self-Identified Gay Thai Men in Bangkok," *Jouvert* 2, no. 1 (1998), ⟨http://152./.96.5/jouvert/v2il/Enteen.htm⟩ (25 July 2002); Penny van Esterik, "Repositioning Gender, Sexuality, and Power in Thai Studies," in *Genders and Sex-*

ualities in Modern Thailand, ed. Peter A. Jackson and Nerida M. Cook (Chiang Mai, Thailand: Silkworm Books, 1999), 275–89.

22 Rosalind C. Morris, "A Ban on Gay Teachers: Education and Prohibition in the 'Land of the Free,' " *Social Text* 15, nos. 3–4 (1997): 54.

23 Moira Gatens, "Woman and Her Double(s): Sex, Gender and Ethics," in *Imaginary Bodies: Ethics, Power and Corporeality* (London: Routledge, 1996), 29–45.

24 Chad Yensabai, "Gay: Sisan Thi Taektarng" [Gay: A different color], in *Krungthep Turakij* (21 October 1999), ⟨http://xq28.hypermart.net/different. html⟩, (12 May 2000).

25 Iemvonmet Thienchai, *Standard Thai-English Dictionary* (Bangkok: Ruamsarn, 1990), 1175.

26 Diana Fuss, "Inside/Out," in *Inside/out: Lesbian Theories/Gay Theories* (New York: Routledge, 1991), 4.

27 Morris, "A Ban on Gay Teachers," 65.

28 Rattachumpoth, foreword.

29 Robert Hodge and Gunther Kress, *Social Semiotics* (Ithaca, NY: Cornell University Press, 1988).

30 Storer; Jackson, "Tolerant."

31 Storer, paragraph 32.

32 Lynne Tirrell, "Derogatory Terms: Racism, Sexism and the Inferential Role Theory of Meaning," in *Language and Liberation*, ed. Christina Hendricks and Kelly Oliver (New York: State University of New York Press, 1999), 41–88.

33 ⟨http://xq28.net/think/4.html⟩ (15 November 2000).

34 Peter A. Jackson, "An Explosion of Thai Identities: Global Queering and Reimagining Queer Theory," unpublished manuscript.

35 ⟨http://xq28.net/think/3.html⟩ (11 December 2000).

36 *The Iron Ladies*, dir. Yongyoot Thongongtoon, 2000.

37 ⟨http://xq28.net/think/5.html⟩ (17 December 2000).

38 It may be noted for the benefit of discussions on the rise of a "modern gay" identity that for these queer Thai subjects at least, the renunciation of the label gay and not its embracing is key to the assertion of manhood in the face of emasculation. Peter A. Jackson, "The Persistence of Gender: From Ancient Indian Pandakas to Modern Thai Gay-Quings," *Meanjin* 55, no. 1 (1996): 110–20; Jackson, "Kathoey⟩⟨Gay⟩⟨Man: The Historical Emergence of Gay Male Identity in Thailand," in *Sites of Desire/Economies of Pleasure: Sexualities in Asia and the Pacific*, ed. Lenore Manderson and Margaret Jolly (Chicago: University of Chicago Press, 1997), 166–90; Storer, "Performing Sexual Identity."

39 *Xq28* experienced "Thai indifference" when three attempts to establish bulletin boards were disallowed by different servers on the grounds that they were "inappropriate" (Sunnie, email communication, "Hi," June 10, 2000).

The latest edition of *xq28.net* has three bulletin boards for gays, lesbians, and friends each.

40 Sunnie.

41 Judith Butler, *Excitable Speech: A Politics of the Performative* (New York: Routledge, 1997).

42 Victor Seidler, "Embodied Knowledge and Virtual Space: Gender, Nature and History," in *The Virtual Embodied: Presence/Practice/Technology,* ed. John Wood (London: Routledge, 1998), 15–29; Berry and Martin, this volume.

43 Xavier Gallard, "Two Pages That May Help Some Families," *The Nation* (2 February 1999), ⟨http://202.44.251.4/nationnews/1999/199902/19990202/ 38445.htm⟩ (15 June 2000).

44 ⟨http://xq28.net/think/4.html⟩ (17 December 2000).

↔ II

Mobile Sites

NEW SCREENS,

NEW SCENES

BADEN OFFORD

Singaporean Queering of the Internet:

Toward a New Form of Cultural Transmission

of Rights Discourse

Sexuality, identity, and human rights are presently being taken up as crucial sites of ethical intervention by queer Southeast Asians.[1] An important tool used by these queer activists to intervene into society is the Internet. Its capacity to provide a space for intersubjective and intercultural communication, allowing discourse around citizenship and notions of belonging and participation not stymied by normative and regulatory bodies, has empowered queer Southeast Asian citizens. This essay explores the nature of this empowerment, relating it specifically to the question of how the cultural transmission of rights discourse and sexual identity through the medium of the Internet has added to the piquancy of domestic, traditional sociopolitical and media discussion in Singapore around the issue of homosexuality.

I do four things in this essay. First, I contextualize the frame of homosexuality and rights discourse in Singapore. As a vociferous representative of the "Asian values" debate through the 1990s, Singapore offers a cogent and important site to examine the tensions thrown up in the wake of new media.[2] Second, I introduce the question of cultural transmission and the value of the Internet, following on the recent work of James Slevin and his analysis of the Internet and society. This conceptual framework is applied to the Singaporean situation. In calibrating the theoretical frame of the essay, I also posit a conceptual intersection between queer theory and the work of Manuel Castells in terms of identity, which is useful in locating activist concerns and the complexity of identity politics in non-Western polities. *Queer* is used primarily in this essay to refer to unruly sexualities, which has a twofold meaning. First, it implicates those sexualities that, by virtue of their identity and practice, are stigmatized and ostracized by and excluded from dominant discourses of belonging and participation in society. Second, it explicitly refers to the activity, energy, and articulation by unruly sexualities in meeting the challenge of those dominant discourses of exclusion. Thus, in relation to Singapore, where the Confucian notion that *legitimate* belonging and *legitimate* participation in society is predicated on the value and measure of heteronormativity, unruly sexuality is a site of civil and state contestation. In this sense, unruly sexuality is therefore both activated and brought into relief by the state's social engineering of heteronormativity. Unruly sexuality, furthermore, has the potential to be transformed into a politicized identity.[3]

Third, I venture into the notion that the Internet has become, for queer Singaporeans, a key strategy of survival and articulation of ways to ameliorate their unruly sexual status in society. Two Web sites are examined to illustrate the nature of strategy on the Internet. Fourth, I conclude by suggesting that the role of the Internet for queer Singaporeans *acts* as a crucial cultural facility of queer sensibility and potential social change and that there is some evidence of its effect on sociocultural everyday life. How far these effects are felt is uncertain territory. But the theoretical frames offered by Slevins and Castells are posited as useful windows through which to understand the intersection among unruly sexuality, identity, and the Internet.

Rights Discourse and Homosexuality in Singapore

Singapore appears to be the last frontier in the Asian region for
positive gay and lesbian developments
—LAURENCE WAI-TENG LEONG, "Singapore," 1997

I can keep people inoculated against certain fads, against infections.
We can't keep influences out.
—LEE KUAN YEW, qtd. in *Time Australia*, 1994

Government control of homosexuality has largely been carried out through a certain official tolerance coeval with strict suppression of homosexual representation in traditional media and the deployment of that representation as a focus of difference between Asian and Western cultural values and attitudes.[4] Singapore outlaws homosexuality, specifically male-to-male sex, with laws that have been inherited from a British colonial past.[5]

In 1996, in its attempt to reinforce the immoral nature of homosexuality, the government instituted guidelines for Internet servers. In the preamble in the section on "Public Morals," the Singaporean Broadcasting Authority Act states, "Contents which depict or propagate sexual perversions such as homosexuality, lesbianism, and paedophilia" are strictly not allowed.[6] This conflation of homosexuality with something like pedophilia is not new. Government representative Wong Kang Seng, at the World Conference on Human Rights in Vienna in 1993, stated, "Singaporeans . . . do not agree . . . that pornography is an acceptable manifestation of free expression or that homosexual relationships are just a matter of lifestyle choice."[7] Here is a nation exhibiting the tensions arising out of the confluence of modernity and postmodernity, "a society that is modern but puritanical."[8] In the face of porous borders, as an active participant in the technologically globalized world, Singapore is braced by local elite reaction—political and social leaders—who reinforce normative representations of family and sexuality. Thus, in terms of homosexuality and rights discourse, Wong Kang Seng also stated at the World Conference, "Homosexual rights are a Western issue."[9]

I argue that homosexuality is constructed as a difference to consolidate an imagined border that somehow delineates Singapore from Western society. In this context it is important to tie this argument to the nature of human rights and what they imply to state and civil society. Here, with regard to the state's rhetorical resilement from the "other" (in Singapore's case, its embedded conflation of homosexuality with the West), Christopher Tremewan has noted, "Human rights, their observance or violation are bound up with questions of state sovereignty and the inviolability of state borders."[10] The civil response in relation to human rights is intrinsically affected by the state's mapping of its sovereignty, specifically by strong rhetoric on cultural values and attitudes indigenous to Singapore's population. Demonizing homosexuality, aligning it with pornography and pedophilia, positing it as a Western issue underscores an imagined cultural border of the nation-state, and in Singapore's case, an imagined border that is based on East Asia Confucian ideology that is embedded in heterosexist governance. Indeed, as Leong writes, "The state is so omnipresent that even the private areas of family and sexuality cannot escape its clutches. The paternalism of the authoritarian state is evident in the way state elites see themselves as responsible for the marriage and reproduction of the population. . . . In this schema of things, heterosexuality and the nuclear family are privileged by the state."[11]

The problems of privacy and sexuality are intrinsic to the whole question of homosexual rights as human rights in Singapore. In its activity of engineering sexual reproduction,[12] the state has taken over private space; in this regard, any kind of sexuality that does not conform to the dominant ideological orientation of procreation is silenced and made invisible. Homosexuality is, therefore, according to the state of Singapore, a Western issue.

The complexity of homosexual identity is replete with nuances. One example is a talk by Alex Au on 21 September 1997 at the Substation in Singapore on "Gay Culture in Singapore." Au stated, "The emerging gay culture is largely inspired by the progress achieved in the West." This is what the government of Singapore seems to fear. It is in this discursive trope that homosexuality (as demonized by Singapore's elite) has its most poignant utility in the context of rights discourse. The crux lies in terms of what privacy holds, means, and suggests. The individual rights that are emphasized (ostensibly) by Western nations, such as freedom of expression, freedom to organize, and the gradual mainstreaming of sexual orientation and sexual rights (among others), are all underpinned by strong notions of privacy. Cerna has observed that "the challenge to the concept of the universality of human rights coming primarily from Asia, has to do with what I call 'private' rights."[13] Unruly sexuality in Singapore is a crucial and powerful site where the contest over what is private is pivotal to the question of the maintenance of the heteronormative state.

It is not so much the fear of individualism from which Singapore elites recoil, but the implications of individual privacy and individual space. Social space is available for the gay Singaporean, but privacy, in terms of sexual identity, is a luxury in Singapore and thus requires covert sexual identities. Private space in Singapore is therefore a critical contour where unruly sexuality, identity, and rights discourse meet. The Internet has become a key contemporary site for exercising and providing private space. What is notable in this is the paradox of private space. It acts as a conduit for self-autonomy and self-representation with visible claims to an inclusive

Mobile Cultures

rights discourse, and at the same time as a source of sustenance for private contemplation and affirmation of self and sexual identity. This is the context, then, that frames homosexual rights discourse in Singapore. It provides the necessary background for understanding the interactional impact of the Internet on queer Singaporeans.

Theorizing Cultural Transmission

When we consider how the Internet is creating new ways for queer Singaporeans to communicate, to articulate and circulate information, and to reach into the everyday social, political, and cultural fabric of life in Singapore, we are attempting to understand specific cultural configurations of connection and communication. In his recent work on the Internet and society, James Slevin has critiqued this new facilitation and reorganization of social relations in terms of what he refers to as a theory of cultural transmission. The specific concern of this theory is understanding the "Internet's interactional impact."[14] Drawing heavily on John Thompson's interrogation of culture and ideology, Slevin outlines the changes occurring in the mediated world via the Internet and how the interactional qualities of the Internet can provide a basis for transforming society. There are certain properties of the Internet, he writes, that distinguish it from other new media in this regard. For example, Slevin convincingly argues that the Internet is potentially highly dialogic.[15] As he puts it, "The Internet clearly contributes to the repertoire of possibilities for the two-way flow of actions and utterances" (79). In terms of the use of the Internet to actively intervene into dominant discourses and regimes of truth, he also argues, "Internet use always involves asymmetries of power and each communicative act has to be successfully 'brought off' by those using it. The transformative capacity of Internet use, that is, the way it can be deployed to 'make a difference,' is thus, among other things, dependent on the characteristics of the individuals and organizations involved, their location in time-space, the institutional arrangements within which they act, and the means which they have at their disposal" (70).

The usefulness of this theory of cultural transmission, however, becomes apparent when trying to make sense of the efficacy and value of Web sites and whether their properties are promoting the facilitation and reorganization of social relations. In judging specific Web sites later on, which are deployed by unruly Singaporean sexual objects, certain aspects of cultural transmission will be used to frame the analysis.

For the purposes of this essay, we will look only at the technical medium of transmission, which, according to Slevin's interpretation of Thompson, consists of the following:

> 1. Fixation. This refers to the medium's capacity to hold or store information. Slevin writes, "The mode of information storage affects the way in which we might approach questions such as who may store information, what kind of information can be stored, who may access the information and to what ends it may be used" (63).
>
> 2. Reproduction. This refers to the dynamic present regarding the access to that information and to what degree it can be reproduced. The intensity of reproduction can occur in myriad forms, through the combination and re-combination of content across different sites.
>
> 3. Participation. This refers to the degree of participation dependent on the skills of those using the medium. As Slevin puts it, "Using the Internet is thus a skilled performance and its successful use is an accomplishment demanding particular capabilities, resources and attentiveness" (65).

In summary, Slevin's theory of cultural transmission is a useful frame in approaching the interactional nature of the Internet. It provides an analytical tool for examining the shifting ground of social relations that new media such as the Internet appear to promote.

Theorizing Queer Strategies of Survival

The edges of gay have been stretching ever since . . .
—E. J. GRAFF, "Sexual Disorientation," 1997

A second key theoretical framework is postulated in this essay to assist in arranging and interpreting the impact and interactional nature of the Internet. It consists of a careful understanding of the way identity and queer theory are deployed and is constructed in terms of *strategies of survival* and *strategies of transformation*. In demonstrating the efficacy of this conceptual coupling, it is useful here to bring in the recent work of sociologist Manuel

Castells, who, in his volume *The Power of Identity,* has conceived of three forms of identity development:

1. *Legitimizing identity:* introduced by the dominant institutions of society to extend and rationalize their domination vis-à-vis social actors . . . [and] fits in with various theories of nationalism.

2. *Resistance identity:* generated by those actors that are in positions/ conditions devalued and/or stigmatized by the logic of domination, thus building trenches of resistance and survival on the basis of principles different from, or opposed to, those permeating the institutions of society, as Calhoun proposes when explaining the emergence of identity politics.

3. *Project identity:* when social actors, on the basis of whichever cultural materials are available to them, build a new identity that redefines their position in society, and by doing so, seek the transformation of overall social structure. This is the case, for instance, when feminism moves out from the trenches of resistance of women's identity and women's rights, to challenge patriarchalism, thus the patriarchal family, thus the entire structure of production, reproduction, sexuality, and personality on which societies have been historically based.[16]

The means by which each of these identity-building processes constitutes society is, according to Castells, implemented thus: "*legitimizing identity* generates a civil society . . . *identity for resistance* leads to the formation of communes, or communities . . . [and] *project identity* produces *subjects*" (8–9). Here, the meaning of *project identity* is the "project of a different life, perhaps on the basis of an oppressed identity, but expanding toward the transformation of society . . . [via, for example] the post-patriarchal society, liberating women, men, and children, through the realization of women's identity" (10).

Castells's conceptual approach allows a specific entry point for the queer theorist. In this essay, the term *strategies of survival* refers to those means necessary for the immediate cessation of oppression or discrimination of the homosexual. This correlates to resistance identities and thus includes the political and cultural mobilization of homosexuality around identity. The strategies employed for the improvement of homosexual life are thus implemented as defensive and deployed within the "dominant institutions/ ideologies, reversing the value judgement while reinforcing the boundary" (9). These strategies are based on essentialist rhetoric and identification.

Castells contends that identities for resistance "may be the most important type of identity-building in our society" (9).

Queer theory, I argue, interlocks with Castells's project identity and to a lesser degree but connected to resistance identity.[17] In this essay the term used to describe this conjunction is *strategies of transformation*. This refers to strategies that are born in and of struggles with civil and state society but that are conscious of the contingent and implicative nature of identity. In this sense, identity is understood reflexively, intrinsic to a holistic meaning of experience, that is, identity experienced simultaneously as a necessity, an "error," and a "fiction."[18] The strategies here are therefore transformative, indeterminate, and inconclusive. As Carolyn Williams states, "It is a politics whose strategies derive not from programmatic prescriptions but from within specific social-political-historical-discursive contexts."[19] They are strategies of connection, of articulation and representation and lived experience. For the purposes of this essay, these strategies, based on Castells's rendering, are useful as a theoretical frame of identity when examining queer Web sites.

Unruly Strategies of Survival: Queer Use of the Internet

There is no way they (gays/lesbians) are going to bury their sexuality as in more traditional cultures. So identity and energy get channeled into various forms of escapism: into partying, sex, the irc, smuggling videotapes and cd-roms, and vacationing in gay hotspots abroad.
—ALEX AU, *Yawning Bread*, 1996

There are, despite sociolegal controls of unruly sexualities, ways that queer Singaporeans are able to survive.[20] Homosexual visibility in Singapore is certainly quiet, but it is evident and growing. That visibility is taking place in civil society, among friends, in families, and through travel. For a gay in Singapore the issue of human rights is faced in two distinct areas. First, there is the state, with its laws, rhetoric, and political values and attitudes. Second, there is the wider society of family, friends, colleagues, sport clubs, religious bodies, and so on. Overall, as Russell Heng Hiang Khng observed in 1995, "The situation for Singapore's gay community seems to be a mixture of exhilarating potential and a fair dose of tension and stress that comes with negotiating within an authoritarian polity for more political and social space."[21]

One of the most significant ways the homosexual activist and voice in Singapore have been able to employ both strategies of survival and transformation has been through the Internet. Wolfgang Kleinwaechter characterizes this new media: "The decentralized Internet is to a certain degree the most organized chaos in the history of mankind. It is unmanageable and uncontrollable. It is a new dimension, a new culture, a new way of communication."[22] Through the use of the Internet and electronic mail, access to cyberspace has allowed gay and lesbian Singaporeans an avenue for dialogue and reflection about their sexuality and its implications across a wide field of concerns. It has facilitated an educational role, a place for gay and lesbian Singaporeans to share their feelings and thoughts regarding a variety of subjects that include activism, the political culture of Singapore, the media's representation of homosexuality, coming out issues, family constraints, gossip, and more. As Laurence Wai-Teng Leong argues, the Internet, together with globalization, *is* challenging the state's silence on civil rights and developing an awareness of gay and lesbian issues.[23] This is not to suggest that globalization is eclipsing local understanding and response. As Deborah L. Wheeler has written in her study of the Internet, global culture, and culture clash in Kuwait, "Adaptation to globalization is part of what creates and maintains local consciousness of self and distinctiveness in a networked world."[24] I believe this can be applied to Singapore too.

The Internet, according to Alan Sondheim, "represents a deep realignment of human community, one which circumvents borders."[25] It is, in fact, a place of intersubjective conversations and dialogue, postings, news, stories, and all manner of analysis. In the 1990s the use of the Internet as an effective space of activism was demonstrated by the plethora of movements that inhabit it. It has given added weight to the fact that "technology never escapes politics."[26]

For many rights activists the Internet represents an interface among individuals within and across polities, individuals who share similar problems and issues, such as political oppression or social exclusion. It is a private but also public space of freedom, where there is autonomy of thought and reflection not usually possible in a carefully controlled society such as

Singapore's. The Internet provides that crucial private space that can act as a conduit of communication among unruly sexualities. This paradoxical characteristic of the Internet, where the boundaries between private and public are blurred, thus makes the possibilities of communication and interaction more diverse, complex, and unruly.

In this sense, for homosexual Singaporeans the Internet is a key space of mobilization and expression. It serves as a cutting-edge bridge of intersubjective conversations about how to negotiate Singaporean state and civil society. The most important and recent study so far on the impact of the Internet on queer Singaporeans is by Ng King Kang, titled *The Rainbow Connection*. This qualitative and quantitative study, although by no means exhaustive, suggests that for many gays and lesbians the Internet has provided a crucial domain for sexual, emotional, and sociological reasons. Ng writes, "In the Internet era, being gay is not the same as it used to be."[27] Kang's work is the first analysis into the benefits of this new media on gay sexualities in Southeast Asia and establishes the evident and explicit link between the Internet and the amelioration of homosexuality, at least in terms of its subjective impact. To gain a sense of how the Internet has come to play such a significant role in Singaporean gay and lesbian lives, a brief background follows.

Singapore is uniquely situated in terms of the technology revolution and the network society. As a technological and global capital hub of the Asia/Pacific it has deliberately guided its future toward a completely "wired" and "intelligent" society. The Singapore government is active in its reimagining of the nation as "Internet Island"[28] and is not shy to deploy a strategy of "cyberboosterism."[29] According to the Singapore Broadcasting Authority's (SBA) information Web site: "Internet use in Singapore has jumped from 100,000 dial-up accounts (in July 1996) to 321,575 by end-June 1998. If we include corporate accounts and users in the tertiary institutes, the total number of Internet users in Singapore is approximately 500,000."[30] This underscores the role that the Internet is having in Singapore. It has become a major form of communication in the corporate, educational, government, and civil sectors. The government's own Web site is promoted with the following mission statement: "To help inform, educate and entertain, as part of our national goal to make Singapore a hub city of the world and to build a society that is economically dynamic, socially cohesive and culturally vibrant."[31]

Mobile Cultures

However, as Slevin points out, this mission statement is difficult to see realized when analysis of the Web site reveals a very insufficient and low degree of interactivity. This demonstrates a key tension between embedded (governmental) sociopolitical and cultural guidelines on sexuality, predicated on the ongoing legitimization of heterosexual identity, and the articulation of (unruly) sexualities, which is predicated on resistance or project identity. The process of legitimizing sexual identity depends on the parameters of dominant institutions, where interactivity is minimal. Resistance identity and project identity, on the other hand, offer a range of interventions that are based on various levels of interaction, and this is where queer use of the Internet plays such an important role.

Although the SBA has guidelines for Internet content disallowing homosexual depictions or its "propagation," there remains little control of personal homepages that can be hosted on foreign servers (for example, Geocities in the United States). From what I can gather from Singaporean gays, the SBA's guidelines are ambiguous, and hosting Web pages on domestic Internet providers can be scrutinized for "offensive" materials. Many Singaporeans therefore choose to use foreign hosts. This applies to political opposition groups and parties as well. However, Clause 10 of the SBA's Code of Practice states, "Individuals who put up personal webpages are exempted from the Class License, unless they are putting up these webpages for business, or to promote political or religious causes."[32]

The gay Internet community of Singapore is characterized by a range of interests that do not fall into one overall, coherent organization. For example, there are a number of HIV/AIDS organizations with a presence on the Web. One of these, Action for Aids: The Act (AFA), is a government-run organization that has an educational role and helps to dispel myths about homosexuality in the process of informing the wider community about HIV/AIDS.[33] There is also a homepage for *People Like Us,* the first group of gay and lesbian Singaporeans to attempt registration; *SiGNel,* a gay discussion list and chat room; and *We Are Family,* which has links to gay Singaporean homepages. At *Utopia,* a Web site devoted to travel and resources in Asia, the gay and lesbian Singaporean community is accessible via links to homepages and information on accommodation, popular spots, cruising localities, organizations, and so on. Via *Sintercom,* an alternative online magazine, Singaporeans can pick up articles and interviews that discuss gay and lesbian issues. A recent example is an interview with Singaporean ilmmaker Madeleine Lim, a lesbian who lives in San Francisco, who left for the United States because "I wanted a lesbian community around me to organize within, to be an active part of. Since that was not possible in Singapore, I decided to explore other countries."[34]

What the Internet thus offers the gay or lesbian Singaporean is greater access to the subjective political, cultural, and social viewpoints of "other" unruly citizens who are not able to participate in the full political and social dimensions of society because of their sexuality. The Internet offers a means of cultural transmission that is multifaceted, asymmetrical, and complex; it represents possible engagement with "others" by circumventing the usually repressive strictures laid down by dominant regimes of truth and power. As Philippe Queau writes, "The Internet phenomenon technically enables transparency from one network to the other. It is now possible to take immense shortcuts between countries, cultures and diverse visions of the world. . . . Internet effectively short-circuits nations and their laws."[35]

Yawning Bread

This section and the next bring the above theoretical considerations and Internet discussion together to focus on an analysis of two Singaporean gay Web sites. The first analysis is of a personal site; begun on 30 November 1996, *Yawning Bread* represents a site that ethically intervenes into Singaporean society and culture. It is the personal homepage of gay Singaporean Alex Au Waipang, age 46; he is of Chinese ethnicity but his main language is English. This Web site is an example of the Internet's interactional impact on Singaporean unruly sexualities as well as the wider community.

In terms of storage, the site is content-rich. Information can be reproduced from many linked sites and informs the user of a wide range of sources. In this sense, the site has its own unique culture of pedagogy, one that is clearly informational as well as dialogic. To draw on the theory of cultural transmission, the site has a high degree of participation, demonstrated by the accessibility of the site owner through email and by the invitation to submit responses and written pieces to the repository of information. Altogether, the site illustrates cultural transmission in a variety of ways, but specifically in relation to rights discourse, identity, and sexuality the site is reflexive, pedagogical, engaged, and dense. In terms of strategies, the site situates itself in strategies of survival and transformation and seeks, through ongoing essays, to engage in the amelioration of homosexual marginalization in Singapore. These strategies inform the nature of the site itself as well as its communication facility and practice. The following analysis of some of the content of this site teases out the way identity, sexuality, and rights discourse are articulated in an environment that is interactive and responsive.

In analyzing this homepage I draw on the conceptual framework offered by George Gerbner, who has theorized about the function of storytelling, because at its most basic level *Yawning Bread* is a site of storytelling and resistance identity. Gerbner argues that "stories that animate our cultural environment have three distinct but related functions. These functions are (1) *to reveal how things work;* (2) *to describe what things are;* and (3) *to tell us what to do about them.*" The implications of these three functions are as follows: *how things work* "illuminates the all-important but invisible relationships and hidden dynamics of life"; *what things are* "are descriptions, depictions, expositions, reports abstracted from total situations and filling in with 'facts' "; and *what to do* stories are about "value and choice."[36]

Yawning Bread offers a site with essays and stories that deal primarily with gay issues, but also with politics, culture, society, and Singapore in general. These writings explicate *how things work, what things are,* and *what to do* in the context of homosexual experience in Singapore. Apart from regular contributions by the site owner, Alex Au, there are also offerings by other gay Singaporeans. The site is thus a repository of contemporary musings, stories, reflections, analyses, and news that are of particular interest to homosexual people in Singapore. The target audience as far as Au is concerned is the gay or lesbian Singaporean, but he hopes that the articles are also accessible to "heterosexual Singaporeans or gay foreigners." He positions his role as a representative of the gay Singaporean by stating, "The 'we' or 'us' that I use in my writing quite often refer[s] to gay compatriots."[37] As far as his own acknowledged agenda goes, Au remarks, "For readers who are homosexual, I hope Yawning Bread can be a catalyst to self-reflection, self-discovery, and a better understanding of where we stand in society, and why we stand where we stand. I hope it is of some help to you in breaking out of any sense of isolation you may have. This page is also meant as a channel for your own self-affirmation. . . . The act of writing is a release, *a lifting of a burden,* a seminal act that establishes yourself, a sense of who you are."[38] Clearly evident is the activist role of the site, activist in the sense of informing, articulating, and presenting perspectives on homosexuality in Singapore. It is not a confrontational site insofar as it offers reflective engagement, not aggressive, overt attacks on Singaporean society. It is an intellectual, transparent space, of discernment, analysis, polemics, and challenge. It is a distinct window into the world of the gay Singaporean. Utilizing the properties of the Internet, the site is a private space of exploration, reflection, and communication with a public concordance.

In terms of *how things work, what things are,* and *what to do* about (homo)sexuality in Singapore, the site offers many stories and essays to consider. Under the rubric of *how things work,* one example is an essay titled "Explaining Singapore (March 1997)." It speaks about the musings of foreign gay visitors to Singapore and the kind of expectations about a society that is assumed to be somewhat of a "police-state." The essay informs the reader about the contradictions of Singaporean society and its view on homosexuality. Au comments, "Singapore is not a gay-friendly country. That's for sure. However, it is not downright oppressive." He highlights the fact that there is a general reluctance to "engage" with homosexuality at a political level. The theme he posits is that Singapore has rather static and fixed public policies that keep "in place anti-gay strictures inherited from a generation ago," but that "no society is monolithic." He argues that despite the presence of antigay sentiment at the workplace and on the social level, there is a response happening by gay individuals making "gay spaces here and there." Characterizing both the gay and nongay situations in Singapore, he explains, "Clearly at some point, gay people will have to negotiate with public policy on these issues, otherwise gay space and gay expression (let alone justice and rights) will remain restricted. Here we come to the irony. People in Singapore, not just gay ones, are reluctant to engage with the government.

Another essay that demonstrates *how things work* is the analysis "*Asiaweek:* Gays in Asia (August 1998)," where Au examines how a gay story appearing in *Asiaweek* basically reduces the issues and problems to superficial information. After scrutinizing the weaknesses of the story, Au argues that it ultimately fails to wrestle with the main problem of "the tension between the individual and society and that between a minority and the state."

Mobile Cultures

A story that fulfills the function of *what things are* is Au's essay "The Why Nots of Human Rights." This essay is a presentation of excerpts and analysis of Singapore's Minister for Information and the Arts George Yeo's speech at a human rights colloquium. Au uses this speech to highlight the facts that underscore Singapore's human rights perspectives. He writes, "In a nutshell, George Yeo's speech re-stated the 'relativist' position. The meaning and appropriate objectives of human rights are relative to the culture and value-system of a society." In this essay, Au goes through the key arguments of Yeo's speech, Asian values, economic imperatives, economic rights, and Western imperialism. He then refutes these positions one by one. At the end of the essay Au contends, "Human rights are something that the local citizens want. And they do not believe that they will automatically slide back to poverty when they get it. It's as simple as that."[39]

"Without Cover of the Covenant" is an essay that also offers the function of *what things are*.[40] The subject of the essay is the International Covenant on Civil and Political Rights (ICCPR) and the problem of Singapore's not being a signatory. This is a political essay and refers to the imprisonment of Chia Thye Poh under the Internal Security Act (ISA).[41] The basis of the essay is to instruct as well as describe to the reader the benefits of the ICCPR, to show that the ISA would not exist under Article 9.[42]

An essay that functions in terms of *what to do,* speaking of "value and choice," is "Essence and Fluidity."[43] A piece about whether sexuality is fluid, it tackles the question of fixed sexual identities and whether people are *essentially* gay, lesbian, or bisexual. As a polemical piece of writing, it offers a purely subjective position on the subject. Another story with a similar function is "Family Values,"[44] in which Au speaks about the intrusive nature of family members into each other's lives. He suggests that this may well be a reason gays and lesbians might wish to move out of Singapore. He writes, "Many gay men and women dream about a new life in Sydney or Los Angeles, to escape the homophobia of their families and this place. They feel the value system here has no place for them."

The significance of *Yawning Bread* in terms of its wider cultural transmission is evident in its use as an intervention into other media, particularly newsprint. In March 2000 a supporting story featured Alex Au and *Yawning Bread* in *Asiaweek*.[45] The Web site is reported as a window into the gay Singaporean mind. In terms of strategy, the article demonstrates its concern with resistance identity; moreover, it demonstrates the value of

Yawning Bread itself as a site of strategy, a place where unruly Singaporean sexuality can speak without the regime of sexual governance that belies traditional media. Unruly Singaporean sexuality is specifically embodied here by the gay Singaporean mind; it represents an articulation of sexuality that is usually elided by the dominant heteronormative values circulating in Singaporean society.

As further evidence, and even more surprising, was the publication of a survey to gauge attitudes to gay-related issues in Singapore. The survey, conducted by Au, collected 251 responses through face-to-face interviews and another 240 responses through the Internet. The survey was stored for public comment and interface on *Yawning Bread*. What is pertinent in terms of our understanding of the Internet's interactional impact on Singapore is that this survey was picked up by the *Straits Times* editor, Irene Ng, in a two-page spread.[46] The survey is used extensively in this article to substantiate changing attitudes about and wider tolerance of gays in general. Here can be seen the explicit impact of the Internet on other modes of cultural transmission. The *Straits Times* also notes Au's attempt to host a forum at the Substation in Singapore to discuss the relationship between gay and lesbian Singaporean citizens and the government's vision of Singapore 21.[47] Notably, permission for this forum was rejected.

An analysis of *Yawning Bread* thus reveals the presence of strategies of survival (and to a lesser extent *strategies of transformation*) in a variety of articles as well as a deeply dialogic dimension in relation to its form of cultural transmission. There is a sense that the purpose of the site is to engage and to interact with other gays and lesbians. Au states, in fact, "In Yawning Bread, I explore the arguments that homosexuality is a natural condition, deserving human rights and respect."[48] *Yawning Bread* thus represents a gay Singaporean's activist space, a site of strategy, of unruly subjectivity, sexuality, and sociopolitical intervention. Curiously, the Web site has ethically intervened into Singaporean society, demonstrated by its use as a credible source in print media both domestically and abroad.

SiGNeL

Given Singapore's current situation, fighting the state on matters of
sexuality is like a praying mantis trying to stop a bull cart.
—Chong Kee, "Fighting the Wrong Devil," 1998

Another important example of the usefulness of the Internet for the homosexual Singaporean community is the news group *SiGNeL*. On any day this
site receives a number of postings, usually on a particular article that has
appeared in the *Straits Times* or perhaps an issue that concerns one of the
subscribers, such as coming out or what to read. The quality of interactivity
on this site is quite explicit. The nature of the communication is highly
dialogic, where dialogization takes place without a central authority. This
meaning of dialogue is useful here in understanding how this site works as a
leavening of unruly sexuality, rights discourse, and Singaporean conceptions of belonging and participation. The strategies of survival and transformation are dialogically embedded. There is an ongoing deliberation and
contest of definitions, position, and direction, the effects of which are
implicated across subjective and social contexts.

Having subscribed to the list and observing the general tenor of the
discussion from 1997 to 1998, I characterize *SiGNeL* as having a certain
degree of serious debate and dialogue, an investigative spirit. This is a
moderated site that demonstrates the intersubjective interaction that can
occur among individuals who are in conversation about human rights,
values, attitudes, movements, influences, government policies, and much
more. It is a space for critical engagement, interrogation, and exchange of
perspectives. This demonstrates what Slevin argues characterizes the potential interactive quality of the Internet. Queer sensibility is tremendously
empowered by its capacity to culturally transmit views via a medium where
the information is two-way and the conventional dichotomy of producer/
receiver is blurred.[49]

Many of the discussions focus on the homosexual dilemma in Singapore.
For the purposes of this section, I examine one of these discussions that
occurred in June 1998 under the title "Fighting the Wrong Devil."[50] The
discussion shows the sophistication of debate that is present on *SiGNeL*. It
also reveals the conversational tone of the exchanges with a sense that the

object of the explication of ideas is not to seek closure but to open up the deliberations. There is, therefore, embedded in this discussion list the property of nonauthoritarian dialogue, which is a key strategy of transformation.

The first posting on this subject is by Alex Au (6 June 1998: 11:44 A.M.), the host of *Yawning Bread,* in which he makes, in part, the following statement on the debate about Asian values and homosexuality: "It may well be that the crux of the matter lies not in societal homophobia, but in the political culture of a place. To fight ignorance and homophobia may be to fight the wrong devil. The primary battleground for us may well be the arena of the political culture."

In response to this (and the key to *SiGNeL* is the ongoing *response* by subscribers) Petrus (6 June 1998: 5:51 P.M.) suggests that the government of Singapore is threatened by the "liberal idea" of the homosexual lifestyle. The discussion revolves around the attitude of the government and its role. Dan (6 June 1998: 11:39 P.M.) believes, "There is this widespread apathy I note in Singapore over most issues in life because many people believe that the government will handle it." This refers to the paternalistic nature of the state and its interference in practically every part of a Singaporean's life. Chong Kee (7 June 1998: 10:44 A.M.) continues the theme: "I understand that the state is now the main block to sexual equality." An anonymous posting (7 June 1998: 2:49 P.M.) speaks to the theme by suggesting that "the best way to negotiate for . . . freedom is not to sit down and lament in agony. . . . All it takes is for everyone, doing a simple social/political act every day to make living in Singapore a whole NEW experience."

Au once again steps in to refine the discussion and to articulate a more nuanced approach (9 June 1998: 9:30 P.M.): "I didn't mean engaging in electoral or party politics. I mean subpolitics, like lobbying, speaking with the press, submitting papers for forums, meeting selected MPS." A redirection of the subject is then posted by Chong Kee (11 June 1998: 3:36 A.M.): "I prefer to believe in the 100 monkey phenomenon—when a critical number of people change to a new consciousness, the whole population will soon follow." His prognosis for an emerging civil society is to "Start with your relatives and friends. Find the nooks and crannies of emerging civil society and help expand it."

Following this there are postings by Simasar (11 June 1998: 4:55 P.M.) and by Liberty (12 June 1998: 12:13 A.M.) about how to fight the state. Au responds to the "critical number" theory by asking, after a lengthy posting

Mobile Cultures

(12 June 1998: 11:07 P.M.), "So if the Singapore government applies the same insistence on promoting its heterosexist agenda, and ban gay visibility in the media the way they banned [Chinese] dialect, would the critical mass in our population also stay with the homophobic side?"

After another reply from Chong Kee (13 June 1998: 2:25 P.M.), the final thoughts on the theme are from Liberty (13 June 1998: 10:28 P.M.), who contextualizes the whole dilemma in relation to the Reformasi movement in Indonesia: "I don't know what are the cost[s] to Singapore for gay rights to be recognised. . . . Just imagine, the huge implications that come with recognising gay rights. It is going to affect everything in Singapore, Military, Education, Family Structure, Housing, Economics and . . . more."

The features surrounding the political nature of Singapore found in this chronotope[51] have been characterized by Melanie Chew as problems the regime will continue to throw up against its citizenry. There is, she comments, a "detached political culture, which results from the lack of a sense of political participation," and also "the *kiasu* culture, characterized by anxiety and conformity." These have produced a cynical attitude toward political institutions and an alienation of citizens from the political process. In the tensions that are explicated above in the various points of view put forward by *SiGNeL* subscribers can be seen an interrogation of Singaporean citizenship in relation to homosexuality and gay identity. Chew ultimately argues for a Singapore that goes beyond the pressures of conformity that lead toward mediocrity. Her argument has a strong resonance with the discussions that take place on *SiGNeL*. She states, "A strong nation is made up of strong individuals who are free and freely choose to join the energies for the common good. And the basis of the strong, free individual lies within the principle and practice of human rights."[52]

The exclusion of gay and lesbian Singaporeans has led to the formation of discussion lists like *SiGNeL*. Such forums on the Internet clearly demonstrate strategies of survival and transformation and underscore the interactional impact of the Internet on the intersection of identity, sexuality, and rights discourse in Singapore. Perhaps the most remarkable feature of *SiGNeL* is its interactive fluidity, as shown in the 1.5-week timeline above. Strategies of transformation are explicit in the way discourses, subjects, positions, and voices change and shift so rapidly throughout this period.

Conclusion: Toward New Forms of Queer Cultural Transmission

I began this essay by noting that research on the Internet in terms of its effects on the sociocultural and political everyday life of queer Southeast Asian citizens is theoretically undernourished. What I have attempted to do here is develop a theoretical frame that is useful in examining the nature of the relationship among Singaporean queer activists, the Internet, and rights discourse. The questions raised included: How do queer Singaporean activists utilize and deploy the Internet in their struggle for human rights in civil and state society? How has it become a useful means of intervention into Singaporean society? Is it possible to see queer activism on the Internet as a radical new form of cultural transmission, and therefore a significant challenge to the status quo? The central argument in this essay is that the Internet *acts* as a crucial cultural facility of queer sensibility and therefore potential social change. The Internet provides the Singaporean queer activist the possibility of engaging in rights discourse without the usual sociopolitical constraints, beyond state and civil society's governance and surveillance of sexuality.

The two Web sites examined illustrate the nature of their form of cultural transmission on the Internet—as deeply dialogic and framed by strategies of survival and transformation. These sites contribute to our understanding of the noncentralized chaos of cyberspace in its creation of new ways of belonging and participation. The consequences of these new forms of cultural transmission have far-reaching effects for the everyday life of the queer Singaporean and, indeed, queer Southeast Asian. At this stage it is difficult to map or gauge entirely the effects of the Internet's interactional impact on Singaporean society, with its embedded discourses on rights and sexuality. But my hope is that this essay goes some way toward an ethical intervention into Singapore's apartheid of unruly sexualities. To quote Zygmunt Bauman and how we might sense the impact of the Internet: "What we and other people do may have profound, far-reaching and long-lasting consequences, which we can neither see directly nor predict with precision. Between the deeds and their outcomes there is a huge distance—both in time and in space—which we cannot fathom using our innate, ordinary power of perception—and so we can hardly measure the quality of our actions by a full inventory of their effects."[53]

Notes

I would like to thank Fran Martin, Audrey Yue, and Chris Berry for their editorial expertise and encouragement and Robert Kostevc for his research assistance.

1 See Donald J. West and Richard Green, eds., *Sociolegal Control of Homosexuality* (New York: Plenum, 1997); Baden Offord and Leon Cantrell, "Homosexual Rights as Human Rights in Indonesia and Australia," in *Gay and Lesbian Asia: Identities and Communities,* ed. Peter A. Jackson and Gerard Sullivan (New York: Haworth, 2001); Barry D. Adam, Jan Willem Duyvendak, and Andre Krouwel, eds., *The Global Emergence of Gay and Lesbian Politics: National Imprints of a Worldwide Movement* (Philadelphia: Temple University Press, 1999); Dennis Altman, "The Emergence of Gay Identities in Southeast Asia," in *Different Rainbows,* ed. Peter Drucker (London: Gay Men's Press, 2000), 137–56.

2 The "Asian values" debate was activated in the early 1990s by Singaporean, Malaysian, and Chinese politicians particularly. Singapore's elder statesman Lee Kuan Yew specifically inculcated a view that East Asian Confucian values are different from Western values. In articulating his view, Yew drew on Confucian emphasis on the family, that in fact the government itself is not above the role of the family. In this formulation of Confucian values, the individual is entirely subservient to the wishes of the family, and embedded in this discourse is the notion of the nation as a protectorate of family values. Moreover, the state is the organ of the family, thus imagined and conceived as genetically, philosophically, and culturally heterosexist. Singaporean traditional media has well regarded the role of the family as the fulcrum of Singapore's success, whereas new media such as the Internet, the subject of this essay, have offered a crucial space for intervening into and challenging the heterosexism of the state and civil society. See Lee Kuan Yew, *From Third World to First* (New York: HarperCollins, 2000), 491–92. For a critique of Singapore's role in the "Asian values" debate, see Armartya Sen, "Human Rights and Asian Values: What Lee Kuan Yew and Le Peng Don't Understand about Asia," *New Republic* 217, nos. 2–3 (1997): 33–41; E. P. Mendes, *Asian Values and Human Rights: Letting the Tigers Free* (Ottawa: Human Rights Research and Education Centre, 1996); Sarah Pritchard, "Asian Values and Human Rights," paper presented at Australian and New Zealand Society of International Law colloquium, University of New South Wales, Australia, March 1996; Chee Soon Juan, *To Be Free: Stories from Asia's Struggle against Oppression* (Melbourne: Monash Asia Institute, 1998).

3 For background analysis of Singapore's state-directed heterosexism, see Lau-

rence Leong, "Walking the Tightrope: The Role of Action for AIDS in the Provision of Social Services in Singapore," in *Gays and Lesbians in Asia and the Pacific: Social and Human Services,* ed. Gerard Sullivan and Laurence W. Leong (New York: Harrington Press, 1995), 11–30.

4   See Laurence Wai-Teng Leong, "Singapore," in *Sociolegal Control of Homosexuality: A Multi-Nation Comparison,* ed. Donald J. West and Richard Green (New York: Plenum, 1997), 127–44; Baden Offord, "The Burden of (Homo)sexual Identity in Singapore," *Social Semiotics* 9, no. 3 (1999): 301–16.

5   Sections 377 and 377a of the Singaporean Penal Code, cited in Leong, "Singapore," 127.

6   Section (e) of the Singaporean Broadcasting Authority Act (Chapter 297), 1 November 1997, states that Internet material prohibited under the Act includes "whether the material advocates homosexuality or lesbianism, or depicts or promotes incest, paedophilia, bestiality and necrophilia"; cited in *Singapore Broadcasting Authority,* 8 July 1998, ⟨http://www.sba.gov.sg⟩ (25 July 2002).

7   Statement by Singaporean government representative at the Vienna World Conference on Human Rights, "Appendix Three," in *Human Rights and International Relations in the Asia-Pacific Region,* ed. James T. H. Tang (New York: Pinter, 1995), 244.

8   Leong, "Walking the Tightrope," 16.

9   Statement by Singaporean government representative at the Vienna World Conference on Human Rights, 244.

10   Christopher Tremewan, "Human Rights in Asia," *Pacific Review* 6, no. 1 (1993): 17.

11   Leong, "Walking the Tightrope," 17–18.

12   Singapore's nation building has been predicated on strong paternal regulation and control of gender and sexual relations. See Geraldine Heng and Janadas Devan, "State Fatherhood: The Politics of Nationalism, Sexuality and Race in Singapore," in *Nationalisms and Sexualities,* ed. Andrew Parker, Mary Russo, Doris Sommer, and Patricia Yaeger (New York: Routledge, 1992), 343–64.

13   Christina M. Cerna, "Universality of Human Rights and Cultural Diversity," in *Regional Systems for the Protection of Human Rights in Asia, Africa, in the Americas and in Europe,* ed. W. Heinz (Strasbourg, France: Friedrich Naumann Stiftung, 1993), 10.

14   James Slevin, *The Internet and Society* (Cambridge, England: Polity Press, 2000, 55); subsequent references are cited parenthetically. Slevin's work is an in-depth examination of the development of the Internet and its relationship to a plethora of contemporary issues, such as the reconfiguration of the state, the processes of globalization, and risk management. He draws theoretically

on Anthony Giddens, Zygmunt Bauman, Jürgen Habermas, Manuel Castells, and John B. Thompson.

15 *Dialogic* in this essay is used to highlight the particular capacity of two-way interaction via the facility of the Internet. But it further underscores the potential dialogic quality that exists in the Internet in terms of its technological facility *and* the interaction among subjects, in this case, unruly sexualities, thereby allowing the sharing of information and the concordance of resistant and creative online community and identity. Dialogic is also used to indicate the presence of a wider impact of the Internet, that is, how it has the potential to impact everyday life through providing a crucial private space for survival. Dialogic then, is used here in the sense that it is an embedded communicative and social tool of the Internet that implicates across subjective and social contexts. How far these dialogic effects go are difficult to assess.

16 Manuel Castells, *The Power of Identity* (Oxford: Blackwell, 1997), 8; subsequent references are cited parenthetically.

17 I am using queer theory here, not so much in terms of its implicit anti-identity critique, as in its discursive deployment of *sexual identity as a strategy*, in its capacity to be an *act* of political, social, and cultural intervention. Such an *act* is substantially unruly by virtue of its challenge to the fixed notions of heteronormativity. However, unruly sexuality, although inherently a resistant sexuality, may not necessarily be a substantive transformative sexuality. Here the work of Judith Butler, Carol Pateman, Michael Warner, Wayne Morgan, and Carolyn Williams is useful in understanding the activity of identity politics in the context of resistance and transformation. There is no unified queer theory, but a project that is engaged in a critical dialectic between essentialist and constructionist positionings.

18 Carolyn Williams, "Identity Politics in the Postmodern," in *Gay and Lesbian Perspectives IV,* ed. Robert Aldrich and Garry Wotherspoon (Sydney: University of Sydney, 1998), 37.

19 Ibid., 38.

20 See Offord, "The Burden of (Homo)sexual Identity," 307–8.

21 Russell Heng, "Tiptoe out of the Closet: A Look at the Increasingly Visible Gay Community in Singapore," paper given at the Emerging Gay and Lesbian Communities in Asia Conference, University of Sydney, Australia, 29 September 1995. For the development of these thoughts, see Russell Heng Hiang Khng, "Tiptoe out of the Closet: The Before and After of the Increasingly Visible Gay Community in Singapore," in *Gay and Lesbian Asia: Identities and Communities,* ed. Peter Jackson and Gerald Sullivan (New York: Haworth, 2001), 81–97.

22 Wolfgang Kleinwaechter, "The People's 'Right to Communicate' and a 'Global Communication Charter,'" *Journal of International Communication* 5, nos. 1–2 (1998): 119.

23 Leong, "Singapore," 142.

24 Deborah L. Wheeler, "Global Culture or Global Clash: New Information Technologies and the Islamic World—A View from Kuwait," *Communication Research* 25, no. 4 (1998): 377.

25 Alan Sondheim, *Being on Line: Net Subjectivity* (New York: Lusitania Press, 1997), 6.

26 Robert Markley, "Introduction: History, Theory and Virtual Reality," in *Virtual Realities and Their Discontents,* ed. R. Markley (Baltimore: Johns Hopkins University Press, 1996), 4.

27 Ng King Kang, *The Rainbow Connection: The Internet and the Singapore Gay Community* (Singapore: KangCuBine Publishing, 1999), iv.

28 Michael Shari, "Welcome to Internet Island," *Business Week,* 1 February 1999, 37.

29 Stanley D. Brunn and Charles D. Cottle, "Small States and Cyberboosterism," *Geographical Review* 87, no. 2 (1997): 340.

30 See Singapore Broadcasting Authority, *Singapore Broadcasting Authority,* 8 July 1998, ⟨http://www.sba.gov.sg⟩ (28 December 2000).

31 Qtd. in Slevin, *The Internet and Society,* 144.

32 Singapore Broadcasting Authority, *Singapore Broadcasting Authority.*

33 Action for Aids: The Act, *AFA Homepage,* 1 January 1997, ⟨http://www.afa.org.sg⟩ (1 November 2000). For example, see "Research Report: The Risks Men Take: Insights from the Anonymous Testing Site," 18, Action for Aids: The Act, *AFA Homepage,* 1 January 1997, ⟨http://afa.org.sg/issue/issue18/prisk.html⟩ (1 November 2000).

34 People Like Us, *PLU Homepage,* 15 July 1999, ⟨http://www.geocities.com/WestHollywood/3878⟩ (30 November 2000); SiGNel, *SiGNel Homepage,* 15 March 1997, ⟨http://www.geocities.com/WestHollywood/3878/signel.html⟩ (25 July 2002); We Are Family, *We Are Family Homepage,* 27 August 2000, ⟨http://www.geocities.com/WestHollywood/Heights/7288/⟩ (30 November 2000); Utopia, *Utopia Homepage,* 13 December 1997, ⟨http://www.utopia-asia.com⟩ (25 July 2002); Sintercom, *Sintercom Homepage,* 1994, ⟨http://www.sintercom.org⟩ (30 November 2000); Madeleine Lim, "Chatting with Madeleine Lim," *Sintercom,* 14 July 1997, ⟨http://www.sintercom.org/sp/interview/madeleine.html⟩ (11 November 2000).

35 Quoted in Carlos A. Arnaldo et al., "Freedom of Expression: A Universal Optique," *Journal of International Communication* 5, nos. 1–2 (1998): 39.

36 George Gerbner, "The Stories We Tell and the Stories We Sell," *Journal of International Communication* 5, nos. 1–2 (1998): 75. I use Gerbner's model here with the caveat that, although perhaps a little narrow and functionalist, it provides a way of seeing how the cultural environment of the Internet, for the purposes of this analysis, animates discourse through various stories.

37 Au, *Yawning Bread* ⟨http://www.geocities.com/WestHollywood/5738⟩ (30 November 2000).

38 Ibid., emphasis added. Subsequent references are to this site.

39 Au, "The Why Nots of Human Rights," *Yawning Bread.*

40 Au, "Without Cover of the Covenant," *Yawning Bread.*

41 Chia Thye Poh, Member of Parliament and academic, was jailed for thirty-two years under the ISA.

42 Article 9 states: "Everyone has the right to liberty and security of person. No one shall be subjected to arbitrary arrest or detention. No one shall be deprived of his liberty except on such grounds and in accordance with such procedures as are established by law." United Nations High Commissioner for Human Rights, "International Covenant of Civil and Political Rights," *United Nations Homepage,* 25 November 2000, ⟨http://www.unhchr.ch/html/menu 3/b/a_ccpr.htm⟩ (1 December 2000).

43 Au, "Essence and Fluidity," *Yawning Bread.*

44 Au, "Family Values," *Yawning Bread.*

45 "Agents of Change," *Asiaweek Online,* 26, no. 11 (24 March 2000), ⟨http://www.asiaweek.com/asiaweek/magazine/2000/0324/cover.4people.html⟩ (30 November 2000).

46 Irene Ng, "Do Gays Have a Place in Singapore?" *Straits Times,* 27 May 2000, n.p.

47 Ibid. Singapore 21's motif is "Everyone Matters." See *Singapore 21,* 1 January 2000. ⟨http://www.singapore21.org.sg⟩ (30 May 2001).

48 Au, *Yawning Bread.*

49 Slevin, *The Internet and Society,* 74.

50 SiGNel, *SiGNeL Homepage* ⟨http://www.geocities.com/WestHollywood/3878/signel.html⟩ (25 July 2000).

51 *SiGNeL* demonstrates the interconnectedness of time and space and thus surely implicates the strategic efficacy of such communication. Understanding chronotope in this way underscores the value of the Internet as a prime and crucial space for connecting the private and the public, where transgression, unruly contest, and interrogation are possible in the most public domains of all.

52 Melanie Chew, "Human Rights in Singapore: Perceptions and Problems," *Asian Survey* 34, no. 2 (1994): 945, 948.

53 Zygmunt Bauman, *Postmodern Ethics* (Oxford: Blackwell, 1993), 17.

LARISSA HJORTH

Pop and *ma:* The Landscape

of Japanese Commodity Characters

and Subjectivity

Ma is the pause, the space between words, between images. It is that
part of the page, of the picture, left untouched, as ineffable white. In
Japanese aesthetics, in any composition, whether verbal or visual, this
absence is also supposed to be savored, enjoyed in its own right. . . .
I'd met Meadowlark shortly after I'd first discovered this idea and was
wondering whether such notions could be applied to a person. Could
one, for example, find meaning in someone's blank spaces, in the
juxtaposition between what was present in his character and what
was quite absent? Certainly Meadowlark appeared to operate on the
narrowest conceivable spectrum. A single ink squiggle in an awful
lot of white space.—GAVIN KRAMER, *Shopping,* 2001

Japanese young people often hang tiny, doll-like "characters" from their
mobile phones, enabling them to signify something about themselves to all
around. In Japanese, the term commonly used to refer to both mobile
phones and other portable communication technologies, like the WAP
phones discussed below, is *keitai,* which means, literally, "portable." Examples of characters commonly hung from keitai include Sanrio's mouthless
kitty known as Hello Kitty and Sony's virtual email pink pet known as
PostPet. At first sight, these "cute" (*kawaii*) characters may seem to reinforce highly conventional gender and sexuality stereotypes. However, the
fact that Hello Kitty has been appropriated, for example, in lesbian dance
party advertisements, indicates things may not be so simple.[1] To understand this, we need to examine two concepts. First, difference in a Japanese

cultural context may not be structured in binary oppositions but may appear in the indeterminate spaces and gaps, which may be understood through a rethinking of *ma*. In particular, kawaii reappropriations inside and outside keitai scapes could be seen to echo the ambiguity and ubiquity signified by ma. Second, the "cute" (kawaii) world—implying childhood or childlike qualities—is not an asexual space at all. Survey data suggest that for many Japanese users, in particular Japanese women users, cute characters may be appropriated to open up possibilities of nonconformist gender roles and sexualities.

This essay seeks to explore the character landscape attached to keitai cultures in Tokyo. Specifically, I explore the sexual and gender reappropriations and identifications apparent within the ongoing negotiations between kawaii and keitai consumer scapes. After recently spending three months in Tokyo, I became increasingly curious about the ways these various characters operate as signifying codes spanning gender and sexual politics. I frame the analysis of the landscape of characters and characterization through a revision of the Japanese notion of ma. Traditionally defined as a space to be contemplated (between images, words, or concepts), it has more recently been redefined as a rhetorical device connoting conceptual ambiguity, which in turn relates to the ambiguity of sexual codes in contemporary Japanese culture. In this way, a renegotiated ma, understood as a space for conceptualizing and practicing the ambiguity associated with contemporary modes of subjectivity, reflects the major shifts forged by the dialogue between kawaii and keitai. Many symbols of modernization and postmodern society, such as PostPet, are defined by conservative groups through the language of either ma abysses or consumer pop (meaningless trash). However, although the language and attached ideologies are ambiguous, they are far from meaningless.

For me, one of the most interesting facts about character culture is that it is a predominantly female preoccupation. Within the terrain of consumerism, the construction of women as consumers in both Western and Japanese culture highlights the various roles provided (or not) for women and female same-sex relations. As will be discussed, character culture as symbolic of female consumption is an important site for performing and representing the complexity of gender roles, specifically alternative female sexualities. The kawaii characters attached to keitai are in fact far from reinforcing traditional female representation within a heterosexual framework.

In particular, "cuteness" as symbolic of female subjectivities within consumer culture is being revolutionized by shifts toward the Internet, specifically mobile phone–based Internet gadgets, portables and gizmos such as the NTT WAP phone (Wireless Application Protocol) DoCoMo.[2] These shifts in the cute also relate to the growing role and visibility of women within the economic and cultural logic of Japan. Following these recent technological changes, the cute is no longer the powerless in need of subversion by lesbian groups but instead a type of enfant terrible that could complicate, as much as lubricate, social relations.[3] In particular, the changing role of women in Japan through vehicles such as new technology and the associated employment can be mapped through the changing role of characters from passive and asexual to active and sexualized. Specifically, because women are seen as the major market for characters it is no accident that changes in characters run parallel to shifts in the female demographics of Tokyo. Maybe in this instance it is not such a bad thing to be left "hanging on the telephone."[4]

Post-PostPet

In their article "In the Company of Strangers," the Sussex Technology Group argue, "The mobile phone is a significant object; it is a guarantee of connection in (and to) the dislocated social world of modernity."[5] Their study, informed by surveys conducted in Brighton, England, attempted to map the spaces practiced and conceived by mobile phone users in relation to Erving Goffman's notion of self-presentation and appropriation.[6] Although their identification of paradoxes surrounding "mobile telephony" consisting of shifting public/private zones and the changing definition of performative, physical, and psychological spaces is of interest to this study, their application of Goffman's theories does not lend itself to a neat translation in a Japanese framework.

As argued by Todd Joseph Miles Holden in "I'm Your Venus/You're a Rake," the roles mapped by genderism in Japanese mediascapes are not identical to those found in the United States.[7] Instead of attempting to stretch and twist a Western theory about space and identity into a Japanese context, I have opened up a revised notion of ma as an appropriated social and psychological space. This notion, as with my investigation into surveying relationships to kawaii modes within keitai scapes, represents an attempt to navigate new roles for gender and sexual difference. Far from definitive, this is a peripatetic exploration of some of the relationships and modes of representation afforded to women and lesbians in Tokyo.

One problem when analyzing character cultures in Tokyo is understanding how individual use can be qualified and quantified as different from the consumer rhetoric espoused by the various companies. While in Tokyo I noticed the ways characters were appropriated and reappropriated by various demographics. However, I found it quite difficult to actually tease out these variations. To map out the identity landscapes, I initially conducted a survey asking questions about the roles characters provided in conventional consumerism and transgressive appropriations.

I was aware of the associated methodological restrictions imposed by survey-based studies, in particular the leading nature of asking set questions, and being sensitive to my own cultural baggage as an Australian ethnographically analyzing an*other* culture. Related to this point was a need to negotiate the cultural and linguistic landscape encountered in analyzing Japanese popular culture. I try to resolve these potential problems by employing a reworked, self-consciously hybrid and contemporary notion of ma.

So, what is ma? Ma is defined as a spatial concept specifically within Japanese linguistics. Ma is meant to be contemplated and enjoyed—a space as meaningful as written characters (*kanji*). My use of ma highlights negotiations between traditional pre-Meiji and contemporary Westernized Japan. The use of a Japanese term by a Westerner could imply a type of exoticization or "otherness" associated with functionalist, early anthropological methods.[8] However, my appropriation of ma is not to resuscitate the original "timeless" concept but rather to survey a self-consciously contemporary discourse that is fraught with contested and often contradictory codes. The notion of ma, as I argue below of the notion of cute (kawaii), is a polysemic and ambiguous one. It began in Japanese writing and in my analysis extends out to represent the complex, and often contradictory, sites afforded to contemporary subjectivity and consumerism. In particular, my renegotiation of ma is as a space not only contested but also encoded with the ambivalence associated with a type of aesthetic blank canvas. The idea of the blank canvas implies a "whiteness" that is simultaneously all colors and yet none.[9] It is both ambiguous and ubiquitous. I suggest that a reworking of ma could reflect the new spaces opened up by the relationship between kawaii and the keitai (including DoCoMo) and help in reconceptualizing cultural and social landscapes accordingly.

In particular, the use of ma to map the ambiguous yet ubiquitous terrain navigated by kawaii and keitai can be witnessed in the production and consumption of the dominant WAP DoCoMo (with three-fifths of the market). These keitais with three roles—mobile phone, handheld computer, and wireless email receiver—are marketed and designed to reconfigure social and communication processes. According to the ads, DoCoMo is an acronym for "Do communications over the mobile network," but as Frank Rose points out in "Pocket Monster," the name is very similar to the Japanese word *dokomo,* which means "everywhere" and "anything."[10] This dokomo spatial organization and logic parallels a reworked notion of the ma, a scape in which kawaii appropriations produce various modes of interpretation, representation, and consumption.

Ma can thus be seen as a scape in which to rethink kawaii and keitai identification, consumption, and processes of desire (*akogare*). In particular, the Japanese social etiquette of not talking on mobile phones in public spaces means that many participants are forced into the mediated scapes of text messages or emails, a spatial terrain that provides different modes and relations to kawaii culture and in turn shifts the users' relationship to the keitai. Within these practices there exist simultaneously productions of both subcultural and mainstream tendencies, global and local vernaculars, personalized and standardized modes of communication and representation. I propose that this ongoing dialogue between self-presentation and transgression in kawaii cultures constitutes and inhabits a space configured according to a revised notion of ma.

The terrain painted by my specific use of ma echoes the *apparently* banal mainstream quality of characters such as Hello Kitty. Hello Kitty seemingly reinforces gender-conservative notions such as femininity as passive and voiceless within an asexual, "childlike" concept of kawaii. This parallels the ambivalence in the seeming blankness of ma. So why would Hello Kitty be appropriated by lesbian subcultures in Japan? This appropriation suggests that "childhood" and the kawaii are far from asexual in contemporary character culture in Tokyo. The results of my survey suggest that it is this aesthetic blankness (or ma) that simultaneously and paradoxically allows for nonconforming sexual and gender identification. The ambiguity and

Mobile Cultures

ubiquity of ma performed by Hello Kitty and friends are precisely what enable her to be appropriated by lesbian identity and sexuality. Her association with girl friendships, like her signifying childhood through kawaii, is far from asexual.

Fieldwork and surveys provide part of the basis for my discussion. The survey was conducted during September 2000 and consisted of a questionnaire through email and postal mail to two hundred Tokyo residents. I made a conscious decision to isolate the study to Tokyo rather than Japan as a whole. The questionnaire was devised through discussions conducted face-to-face with residents met while I was in Tokyo from February to May 2000. During this time I questioned many participants about their own or others' use of and identification with characters, particularly in reference to characters attached to keitai.

These initial informal surveys attempted to understand the significance of characters in various social groups. In this study I was careful to encompass a range of different social backgrounds, aiming for a rough balance of men and women, both heterosexual and homosexual, of various ages spanning different employment fields. The survey consisted of questions pertaining to lifestyle issues and the respondents' thoughts about and relationship to characters such as Hello Kitty. From this survey I chose forty respondents for further discussion and questioning. I do not claim that this study represents all of Tokyo's residents but rather a sample study informed by the active respondents.

The demographics of the final survey consisted of 40 percent lesbians, 40 percent heterosexual women, 10 percent homosexual men, and 10 percent heterosexual men between the ages of 21 to 40. It is interesting to note that sexual preference in the category of women did not mark a difference in use of and identification with characters, although Hello Kitty seemed less preferred by heterosexual than homosexual women. In the male demographic surveyed, there seemed to be a preference for less well-known characters. From the survey, 82 percent identified with one or more characters (no more than five), and 16 percent rejected characters for their mainstream status, often identifying them as a "fad"; 2 percent were uncommitted. Of the 82 percent who identified with characters, 74 percent claimed that the chosen character or characters signified some personal meaning.

Of those surveyed, 75 percent attached characters to their keitai. This category was marked by a predominantly female demographic. Of the participants, 60 percent had their own Internet service (either through the home computer or WAP mobile phone). This was a surprisingly high percentage considering it has been claimed that because Japan is the most expensive country for Internet service providers, only 20 percent of the population have their own Internet service.[11] Of this percentage, only 30 percent had online characters such as PostPet.

The questionnaires quickly began to demonstrate that throughout all the variables, some constants, particularly in relation to gender and sexuality, could be mapped. Identification with characters illustrated three interrelated points of negotiation. First, the cute, explicitly tied to the terrain of characters, was changing in accordance with shifts in new technologies and global tendencies. This change paralleled the shifting status of the prime consumers of characters: women. Second, the notion of cute occupied a particular relationship to adulthood and sexual identity rather than the frequently desexualized category of childhood as often assumed by adults. Third, the fashioning and consuming of characters in Japanese popular culture demonstrated simultaneously mainstream and subcultural affiliations.

From the survey, Hello Kitty was the most used example and provides material for an interesting discussion. Most participants were able to quote the characteristics attributed to Hello Kitty by the company Sanrio almost word-for-word and stereotype the marketed audience as "young girls (or women who want to be like young girls)"; however; Hello Kitty was frequently reappropriated into "other" modes of representation and identification. The most noted attitude toward Hello Kitty's possible transgressive roles was the fact that character culture provided a space for humor to be deployed. In addition, Hello Kitty explicitly and implicitly represented same-sex, in this case female-to-female, relations, although consumption by males was on the rise.

Of those surveyed, 90 percent identified the characters as coming from ideal, middle-class families with lots of friends, and the initial market for characters such as Hello Kitty as children. The fact that the characters are animals role-playing human characters was noted by the respondents, but it was not a major focus of interest. The use of animals seems to be just a device to employ degrees of cuteness while playing into Japan's popular cultural focus on childhood.

Significantly, almost all participants recognized the ability of the cute in many character cultures to afford individuals a space in which to negotiate taboo notions such as sexual identity. Although this was quite hard to map, as many attributed this activity to "others," the notions of gender and, more specifically, same-sex relations were loud and clear. When stereotyping markets, participants articulated various characters to same-sex preoccupations. And although the cute was understood as initially a female concern, this was also changing quickly.

When questioned about the significance of characters in terms of sexual symbols or categories, participants unanimously commented on the characters' lack of sexuality as relating to cultural taboos. However, all participants noted that they were aware of "others" who appropriated the characters, especially the "Lolita complex" of heterosexual men fetishizing Hello Kitty while simultaneously interested in its primary market of high school girls.

One interviewee, a Japanese heterosexual female art student, said, "Hello Kitty, My Melody, and Kiki Lara are so romantic if the owners are adults. But when men have them, that's weird!!!" One heterosexual male participant, who collected the droopy panda Tare Panda, claimed, "I don't know, he's just so cute, he's irresistible." And one female heterosexual claimed, "The character goods are also for boys. Manga comics produce many recognizable characters and the boys also get taken into the fashion. Like girls, they attach straps on the mobile phones, have key rings, watches, etc. Difference is, the boys are more open-minded and take interest in alternatives as well. They are clear about stating their identity by character goods. . . . *Otaku*-people, *manga*-manic (people over 20, tending to be professionals or businessmen) tend to relate the sexual contents of cute characters to girls, to feel as if the character existed as his girlfriend, or to feel like a girl."[12]

Kawaii Is Not Japanese for Kitsch

Kawaii in Japanese means cute and refers to the notion of childlike. To a Westerner, it is easy to identify the cute as kitsch in the classificatory framework associated with modernism's definition of popular culture. From the Frankfurt School to Clement Greenberg, the denigration of the popular has defined it as contaminated by the mindlessness of mass production. Greenberg's 1939 definition of popular by using the German word associated with the Berlin Olympics propaganda of the time—the kitsch—illustrated the strong political agenda of the West to create oppositions between high and low culture.[13] The explanation of the kawaii in terms of kitsch reveals more about Western inabilities to comprehend popular culture than it does about Japan itself. In turn, it makes clear that although global popular culture may be ambiguous and ubiquitous, it is far from a homogenized terrain.[14]

In between the black-or-white binary canvas of modernism there is no space afforded to the "blankness" of ma. In other words, the reworked notion of ma that I am deploying here, like the concept of kawaii, represents a type of ambivalent *in betweenness* in popular culture rather than an opposition between popular culture and its "other." In this way, discussion of the kawaii attracts the same debates and critiques surrounding rethinking "popular culture" in postmodern frameworks.[15] It is the ambiguity and ubiquity of kawaii characters such as Hello Kitty that in turn renegotiates the "otherness" of childhood within a duplicitous and paradoxical space: "Some Japanese men are drawn more to the typical owner of cute merchandise than to the merchandise itself. The cuteness of a giggling girl clad in a Hello Kitty jumper isn't entirely innocent. It ties in to what is well known in Japan as *Lolicom,* the Lolita complex. The phenomenon of the little girl as sexual abounds in Tokyo: Vending machines sell schoolgirls' used panties, which the girls sell to middlemen; "image bars" specialize in escorts dressed in school uniforms."[16]

In this quote from her article "Cute Inc.," Mary Roach outlines the often contradictory processes associated with the notion of cute culture and what it provides and performs in terms of gender and sexual roles. Character culture, from *manga* and *anime* to kawaii, demonstrates the diverse functions of sexual identification and gender role playing. In turn, it is capable of subverting and transgressing Japan's repressive and strict censorship codes. However, as in many studies of kawaii character culture, there is a failure in Roach's work to extend research and analysis into female representation and identification beyond heterosexual frameworks.

As David Buckingham identifies in "Electronic Child Abuse? Rethinking the Media's Effects on Children," the category of childhood is often defined by adults and thus positioned as "other."[17] In this binary model, childhood is illustrated as naïve, asexual, vulnerable, and powerless. In Western popular culture, the combination of childhood and sexuality is often seen as oxymoronic while also firing debates around moral bankruptcy. Especially within the plurality and cultural relativity of postmodernism, characters symbolizing childhood have become leaking and fluid modes open to the various positions of the debate.[18]

In delving into kawaii, we venture into the land of desiring childhood. The notion of childhood is ineluctably linked with the field of advertising, "pester power" being one of the most powerful forces in family buying. In the West, subcultures are defined by a historical linkage between the birth of popular culture and the teenage consumer in the 1950s (and its emergence in the United States of the 1930s); in Japan, mass consumerism and buying into subculture are not about youth cultures but child cultures: "We in the U.S. are said to be a youth society, but what we really are is an adolescence society. That's what everyone wants to go back to. In Japan, it's childhood, mother, home that is yearned for, not the wildness of youth."[19]

Childhood in Japan is openly a site for adult preoccupation. In "The Marketing of Adolescence in Japan: Buying and Dreaming," Merry White identifies a great difference, both conceptually and pragmatically, between definitions of American and Japanese teenagers. For a long time the definition of Japanese teenager represented a type of "betweenness," a "bridge between childhood and adulthood."[20] As I have argued, the kawaii presents a type of in between space paralleling my appropriation of ma. This in betweenness or "blank canvas" both enables a rethinking of gender and age and gives a voice to the traditionally silenced site of sexuality in Japan. So the kawaii is more about the *idea* of childhood rather than being a site actually occupied by children. According to Japanese teen magazine *CREA*, as cited in Kinsella, kawaii is "the most widely used, widely loved, habitual word in modern living Japanese."[21] Kinsella goes on to argue that the cute craze supposedly began in 1970, when a fad for handwriting in big, rounded characters spread among teenage Japanese girls: "Scholars who studied the phenomenon dubbed it Anomalous Female Teenage Writing. Kids called it *burikko-ji*, translated as 'kitten writing' or 'fake child writing.' At one point in the mid-80s some 55 percent of 12- to 18-year-old girls were using it."[22]

The arena of the kawaii has attracted much analysis, particularly from Western theorists. These studies have attempted to cover much ground in rethinking female representation in the changing fabric of contemporary Japanese culture, because the stereotypical consumer especially of the kawaii is female. I next briefly present two different approaches and arguments surrounding the ambiguous and ubiquitous landscape that tackle notions of female representation. The two approaches are exemplified by the different theories, written around the same time, espoused by anthropologist Brian McVeigh in "Commodifying Affection, Authority and Gender in the Everyday Objects of Japan" and sociologist Sharon Kinsella in "Cuties in Japan." Both theorists argue that the kawaii is important in rethinking the place of females in contemporary Japanese culture while simultaneously identifying the kawaii as a space of both ambiguity and ubiquity. In addition, both arguments highlight difference in terms of females through the filters of age categories. For McVeigh, the kawaii is symbolic of social power relations in Japan. McVeigh adds that "cuteness does not merely reflect the social world; rather, via communication, it constructs gendered relations."[23]

While McVeigh outlines ambiguity and ubiquity as part of kawaii, he argues that the kawaii results in reinforcing while simultaneously "softening" traditional power relations. His use of gender roles is homogenized into binary relations; while kawaii may be part of gift giving and thus various forms of relationships, McVeigh neglects to extend gender and sexuality beyond the heteronormalities where they remain problematically fixed. One is left thinking that the kawaii is essentially conservative and merely symptomatic of cultural change. Kinsella, on the other hand, maps the translation of the kawaii as an actively subversive space. In this way her understanding of the kawaii is comparable to my reconfiguration of ma, a "blank canvas" where such "voiceless" categories as female sexuality can be performed, all under the veneer of seemingly reinforcing traditional power relations.

McVeigh's later essay, "How Hello Kitty Commodifies the Cute, Cool and Camp: 'Consumutopia' versus 'Control' in Japan," is less reductive in its evaluations of codes for subjectivity within the kawaii site of Hello Kitty.[24] Once again McVeigh's exploration of female representation is predominantly within the variables of age rather than sexual difference. The argument, informed by surveys, constructs "consumutopia" (self-autonomy or counteridentification to the banality of popular, consumer culture) against "control" (a reflexive mode for thinking about Japanese culture). McVeigh sees Hello Kitty's diversity as allowing her to present different female modes of self-representation/identification from childhood (cute) to adolescence (cool) and womanhood (camp). In particular, his alignment of female adulthood with the category of camp demonstrates Hello Kitty's role as extending not only gender and age but also sexual categories. In this text, McVeigh seems to reiterate Kinsella's position of the kawaii as a meaningful site for representing or prefiguring diverse subjectivities, in particular female same-sex relations or "kitty flip."

Kitty Flip: The Gift of the Gap

As Kinsella and McVeigh argue, kawaii character culture such as Hello Kitty has been so successful because it plays into the Japanese tradition of gift giving.[25] The gift in Japan is often used to express unspeakable relations and "in between" social spaces. The gap signified by the need for gift giving thus demonstrates cute as occupying a type of reworked ma space. Here the kawaii is absorbed into consumer categories of contemporary Japanese popular culture while also echoing the traditional role as a type of conventional ma "gap filler."

Kawaii culture also presents a reconfiguration of the relationship between subcultural and mainstream within gender and sexual roles, similar to that often performed by media such as manga (comics). Mark McLelland in "Male Homosexuality and Popular Culture in Japan" maps a notion of homosexuality in Japanese media, specifically manga. As noted by McLelland, there has only recently been information available on male homosexuality in Japan, with still very little research done in relation to Japanese lesbians. McLelland's reflective analysis convincingly argues against Dennis Altman's theory of "global queering," highlighting the vertical imposition of such a model as a type of "cultural imperialist queering."[26] While arguing that gender flexibility is often collapsed into sexual difference in Japanese popular culture, McLelland is quick to point out that Japanese understandings of sexuality and gender roles do not neatly tie into Western frameworks and thus need to be "differently conceptualized."[27] He demonstrates this point through the representations of homosexual love in Japanese popular culture that would be "unimaginable" in the United States or Europe. And yet, the sexual freedom and diversity provided by characters in comics and animations do not necessarily lend themselves to translation into actual lived experience. Rather, McLelland argues, Japan still suffers from the confusion between same-sex desire and cross-dressing/"transgenderisms."[28] Although this may be the case for sexual representation in manga, a different argument could be put forth in relation to the seemingly asexual but definitely gendered kawaii characters. On one hand, characters such as Hello Kitty could be seen to reinforce sexual repression through attributes such as their lack of genitalia; on the other hand, the fact that these characters are gendered but not sexualized makes them a perfect site in which to break with simplistic gender-sex collations.

In the wake of global technologies and Japan's embrace of the Internet is a growing divide between characters such as PostPet and Hello Kitty and those from manga and anime. While characters such as Hello Kitty seem to be enjoying the visibility afforded by new media in the light of the Pokemon phenomenon, arguments have been put forth that new technologies are draining the imagination and creativity surrounding *otaku* culture (the culture of people obsessed with magna and anime).[29] Critic Hoki Hamano argues that the increased exportability of okatu culture is leading to a decline in product quality.[30] In this case, the growing access and visibility of mass repetition and appropriation inherent in Internet technologies is leading to debates surrounding quality versus quantity and original versus copy. Here, okatu culture is put in direct conflict with non-manga and non-anime characters such as Hello Kitty, PostPet, and Pokemon. This argument echoes a type of Greenbergian modernist argument in which kawaii characters such as Hello Kitty are contaminating the purity or originality of okatu culture. This is a simplistic and conventional argument, but it does bear witness to the reconfigurations of Japanese contemporary culture by kawaii characters as symbolic of new technologies. Specifically underlining the quasi-modernist debate is the contested terrain of cultural renegotiations of ma in which notions about gender and sexuality are at the heart.

Hiroki Azuma argues that Japanese kawaii characters are far from suffering a loss of aura in the light of mass reproduction outlined in Walter Benjamin's 1936 "The Work of Art in the Age of Mechanical Reproduction." Azuma states that although characters are initially without an aura in their mass production, they are quickly personified and personalized. Using the example of the character Toro from the Playstation software *Dokodemo-Issyo*, Azuma argues that although characters always remain within a limited range of possibilities and roles as sketched by the program designer, it is their ability to befriend consumers that gives them an aura. In other words, within character culture a reproduction can also be simultaneously an original, suggesting once again the ambiguity characteristic of ma space.

Azuma argues that characters are "reproductions with aurae," reflecting major changes in Japan's cultural and social fabric: "Loving a character and feeling like a character; these are not just hobbies but ways to live in the age of [the] postmodern."[31]

Lending weight to Azuma's argument, one survey respondent emphasized that the character attached to the keitai personalized the mechanical nature of new communication technologies.[32] Here the presumptively mainstream character is appropriated by the user to encode the standardized, mainstream keitai with a subcultural and personal signifier. The attached character operates as a ma space transforming the blankness and mainstream quality of the keitai into a personal signifier. But one design student noted, "Even though I said that the character gives some personal identity to the product (the keitai), I may be wrong. People just attach it just because it looks cute and erases the mechanical image of the mobile phone. For me, it personalizes communication." Or, as one respondent, a heterosexual female design student, suggested, "Attaching the character to the mobile phone gives something special to the owner because the mobile phone is a product and nothing personal (everyone has the same model). It gives a personality to add a character. But now everyone is doing this, the meaning of identity has become obscured by attaching character goods. These days, young people attach 'non character goods,' such as feathers and pebbles. But it's hard to say, because both genders and all age groups are obsessed with character goods."

Azuma's argument highlights the need to reconceptualize the kawaii, alongside the ma, in the light of character culture. In particular, the kawaii, like the ma, is capable of simultaneously representing and silencing sexual difference and identity. Both terms are fraught with tensions between the old and the new, the copy and the original, the lived and the imagined. In turn, they are both capable of being open signifiers in which blankness can be used to represent diversity while conversely, and problematically, avoiding representing it.[33] The ma, like the kawaii, is ambiguous and yet ubiquitous. Each can be seen as a form of poetic contemplation in the frenetic pace of Tokyo and also as a deafening silence or background to the perpetual grappling between the old and the new.

As mapped by Kinsella, kawaii has grown from a once linguistic reappropriation in the form of the "kitten writing" in the 1970s to a visible saturation across all forms of popular culture, from fashion to music.

Through the translations and transitions of the kawaii one set of "characteristics" has remained: it has represented and continues to represent in between concepts through its ability to be simultaneously ambiguous and ubiquitous. In turn, the space of ma, once a conceptual site between linguistic symbols, can now arguably be reworked as a notion echoing the language of the kawaii. This is particularly apparent within the "blank canvas" of the seemingly voiceless quality of kawaii sexuality.

As Kinsella argues, the kitten writing of the 1970s saw Japanese youth rebelling against traditional Japanese culture, particularly by reconfiguring Japanese words, citing the example of the term *kakkoii* (cool or good) being intentionally mispronounced and misspelled as *katchoii*. Perhaps in the context of my argument here, the most telling example of this intentional subversion was the phrasing of "sex" as *nyan nyan suru* or "to meow meow."[34] Following that line of logic, Hello Kitty is capable of representing paradoxical duplicity. Her seeming mouthlessness and lack of genitals are misleading. Her kawaii is both sexual and a space for exploring repressed sexuality in Japan. An initial reading of character culture would seem to suggest that the characters reinforce heterosexuality by placing women as mainstream consumers into passive roles of heteronormality. However, my survey results indicate that this is not the case, particularly as the kawaii of the character landscape is often appropriated to play out the sexual repression associated with Japanese culture. One interviewee, a lesbian office worker, claimed, "Hello Kitty is being more and more used by men. This has to do with heterosexual men wanting to obtain the stereotypical user of Hello Kitty, which is high school girls. But I find this weird because Hello Kitty for me has always been about girls being with girls, whether as in just friends or sexual. The great thing about Hello Kitty is because it is cute—i.e. passive—it is easy used to stand in for unspoken sexuality."

I asked one respondent about the significance of using Hello Kitty as a mascot for Japanese lesbians. She replied, "Everyone knows and thus identifies with Hello Kitty. She symbolizes girl friendships." I then asked what the difference was between Hello Kitty as a symbol for heterosexual girlfriends and homosexual girlfriends. She replied, "Hello Kitty is about girls. She is about girls with girls. She is about one gender, not one sex." This comment makes fairly obvious sense in light of Hello Kitty: she has no genitalia and arguably no mouth.[35] But Hello Kitty is clearly a female, and this is one of the key attributes in character culture: they have a gender but no sex.

Returning to McLelland's argument, character culture could be seen to highlight the way Japan conceptualizes same-sex relations and gender codes of masculinity and femininity as different from Western assimilations about the relationship between gender and sexual norms. In this way, character culture affords a type of renegotiated ma space for exploring gender through same-sex relations, a type of in betweenness rather than a highlighting of differences between genders. This allows the characters to symbolize the cute and a longing for childhood while being the object of fetishistic appropriations, without coming under the big sandpapering hand of Japan's censorship laws.[36] As one Japanese student said in relation to the role of character cultures and queer categories, "The cute image breaks stereotypical images about sexual categories. For example, sex relates to sinfulness in religion or morality, but putting sex and character goods together makes the image softer and more socializable and fun to others as well as queer culture."

Dot to Dot: Mainstream Coloring on the Global Canvas

My discussion so far necessitates a clarification of the distinction between theories of cultural imperialism (or imported culture) and globalization. Cultural imperialism presents a model of vertical imposition where power is understood as a binary between powerful and powerless. On the other hand, globalization, as opposed to cultural imperialism, demonstrates the need to be able to think about power as a shifting inbetweenness. In this way, the grayness of globalization and what this provides for thinking about consumerism and sexual identity echoes the inbetween space of ma. As Chris Barker points out, globalization is a process of both fragmentation and homogenization, unlike cultural imperialism (often known as Americanization), which is a vertical model where power is oppositional and imposed.[37]

In his 1990 discussion of globalization, Arjun Appadurai argues that if there are indeed global frameworks and forces, they are saturated with ironies and resistances.[38] In particular, this is evidenced by the paradox of seemingly "passive" Asian consumption of Western patterns in popular commodity culture. This is nowhere more evident than in the space of the kawaii, which Kinsella argues was initially borrowed, or in this case "seemingly passively consumed," from Western frameworks. The fact that Hello Kitty was born in London in 1974, according to her Sanrio Web site, and is very white does not detract from her reappropriation and perpetual reinvention, which have seen her become a global symbol for the Japanese notion of kawaii throughout the world. Hello Kitty may be recognized around the world, but she is far from a homogenizing force. As I have argued, she is capable of representing many things to many people, often representing simultaneously contradictory forces, particularly in relation to gender and sexuality.

The Whole World in Her Hand

The seeming passivity and mouthlessness of characters like Hello Kitty may appear to represent a type of sexual and gender inequality in which the feminine is marked by passive asexuality. However, the kawaii and its tie to childhood are by no means untainted by sexual identity. These characters have the ability to support conventional gender relations while also providing a site for nonconformist gender roles and sexualities. In turn, the associated signification of women's shifting status as prime consumers parallels the increased complexity and diversity performed by characters in the terrain of new technologies.

To return to the spatial organization suggested by the reappropriated notion of ma, the scapes of kawaii and keitai culture are renegotiating gender and sexual representation and identification. The spaces of ma, like the kawaii scapes, are transformed and reconfigured by keitai logic; this is particularly prevalent in relation to women. As the roles of kawaii characters are transformed by the possibilities of this "mobile culture," so too are women finding that new social and psychological spaces are opening up, as demonstrated by the movement of women like DoCoMo's senior manager Mari Matsunaga into senior corporate positions.[39] Far from silent and passive, appropriations of kawaii characters reflect the anything-but-empty space of ma. Both demonstrate the paradoxes and shifts associated with modernity. Similarly, both ma and kawaii enable the configuration of new categories of gender and sexual identity.

Kawaii culture reflects the ambiguity and ubiquity of consumerism. In turn, as keitai discourses begin to renegotiate communications through often unfamiliar cyberspaces, they utilize the familiarity of kawaii to induct consumers. Thus, ma can be a space used to conceptualize and practice modes of subjectivity inside and outside the keitai. Ma then becomes a site imploding with subcultural and mainstream, global and local, and personalized and standardized tendencies, and makes the "choice" of kawaii characters much more than a simple exercise of consumer preference, as demonstrated by the sample survey conducted for this project.

Lesbian musician Michiru Sasano, daughter of one of the most powerful women in Japan, Teiko Sasano, states, "Up until now, women have lived in the age of men—with its competition, materialism and disunion. But Japanese men seem to have lost their *joie de vivre*. I think I understand why. They have never developed a sense of their inner self."[40] Could Michiru Sasano's words be interpreted to mean that men have been unable to develop their own sense of character because they lack access to the diverse gender and sexual roles (or ma space) signified by kawaii characters like Hello Kitty? Who says you can't buy character?

Notes

1 One example was the use of "kitty" in the naming of Kitty Flip, a lesbian club night every third Saturday in Shinjuku.

2 NTT is the major telecommunications company in Japan. These new WAP phones afforded a growth in Internet accessibility and use and in turn demonstrate a new type of cute character representation inside rather than outside mobile phones.

3 An example of cuteness as powerlessness is Tare Panda, "a genderless sandbag of a bear so weak that it cannot walk, but has to roll slowly from place to place" at 2.75 meters per hour, according to company literature; cited in Mary Roach, "Cute Inc.," *Wired* 7, no. 12 (December 1999), ⟨http://www.wired.com/wired/archive/7.12/cute.html⟩ (25 July 2002).

4 I recognize that as I am writing this I am surfing a use-by date. One of the problems with mapping the terrain of character culture in Tokyo is that, like all fashions, these characters will soon be left in the 100-Yen shops and outdated. As indicated by my surveys, characters attached to mobile phones are quickly being made outdated by the virtual characters. So why choose something that is so flexible and transitory? It is for these very reasons that charac-

ter culture is so interesting. Not only is it marked with current market forces and consumer politics, but it also bears witness to the discourse intersecting the ephemeral notion of "popular" within the cultural fabric of Tokyo.

5 Sussex Technology Group, "In the Company of Strangers: Mobile Phones and the Conception of Space," in *Technoscapes,* ed. Sally R. Munt (London: Continuum, 2001), 205.

6 Erving Goffman, *The Presentation of Self in Everyday Life* (London: Penguin, 1959).

7 Todd Holden, "'I'm Your Venus'/'You're a Rake': Gender and the Grand Narrative in Japanese Television Advertising," *Intersections,* no. 3 (January 2000), ⟨http://wwwsshe.murdoch.edu.au/intersections/issue3/holden_paper1.html⟩ (10 October 2000).

8 A good example of an attempt to question the functionalist tendencies of traditional Western frameworks of anthropology is Edward W. Said's *Orientalism* (London: Routledge and Kegan Paul, 1978). Said highlights the fact that many earlier studies of Eastern cultures by the West were problematic as they neglected to engage in processes of reflexivity.

9 This notion of "whiteness" as "all colors and yet none" is discussed in Richard Dyer's "Whiteness," where he takes up arguments surrounding Anglocentrism as seemingly "neutral" in relation to Anglo and non-Anglo relationships and representation in films. Richard Dyer, "Whiteness," in *The Matter of Images: Essays on Representation* (London: Routledge, 1993), 141–63.

10 Frank Rose, "Pocket Monster," *Wired* 9, no. 9 (September 2001): 128–35.

11 Stephen Lunn, "The Big Mo Wins in Japan," *The Australian,* 9 November 2000, media section, 13.

12 Responses were in English, and therefore idiosyncratic grammar and spelling have not been changed.

13 Clement Greenberg, "The Avant-Garde and the Kitsch," in *Kitsch: The World of Bad Taste,* ed. Gillo Dorfles (London: Studio Visa, 1969), 116–26.

14 Both Holden and Clammer highlight, specifically in relation to advertising and female representation in Japan, that Western theories about popular culture and mass media cannot just be superimposed on "other" cultures. Holden and, in less detail, Clammer use the example of Erving Goffman's theories to illustrate the inadequacies of "importing" Western frameworks for thinking about popular culture into Japan. See Holden; John Clammer, "Consuming Bodies: Constructing and Representing the Female Body in Contemporary Japanese Print Media," in *Women, Media and Consumption in Japan,* ed. Lise Skov and Brian Moeran (Surrey, England: Curzon Press, 1995), 197–219.

15 This specifically relates to the argument that the one defining characteristic of postmodernism's various trajectories is that popular culture is the focus,

unlike modernism's negation of popular culture as "other" and "low" culture. See Jim Collins, "Postmodernism and Television," in *Postmodern After-Images: A Reader in Film, Television and Video,* ed. Will Brooker and Peter Brooker (London: Arnold, 1997), 192–207.

16 See Roach.

17 David Buckingham, "Electronic Child Abuse? Rethinking the Media's Effects on Children," in *Ill Effects: The Media/Violence Debate,* ed. Martin Barker and Juliana Petley (London: Routledge, 1997), 32–47.

18 A great example of this was American evangelist Jerry Falwell's argument that one of the Teletubbies was advocating gay rights. Falwell observed that one of the characters was a purple male (although they have no genitalia) who carried a red handbag and whose antenna was shaped in a triangle. Purple, plus triangle, plus handbag equals gay! Ashleigh Wilson, "Unbridled Innocence," *The Australian* (12 October 2000), media section, 18.

19 Cited in Roach.

20 Merry White, "The Marketing of Adolescence in Japan: Buying and Dreaming," in Skov and Moeran, 255.

21 Sharon Kinsella, "Cuties in Japan," in Skov and Moeran, 221.

22 Qtd. in Roach. The quote refers to Sharon Kinsella's discussion of Yamane Kazuma's research into cute handwriting (between 1984 and 1986). Kinsella, 222.

23 Brian J. McVeigh, "Commodifying Affection, Authority and Gender in the Everyday Objects of Japan," *Journal of Material Culture* 1, no. 3 (November 1996): 293.

24 Brian J. McVeigh, "How Hello Kitty Commodifies the Cute, Cool and Camp: 'Consumutopia' Versus 'Control' in Japan," *Journal of Material Culture* 5, no. 2 (July 2000): 291–312.

25 Kitty Flip, as pointed out earlier, is a name used by a homosexual Shinjuku club for lesbian and female bisexual nights. The notion of "gift," as articulated in most Sanrio advertisements, is intrinsic to the concept of giving a gift of Hello Kitty. Here, Sanrio has capitalized on the Japanese tradition of gift giving.

26 Dennis Altman, "On Global Queering," *Australian Humanities Review,* 2 (July–August 1996), ⟨http://www.lib.latrobe.edu.au/AHR/archive/Issue-July-1996/altman.html⟩ (25 July 2002).

27 In this case, McLelland illustrates the inadequate models for thinking about Japanese homosexuality used in Barbara Summerhawk, Cheiron McMahill, and Darren McDonald, eds., *Queer Japan: Personal Stories of Japanese Lesbians, Gays, Bisexuals and Transsexuals* (Norwich, VT: New Victoria Press, 1998); Mark McLelland, "Male Homosexuality and Popular Culture in Japan,"

Intersections, no. 3 (January 2000), ⟨http://www.ssshe.murdoch.edu.au/intersections/issue3/mclelland2.html⟩ (21 October 2000).

28 Dharmachari Jnanavira argues that Japanese tradition has a long history of same-sex relations. Jnanavira uses Michel Foucault's notion of archaeology from *The History of Sexuality Volume 1* to map Japan's long history of same-sex relations and makes a very convincing argument for why Western models for defining sex, often attached to gender, are simplistic, inadequate, and problematic. Referencing the theories of the famous Japanese psychologist Doi Takeo to discuss the differences between Japanese and American same-sex relations, Jnanavira argues that whereas Western cultures value relations between men and women, Japan focuses on the relationship *in between* men and *in between* women. In other words, ma is negotiated between women or between men, rather than between men and women. Dharmachari Jnanavira, "Homosexuality in the Japanese Buddhist Tradition," *Western Buddhist Review* 3 (1999), ⟨http://www.westernbuddhistreview.com/vol3/homosexuality.html⟩ (25 July 2002).

29 As argued by Staff, "Okatu Culture Set for Extinction?" *Kobe Shimbun,* 7 November 2000.

30 Hoki Hamano, "Japanese Anime: Quality and Quantity," *Chuo Koron* (September 2000), ⟨http://www2.chuko.co.jp/koron/back/200009.html⟩ (19 April 2001).

31 Hiroki Azuma, "Ontological, Advertising, 'Character,'" *Kohkoku* 41, no. 2 (March 2000): 6.

32 Sanrio says characters such as Hello Kitty are a form of social communication, part of a gift-giving tradition that seeks to befriend. The character attached to the mobile phone demonstrates the ma between public identifications being contested within an electronic *space* and a commercial and yet personalized *place.* Sanrio Co. Ltd., "Hello Kitty Special Feature," ⟨http://kitty.sanrio.co.jp/characters/kitty/kitty.htm⟩ (20 November 2000).

33 While in Tokyo I interviewed some visual artists for an article I wrote on "alternative" art spaces in Tokyo for *Art Asia Pacific* (January 2000). In one interview, the artist would not elaborate on the art apart from saying that it was about ma. In this way ma operates as a tool for evasion.

34 Kinsella, 225.

35 This is discussed when Roach interviews Sanrio's Yuko Yamaguchi (the designer of Hello Kitty for the past nineteen years), who argues that Hello Kitty has a mouth but it is covered in fur.

36 Recently, Japan's methods for censoring books and printed matter changed from ink, which could be faded by lemon juice, to sandpapering.

37 Chris Barker, *Television, Globalization and Cultural Identities* (Buckingham, England: Open University Press, 1999).

38　Arjun Appadurai, "Disjuncture and Difference in the Global Cultural Economy," *Public Culture* 2, no. 2 (1990): 1–24.

39　Kay Itoi, "Rising Daughters," *Newsweek* 135, no. 14 (April 3, 2000): 45. Also see Timothy Stocker, "The Future at Your Fingertip," 4 October 2000, ⟨http://www.tkai.com/press/001004_independent.htm⟩ (25 July 2002).

40　Qtd. in Itoi, 45. Teiko Sasano has served in the House of Councilors since 1989.

SANDIP ROY

From Khush List to Gay Bombay:

Virtual Webs of Real People

South Asian Queers on the Internet

If you search the word "gay" on one of the popular search engines on the Web, it shows up some 6,950,000 hits. If you search on South Asia, it brings up some 346,000 matches. When you search on both, it comes up with some 8,040. A far cry from 6,950,000, but not bad given that in 1986, the first ever issue of *Trikone Magazine* for South Asian lesbians and gay men commented, "Even in America the number of gay South Asians who identify themselves as such is virtually nil."[1] The phrase "*even* in America" is worth thinking about. Implicit is the hypothesis that if ever there was a place where South Asians could express their sexuality it would be America. This is not an uncommon notion, nor is it necessarily untrue. But it does become increasing problematic for those who are trying to build movements in parts of the world like South Asia where they must spend a lot of time explaining why their conception of gay, lesbian, bisexual, and transgender (GLBT) issues is not simply a regurgitation of hegemonic models of GLBT movements in America.

Much has changed since that first issue of *Trikone,* not just for GLBT South Asians in America but also for those in South Asia itself, especially India. The gay scene in India has been more and more visible in the past few years, with magazines, groups, parties, film festivals, and even an attempt at a "freedom march." The South Asian gay movement, at least in terms of publications and groups that focused on issues of homosexuality, actually predates the Internet. Both *Trikone Magazine* in the United States and *Bombay Dost,* the first gay magazine in India, started long before the World Wide Web meant anything to anyone—in 1986 and 1991, respectively. But it is interesting to wonder if the movement could have spread so rapidly, connecting people as far apart as Oklahoma and Colombo, Fiji and Delhi, without the Internet.

At the same time, what role does the Internet play in the prevailing assumptions about GLBT issues being essentially Western issues? Will the very speed of dissemination that the Internet provides create a borderless world where the American concept of a gay movement can spread like a virus and infect all cultures? Does it now just take a modem to start a movement? And once that movement gets off the ground, will it merely borrow from existing movements in the West? Will countries with fledgling GLBT movements risk losing the process of building a movement that is about them and their needs and end up assimilating into Western models because they are more accessible? What happens when the seeds of the movement are sown by members of their diaspora in the West? Is there a danger that the Internet will not only pull together people across oceans but at the same time offer them ready packaged visions of a GLBT movement that does not account for cultural differences? Or will cultural differences cease to matter in a well-homogenized "gay world"?

As the editor of *Trikone Magazine* since 1994 and a board member of Trikone, a San Francisco Bay area-based support group for GLBT people of South Asian heritage, I have the opportunity to witness the growth of the movement and the role the Internet has played in that. This essay incorporates those experiences and uses several articles on various aspects of queer organizing on the Internet, including interviews conducted with activists based in India and in the West. Some of them have been long-time activists involved in the movement in various groups from before the everyday proliferation of Internet. Others have actually cut their activist teeth on the Internet, having been instrumental in forming online groups. Although this essay attempts to present a diversity of voices in terms of levels of activism and gender, almost all the voices represented are those of Indians. Though groups in the West like Trikone identify themselves as South Asian, the fact remains that of all the countries in South Asia, the most active lesbian/gay groups are in India. Not surprisingly, Internet activism is also the most active there, and access to computers is also higher compared to neighboring countries. Sri Lanka has an active gay group called Companions on a Journey that has email access, and some of the other countries in the region have their own email discussion groups, but the movement is still in relatively early stages in most of the countries of South Asia.[2]

Queer South Asian Road Map

The queer South Asian journey on the Internet started through an email discussion group called the Khush list.[3] South Asian cultures have few words that stand in for "gay." Most existing words are either clinical terms or derogatory terms that describe certain sexual acts. *Khush,* which is a literal translation of the word "gay" (as in "happy"), has been gaining currency in some South Asian queer circles as the word of choice for gay. Devesh Khatu and his friend, Marty, started the Khush list in 1993 when they met each other at a university in Texas. The purpose of the list was to use the Internet to connect queer South Asians. Although Internet users largely came from either universities or some large companies at that time, almost one hundred people signed up within a few months of its inception.[4] The Khush list currently has over six hundred members scattered all over the world. The first major offshoot of the list was SAGrrls, a list meant for South Asian lesbian and bisexual women only.[5] This was followed by another women-only group, desidykes.[6]

As the Internet took off and more and more people started having access to the World Wide Web, it became much easier to create and manage groups. Initially hosting and maintaining an electronic group like the Khush list required a fair amount of computer expertise. Now the ease of creating the list through such Web sites as *www.egroups.com* (now *groups.yahoo.com*) has spawned many lists, whether they are dealing with coming-out resources for South Asian parents, or a group for gay and bisexual men of Indian origin but living in Fiji-Australasia.[7] The proliferation of electronic discussion groups is also accompanied by many existing South Asian LGBT groups putting up Web sites. *Trikone* was the first ever queer South Asian Web site to be hosted online, in 1995.[8] Now many other groups, such as *SALGA* in New York, *Trikone-Tejas* in Austin, Texas, and *Humsafar Trust* in Mumbai, have their own sites, which provide information about the groups' activities, upcoming events, even a list of gay-friendly therapists and counselors.[9]

South Asians in the diaspora certainly have had a head start, at least as far as access to the Internet is concerned. It is not surprising that lists like Khush and Web sites like *Trikone*'s originated in the West. As the digital revolution spread, the West has seen the proliferation of personal computers in homes. That affords the privacy for queer South Asians to log on and check out chat rooms on *www.gay.com* or spend endless hours on the Internet Relay Chat (IRC). In recent years, the Internet has also impacted countries in South Asia. The proliferation of cyber cafés in India means checking email is not so difficult anymore; as a result, more and more South Asians are logging on. It is noteworthy that the more locally focused Gay Bombay list actually has more members than the more international Khush list.[10] Gay South Asians in the West and in South Asia have set up city-based lists as a means of communication among people in those cities or others visiting them. A difference, however, is the nature of the groups. Groups in the West are identity-based queer groups and try to provide content and services that are both South Asian and queer in nature because there are plenty of non–South Asian queer resources and information already available. Groups in India, however, are just queer (Indian ethnicity being a given) and can be much broader in the scope of their content and services. For example, gay men worried about the poor quality of condoms in India and whether they will break during anal sex can buy recommended condoms from the *Humsafar Trust* Web site in Mumbai. However, a gay South Asian man in San Francisco would probably just go to a local pharmacy to pick up such condoms and not think of going to the *Trikone* Web site for them. This is a critical point because it illustrates the limitations of the diaspora in the movements of the homeland. Groups like *Trikone* may have provided inspiration and ideas to activists in countries like India, but in the end their agendas are somewhat different and the diasporic groups have to realize that their role in the movements in their homeland will essentially be as supporting actors. Diasporic South Asian GLBT groups are primarily about creating a space and visibility for South Asian issues inside the largely white gay mainstream. Once they have done this to some extent, the groups often end up pushing for GLBT visibility in their parent diasporic communities. Groups in South Asia are much less interested in the ramifications of being "Indian *and* gay" than being "gay *in* India."

Who's Online and Why?

All the varied sites and email discussion groups would not amount to much if no one accessed them. What can South Asian queers find on the Internet that they cannot find in other places? In an email interview in October 2000, Sunny, a 20-year-old South Asian man living in London, wrote, "The first thing I discovered on the Net was chatrooms (in particular, IRC and *gay.com*), where I learnt about clubs in and around London—which can be very useful. With the chatrooms, came file attachments—and porn (another way to learn about sex before actually having sex). There wasn't anything South Asian based—but you sometimes meet Indians online and they can tell you about their experiences. For the youth it remains a place to learn about safe sex without going ahead and risking the danger of having unsafe sex."

For a gay man living in a small town in India, the Internet can be a godsend. Barun, a 20-year-old man living in the northeast of India, said simply that the Internet has been "like manna from heaven. Through it I can talk and make friends with other gay guys around India and the world as well as get access to gay materials while remaining anonymous. Now it has come to the stage where very soon I hope I will have gay friends in real life and it's all thanks to the Net."[11]

The importance of anonymity and privacy in a country of over a billion people cannot be overstated. The Internet has suddenly opened a gateway to information and images that otherwise would not be accessible. In a community where people did not have real venues to meet other people like themselves, the *Trikone* classifieds page had always been very popular. Most of the ads are now placed on the *Trikone* Web site, which can be accessed every day and use email addresses instead of postal addresses. The email personals are a quick way of connecting with other people instead of relying on the vagaries of the postal system. Although *Trikone* is well established in the San Francisco Bay area, many of the personals are placed by South Asians in the area who do not necessarily come to *Trikone* events. They are perhaps not yet ready to be out in the community where someone might know them. The Internet and Web sites like *Trikone* offer them a way of connecting with other queer South Asians at their own pace. The Khush list has actually been described as "a community-space in cyberland—for many, it may be the only South Asian queer space available."[12] A queer

South Asian Web site in Canada, *khushnet.com,* even provides personal ads with the catchy slogan, "Nobody knows I met my boyfriend through KhushNet's personals."

Email is used even for counseling. *Trikone* recently received an email from a young man of South Asian origin living with his family in a rural part of the United States who was very isolated. He desperately wanted to talk to a queer South Asian person about marriage pressures he was being subjected to, which he felt other mainstream gay groups could not relate to. Email provided a way to counsel the person that was private and did not involve long-distance calls that could provoke questions from his family. In an email interview in October 2000, Geeta Kumana, project coordinator for Aanchal, a helpline for women in Mumbai, wrote, "The Internet is a very important tool in the Aanchal organisation, as women who want to come out can do so over the Net. Hence, I insist on a hotmail account for Aanchal because it is confidential and only I can access it as of now. It helps with women being assured of their names or issues being confidential." Realizing the potential of the Internet, Sappho, a group for women that started up in Calcutta recently, immediately started raising funds to go online.[13]

The speed of the response one gets from the Internet is another major advantage. Every month the email discussion lists receive postings looking for information on gay life from people traveling to South Asia. These emails generate an immediate response from a wide variety of readers. The only way to do this previously was to place an ad in a magazine such as *Trikone.* This required coordination well in advance. Web sites such as *gayDelhi.com* can provide listings for upcoming parties in Delhi (as well as updates of cancellations or venue changes) and disseminate that information fast. It is no wonder that *gayDelhi.com* receives about six hundred visitors per day.[14] When *Bombay Dost* went online it received twenty thousand hits within three months even though it was not registered with any of the search engines. Editor Ashok Row Kavi revealed in an email interview in October 2000 that the cyber edition means they can run longer stories that do not fit in the print edition as well as reach readers directly without distribution networks and retail stores, which may not want to carry a gay magazine. He appreciates the reach of the Internet, citing three specific email messages that *Bombay Dost* received: "One from a Mexican NGO which wanted to know how we had sex-mapped Bombay (Mumbai) city, another from China which sought a visit for its 'official' delegation and the third from the USA, from a research student who wants to work as an intern with the Humsafar Trust after reading about our work on our website." In fact, email has helped activists in South Asia and those settled in the West interact with each other at a much more intensive level. Whether it is an Indian student in the United States posting on the gay Calcutta list to find out what is happening there when he visits during Christmas or activists in Sri Lanka sending out an update on a homophobic incident involving the Press Council, the traffic is two-way and no longer dependent on postal mail that could have a two- to three-week turnaround time.[15]

Many Faces of the Internet

The Internet was first used (and is still primarily used) as a place to store information that can be easily accessed by others and as a way for people to get in touch with each other and discuss issues. That was the main purpose behind starting the *Gay Bombay* discussion group. Although the Khush list was a worldwide virtual community of GLBT South Asians, a subscriber in Mumbai felt the need for a similar list that catered to the interests of people in Mumbai.[16] Mumbai already had an established gay group and magazine, and the egroup proved a resounding success.[17] Webmaster Bhavesh explains the philosophy behind the group: "We wanted to create a safe space for people who wanted to come to terms with their sexuality, but could remain anonymous if they so desired. More importantly, the idea was to create a non-sexual forum where people could join in and relax without the pressure of having to participate in sexual conducts and advances."[18] The group soon reached a membership of over one hundred and people soon wanted to meet others on the list. Eventually the group decided to have a physical meeting at a local McDonald's. In a July 2000 email interview Bhavesh explained, "We chose McDonald's because it was a family-oriented space and did not assume gay connotations if you were seen there." The meeting was very successful and soon led to others and to outings, movie nights, parties, and even a couple of PFLAG-style meetings for parents and families.[19] What started as a virtual group has now become a much more flesh-and-blood one, fostering a sense of community.

Vikram, a Bombay-based journalist involved with gay community issues, feels that the very middle-class nature of the group helped people bond and find issues in common. He maintains, "Richer guys have their own resources, they can become passport princesses (gay men who can air their gay side on holidays abroad), and are rarely interested in community development."[20] In an October 2000 email interview he elaborated: "Poorer guys have fewer options—they often have to get married, or if they are very effeminate they get absorbed into the *kothi* (men who are penetrated) culture. The Gay Bombay guys are in between. There are a lot of middle-class professionals, so there is a chance of them getting jobs, leaving the family, becoming self-supporting and creating lives of their own. They can think of leading gay lives, and they needed support. You won't find them marching in the streets or doing anything too overt. They would feel they have too much to lose in the sort of balance they are building in their lives. But they are also willing to have things like the parents' meet—or to pay to have parties."

Whereas the *Gay Bombay* space helped create a social space for its members, some other lists were formed with a much more activist agenda in mind. For example, the LGBT India list was formed primarily as a means of communication among different groups scattered all over India.[21] In 1999 the Walk for Freedom and Friendship in Calcutta grew out of Internet discussions and could not have been executed without the Internet. The Internet was also used to mobilize opinions in a campaign to confront an Indian politician who had used the term "homosexual" as a slur in an election campaign. When the Press Council of Sri Lanka said that lesbianism was a sadistic deviant act, the International Gay and Lesbian Human Rights Commission was able to use the Internet as a way of quickly getting the information out to networks of activists all over the world, encouraging them to write letters of protest. Likewise, when a married lesbian was horribly abused by her husband, a support group in Calcutta, Counsel Club, was able to use the Net to enlist the help of activists all over the country.

When *Trikone* organized DesiQ2000, an international meeting for LGBT South Asians, in San Francisco in 2000, the Internet proved to be an indispensable tool. In an email interview, Madhuri Anji, who was cochair of *Trikone* at the time, lists the main ways the Internet was used to put the conference together: "Communication using egroups to reach groups of people at once and minimize phone tag, publicity (it was worldwide and cheap—in fact the Web was one of the few places we had our conference logo in color), research for finding venues, cheap tickets, and outreach to South Asia (which would otherwise be slow and expensive)." Email helped organizers in San Francisco obtain immediate information when some of the international delegates in India and Bangladesh were refused visas. Precious time was saved in this way and it enabled a record number of attendees from abroad to come to the conference.

Another major use of the Internet is to create a safe space. Ironically, the very anonymity that creates a comfort zone for some can also jeopardize the sense of safety for others. Mala Nagarajan recalls, "I remember the amazing rush that came over me when I discovered the presence of other South Asian queer folk [on the Khush list]. But soon that rush disappeared as I experienced the dual-edged sword of sharp personal jabs or complete dismissiveness aimed at women who expressed themselves on the list."[22] The cloak of anonymity around the Internet led some men to make rude and insulting comments about women whose viewpoints they disagreed with. Women who had posted on other issues suddenly started receiving private solicitations from male members seeking marriages of convenience. Ultimately, several women started sAGrrls, a list expressly for South Asian queer women. To preserve the integrity of the group, the members decided to operate as a word-of-mouth and referral-only list. Jasbir Puar, who helped start the list, commented, "Many women told me that in the first years of the list that they were so thankful to find out that such a list was there and to be able to be on it, that actually posting mail was secondary to the security of knowing that a community was there for them."[23]

Safe space, organizing, social events, counseling, activism—what about the promise of e-commerce that all the dot coms are based on? The Internet has had a mixed track record as a business opportunity for queer South Asians. With easy access to gay stores and paraphernalia, one would think the anonymity would actually work to its advantage, especially for those who do not live in big metropolitan areas. In India, the Humsafar center sells its magazine *Bombay Dost,* condoms, and other services through the Internet. The proprietor of *khushnet.com* (note the domain ".com" as opposed to ".org") readily admits that as a business venture, it has not quite taken off. He hopes at least to cover costs.[24] Bhavesh, who maintains the *Gay Bombay* Web site, says, "The people who become regulars at Gay Bombay, the family as I call them, often contribute whatever they can to make events possible. This contribution is voluntary. If we fall short, the core group (regulars) chip in the money." Bhavesh also notes that as costs for hosting the site increase, there is a need for a more systematic approach to covering costs of the digital revolution.

Double-edged Sword

Despite its many obvious advantages, the Internet comes with its own baggage as well. The very convenience of the Internet can lull people into a comfortable sense of "keyboard activism," forgetting that the real grass-roots organizing still needs to be down on the ground, in community forums, protest petitions, and mailers. The South Asian LGBT movement (whether in the West or in South Asia) has often suffered from the lack of a visible face. Very few people are willing to take the risk of being out in the community. There is a danger that "keyboard activism" on the Internet can aggravate that.

The democracy of the Internet means anyone with access can set up an email group; it takes much more blood, sweat, and tears to set up a real group. Thus, groups like *Gay Delhi* and *Gay Bombay* are not really affiliated with any particular gay group in those cities. This allows these groups to be more organic and free-flowing and somewhat easier to keep going. On the other hand, there is also a lack of accountability and the controls (such as a board of directors, meetings, by-laws) that keep a group honest. Anyone who has access to technology and finances is able to set up a Web site. There have been instances where a site or electronic group has been at loggerheads with a real on-the-ground group. For example, a Web site called *gay India* claiming to be "the Web portal for India" came out denouncing Humrahi, the established gay support group in Delhi, which has an office and regular meetings. Putting aside the exact nature of the conflict, what the issue threw into sharp focus was the fact that there was little one could do to check the credibility of the claim when a site called *gay India* promoted itself as the official Web site for the Indian gay community. Scott Kugle, an activist who has lived several years in South Asia, observes, "Setting up a support group is hard work, requiring years of effort by a team of committed people who are known by a wide community of people and are accountable to them. In contrast, a person can set up a webpage with only financial resources, under a false name, with no sense of accountability. The claims and information of a web-site may not be verifiable; the personal agenda behind it may remain obscure."[25] Thus, a virtual community could end up competing directly with a real community instead of complementing and enhancing it.

Another danger of the Internet is the very thing that makes it a godsend in other ways: its ease of use. The ease of use and short response time can become very seductive and alluring; eventually, it becomes hard to resist the temptation of working only with people who have access to the Internet. For example, in editing *Trikone Magazine,* it is much easier to deal with contributors who can turn in their articles via email; one does not have to rely on the postal system, can squeeze in articles under the wire, and, best of all, the back and forth of the editing process becomes a breeze. But not everyone has access to the Internet and the danger is leaving out the voices of those whose Internet access is patchy or nonexistent. Thus, the digital divide could have a very real impact in slowly squeezing out the voices of those who are not just a mouse-click away and whose response time is longer than twelve hours. Members of the *Trikone* board realized this when we found that board members who had easy and everyday access to email often ended up discussing issues on email and taking decisions without the full participation of those who checked their email only once a week.

Vikram, a journalist in Mumbai, admits in an email interview that the main users of the Internet in India will be the English-speaking upper middle class for some time to come. Thus in a sense, the demographics of the Internet-based gay Bombay community could be obviously skewed, but he sees cyber cafés spreading the Internet to a much wider population group. He writes, "At the moment I'm sitting in a small cyber café next to my place. It started off three years back in a driving school, where the owner placed three computers. Today it's almost taken over the driving school. It used to be mostly yuppies, foreigners and students. Now there's a lady who looks like a grandmother sitting next to me, there's a middle aged man a few PCs away and the owner is helping a couple of guys, who clearly don't look like they speak English well, learn how to use the Net." He clearly sees that diversity in the gay Bombay profile in terms of more people from small towns logging on as well as people with different proficiencies in English. He does not view *Gay Bombay* ever being a really grassroots group, but he says that "within our target audience, which is an expanding one, I think we'll be able to straddle a reasonably high spectrum (gay men from a reasonably large socio-economic range)."

The digital divide and the anonymity of the Internet can also foster disconnections even as it potentially creates new connections. For example, the Internet discussion group, lgbt-india, was set up by a group of gay men with the hope of building a "common activist agenda" that would take into account important issues from every community segment. However, some lesbian and bisexual women's support groups perceived that the Internet connectivity gave the illusion of a single coalition without actually empowering women's groups. They felt that gay men appropriated their voice without their consent by including the "l" of "lesbian" in the title of the egroup.[26] The gender divide was also what prompted the creation of the SAGrrls list. While there is still a gender divide on the Internet due to age-old factors like economics, for example, in the kinds of jobs South Asian lesbians and bisexual women hold compared to gay men, Madhuri Anji expresses in an email interview that the divide is narrowing.

The gender divide is also apparent in India, where Geeta Kumana feels that the reasons fewer women have access to the Internet are still rooted in patriarchy. Married women who stay at home to raise a family are less likely to access the Internet through cyber cafés, whereas men have more access through their workplace. Very few women have the economic power to buy a computer for their own use. She writes in an email interview, "In LGBT groups, there are definitely more men on the Net than women, mainly because the lesbian bisexual lobby is so small compared to the gay male lobby and so many more women are less visible than the men. If you look at all the lists, Khush, Gay Bombay, etc., they are mainly male dominated." It can be a self-fulfilling prophecy: the fewer women who are online feel uncomfortable being visible because of the lack of numbers, leading to new women coming online feeling there are no women present and dropping out.

Some activists are concerned that as gay issues become more visible in India, the backlash will try to peg it as a corrupt Western influence. As the Internet opens the movement up to many more resources around the world, paradoxically the potential for backlash and the charge of Westernization also increases. This argument reached fever pitch when Deepa Mehta's film *Fire* (1997), about two housewives in Delhi falling in love with each other, was released in India. Mehta, who lives in Toronto, was accused of injecting decadent Western values into Indian culture. Vikram in Bombay says it is futile to spend too much time fighting charges like that because "one would be silly trying to pretend that the gay identity does not have

Western roots. Of course it does—as do a million other things in Indian culture, from cricket onwards. Is that making any of them any the less 'Indian' or acceptable? India, as a whole, on gay issues and everything else, does pretty much what it likes and doesn't bother about questions about source or authenticity." Giti Thadani, one of the early lesbian activists in India, made the same point several years earlier. She writes, "It is all right for the feminists to use the terms Marxism, socialism, communalism, all of which have either originated outside India or are English words. Whereas these have been adapted and contextualized to different Indian situations, the word 'lesbian' is singled out as only being Western property."[27] All the Internet allows is easier access to many of those ideas. Certainly, it provides budding groups in different countries access to Western gay resources, but it would be insulting the intelligence of many of these activists to assume they would need to blindly copy Western models of activism like street marches, Pride parades, or the in-your-face ACT-UP style of demonstration. The activism that develops in a country is suited to the ground realities there; otherwise, it has little hope of making much headway. Ashok Row Kavi readily admits that he conceived the idea of *Bombay Dost* after a visit to Canada for an international AIDS conference in 1988: "It was my first visit to the American continent, and I was shocked by the aggressiveness with which the American gay community fought for funds. I also realized they don't think there is a gay community outside America. So when I went back to Bombay, I formed the editorial collective of *Bombay Dost* with some friends."[28] However, few would call *Bombay Dost* and *Humsafar Trust* divorced from the ground realities of India; its counselors are trained to do outreach in the streets and toilets and railway platforms to educate on safe sex, and to work with the All India Institute of Medical Sciences to produce pamphlets on how to use condoms and with legal experts to decriminalize homosexuality in India. Recently, researchers have uncovered many depictions of homosexuality in ancient and medieval Indian texts; these will certainly help strengthen the argument that homosexuality is nothing new to India, though gay activism may be a relatively recent import.[29]

Certainly, the Internet cannot be a substitute for activism on the ground. Whether it is outreach work at a cruising site or cajoling a quiet member at a social gathering to speak and be comfortable, direct contact has no real substitute. The Internet can foster a certain passivity; the vast majority of Internet group members tend to rarely post, becoming instead consumers

Mobile Cultures

of discussions. Likewise, people can feel they have done their bit by for-warding along an email petition without really doing something about it. Ashok Row Kavi, who has put in many years of activism on the streets of Mumbai, emphasizes, "The pitfalls are, firstly, when we mistake letting off hot air and steam on the Net itself as actual activism. Also, one big danger is you can be monitored on the Net by people inimical and hostile to you or your agenda." He cites an incident that ensued on the Khush list in 2000, when some people who had not been in any way involved with the creation of Khush Toronto (the gay South Asian support group there) felt free to discredit the group online. Row Kavi writes caustically, "Sorry I don't like these cyber *kshatriyas* [warriors]. I'll rather fight my battles in the gullys and gutters of Gaziabad in India than with aseptic assholes living in Arkan-sas, USA." *Gay Bombay* discovered this when its original Internet service provider pulled the plug on it in 2000 for links to pornographic content. Its files were subsequently hacked into and deleted. Even though the site itself has no pornography or frontal nudity, Webmaster Bhavesh says that classi-fied ads people post could have such links: "But I am told other sites (hosted by the ISP), more mainstream ones, have more graphic and hot content."[30]

Looking Ahead

In the brave new world of dot coms and dot orgs, what does the future hold? In the West, where the Internet first took off, it has certainly been a boon for connecting queer and questioning people who feel the isolation of being a double minority. As a South Asian queer growing up in a small university town in the Midwest where one's father is a professor, it is hard not to feel isolated. Such a person would always stand out in the local campus LGBT organization. At the same time, the tight-knit South Asian community can be quite claustrophobic. The Internet has enabled a sup-port structure and network. The *Trikone*-organized DesiQ2000 conference was a way of putting faces to this virtual community. The Internet has given identity-based organizing a boost that before could be obtained only if one lived in a city like New York or Chicago or in the Silicon Valley, which has high South Asian populations. When a gay Pakistani American activist, Ifti Nasim, was assaulted in a restaurant in Chicago in March 2001, the various LGBT South Asian groups were quick to use the Internet to coordinate statements condemning the assault and demanding it be treated as a hate crime. Former executive director of the National Gay and Lesbian Task Force Urvashi Vaid points out that it is vitally important to be out in both South Asian communities in the West as well as the mainstream queer organizations that have few South Asians: "It is vital for South Asian GLBT activists to establish visibility inside South Asian communities, and inside our families of origin. This is because our lives are barely visible to the majority of our own people. It is important for GLBT South Asians to be outspoken inside mainstream queer worlds because we need to join the struggle to challenge racism inside our own communities and in the broader society. As immigrants, and sons and daughters of immigrants, there is much that we can add to the debate in this country on race."[31] The Internet is already playing a major role in providing this visibility as well as the basics of a support structure for when this visibility provokes a back-lash. For while the activists in South Asia have to fend off accusations about homosexuality being a Western import, the South Asian activists in the West have to constantly defend themselves against accusations of bringing shame on a community that has prided itself on being a model minority.

Back in India, Ashok Row Kavi writes, "The next important task is not just increase coverage but also to deepen the base of the movement. Hardly one out of a 1,000 Indians have access to computers or to the Internet. So we are thinking of manufacturing e-mail addresses for transgendered persons, working class (Marathi speaking/Hindi speaking lesbians) and poor gay men and male sex workers and further teaching them how to access the Net. We are thinking of a 'cyber corner' at the Humsafar Centre so the poor gay men and *hijras* (who are not even allowed to enter cyber cafes) can access computers."[32] Geeta Kumana at Ananchal hopes that the future will see more and more women online: "India has a long way to go in educating women. Once that barrier is crossed, more and more women will be on the Net."

Mala Nagarajan looks at women-only lists like SAGrrls and DesiDykes and sees three issues they will need to confront in the future. "The first," she writes, "is members within the group recognizing and actively challenging their own positions of privilege. Even with a defined charter, a South Asian queer women-only defined list does not mean it is a space free of other assumptions or privileges. For example, individual postings regularly as-sume everyone on the list lives in the US or North America, everyone is of a particular class (i.e., middle class or upper middle class) or everyone is of a particular political philosophy." The other two issues deal with whether to keep the list restricted or open (especially in terms of transgendered people, non–South Asians, and even men) and a need to get more volunteers to manage and administer the list. But she affirms, "The overwhelming feeling from South Asian queer women-only spaces is one of empowerment. And as long as it is, women-only spaces will survive."[33]

Bhavesh states in an email interview that his primary aim for the *Gay Bombay* Web site is to "provide information, legal position, and how does one go about a gay lifestyle. So while providing this information, I also tried to make it a complete lifestyle site with a poetry section and story section. In short, I'm trying to make a gay positive site, which would make you feel good about being gay, try and take away those guilt feelings." The Web site and the list obviously struck a chord; the list now has over one thousand members. He states, "For me, gay Bombay is a family that I chose, and it's a family and space that I will not trade for any in the world."

The Internet is here to stay, and its influence will only be broader and more pervasive in the coming years. Those who fear that it will become a means to propagate one cultural model of GLBT movement both overestimate its power and underestimate its target. Just because an Indian gay man in Hyderabad wears jeans does not mean he has been incorporated into the Western cultural model; it may merely be that he is strategically using what he finds useful in it. The pressure to push a homogeneous message of what gay culture should look like, how gays should act and think will always be there. The Internet can be an effective conduit, but unlike many other methods of communication it works both ways. A Web server in Delhi and San Francisco can propagate both viewpoints with equal emphasis. Certainly, activists in the West, including South Asians, have more access to resources that could be harnessed in diasporic movement building; naturally, they will want to use those resources to fashion a movement in a way that feels acceptable and right to them. But it would be simplistic to assume that movements in South Asia are naïve enough to passively absorb any points of view being fed to them unquestioningly. If anything, the chaos of the Internet hopefully will lead to more clashes of ideas and suggestions that will help fashion GLBT movements that will be free to borrow or reject ideas from movements in the West. To this author, the concern is not whether the Internet is a tool for a global homogenized gay movement; rather, the question that should be raised is whether the Internet is becoming the *only* tool (or the most convenient one) for building a gay movement in different parts of the world. That is when the questions about who has access to the Internet threaten the integrity of movements. That is when the Internet can breed and nurture a false sense of community and movement and consensus when there may in reality be none. It is important to realize that for all the visual polish of its user interface, the Internet is really a faceless, amorphous entity. It is a convenient entity, but it is not a living one. The danger lies in treating it as if it were.

Whether it is used to find porn, lovers, support, books, or just people like you, the Internet will become a more and more important tool in organizing. Used judiciously, the virtual communities it creates can actually help forge real communities. The future will show how this brave new cyber world can coexist with and complement more traditional notions of community organizing. But it is wise to remember that the eworld is still a virtual world and has its limits. As the members of *Gay Bombay* discovered, it eventually required a real-life meeting at McDonald's to move on to the next step. But an effective combination of the cyber world and the real world can help the movement grow stronger and be more effective as it connects South Asian queers all over the world, separated by oceans and many time zones.

Notes

1 Suvir and Arvind, editorial, *Trikone* 1, no. 1 (1986): 1.
2 Companions on a Journey can be contacted at *coj@sri.lanka.net*.
3 Khush list can be contacted at *khush-list-subscribe@yahoogroups.com*.
4 Chandra S. Balachandran. "Desi Pride on the Internet: South Asian Queers in Cyberspace," *Trikone* 11, no. 1 (1996): 18. *Desi* is a term South Asians use to describe themselves. It is derived from *desh* which means "land" or "homeland."
5 SAGrrls can be contacted at *sagrrls-subscribe@yahoogroups.com*.
6 Desidykes can be contacted at *desidykes-subscribe@yahoogroups.com*.
7 ⟨www.egroups.com⟩ was a Web site that allowed Internet users to create their own email discussion lists. It also managed the lists for them. Recently acquired by Yahoo, this Web site is now located at ⟨http://groups.yahoo.com⟩.
8 The *Trikone* Web site is located at ⟨http://www.trikone.org⟩.

9   SALGA, *Humsafar Trust,* and *Trikone Tejas* can be contacted at ⟨http://www.salganyc.org⟩, ⟨http://www.humsafar.org⟩, and ⟨http://www.main.org/trikonetejas⟩, respectively.

10   The *Gay Bombay* Web site is located at ⟨http://www.gaybombay.com⟩.

11   Qtd. in Vikram, "Cybergay," *Bombay Dost* 7, no. 1 (1999): 8.

12   Balachandran, 19.

13   Sappho can be contacted c/o A.N., P.O. Box EC-35, Calcutta-700010, India.

14   Shrinand Deshpande, "Point and Click Communities? South Asian Queers Out on the Internet," *Trikone* 15, no. 4 (2000): 7.

15   Gay Calcutta list can be contacted at *gaycalcutta-subscribe@yahoogroups.com.*

16   Deshpande, 6.

17   *Gay Bombay* list can be contacted at *gaybombay-subscribe@yahoogroups.com.*

18   Deshpande, 6.

19   PFLAG is a support group for parents and friends of lesbians and gays.

20   Qtd. in Jay Vithalani, "Passport Princesses," *Bombay Dost* 7, no. 1 (1999): 17.

21   LGBT India list can be contacted at *lgbt_india-subscribe@yahoogroups.com.*

22   Mala Nagarajan, "SAGrrls and Desidykes: Women on the Internet," *Trikone* 15, no. 4 (2000): 8.

23   Qtd. in ibid., 9.

24   Despande, 7.

25   Scott Kugle, "Internet Activism, Internet Passivism," *Trikone* 15, no. 4 (2000): 11.

26   Ibid., 10.

27   Giti Thadani, "No Lesbians Please: We Are Indian," *Trikone* 9, no. 2 (1994): 6.

28   Ashok Row Kavi, "An Indian Original," interview by Sandip C. Roy, *Trikone* 8, no. 3 (1993): 5.

29   Ruth Vanita and Saleem Kidwai, *Same-Sex Love in India: Readings from Literature and History* (New York: St. Martin's Press, 2000).

30   Deshpande, 7.

31   Qtd. in Sandip Roy-Chowdhury, "Coming Out, Coming Home," *India Currents* 14, no. 6 (2000): 40.

32   *Hijras* are a religious community of men in South Asia who dress and act like women. The term often loosely translates as eunuchs or hermaphrodites, although hijras may be neither.

33   Nagarajan, 9.

↔ III

Circuits

REGIONAL

ZONES

KATRIEN JACOBS

Queer Voyeurism and the

Pussy-Matrix in Shu Lea Cheang's

Japanese Pornography

This essay considers a Japanese-produced digital sci-fi porn film, *I.K.U.: A Japanese Cyber-porn Adventure*, by Taiwanese American filmmaker Shu Lea Cheang and the ways it rehearses a future condition for electronically networked sexual communities.[1] *I.K.U.* departs from the much-hyped "newness" of new media and liberatory queer discourses that attend the World Wide Web. The film is partly inspired by Ridley Scott's *Blade Runner* (1982) and offers a keen meditation on the globalization of sexual agency, often defined in commercial advertising by a capacity to traverse gender and national boundaries independent of material conditions. Marketing strategies construct a global queer subject who purchases services instead of taking an activist position in sexual minority groups. Rather than gesturing toward sexual transgression defined by the entrepreneurs of online chatrooms or cybernetic designer wear, Cheang's curiosity lies in improvising within the realm of subversive eroticism disguised as "Japanese pornography."

Cheang's Japanese pornography offers a statement on globally distributed eroticism and cybersexual commodification. Not unlike Arjun Appadurai's notion of social practices articulated within a globalized imaginary, *I.K.U.* symbolically locates sex practices and pornographic consumption in the realm of transnational cultural production.[2] The frame of analysis of porn production and consumption moves from nation-states to "inbetween cultures where the edges of cultural belonging tangle and blur, the zones in which processes of translation hybridity and (mis)understanding occur, where meaning is formed and deformed, where national histories are made and unmade, buried and disinterred."[3] Bearing cultural hybridity in mind, this essay does not aim to research the influence of Japan's pornographic cultures on Cheang's work, nor measure responses to Cheang's work in Japan.[4] Instead, I contemplate Cheang's refiguring of Japanese pornography with reference to globalized notions of space, queer pornography, and feminist discourses.

I.K.U. uses porn conventions to critique mainstream porn. The movie casts seductive porn figures in cyberspace as mobile flows, financially supported by the transnational corporation Genom. Cheang depicts and works in the same modes as global capital flow to critique and subvert that order. *I.K.U.* is a feminist intervention into the debate over and practice of corporate mainstream porn, by emphasizing the subversive sexual agency of its female characters. This is particularly significant in relation to the representation of female sexuality in Japanese porn as "soft," maternal, passive, and centered on organs that cannot be publicly denoted. It challenges this last description particularly in its overt positing of "pussy as matrix." The matrix is an invisible network, a virtual reality that holds power over netizens by connecting them to anonymous others and by immersing them in manipulated environments. Cheang predicts that women will take part in building magnetic sexual environments or pleasure domes based on female "pussy" pleasures rather than hard phallic sexuality shown in mainstream porn. She predicts the globalization of "pussy power," or porn artists who seduce consumers in unexpected ways. The movie speaks to straight male viewers in many of its conventional porn scenes, yet also includes female and "queer" viewers. Queer viewers are exposed to underground cult figures and digital cut-up techniques that demonstrate the impossibility of any "natural" sexuality in pornography. The movie is a queer art experiment that reconfirms once more the radical potential of digital technologies as decentralized sites of porn activism. The film is significant for the ways it works in and through "real" activist sites as well as porn-consuming "queer" Internet communities.

Both queer activists and porn consumers experience sexual identity as indeterminate and elastic. Annamarie Jagose's *Queer Theory* describes queer as "a category in the process of formation . . . an umbrella term for a coalition of culturally marginal sexual self-identifications which has developed out of a more traditional lesbian and gay studies."[5] Cheang's work depicts the formation of queer collectives by matching commercial porn engines with the new media underground.

I.K.U. constructs an empire of the senses, where computer chips programmed with sexual desires drawn from data bank memories are easily inserted into the body of flesh. Citizens purchase an erotic moment that requires the participation of an android, or "coder," who activates the full potential of the carnal-erotic event. These coders are not so much objects of desire based on some lack, as a psychoanalytic explanation of sexual desire would have it, or technologically advanced "pleasure workers," as depicted by the characters Pris and Zhora in *Blade Runner*, but, more simply, a kind of necessary plug-in that catalyzes the erotic event.

I.K.U. shows fragments of a futuristic queer unconscious, loosely inspired by and irrespective of Japanese porn conventions. Furthermore, *I.K.U.* can be seen as an allegory of the political and moral economy of current transnational corporations and censorship agencies as they increasingly restrict, and in some cases disable, online queer communities. This essay seeks to identify how Cheang's work offers a model for highlighting and questioning political mechanisms of surveillance.

The essay further investigates Cheang's queering of new media cultures. First, due to its unusual, almost satirical content and flamboyant technostyle, this Japanese movie is destined to become part of a global underground through appearances in film festivals, video dubbing, DVD burning, and Internet distribution. The essay shows that *I.K.U.*'s iconoclastic vision responds to new developments in censorship legislation. Second, *I.K.U.*'s vision of queer sexuality is centered on the loss of communities as bounded and consistently reinforced entities. It alludes to the disruption of queer enclaves and the reappearance of a patriarchal order in the form of a corporate phantasm whose unity is embodied satirically in the film by the trope of a "digital penis." This phallocentric scenario is at once hardcore pornography and a critical intervention into the patriarchal premises of the genre of hardcore pornography. Analyzing Cheang's digital hardcore porn as a visionary statement about sexuality and post-Internet culture, the essay speculates about her fabling of "queer," "queer Asian," and "Asian diasporic" communities as they exchange pornography and adapt to the current climate of censorship wars centered around Internet pornography.

Cheang is a trickster agent of digital capitalism. A self-professed "digital drifter," she makes Web art on the institutional servers of establishment museums, such as the Guggenheim Museum in New York City and the NTT Inter-Communication Center (ICC) in Tokyo, as a way of cyber-squatting. A Taiwanese-born media artist who assembles work and audiences in high-tech capitals and developing cyber worlds, Cheang has been noted to identify with the "cowboys" and "Indians" of new technological frontiers. Gina Marchetti explains: "As an Asian woman, she represents the 'aboriginal' on the borders of a culture traditionally defined by white, First World men. As a 'homesteader,' she has positioned herself in a world where she may not always find a receptive welcome as a civilizing force amidst digital slavery."[6] Lawrence Chua, a writer who joined Cheang on a long-distance travel journey for *Buy One Get One* (1997), a video/Web installation Cheang made for the NTT-ICC in Tokyo, describes the itinerary-movement of drifting through nations: "The qualities of homelessness in a corporate moment were starting to register as we bounced between cities: there was a difference between being homeless on the streets of New York and homeless on a Thai Airways airflight, rebounding back to Bangkok after being refused entry into Shanghai. . . . We followed the routes of power off the acknowledged paths of commerce into the techno-bush. Home became a circular motion, a sometimes violent revolution on an uncertain globe. It was an odd circuit we followed. It could not have been otherwise."[7] As with any entrepreneurial agent of global capital flows, it is now standard practice for artists to be equipped with the staple technologies of transition—the mobile phone, the high-end laptop, the air ticket, the hotel stub—and to undertake their work in deterritorialized modes. In *Buy One Get One,* Cheang and Chua registered the influence of cultures, responded to erratic global flows of capital, and rehearsed concepts of space, speed, and desire that were soon to be appropriated by dot com companies in their search for a global navigator/consumer.

Clicking on the nipple in the center of the *Buy One Get One* homepage, viewers can start viewing Cheang's Web design and follow her travel paths through the cities of Seoul, Shanghai, Bangkok, Harare, Beirut, and Johannesburg. In Johannesburg, Chua observes, "You maneuver the streets, trying to lose your skin. With a suitcase of privilege in your once colored hands, you try to become another transborder data flow, skimming the surfaces of oceans, looted banks, whole cities still glittering under siege."[8] *Buy One Get One* commented on the precarious guilt that digital drifters experience, like so many diasporic peoples, when confronted with cultures defined (and ruined) by coherently materialized divisions, such as "black" or "white" neighborhoods, within the local geography.

Cheang's work has often relied on a cultural rhetoric of deconstruction of race and gender. In the predigital video and audio installation, *Those Fluttering Objects of Desire* (1993), viewers investigated the act of exchanging ethnic identities and prejudices through mass media communication. The installation was based on a Times Square peepshow and phone-sex lines, inviting audiences to respond to mutated "exotica" shows. Viewers acquainted themselves with different art media and artists' confessions of interracial desire while adopting voyeuristic viewing mechanisms.

Cheang's more recent Web installation, *Brandon* (1998–1999)—built as hyperactive afterlife commemorating a gender-crossing individual from Nebraska who was raped and murdered in 1993 after his passing as a male was revealed—presents viewers with the opportunity to enter fantasy spaces based on gender exchange. Drawing from the writings of Michel Foucault, a site called *Panopticum Interface* displays online prison cells based on Jeremy Bentham's principle of the panopticon, a space of surveillance that is at once material and imaginary wherein subjects are trained to self-regulate behavior. In an interview with Cheang, Kimberly SaRee Tomes notes that Cheang consistently uses the Web to build underground zones: "Cheang decodes the language of technology in order to mutate existing languages into forms that open up alternative spaces in which to create new communities and relationships. In her own words, she has evolved from 'developing artist to hi-tech aborigine' in her drive to explore cyperspace and to understand the possibilities it offers to alternative communities."[9] Cheang's work shows experimental models of artistic collaboration and queer socializing in today's privatized new media spaces that are increasingly governed by customer profiling and state and corporate censorship.

For instance, the movie *I.K.U.* does not explicitly address lesbian and gay viewers, but rewrites heterosexual viewing pleasures for a mixture of straight and queer audiences. As a low-budget sci-fi porn movie, *I.K.U.* has been released only at independent film festivals, but it invites further dissemination and alteration of its queer content through forms of Internet communication and sampling. As stated in the *I.K.U.* promotional Web site, the movie is "ready to be downloaded and recreated in hundreds of variations with little effect on the ultimate quality of the film."[10] However, as Marchetti notes, Cheang's work is profoundly ambivalent about new media and the Internet as distributor of queer art and activism. A struggle between artists and corporate activists was a major theme in Cheang's first feature-length movie, *Fresh Kill* (1994), which offered a dystopian vision of computer networks as "sites for struggle, disruption, and intervention."[11] Cheang's work depicts virtual spaces as sites for agitation and activism as well as conduits for transnational commerce and the dissemination of commercial propaganda. Her work shows an acute awareness of the contradictory nature of new media technologies in their capacity to enable a new climate for sexual openness and tolerance within straight and queer communities.[12]

I.K.U. situates viewers as queer subjects who are excessively sexualized by Internet culture. *I.K.U.*'s cinematography is equally influenced by Japanese commercial animation porn (*hentai*), whose explicitly pornographic scenes offer a mixture of consumer fetishism and violent-erotic imagination, and by marginal feminist waves of pornography. Both products speak to different youth and adult audiences but have a prolific and hybridized existence on the Internet. For instance, a free preview tour for a hentai porn site introduces the sci-fi story *The Naked Earth,* which shows a cult of android Amazons engaged in fierce combat with violent monsters. After some women have been strangled, raped, and murdered by the tentacled monsters and we see their corpses bleeding from between the thighs, one Amazon urges the Amazon headmistress to make an exit. The headmistress replies, "Escape is not an option, my child!" as the page scrolls over to membership sign-up information for the porn Web site. On the upper left corner of the page, a pop-up sales window displays the popular phenomenon "dickgirl" (girl with penis) rhythmically sucking a soft and elongated penis. Dickgirl is the soft and humorous, infantile-feminine counterpart to the violent monster. She happily sucks her fantastically engineered and *soft* genital for voyeuristic audiences.[13] Dickgirl is a common figure in Japanese hentai who speaks to male and female audiences, yet she can also be seen as a popular character to be appropriated or "queered" by women's communities in their quest for transgender constructions of the female body.

Japan has a very prolific animation industry and hosts new generations

Mobile Cultures

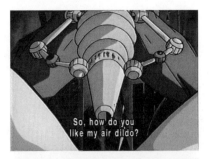

Still images from the animated cartoon *La Blue Girl 4: The Perverted World of the Haunted Sword*. Miko is being approached by a ghostlike character, "micro Ninja," who pretends to want to satisfy her with a giant air dildo but secretly inserts a control device inside her vagina and says, "The womb is the center of all woman. If you can take control of the womb, then you can take control of the woman."

of commercial artists to reinvent porn codes for male and female, straight and queer audiences. *I.K.U.* samples and subverts such codes in Japanese and transnational contexts. The movie is introduced with a scenic presentation of "queered" porn stars. In the seclusion of an elevator, protagonist Reiko No. 1 (played by Tokitoh Ayumu, an erotic actress from Japanese satellite television) meets Dizzy, the *I.K.U.* runner (played by the black transgender cult figure Zachery Nataf).[14] Shots of Dizzy's hands on Reiko's breasts and pubic area are followed by a dialogue in which Reiko begs to touch Dizzy's penis. Dizzy diverts Reiko's gaze from his genitalia and sends her off onto a more expansive sexual universe, initiating her into a world of strip dancers and bondage masters, autoerotic drag queens and sassy school girls, pink girls eating jelly dildos, and mistress mentors who teach masturbation techniques and reload her burnt-out system after she crashes on the Tokyo Rose virus.

In the closing scene of the movie, Reiko No. 1 rejoins Dizzy inside the secluded elevator and wants to have sex with him again. Determined once again to touch Dizzy's penis, Reiko discovers that Dizzy is a postoperation transgender male. Reiko's acceptance of Dizzy's unusual penis is carefully registered as we observe her salaciously licking Dizzy's pubic hair and genitals. This shot is significant, as it would normally be censored in Japanese pornography. It also produces an important moment of confusion as viewers confront the lack of boundaries of sexual orientation and constitution in the protagonists.

New concepts of queerness are proposed in *I.K.U.* by immersing viewers in subversive film aesthetics. *I.K.U.* shows bodies aroused by an aesthetic of mobility, fragmentation, and rotation, emphasized in the film by chopped up editing on noisy techno-beats, constantly shifting camera angles, and layered visuals as subversive attachments, all destined to create a new type of somatic viewing experience. Viewers hover in hypererotic nausea as they adapt to the film's shifting platforms as well as shifting sexual scenes. *I.K.U.* translates movement-dynamism from one form of reality to another: from kaleidoscopic "live" sexual numbers to fantasy-animations and from sci-fi plot to routine porn conventions. Movement itself becomes characteristic of the queer image, as Gilles Deleuze understands such images: "An image is a center of dynamic exchange whereby movement steps up (is contracted) or steps down (is redilated) from one dimension of reality to another, and therefore is always in the middle (it is a site of passage and exchange in a

Still images from *I.K.U.: A Japanese Cyber-porn Adventure.* A recurring image is the animated "digital penis" depicted as if shot from "inside a female cavity being penetrated."

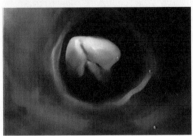

field of exteriority, it is a milieu)."[15] *I.K.U.* shows pornographic bodies as "in-between" technologies, focusing on speed, movement, and cyberspace as catalysts of desire. Multishaped bodies and bodily cavities are filmed and painted with software programs, connected through dizzying editing techniques and camera angles. We can see subjects in moving vehicles, fast cars zipping through tunnels, vaginal cavities and mobile cages for bondage rituals, and blow-up dolls flying onto the stage and attaching themselves to subjects. Movement creates sequences of images for viewers who desire to experience diverse forms of sexual orientation and pornographic genres.

I.K.U. also playfully cites the genre of Western hardcore pornography. However, the movement-aesthetics destabilize hardcore pornography's feature of maximum visibility, as defined by Linda Williams: "to privilege close-ups of body parts over other shots; to overlight obscured genitals; to select sexual positions that show the most of bodies and orgasms; and, later, to create generic conventions, such as a variety of sexual 'numbers' of the externally ejaculating penis."[16] Williams's *Hard Core: Power, Pleasure and the "Frenzy of the Visible"* argues that hardcore pornography juxtaposes transparent shots of the ejaculating penis as "evidence" of pleasure with a quest for the mysterious realms of female pleasure. Female pleasure is suggested rather than externalized, and is depicted as a seductive out-of-control attitude of the interior female body. Whereas male pleasure can be portrayed around moments of external evidence, female pleasure is constructed around a "frenzy of the visible," as Williams writes: "While it is possible, in a certain limited and reductive way, to 'represent' the physical pleasure of the male by showing erection and ejaculation, this maximum visibility proves elusive in the parallel confession of female sexual pleasure."[17] As indicated in this essay, *I.K.U.*'s showcasing of hardcore porn is a new instance of cross-cultural porn exchange and hybridized imagination.

Borderline Aesthetics and Digital Distribution

I.K.U.'s queer content and aesthetics will likely generate different responses in various Asian and Western cultures and diasporic communities. One Asian American respondent to the *I.K.U.* questionnaire, which I distributed online after *I.K.U.*'s screening at the Asian-American International Festival in July 2000, saw the movie as making a statement about transnational sexualities in relation to "Japan": "To me the film is about border crossing and the blurring of gender, racial, and national boundaries. I suppose the film is also about technology and how it has come to shape, define and most importantly liberate our identities. To contextualize it in the Japanese society, one of the most homogeneous and orderly in the world where difference (on the surface) is to be frowned on and where people know their place, the film is part of the pop-culture releases of the suppressed energies and chaos! The film in that sense is subversive. I would also add that it is much more so than its *anime* counterparts!"[18] *I.K.U.* is an instance of *fabled* geography, produced in Japan and influenced by Japanese pornography, but placed in a transnational cultural framework. Cheang's workspaces and fictional spaces are typically located outside cultural establishments or demarcated cultural regions.

Her work is in line with recent trends in cultural studies and visual anthropology, which would question the notion of "Japanese" porn as a geographically marked repository of culture, and rework it as a network of "zones" or "sites" where different aspects of cultures collide and mutate.[19] Arjun Appadurai's *Modernity at Large: Cultural Dimensions of Globalization* proposes that we view cultures in terms of irregularly shaped metaphors of space or "-scapes." Such amorphous metaphors rely on the role of hybrid fantasies as much as regional/national geographies. Sexual fantasies are modulated by historically situated subjects and technologies, and practiced and shared in everyday communication. Appadurai believes that the social imagination becomes "a central force to all forms of agency . . . the key component of the new global order."[20] Marchetti argues that Cheang's work has for many years hinged on "queerscapes" as transnational zones that enable new perspectives on gender and sexual orientation. Queerscapes are enabling networks that question and transcend "localized gay/lesbian/ bisexual/transgender human and civil rights initiatives and move into the wider arena of critique of the myth of identity, the patriarchy, heterosexism, and the tyranny of traditional gender norms."[21] Queerscapes develop new concepts of space, gender, and sexuality as they permeate the plural en-counters between local and global citizens. Cheang's work and porn movie exemplify Appadurai's concept of geography, indicating that queerscapes consist of zones of encounter figured on ephemeral queer communities.

A theoretical framework for queerscapes can also be developed out of the Deleuzian notion of "minorities," subjects-in-making who communi-cate, drifting in and out of specific sites, communities, and nations. John Rajchman explains that Deleuzian minorities are undefined subjectivities that introduce "other" or "unknown" parameters of space and time: "A minority is always somewhere a 'people to come'—our minorities are those 'future people' we might yet become. But we are thus 'peoples' in a very different sense from what modern political thought calls *the* people. A minority is rather *a* people, a people not completely defined or deter-mined."[22] In *I.K.U.*, coders are people who do not have a clear future, do not have histories of minority status, but formulate revolution as moments of "becoming." Becoming, as defined by Gilles Deleuze and Félix Guattari, evokes new conceptions of time and space: "Unlike history, becoming can-not be conceptualized in terms of past and future. Becoming-revolutionary remains indifferent to questions of a future and a past of the revolution: it passes between the two."[23] Rajchman explains that such revolutionary forces are "diagnosed" rather than "enlived" historical moments. They have a "pragmatic" rather than a "mystical" lineage as "a question of novelty and singularity, of what we can't yet see or think in what is happening to us, new forces which we must nevertheless diagram or diagnose."[24] *I.K.U.* seeks out porn viewers as self-conscious dispersed catalysts of desire rather than communities made up of homogeneous subjects. Cheang explains in an interview that she sees dispersion as a direct result of Internet culture: "The Internet is the most interesting area for the porn industry, as people download images. If you stretch the imagination a little bit, what gives somebody an orgasm? Traditionally it would be the centerfold of *Penthouse* magazine. The centerfold has a pubic area and people touch that and masturbate and come all over the picture. That is the traditional way. Now there are so many porns available and the entire computer drive is swamped and you can look at it anytime."[25] Cybersex killed the centerfold and gave viewers the sensation of being "queered" through ongoing encounters with multiple and transformative partners of desire.

Theorists have documented how the Internet has facilitated transnational queer exchanges and how the support of global networks has transformed the gay, lesbian, and transgender communities in many parts of the world. For instance, Mark McLelland's essay in this book shows that Internet communication is creating specific types of Japanese homosexuality different from the development of Westernized gay identities. Japanese men apparently use Internet communication to develop sexual "playtime" modes that do not correspond to public gay cultures in the Western world.[26] Even though the Internet provides new forms of sexual communication in many different cultures, Japanese men employ the Internet to respond to specific historical circumstances. McLelland notices a high level of tolerance by Japanese mainstream society for homosexual men and their Internet "playzones" in Japan, so long as they do not interfere with the reproductive role of men within the marriage relationship. Japanese gay men's fusion of sexual, social, and political interests may have been facilitated by contact with Western gay/lesbian organizations, but this type of contact does not automatically benefit other gender and ethnic communities in Japan. Women and lesbian communities do not have equal access to sites of public sexuality, even though growing Internet sites such as *Ruby in the Skye with Sitrine* are creating venues for women to chat, exchange information, and set up meeting points for actual and virtual seduction.[27] The participation of Japanese women in global sexual communities will depend on their ability to adopt the roles of networked queer consumers as well as participate in Internet sites with local or communitarian concerns.

As McLelland and Veruska Sabucco both discuss further in this volume, it is also important to mention that since the 1970s Japan has cultivated a distinct tradition of women's erotica magazines (*manga*) where female producers have constructed sexual personas peculiar to markets for female readerships. This has enabled Japanese women to be trained in a cultural form that has since been transferred to the Internet. Contiguous with literacy in computer-mediated communication and the World Wide Web, interaction with erotica products online enhances the possibility for women to develop literacies not limited to the cultural form of erotic manga.[28] That is, a radical contingency emerges wherein erotic manga intersect with electronic forums that might include chatrooms, mailing lists, health information, and educational resources, not to mention the glory of becoming a player in the online stock market. One recent manifestation of manga culture that seeks to extend processes of youth identity formation within an exchange economy is the World KiSS Project. This project attracted erotica doll creators both in Japan and internationally to explore the viral life of commodity forms by exchanging transformed versions of sexy dolls. As Anne-Marie Schleiner observes, "The process of creativity employed by KiSS artists is a form of cultural sampling, hacking, and appropriation, a form of play from which new configurations emerge. She adds that the international audience of World KiSS is creating an interactive counterculture open to fantasies that deviate from the sexual norms: "As an open source strip doll player, the World KiSS Project allows its users to insert their own erotic fantasies into the mix rather than relying on a particular industry to feed its users prepackaged sexiness. The World KiSS Project is a global collaborative experiment for how to play with sexy interactive dolls and avatars, allowing queer, hetero, female-friendly, fetish, Goth, Japanese bondage, *anime* tingles, . . . and other fantasies to be distributed and exchanged."[29] The World KiSS project assumes that forms of porn activism can be stimulated and enriched by the global Internet economy.

The Phantasm of Phallic Feminism and Censorship

As argued earlier, Cheang's struggle to make "anxious" commodity pornography is visible in *I.K.U.*'s queer aesthetics. Shot in Tokyo, one of the global cities of porn production, the movie casts Japanese porn actresses who lure viewers with their naked display and gyrations of sexual pleasure as they approach climax. Yet this routine code of porn cinema is disrupted throughout the film's fragmented narrative by the appearance of various digitally animated sequences. The most important of these involves the work of a digital penis in the penetration scenes. Traditionally, the penetration scene in much mainstream Japanese porn is censored, yet this imposed limit has often encouraged filmmakers to establish a new code for porn by substituting the moment of censorship with a fetishized mosaic edited onto the genitalia. A correlation to this practice may be seen in Bombay cinema, where erotic love scenes are implicitly rather than explicitly shown, with the seemingly spontaneous outbreak of song and dance routines interjected in the film's central narrative. In *I.K.U.*, Cheang plays with the Japanese code in conjunction with painterly 3D digital effects to reconstruct the representation of female and male genitals and the act of penetration.

The remarkable scenes with a digital penis comment on the paranoid scene of Internet censorship in the United States, Japan, and elsewhere. Triggered partially by the controversies over Internet child pornography, new conservative censorship legislation places responsibility for administering online regulation in the hands of Internet service providers (ISPS). One effect of this has been an increase in the disabling of online sexual communities in which participants often distribute depictions of minors engaged in sexual activities. This is particularly the case in the United States, where commercial host portals such as egroups, Visto, Yahoo, and Excite have disabled legal adult Web sites for gay communities where "obscenities" such as pictures of urinating boys are exchanged. Because the sites are hosted by corporate host portals as free services, the portals are "free" to set any terms of service (TOS) they choose. For instance, the *Visto.com* TOS reads: "We reserve the right to terminate any subscriber, without disclosure of specific reason for said termination, at our own discretion, if we deem that such termination is in the best interest of Visto Corp."[30] It is important to note that the corporate control on adult sites is indeed damaging the educational and social functions they perform. Some of the moderators of censored sites have maintained extensive discussions about nudity between children and nonparental adults to resist a generalized representation of this taboo area of sexuality.[31]

Whereas depictions of nude minors in gay and lesbian networks are a cause of moral outrage in the United States, these depictions are tolerated in other cultures, such as Japanese live and animated pornography. Mark McLelland notes in his essay on Japanese erotic online manga that "scatological references may appear obscene to a western audience, but they are in fact commonplace in Japanese media." Discussing the Web site *Saki's Room* and illustrations with urination and masturbation themes, McLelland suggests that "the most troubling illustration for a western viewer involves scenes depicting interplay between male minors."[32]

The fear that the Internet kindles an upsurge of "deviant" sexualities produces chaotic policymaking by networked legislators and corporations in their attempt to control electronic information. In his astute overview of Internet censorship in the article "Censorship 2000," John Perry Barlow of the Electronic Frontier Foundation (EFF) stated, "Now, all over the planet, the mighty have awakened to the threat the Internet poses to their traditional capacities for information control." A historically unprecedented conglomerate of scattered collectives and individuals posing as nation-states, local governments, corporations, religions, cultural groups, information distributors, and information "owners" participates in the construction of ethical values surrounding Internet communication and sexuality. Barlow believes that there is a sudden global epidemic of virtual censorship. He explains that nation-states such as Switzerland, England, and France, as well as international organizations such as the G8 (group of eight industrial nations), are desperately seeking to turn telecommunication carriers and Internet service providers into the "content cops of the Internet," whereby companies would be required to block their customers from accessing certain sites proscribed by various authorities. Barlow also believes that a transnational culture of censorship will easily result in the political suppression of marginal groups as it creates a tide of chaotic intolerance: "Within narrower contexts, suppressing the expression of gays, women, heretics, traitors, and troublemakers is politically popular."[33] It would not be hard to imagine that such a "glocal epidemic of virtual censorship" will easily target the work of pornographers who touch on areas of censorship and whose visions are not supported by corporate interests.

Just like the World KiSS artists, Cheang encourages viewers to reproduce alternative erotica, meanwhile spreading a cyberfeminist message that "the pussy is the matrix" and that viewers with marginalized backgrounds can participate in a critique of globalized porn. This point is emphasized by the filmmaker in reference to the representation of women in Japanese porn: "In Japanese film and porn, there is also a lot of abuse of women. There is that kind of force, that is, you have to force women to have sex. I couldn't quite understand and I was trying to go against that. In *I.K.U.* women become active and this happens with a certain purpose."[34] The movie develops the role of female agents as coders and emphasizes their access to gender-fluid digital genitals.

Using Japanese popular culture as cognitive context, Anne Allison has argued in *Permitted and Prohibited Desires* that female bodies in manga for men are typically "smooth and 'natural,' naked, and unadorned . . . yet almost always interrupted by the sharp edges found on the cyborg like bodies of men."[35] Based on the observation that most Japanese manga show men and animals as "sharp" brutal figures who assault females, Allison proposes that Japanese popular culture constructs essential gender differences: "Gender is constructed as a difference between two kinds of identities and ontologies—one impulsive, narcissistic, and machinelike: the other stable, continuous and naturalistic—and 'sex' is the act and relationship of the one trying to break down, break into, and break away from the other."[36] Allison distinguishes Western "phallocentric" gender differences, where individuals internalize the phallic threat issued by the father, from Japanese "infantile" gender differences, where femininity is a maternal, soft arena that nurtures and wraps the male.

I.K.U. criticizes Japanese portrayals of femininity and highlights females as single agents who arrange and enjoy sexual encounters. One Asian American woman who responded to the *I.K.U.* questionnaire stated that the movie reinforces female pleasure, for instance, by repeatedly showing oral sex: "There is far more oral sex received by women in this film than in any other films I have seen."[37] The explicit "pussy shots" in the movie make a clear break with Japanese obscenity laws that have an absolute prohibition on the showing of pubic hair and genitalia. As noted earlier, penetration is traditionally censored in Japanese pornography, but is reintroduced in *I.K.U.* by means of a digitally designed, colorful, erect penis shape penetrating humans and androids when they are about to orgasm. The digital penis is a device that is inserted to give pleasure and measure satisfaction. The digital penis does not ejaculate, but enters the male/female, straight/queer android through the vagina and/or anus as a genital or a fist, giving pleasure to the subject and extracting precious data about the machine-manipulated state of orgasm. The digital penis goes beyond "phallocentric" and "infantile" forms of masculine craving as it is portrayed as a gender-fluid fantasy object used by both genders. The digital penis is shot from the point of view of "digital pussy"; we can observe the huge fantasy-object as it enters the traditionally censored female cavity and pleasure zone. The digital penis is a prosthetic device that is used to access interior data stores inside body cavities. The film suggests that such data need to be retrieved from vaginas rather than protected and concealed from gazing eyes.

Cheang explains that it was very difficult to confront sexual taboos around nudity, pubic hair, and genitals in collaboration with Japanese actresses and porn stars: "Working with porn actresses was the only way we could get people to take off their clothes. There is no other way. In Japan only porn actresses will take off their clothes. I have a great relationship with the actresses and specifically Tokitoh Ayumu [who plays Reiko No. 1]. I am so grateful that she dared to show her pussy in the opening elevator scene. Or the elevator scene in the end when she starts sucking the transsexual character, Dizzy. We prepared her for that. When Zach Natafy took off his pants she went down on him like that. I was almost crying because most people have such trouble with that shot."[38] As stated earlier, the "sucking scene" reveals that Dizzy is a F2M transgender individual and that his female genitalia were turned into a penis by means of an operation. The scene also makes a powerful statement against censorship regulation by explicitly showing pubic hair and genitals.

Allison notes that censorship mosaics and tags on female genital areas in Japanese porn convey to the viewer that the pussy is a forbidden orifice that contains a smutty and dirty substance. At the same time, the tag posits the vagina as a sacred zone that needs to be protected from assault by outsider forces. The protection of the pussy as a sacred/taboo zone has been accompanied by a larger obsession with the nonphallic penetration of other orifices, notably female anuses that get penetrated by animals, ghosts, and cyborgs. Allison summarizes: "[There is a] preponderance in Japanese media of peepshots up the skirts of girls and women at the ever-present white underpants; the fetishization of body parts other than genitals, such as buttocks and breasts; the infantilization of females, who are (or made to appear) prepubescent and lacking pubic hair; and acts of sado-masochism in which there is no genital copulation, stimulation, or exposure. The images all avoid the realism of genitalia, which center the state's definition of both sexuality and obscenity."[39] Sexuality is constructed beyond a fascination with the ejaculating penis, and women are shown to possess a sacred, untouchable kernel of "femininity" that has historical and cultural antecedents in Japan.

By emphatically declaring "The pussy is the matrix," Cheang defuses Japanese constructions of femininity as well as stereotypes of maternal procreation. *I.K.U.* indicates that gendered metaphors of sexuality are being thoroughly revised by communication technologies. As a playful critique of the new commodified cultures of cybersex and queer navigators, the movie portrays computer networks as mediating agencies that make sexual revolutions available to minorities as well as corporations.

Conclusion

Shu Lea Cheang shows that digital drifters need to be thoroughly collusive with the machinations of commodification to be able to reach global online communities. The question that arises, and continues to plague cultural studies debates, is the extent to which one can obtain, acquire, or interject resistant pornography without simply glorifying the supposed capacity of consumers to function as political actors. As *I.K.U.* has only recently been released in independent film festivals in Europe and the United States, it is too early to research its impact on specific queer communities and sexuality debates in Asian cultures. The movie, however, makes an important contribution to research on global and diasporic queer communities as it shows that queer Asian communities are changed through the transnational culture of Internet pornography. *I.K.U.* can be seen as an "anxious" commodity product meant to mimic and destabilize global pornography, radicalizing the viewer and thwarting his or her construction of exotic subjects and taboo areas of the human body. As Cheang states in a recent ⟨nettime⟩ interview with Geert Lovink: "In every sense, it meant to subvert 'the worldwide male dominance and patriarchy,' the hard on dick that upholds.

Here I want to distinguish my practice from that of art porn which I consider to be a soft industry domain. *I.K.U.* confirms cyberporn as Corporate operation of level 7 hard and soft fusion. Ultimately, *I.K.U.* severs the cumbersome tentacles of the wired 90s' cyborg entity and initiates the body as a gigabyte hard drive, self-driven by a programmed corporate scheme. It updates vns Matrix's 'The clitoris is a direct line to the matrix' by claiming 'The pussy is the matrix.' "[40] In so doing, *I.K.U.* critiques the emergence of upwardly mobile transnational queer viewers who escape in electronically mediated transgressions of race, gender, and nationality without becoming part of activist communities.

This essay has shown that *I.K.U.* blurs porn genres and complicates the study of cultures, situating queer viewers as transmutative and spatialized subjects who constantly move among sexual cultures and spaces where sexual encounters take place. However, the movie differs from commercial pornography in its attempt to attack censorship mechanisms and gender constructs in Japan and the United States. Cheang's Japanese pornography offers a model for global consumers to be artistic and queer respondents to pornography, as it struggles to produce/consume porn images through restricted theatrical release and online distribution mechanisms that circumvent censorship legislation, corporate aesthetics, and an outburst of global paranoia.

Notes

1 I am indebted to Ned Rossiter, who responded to various drafts of the essay and made a grand contribution to the final version. I would like to thank Shu Lea Cheang for kindly answering my questions, for stimulating dialogue around cybersex, and for giving me feedback to my work in progress. Thanks also to Gina Marchetti, Peter Oelhlkers and Shujen Wang for providing key ideas and ongoing support.

2 Arjun Appadurai, *Modernity at Large: Cultural Dimensions of Globalization* (Minneapolis: University of Minnesota Press, 1996), 31.

3 See Scott McQuire's description of cultural hybridity in "Electrical Storms: High Speed Historiography in the Video Art of Peter Callas," in *Peter Callas: Initialising History,* ed. Alessio Cavallaro (Sydney: Dlux, 1999), 31.

4 This type of influence study is partly impossible because *I.K.U.* has not yet been released in Japan. The film premiered at the Sundance Festival 2000 and

has since been featured in film festivals in Copenhagen, Montreal, New York, and London.

5   Annamarie Jagose, *Queer Theory* (Melbourne: Melbourne University Press, 1996), 1.

6   Gina Marchetti, "Counter-Media and Global Screens: Recent Work by Shu Lea Cheang," paper presented at the annual meeting of the Society for Cinema Studies, Chicago, March 2000.

7   Lawrence Chua, "An Odd Circuit: Shu Lea Cheang's Online Road Trip," *Art Asia Pacific*, no. 27 (2000): 51.

8   Ibid.

9   Kimberly SaRee Tomes, "Shu Lea Cheang: Hi-Tech Aborigine," *Wide Angle* 18, no. 1 (1996): 4.

10 *I.K.U.* promotional Web site, 12 June 2000, ⟨http://www.I-K-U.com⟩ (24 August 2000).

11 Marchetti.

12 Marchetti.

13 *Naked Earth,* 12 April 1999, ⟨http://www.nakedearthcomix.com⟩ (15 September 2000).

14 Other cast members include actresses chosen especially from the Japanese erotic world, such as AV actresses, magazine models, and strip club dancers. Also, Japanese rope artist Akechi Denki makes a special appearance to tie up Reiko.

15 Brian Massumi explains the Deleuzian definition of the image as derived from Henri Bergson. According to Bergson, the human body does not produce or consume images; the human body is an image. *A User's Guide to Capitalism and Schizophrenia: Deviations from Deleuze and Guattari* (Cambridge, MA: MIT Press, 1996), 185.

16 Linda Williams, *Hard Core: Power, Pleasure, and the "Frenzy of the Visible"* (Berkeley: University of California Press, 1989), 46.

17 Ibid., 48.

18 "Re: *I.K.U.* questionnaire," 20 August 2000, personal email (20 August 2000).

19 Susan Pointon also works with the notion of Japan as a "porn zone" in her essay "Transcultural Orgasm as Apocalypse: *Urosukidoji: The Legend of the Overfiend,*" *Wide Angle* 19, no. 3 (1997): 41–63. The concept of "zone" is taken from Dwight Conquergood's essay "Rethinking Ethnography: Towards a Critical Cultural Politics," *Communication Monographs* 58, no. 2 (1991): 186. Pointon applies this notion to her study of Japanese anime, arguing that they have adopted Western features and are very popular in American student communities.

20 Appadurai, 31.

21 Marchetti, referring to Appadurai, and Fran Martin and Chris Berry's "Queer'n'Asian on the Net: Syncretic Sexualities in Taiwan and Korean Cy-

berspaces," *Critical InQueeries* 2, no. 1 (June 1998): 67–94. Marchetti invites us to imagine a notion of "queerscape" beyond Appadurai's five dimensions of global cultural flow (i.e., ethnoscapes, mediascapes, technoscapes, finance-scapes, and ideoscapes).

22 John Rajchman, "Diagram and Diagnosis," in *Becomings: Explorations in Time, Memory and Futures,* ed. Elizabeth Grosz (Ithaca, NY: Cornell University Press, 1999), 51.

23 Gilles Deleuze and Félix Guattari, *A Thousand Plateaus: Capitalism and Schizophrenia,* trans. Brian Massumi (Minneapolis: University of Minnesota Press, 1987), 292.

24 Rajchman, 46.

25 Personal interview with Shu Lea Cheang, New York, 30 July 2000.

26 McLelland shows that Japanese men actively use the Net to advertise for partners and make "electronic cruising" efforts enabling them to secretly and efficiently arrange private meetings in designated spaces.

27 *Ruby in the Skye with Sitrine,* 14 May 1999, ⟨http://www2.big.or/jp/~cham⟩ (19 September 2001).

28 See Mark McLelland's work in this volume and his "No Climax, No Point, No Meaning? Japanese Women's Boy-Love Sites on the Internet," *Journal of Communication Inquiry* 24, no. 3 (2000): 274–91. His essay is based on an analysis of women's erotic Web sites.

29 Anne-Marie Schleiner, "Open Source Art Experiments: Lucky Kiss," 26 November 2000, ⟨www.nettime.org⟩ (15 November 2000). For more information about the Lucky Kiss Project, see the Web site ⟨http://www.opensorcery.net/luckykiss_xxx⟩ (3 January 2001).

30 Visto Terms of Agreement (TOS), 24 May 1999, ⟨http://www.visto.com⟩ (3 January 2001).

31 Information gathered from diverse anonymous sources, correspondences between moderators and members of adult sites hosted by egroups and Visto.

32 McLelland, "No Climax," 283–84.

33 John Perry Barlow, "Censorship 2000," 1 July 2000, ⟨http://www.nettime.org⟩ (12 July 2000).

34 Personal Interview with Shu Lea Cheang, New York, 30 July 2000.

35 Anne Allison, *Permitted and Prohibited Desires: Mothers, Comics, and Censorship in Japan* (Berkeley: University of California Press, 2000), 73.

36 Ibid.

37 Answer to *I.K.U.* questionnaire, received 31 August 2000.

38 Cheang interview.

39 Allison, 150.

40 Geert Lovink, "Interview with Shu Lea Cheang," 30 December 2000, ⟨http://www.nettime.org⟩ (30 December 2000).

OLIVIA KHOO

Sexing the City:

Malaysia's New "Cyberlaws"

and Cyberjaya's Queer Success

We are now standing at the site of the cybercity, a city that would
bring us to the next generation and beyond . . . not just a place where
companies involved in information and multimedia technology can
operate in, but one in which creativity and innovation can thrive.
—DR. MAHATHIR MOHAMAD, *Cyberjaya* Web site

Malaysia stands at an interesting point in its development as a nation tied to
the new information technologies.[1] On the verge of becoming a regional
leader in the provision of infrastructure and cyberlaws for multimedia
businesses if Prime Minister Mahathir's vision for Cyberjaya goes according
to plan, Malaysia is also an interesting example from which to look at the
rise of the New Asia over the past two decades, driven by market forces and
heralded by the growth and increasing global prominence of Asian modernities and economies.[2] The "New Asia," built through economic restruc-
turing, regional integration, and technological growth, has been envisioned
as an area that is "modern and prosperous, self-confident but cosmopolitan, peaceful and united, cultured and humane."[3]

From a different critical trajectory, the New Asia has also been constructed in part by the idea of a "queer Asia."[4] Using the case surrounding
the conviction of Deputy Prime Minister Anwar Ibrahim for sodomy as an
example, this essay situates Malaysia's stance on homosexuality within both
the nationalist and regionalist discourses constructing contemporary Malaysia as a modern and technologically sophisticated society. I argue that the
technological utopian discourse embodied by Cyberjaya sits uncomfortably

with local and often critical lesbian, gay, and queer (LGQ) discourses in Malaysia that have proliferated in cyberspace as well as the conservative and nationalistic discourse of Anwar as sodomite that Mahathir has publicly touted, complicating Malaysia's drive to establish itself as a major player in the world capitalist trade order.

Malaysia's push into the arena of information technologies is largely a result of the development of Cyberjaya, the "intelligent city," as it has been dubbed by the government.[5] Cyberjaya is an ambitious (U.S.$10 billion) technology zone backed by the Mahathir government. It forms the "nucleus" of Malaysia's new Multimedia Super Corridor (MSC), which links Kuala Lumpur to its new international airport.[6] The government has planned and promoted the MSC as a home for both local and international companies to kick-start the development of the local information technology sector. The government is to provide infrastructure and "cyberlaws" to govern the use of information technology. Companies such as Microsoft, Intel, Nokia, and British Telecom have already joined up and will move into the "city" when the infrastructure is complete. A new Multimedia University opened up in Cyberjaya at the beginning of 2000 with over three thousand students already enrolled; the population of Cyberjaya is growing, and the city of Kuala Lumpur itself is transforming.[7] This essay addresses how the development in information technologies has also led to changes in the social and political characteristics of the city of Kuala Lumpur and Malaysia more generally.

The economics involved in the development of Cyberjaya and the optimism tied up with its hoped-for financial success for the Malaysian market is not, of course, free from politics. The promotion of Cyberjaya both to Malaysians and to the rest of the world has been inherently political, as well as cultural. Not only is Cyberjaya being created as a self-sufficient "intelligent city," but it also stands for the future of new technologies in Malaysia and Asia tied to "creativity and innovation," as well as to discourses situating Malaysia within "Asia" and to organicist notions of "Asian values."[8] Thus, nationalist and regionalist tendencies on the one hand are being played off against globalizing discourses on the other. As such, Mahathir's rhetoric of "opening up" the nation to foreign investment does not entail an equal enthusiasm for foreign—that is, Western—"influence," including that of homosexuality. While I do not wish to rearticulate the debates surrounding the concept of global queering,[9] I do wish to look at how discourses of globalization and of regionalism constitutive of the New Asia are inflected by discourses surrounding local sexual politics.

Homosexuality is illegal in Malaysia, according to both state and Islamic law.[10] The latter is applicable only to Muslims. Although constrained in expressing their sexual identities freely *offline,* gays and lesbians are articulating their sexuality and forming communities *online* in new national and transnational spaces.

The effective political silencing of former Deputy Prime Minister and Finance Minister Datu Seri Anwar Ibrahim using a discourse of sodomy is one that I wish to reinflect by looking at how support for Anwar on the Internet by gay and lesbian communities in Malaysia entails political and cultural visibility and a certain vocality. Anwar Ibrahim was deputy prime minister and finance minister of Malaysia until September 1998. He was widely regarded as the man being groomed to take over Mahathir's place as prime minister until disagreements over the management of the country's economic affairs and Anwar's push for reform within the government caused a rift between the two men. This essay draws together the (dis)articulation between the discourses surrounding Anwar Ibrahim, the official Cyberjaya discourse, and the local LGQ discourse. Gays and lesbians are also actively participating in the construction of Cyberjaya.[11] Is there, therefore, a national stake in Cyberjaya's queer success?

Electronic Mailing Lists and
the Visibility of Women's Groups in Malaysia

Due to the demonstratively punitive consequences for being gay or lesbian in Malaysia, as witnessed by the gross mistreatment of Anwar Ibrahim during his police custody, trial, and imprisonment,[12] Malaysian gay and lesbian communities are extremely closeted.[13] Consequently, figures relating to the size of these communities cannot be accurately obtained. Many communities have mobilized on the Internet, however, particularly through electronic mailing lists. This is a relatively recent phenomenon, most lists having been founded between 1998 and 2000.[14]

For this essay, I conducted in-depth online interviews with fourteen participants from three electronic lists: Women Who Love Women (WWLW),

Malaysian Lesbian Network (MLNI), and Singaporean and Malaysian Bisexuals and Lesbians (SAMBAL).[15] As such, the observations in this essay focus mainly on women's groups. There are two significant reasons for this. First, to my knowledge, there is no electronic group specifically for Malaysian gay men on the Internet.[16] More general lists for gay Asian men do exist, such as 4AsiaGays administered by Utopia, but these lists are more for making sexual contacts with other Asian men, and so my questionnaire proved to be unsuccessful in such a forum.[17] Second, had there been such a list, I would almost certainly not have been allowed to participate in it, not being a gay Malaysian male. The three lists that I did join had very strict identity-based membership criteria: membership is available only by introduction from another list member or after undergoing intensive screening by the list owner/administrator.[18]

A further reason for a particular focus on women's groups is to examine the role of women in the New Asia. There are new spaces opened up by technology and a certain gender politics that leads toward the public sphere, which Mayfair Yang defines as "a new space established by modernity as the space of public discourse and debate, cultural and ideological production, and mass-media representation." Yang notes that the public sphere is traditionally and predominantly a masculine space.[19] On the Internet, however, this is not necessarily the case. In fact, once invisible constituencies of Malaysia's society, such as lesbians, are now brought together and made visible on the Internet (on Web sites, search engines, etc.). Malaysian political scientist Farish A. Noor writes, "The arrival of the Internet has become the solution to the problem for many of those constituencies that feel that they were somehow left out or not given a space in the discursive economy of the nation."[20] Anwar's trial was not simply about male homosexuality/sodomy, but also about how Mahathir is currently mobilizing antihomosexual sentiments in Malaysia. This is of particular concern to women's groups, given the existing silence surrounding female sexuality in Malaysia. Indeed, many of my interviewees felt that women's groups such as Pink Triangle (Malaysia) should be doing more for the wider gay/lesbian/bisexual/transgendered community in terms of voicing shared concerns.[21]

The research for this essay was almost entirely Internet-based, involving Web sites that feature alternative news articles about recent economic and political developments in Malaysia. Not only is the Internet able to provide the most up-to-date source of information, but this information also would not have been otherwise publishable in Malaysia, given the state's control of the media.

Although not always directly quoted, the comments of my interviewees frame the entire essay. The majority (six) of my interviewees were from Kuala Lumpur, of Chinese background (eight), with no particular religious affiliation, in their early to mid-twenties, and identifying as lesbian (the six from Kuala Lumpur). These demographics—being queer and Chinese in Malaysia—situated them within Malaysian society as marginal in their ethnicity, their religious background, and their sexuality. Yet, from this position, they still felt more comfortable speaking than, for example, an Islamic woman.[22] Although these electronic lists were also transnational spaces with members from the diasporic Malaysian community, those I interviewed were either still living in Malaysia or had spent a significant portion of their life there and had just moved, and were therefore directly affected by Kuala Lumpur's new developments in information technology and the public's reaction to the Anwar Ibrahim situation. To see how diasporic Malaysians are affected would be another research issue altogether.

City Transformations and Cyber-success:
Mahathir's 20:20 Vision

Standing at the site of "his" cybercity, what does Dr. Mahathir see?

Wawasan 2020 (Vision 2020), introduced in 1990, is Mahathir's national campaign aimed at transforming Malaysia into a fully developed and technological nation by the year 2020.[23] The embodiment of Vision 2020 is to be the MSC, which is intended to propel Malaysia into position as an Asian leader in information technologies.[24]

For a foreign company to acquire MSC status and the benefits conferred with such a status, it must prove that it is a provider or heavy user of multimedia products and services and that it will employ a substantial number of knowledge workers; most significant, it must also outline how it will transfer technology and knowledge to Malaysia or otherwise contribute to the development of the MSC and the Malaysian economy.[25]

These new transformations for Kuala Lumpur as a result of its opening up to foreign direct investment are also articulated in tandem with discourses of "Asian values" that situate Malaysia within regional ties. The vision for Cyberjaya, and the premise on which it is built, is that it be a city "where man, nature and technology live in harmony." This catch-cry is on all of Cyberjaya's promotional material, printed on environmentally friendly recycled cardboard and illustrated with pictures of grasshoppers perched on the end of modem lines, daisies with data chips, and the like.

Not only does Mahathir want a technological city, however; he also wants it to have a certain moral foundation, strong in spiritual values and that which is seen to be "natural." In his third book, *The Voice of Asia: Two Leaders Discuss the Coming Century* (cowritten with Japanese politician Shintaro Ishihara), Mahathir writes that a country isn't developed "if it has money and technology but lacks firm moral values. . . . Many Western societies, for example, are morally decadent. . . . To us, that is not development. You must maintain cultural and moral values. We do not want to be just a rich country." Mahathir lists homosexuality among these moral deviances.[26]

In further promotional material, Cyberjaya has been touted as "a balanced environment of enterprise, commercial, and residential zones with recreational areas, including facilities for disabled and vulnerable groups."[27] Who are these vulnerable groups, and how far does Mahathir's benevolence extend?

To negotiate the competing discourses offered by Mahathir to Malaysians, I want to explore how Cyberjaya's newly formed cyberlaws and promises that the Internet will be censorship-free intersect with the real consequences of being gay or lesbian in Malaysia and on the Internet.

Cyber-legalities and Political Legacies

One of the key elements of the MSC is the framing of the world's first comprehensive framework of cyberlaws and the world's first Multimedia Convergence Act. The Malaysian government will now be operating under this new code of cyberlaws designed to create cyber-success (*jaya* means "success" in Malay). A new national administrative capital for Malaysia is being built at a site now called Putrajaya, which will be an "egovernment," a paperless administrative center. Already, the weekly meetings of the Ministry of Energy, Telecommunications and Posts are paperless; they are linked internally.

There are no uniform international cyberlaws in place; therefore, Malaysia has enacted its own set. At the time of writing, four acts have been passed covering computer crimes (Computer Crimes Act 1997), copyright (Amendments to the Copyright Act 1997), telemedicine (Telemedicine Act 1997), and digital signatures, which verify electronic transactions or communications (Digital Signatures Act 1997). These cyberlaws are intended to protect intellectual property rights and create an environment where multimedia industry and online transactions (ecommerce) can take place securely and successfully. In addition to these cyberlaws, the Malaysian government has committed to a ten-point "Bill of Guarantees," which, although not legislation as the cyberlaws are, operates as "promises" made by the government. It includes assurances of providing a world-class information infrastructure; allowing unrestricted employment of local and foreign knowledge workers; becoming a regional leader in intellectual property protection and cyberlaws; and *no Internet censorship*.[28]

In Malaysia freedom of speech is a constitutional liberty, although the courts may pass laws that qualify this liberty in relation to public order, security, morality, or defamation. The courts have generally taken a narrow approach to free speech, choosing instead to uphold the other concerns mentioned. Such an approach will almost certainly apply to information on the Internet as well. Malaysia's cyberlaws will be held to apply to MSC companies. However, in terms of Internet censorship, what may appear objectionable in Malaysia may not be the case in another country. A set of legal as well as practical issues with cultural and political implications will also arise from having unregulated Internet access and use by MSC companies but restricted use by non-MSC companies and individuals.[29]

I am interested in how these cyberlaws will translate across queer communities. Ethnic and sexual marginality renders queer groups in Malaysia extremely "vulnerable," even on the Internet, as governed by these new cyberlaws. Mahathir has promised that Cyberjaya will be "user-friendly" and that online access will become available from almost everywhere in the city. This forms part of his Vision 2020 for the future of Malaysia tied to new technology. Thus, in relation to Mahathir's rhetoric of a progressive and successful "global city" with free information for all, these cyberlaws sit uncomfortably with official government laws concerning homosexuality. Indeed, several of my interviewees were of the belief that the development of Cyberjaya was an attempt not so much to increase the information flow within Malaysia as to have a more controlled Malaysia under Mahathir's gaze. The possible regulation or surveillance of LGQ content via either the new cyberlaws or existing laws on free speech is clearly discrepant with the stated desire for Cyberjaya to help "disadvantaged communities" and "vulnerable groups." Paradoxically, Mahathir and his ruling UMNO (United Malay National Organisation) Party want both to modernize Malaysia, advocating liberal trade in the Asia Pacific and implementing export-oriented economic strategies, and yet keep Malaysia tied to the notion of Asian values by rallying against "Western" liberalism and foreign influence.[30]

Unlike Mahathir, Anwar, as the media perceived and I elaborate below, was able to "demonstrate . . . how Muslims can indeed be a force in the modern global economy without compromising their beliefs and traditions."[31] The accusation of sodomy against him may have been a politically motivated response to this, as sodomy is against Muslim law. Apart from one interviewee who characterized Anwar as "disgusting" for not disclosing his (homo)sexuality to his wife, most of the people I interviewed did not believe that the charges of sodomy were "innocent" or free from political motivation. The judicial aspects of the case and whether the charges were politically motivated are not my direct concern in this essay.[32] Rather, I am more interested in how the media emphasis on the question of his sexuality and sexual practices was used "to exploit and manipulate homophobic sentiments among the Malaysian public."[33] To view this aspect of the case, it is necessary to look at what Anwar Ibrahim seemed to represent to Malaysians.

Alvin Toffler, a renowned futurist author and member of the International Advisory Panel of the Malaysian MSC, issued a statement on MalaysiaNET dated 17 November 1998 that he would resign if Anwar was not released from prison unharmed as soon as possible. He also suggested that other members of the Panel, on whose investments the MSC depends, would follow with their resignations. Toffler wrote, "I do not agree, as Prime Minister Mahathir has argued in response to my appeals, that the MMSC project is purely a business matter and has nothing to do with politics. The 'cyberlaws' that he promised investors—complete freedom of access to information, and other Third Wave freedoms, are, in fact, clearly political. The creation of an Asian Silicon Valley is itself inherently political."[34]

Comparing Malaysia's MSC to California's Silicon Valley seems to suggest an Asia following the West in its development of a zone for information technology. This version of a globally engaged New Asia is one that Mahathir has been reluctant to endorse. Anwar Ibrahim, on the other hand, embodied such a vision.

"The Asian Renaissance": Malaysia and the New Asia

Despite the fact that Anwar was viewed as Mahathir's successor, the differences between Mahathir and Anwar were marked, particularly as highlighted by the local and foreign media. Dr. Mahathir was seen as intractable by the foreign press and as a conservative both locally and overseas. Anwar, on the other hand, was described by *Asiaweek* as "a true Asian renaissance man." Malaysia's *Sunday Star* suggested that he "epitomi[zed] the new generation of Asian leaders who are steering their nations into the new millennium," and Alvin Toffler wrote of Anwar, "[He] seemed the very symbol of the 21st-century, globally linked economy Dr Mahathir wished to build: a worldly, sophisticated Muslim leader who has called for women's rights, freedom of the press, and other Third Wave advances."[35] Anwar in fact wrote a book entitled *The Asian Renaissance* in which he discusses "the rise of Asia as the centre of global economic activity."[36] In an interview in *The Australian,* Anwar said that a new Asia would emerge from the economic crisis that would be "more confident, more mature and liberal and democratic. . . . There will be a transformation to build a new Asia."[37]

Anwar Ibrahim was thus a major proponent of a new Asia. This image in the West was promoted by his PR people. Mahathir, in contrast, appeared abrasive before the international media. There were also comparisons made to President Suharto in Indonesia at that time, in relation to charges of cronyism and nepotism. Suharto was forced to leave office, and there were pressures on Mahathir by opposition political parties and members of civil society to do the same.[38]

In contrast to Anwar's "liberal and democratic" notion of a new Asia, the regionalism that Mahathir sought to promote was a closed regionalism.[39] Mahathir clearly situates Malaysia as an Asian country that is culturally different from nations in the West.[40] His culturalist brand of regionalism operates to mediate against the increasing globalization and transnationalization of capital through foreign investment into Malaysia and fears of an ensuing cultural disintegration.

Mobile Cultures

As Leo Ching argues, a region is "a discursive construct, rather than an empirical reality."[41] The idea of an economic regionalism has been manipulated by Mahathir to serve the culturalist and religious ideologies of his ruling UMNO Party and the Muslim majority in Malaysia that backs it. Through a discourse of closed regionalism, the internal difficulties within the Malaysian political scene could be suppressed, rather than opened up to scrutiny.

Opposition came, therefore, in the form of Anwar Ibrahim, representing a New Asia of reforms and openness to both the region and to global economics in general. According to Anwar, not only was economic reform necessary, so too was political reform.[42] Anwar was behind a general *reformasi* (reform) movement. However, there are no clear definitions of what these reforms might be, and certainly none in relation to sexuality laws in Malaysia. In the way then Deputy Prime Minister and Finance Minister Anwar Ibrahim was constructed by the media and by political commentators, his silencing was also the official "silencing" of homosexuality.

Although Anwar did not publicly champion gay rights in national politics, his political silencing is also tied to a silencing of homosexuality through the charge of sodomy against him (a sacrilegious act to the Muslims, linking him to Western influences). Yet, as Foucault has written, since the nineteenth century sodomy has been viewed not just as an *act* that one commits but also as something beyond that act: "the psychological, psychiatric, medical category of homosexuality was constituted from the moment it was characterized . . . less by a type of sexual relations than by a certain quality of sexual sensibility, a certain way of inverting the masculine and the feminine in oneself. Homosexuality appeared as one of the forms of sexuality when it was transported from the practice of sodomy into a kind of interior androgyny, a hermaphrodism of the soul."[43] In other words, sodomy began to operate as a sign, standing in for a particular type of person and a new kind of signifying body. In this case, it promoted Anwar as a representative of the New Asia, one that was being transformed (corrupted, according to Mahathir) by Western influence.

Quoted in the BBC News, political commentator Professor Liefer notes, "The significance of the particular charge of sodomy is that the actual charge is anathema within Malay culture, and therefore the object of the exercise is to destroy Anwar Ibrahim politically so that he will never again have any kind of effective role in Malaysian politics."[44] Anwar's prison term thus also results in his political obscurity; he won't be due for release until 2014, when he will be 64 years old.[45] Once released, he is barred from sitting in Parliament for a further five years according to Malaysian law. Tan Beng-Hui writes, "Most [in Malaysian society] have been brought up to view homosexuality as a disease, a perversion and an unnatural state of being. How then could they effectively combat accusations that stemmed from the same premises [in order to defend Anwar]?"[46]

One of my interviewees also believed that the Anwar situation was a political maneuver, that it was "another case of the injustice of the Malaysian system and not about him being gay. I hate that the two are confused." This interviewee noted that all of the parties involved in the case are Muslim, yet they were being tried in a civil court and not in the syariah Muslim courts. According to this interviewee, the judicial system is too closely linked with the government for a fair trial.[47]

Whether Anwar is indeed a homosexual is not the point. What is interesting is how the discourses are "confused" and how the ideology of Anwar as sodomite functions in relation to national politics, particularly at this historical juncture in Malaysia's push into the arena of information technologies. The case is particularly interesting in that the charges brought against Anwar are rarely raised to such a high profile in Malaysia. There is no centralized record of sodomy cases that have come before the Malaysian courts, and although there have been convictions concerning consenting adults, sentences have usually been less than three years.[48] Anwar was jailed for fifteen years in total.

Anwar was sacked as deputy prime minister on 2 September 1998.[49] He was initially arrested under the Internal Security Act (ISA), which allows suspects to be detained for sixty days without being charged or put on trial.[50] Rallies and protests for him were held on the streets on 18 September in the northern town of Kota Bahru, where some fifty thousand people attended. This was followed by a series of demonstrations showing an unprecedented level of antigovernment sentiment and protest. A huge rally was held on the eve of the closing ceremony of the 16th Commonwealth Games on 20 September, when the world media were present. Anwar was arrested at his home that very evening.[51]

In April 1999, Anwar was sentenced to six years imprisonment for "abuse of power" in using his position to stop a police investigation into sexual allegations against him. In a second trial on 8 August 2000, he was sentenced to a further nine years for sodomy. Anwar's adopted brother, Sukma Darmawan, was also found guilty of sodomizing the family driver, Azizan Abu Bakar, and of abetting Anwar in his offence.[52]

Anwar on the Internet: Political Discourse as
a Site of Cultural Production

Anwar's case and the Malaysian public's response to it was thus not just about his sexual practices, just as debates around homosexuality are never just about sex but also involve other issues, such as national politics. Anwar's lawyer, Pawancheck Marakhan, has also suggested that the situation was more political than judicial: "Because it is a politicized trial, it won't be solved by the courts. It will have to be solved out there among politicians, and with the populace."[53] What, then, are the people doing? Much public protest has been stifled by the government. During Anwar's first trial for corruption in April 1999, there were large-scale and vocal demonstrations held on the streets. During the second trial, there was little protest and public support had visibly waned. Whether this was due to "Anwar fatigue" or to fear of the government is uncertain.

Internet activity regarding Anwar Ibrahim, however, did increase around the time of both trials, suggesting that support for him might have moved there. An Internet campaign called the Free Anwar Campaign was launched simultaneously in Malaysia, Australia, the United Kingdom, and the United States just days before the verdict in his sodomy trial.[54] The Web site urged supporters to write letters to Prime Minister Mahathir, the Malaysian king, human rights organizations, and their own government to appeal for Anwar's release. Facing government sanctions, Anwar supporters appear to have resorted to the anonymity and reach of the Internet. Obviously, not all Anwar supporters are members of the queer community, yet many of the publicly vocal queer community have been responsive to and supportive of his case. The Internet has played a vital role in mobilizing and developing the queer community in Malaysia and also in making more information available. And it has become a site for resistance to the government, making it "a very real challenge to the existing hegemony."[55] As Bob Paquin writes, "The fact that Malaysian citizens have been able to obtain relatively un-biased news on the Anwar trial and the 'reformasi' campaign exemplifies the increasing difficulty governments have in managing the flow of information within their borders—even when they control the major print and broadcast media. Within days of Anwar's arrest, offshore Web sites sprouted by the dozen offering a combination of news, analysis and essays, and serving as repositories for press statements and letters from prison from Mr. Anwar himself. . . . Ironically, the fact that Malaysians are in a position to make use of digital media reports is due in large part to the government's efforts to transform the country into a kind of information technology mecca."[56]

Anwar himself has been able to send out his writings from prison instantaneously to a wide audience. So that the government cannot bring an end to this material by simply closing down a single site, the Anwar site has been mirrored in different geographical locations.[57] Outside of the national border and held in an electronic location, these images and texts can be accessed but not destroyed.

Ashley Lee, a 26-year-old journalist from Kuala Lumpur and a prominent member of Malaysia's gay community, has commented on the role of the Internet in mobilizing the gay community: "The gay community is growing. Many gay saunas and pubs have been opening up to cater to this increase. Gay men are also becoming more open about their sexuality." He also attributes this growth to the Internet: "We are all logged on to the Internet. We have chat lines catering to Malaysian gays. We have chat parties where we meet the people we have been chatting with." He even suggests that his sex life increased during Anwar's two-year trial for sodomy: "During the Anwar trial it was easy to get lucky. After he was sacked my sex life escalated. Many people wanted to experiment with gay sex."[58] The Internet is thus enabling the LGQ community to operate and mobilize both because of and quite apart from the Anwar campaign.[59]

In this way, Anwar support and queer mobilization are evident on the Net in both imbricated and disarticulated ways, enabling the formation of a kind of reverse discourse.[60] One of my interviewees who is involved in the development of Cyberjaya suggests that "it will become increasingly visible [to the government] that not all information on the Net will be favorable within their vision of shaping the nation." Mahathir's Vision 2020 may thus not be as clear as he expected. The nationalistic discourse of Anwar as sodomite, the technological utopian discourse of Cyberjaya with its attendant cyberlaws, and the resurgent LGQ discourse on the Internet all chal-

Mobile Cultures

lenge Mahathir's clear vision for Malaysia's future, despite his efforts to restrict and contain it.

Conclusion

Repression and "vulnerability" are thus able to find new ways of voicing same-sex desire through online communities, highlighting the increasing emergence of LGQ sexualities and cultures tied to the development of information technology in the region. Thus, sexuality in Malaysia is able to travel from its site of marginality to assume global mobility through the Internet, while maintaining political discourse as a site of local production and contestation.

Internet groups for LGQ Malaysians are forming "virtual communities" that are regional in shape and scope.[61] The participation of other diasporic LGQ Malaysians also informs this. As Leo Ching writes, regions and regionalism are "important sites where the contending forces of global integration and local autonomy converge."[62] The transnationalization and globalization of capital do not correspond to a convergent globalization of sexual identities. Rather, online participation is a way for the local community to assert agency through integration, collaboration, and a sharing of differences—rather than their suppression.

Separate from direct action for Anwar, electronic mailing lists are also helping to construct emerging national, regional, and transnational sexualized communities where women and men can chat, meet up, and organize social and political activities. The significance of cyberspatial technologies is that they transform traditional ideas about (mass) communication, creating new social spaces. The space of New Asia on the Internet, tied to Cyberjaya's queer success, is one that is emerging slowly but successfully, and it will continue to shape Malaysia's future, despite myopic remonstrations to the contrary.

Notes

1 Malaysia is located on the Malay peninsula in Southeast Asia, south of Thailand and Vietnam and north of Indonesia. It is a country of diverse ethnic

communities and religions. Malays constitute the majority of the 23 million population (60 percent), with significant Chinese and Indian minorities (30 percent and 9 percent, respectively). The rest of the population consists of other ethnic minorities such as Eurasians and indigenous Malaysians. Islam is the official religion of Malaysia under the Federal Constitution, although Buddhism, Taoism, Hinduism, and Christianity, among other religions, can also be practiced freely. See *Department of Statistics: Malaysia* Web site, ⟨http://www.statistics.gov.my/⟩ (5 March 2001).

2   The *Cyberjaya* Web site is ⟨http://www.cyberjaya-msc.com/⟩ (5 March 2001). The official site for the Multimedia Super Corridor (MSC) is available from ⟨http://www.mdc.com.my⟩ (5 March 2001).

3   "East Asia Economic Summit Ends with Call for Building New Asia," *Xinhua News Agency,* 15 October 1999, ⟨http://www.xinhuanet.com/english/index. htm⟩ (5 March 2001). See also "Editorial: The End of Politics: The Market Is Moving Force behind the New Asia," *AsiaWeek* (23 November 2000), ⟨http://www.cnn.com/ASIANOW/asiaweek⟩ (August 2000). This "New Asia" is to be built out of the economic crisis that hit the region in the late 1990s.

4   Dennis Altman has written that a "New World of 'Gay Asia'" is emerging, linked to modern Asia and to the self-conscious creation of Asian homosexual identities. Dennis Altman, "On Global Queering," *Australian Humanities Review,* no. 2 (July–August 1996), ⟨http://www.lib.latrobe.edu.au/AHR/home. html⟩ (5 March 2001). See also "The New World of 'Gay Asia,'" in *Asian and Pacific Inscriptions,* ed. Suvendrini Pereira, a special book edition of *Meridian* 14, no. 2 (1995): 121–38; *Defying Gravity: A Political Life* (St. Leonard's, U.K.: Allen and Unwin, 1997); and most recently *Global Sex* (Chicago: University of Chicago Press, 2001).

5   Plans for Cyberjaya and the MSC were first unveiled in late 1995. Hitches in its smooth development have included the economic crisis that hit the Asian region in 1997–1998 and the Anwar Ibrahim situation, which saw some potential investors reconsidering or delaying their move into Cyberjaya. See "Is Optimism about the MSC Justified?" *Bits & Bytes: MSC.Comm,* ⟨http://www. mdc.com.my/msc.comm/html/b_n_b01.html⟩ (5 March 2001).

6   The MSC spans an area of fifteen by fifty kilometers, stretching from the city of Kuala Lumpur to the Kuala Lumpur International Airport. *Multimedia Supercorridor* Web site, ⟨http://www.mdc.com.my⟩ (5 March 2001).

7   Cyberjaya was officially launched by Dr. Mahathir on 8 July 1999. The MSC was launched on 1 August 1996. Cyberjaya is to be developed over two phases, the first to be completed by 2006 and the second by 2011. It is expected that by 2011, Cyberjaya will be a city with a working population of 50,000 and a living population of over 120,000. *Cyberjaya* Web site.

8   The epigraph on the official Cyberjaya Web site reads, "Business civilises the

world, while nature heals and inspires. Place them together for work and play and watch a bonding of creativity and innovation."

9   Chris Berry and Fran Martin's essay in this volume, "Syncretism and Synchronicity: Queer'n'Asian Cyberspace in 1990s Taiwan and Korea," provides a nuanced rearticulation against a homogenizing view of global queering. The essay is a revised edition of an earlier version published in *Critical InQueeries* 2, no. 1 (1998): 67–94.

10 "Malaysia Stands by Anti-sodomy Law," *International Lesbian and Gay Association,* 13 June 1999, ⟨http://www.ilga.org/Information/Legal_survey/Asia_Pacific/supporting%20files/malaysia_stands_by_anti.htm⟩ (5 March 2001).

11 One of my interviewees is directly involved in Cyberjaya's development.

12 Newspaper articles and photographs released around the time of Anwar's arrest show evidence that he was beaten while in police custody. See *Berita Reformasi,* ⟨http://www.geocities.com/Tokyo/Flats/3797/berita.htm⟩ (5 March 2001).

13 *Dragoncastle's Gay Malaysia* Web site warns, "Malaysian society is not very tolerant of gays. The places listed here [for gays and lesbians] can change frequently. If you know of any new bars or clubs, or any changes to any of the places listed here, please let us know. Beware of police when cruising outside." ⟨http://www.dragoncastle.net/malaysia.html⟩ (5 March 2001).

14 As of December 2000, MLNI (founded on 6 November 1998) had fifty-one members; WWLW (founded on 10 April 2000) had seventy-two members, and SAMBAL (founded on 10 October 1999) had seventy-nine members. Note that some of my interviewees are members of two or more of these lists.

15 All three lists are *@egroups.com* ⟨http://www.egroups.com⟩. The description for SAMBAL reads, "The SAMBAL (Singapore and Malaysian Bisexual and Lesbian) E-mail List is an interactive e-mail list for lesbians & bisexual women from Malaysia and Singapore to come together to discuss Malaysian/Singaporean lesbian and bisexual women's cultural, social and political experiences/issues in cyberspace. . . . We define Malaysians and Singaporeans as women born in and/or have ancestral and cultural ties from or descending from these two countries. . . . The list is intended as a forum and support group and discussions can include announcements of community events, gossip, matters of earth shattering importance (or not), your astrological sign, or simple networking."

The WWLW list describes itself as "a private forum, for women only. The mailing list encourages friendship between women, plus, provides a host of other resources, such as women activities, places to hangout, books to share, and more."

The description for MLNI reads, "The Malaysian Lesbian Network International is an international, private mailing list for Malaysian lesbians only.

Messages may include discussion topics, community announcements, social support and networking."

16 *SayangAbang* (darling brother), a site for gay Malaysian men in Malay, is available from ⟨http://www.voy.com/64821⟩ (18 July 2002). There is, however, no general public listserv group that is specifically for Malaysian gay men.

17 There is not much traffic on this list, although over one thousand people subscribe to it. Almost all posted notices were in relation to men seeking to meet up with other men while traveling to different Asian destinations. *Malaysian Gay and Lesbian Club,* ⟨http://webnection.com/mgle⟩ (18 July 2002), based in San Francisco, consists mainly of diasporic Malaysians who meet in the San Francisco Bay area. This group also did not return any questionnaires, as my questionnaire stated that I wished to interview those who were still residing in Malaysia or had been there long enough and recently enough to be affected by the recent developments in the country. In December 2000, 4Asia-Gays had a membership of 1,276. It does not have any strict membership criteria. Its description states broadly, "Asia's gay scene is blossoming. . . . Share up-to-the-minute information on places where gays dance, work-out, party, eat, shop, date and cruise." ⟨http://www.egroups.com⟩ (5 March 2001).

18 For general Web sites on gay and lesbian Malaysia, see *Out in Malaysia,* "for everything gay and lesbian in Malaysia," ⟨http://www.outinmalaysia.com⟩ (5 March 2001). See also *Dragoncastle's Gay Malaysia,* which provides information on various bars and cruising spots in Kuala Lumpur, Johor Bahru, Kota Kinabalu, and Penang; and *GayCapitalKL,* ⟨http://members.tripod .com/gaycapitalkl/⟩ (5 March 2001).

19 Mayfair Mei-Hui Yang, introduction to *Spaces of Their Own: Women's Public Sphere in Transnational China,* ed. Mayfair Mei-Hui Yang (London: University of Minnesota Press, 1999), 2. Yang is elaborating on Jürgen Habermas's notion of the "public sphere" in *The Structural Transformation of the Public Sphere: An Inquiry into a Category of Bourgeois Society* (Cambridge, MA: MIT Press, 1989).

20 Farish A. Noor, "The Other Malaysia," *Malaysiakini,* 30 September 2000, ⟨http://www.malaysiakini.com/archives_column/farishnoor_column309 2000.htm⟩ (5 March 2001).

21 Note that Pink Triangle is a lesbian group, as its name suggests. Tan Beng-Hui has written an excellent article that raises many questions in relation to the role of women's groups in making homosexuality in Malaysia more visible. I acknowledge her work in this area. "Moving Sexuality Rights into the New Millennium," *Women in Action* 1 (1999), ⟨http://www.isiswomen.org/wia199/ sex00006.html⟩ (15 August 2000).

22 Most of these women were relatively "out," and many did not see a connec-

tion between their religious affiliation or ethnic background and their sexuality. I did not, however, receive a single response from an Islamic woman. Islamic women did not seem to be as active on the email lists as Chinese women from different religious backgrounds. It may be that Islamic women are either forming communities in specifically Muslim online arenas, such as *Khanaye Doost* for Iranian lesbians, ⟨http://www.geocities.com/khanaye_doost/welcome.html⟩ (5 March 2001), and *Queer Jihad*, a site for queer Muslims, ⟨http://www.well.com/user/queerjhd⟩ (18 July 2002), or else are too afraid to disclose their sexuality. In the predominantly Muslim countries of Iran, Afghanistan, Saudi Arabia, Libya, and Sudan, homosexual acts are capital offences. Most existing Web sites and communities for queer Muslims such as the two mentioned tend to be U.S.-based. Lakshmi Chaudhry, "Virtual Refuge for Gay Muslims," *Wired* (8 May 2000), ⟨http://www.wired.com/news/print/0,1294,35896,00.html⟩ (5 March 2001).

    In the specific case of Malaysia, I can only speculate about the lack of Internet activity by Muslim women on Malaysian lists for lesbians by citing Aihwa Ong's article, "State vs. Islam: Malay Families, Women's Bodies, and the Body Politic in Malaysia," in *Bewitching Women, Pious Men: Gender and Body Politics in South East Asia,* ed. Aihwa Ong and Michael G. Peletz (Berkeley: University of California Press, 1995), 159–94. Ong discusses how Islamic resurgence from the 1980s to the early 1990s reinscribed urban, middle-class Malay women into traditional roles. She writes, "The moral economy of resurgent Islam gave women little choice but to inscribe themselves into a 'traditional' subordination even when that position was itself an invented tradition" (185). Perhaps such a return to traditionalism has also resulted in less participation in the new media technologies for Islamic women who may also identify as lesbian, because the Islamic resurgence in Malaysia is ongoing.

23   Mohamad Mahathir and Shintaro Ishihara, *The Voice of Asia: Two Leaders Discuss the Coming Century,* trans. Frank Baldwin (New York: Kodansha International, 1995), 18.

24   In the Sixth Malaysia Plan, information technology was earmarked as one of the five key technologies that would launch Malaysia as a fully developed country. The other categories highlighted were automated manufacturing technology (AMT), advanced materials, biotechnology, and electronics. Government of Malaysia, *Sixth Malaysia Plan 1991–1995* (Kuala Lumpur: Kuala Lumpur Government Printers, 1991), 203–4.

25   ⟨http://www.mdc.com.my/msc.comm/html/quicklinks02.html⟩ (October 2000). Since the writing of this essay, over one hundred companies have been granted MSC status, with at least eighty already operating and the others setting up their operations.

26   Mahathir and Ishihara, 20. Mahathir has suggested that he will tolerate some

Western influences, "But there is a limit." In "Dr. Mahathir's World Analysis," *Mainichi Daily News,* 15 February 2000, he recounted how he had lunch with French President Jacques Chirac and said that he respected French culture and had no objection to their drinking wine with their meals: "We don't go around saying, 'Your way is wrong. Our way is right!' But there is a limit. For example, in Western culture they accept homosexuality, including promoting homosexual practices among school children. We cannot accept this. We admit that some people are born with their sexuality mixed up. That is not their fault. But to promote homosexual practices actively as is being done in some European countries is to purposely promote abnormality."

27 At Cyberjaya's official Web site.

28 Available from the MSC Web site, ⟨http://www.mdc.com.my⟩ (5 March 2001).

29 For a more thorough analysis of the legal implications of this censorship double standard, see Adeline Wong and Brian Chia, "E-com Legal Guide Malaysia," ⟨http://www.bakerinfo.com/apec/malayapec.htm⟩ (5 March 2001).

30 David Martin Jones recounts the meeting of the CEOs of companies considering investment in Cyberjaya; when they met in July 1999 in Kuala Lumpur, they were greeted by a giant billboard image showing rioters demolishing a car. The message above the image warned, "Foreign Influence is a Threat to National Security." Jones, "What Mahathir Has Wrought," *National Interest Magazine* (Spring 2000), ⟨http://www.nationalinterest.org/issues/59/JonesD Mextr.html⟩ (5 March 2001).

31 "Anwar's New Asia," *Asia Pacific Management News* (29 January 1998), ⟨http://www.apmforum.com/news/apmn148.htm⟩ (5 March 2001).

32 Although Anwar's trial clearly was not entirely unbiased; for example, there were inexplicable date changes made to the sodomy charge and legal maneuvers to keep Mahathir from having to testify in court despite his public assertions that he had proof. See Ian Stewart, "Second Jail Term for Anwar," *South China Morning Post,* 9 August 2000, ⟨http://scmp.com⟩ (15 August 2000).

33 Tan.

34 *MalaysiaNET* Web site, ⟨http://www.malaysia.net/Anwar_Ibrahim/anwar_ ibrahim.html⟩ (5 March 2001). In the quotation by Toffler, MMSC refers to Malaysian Multimedia Supercorridor. Throughout this essay I have simply used the abbreviation MSC. Note that Toffler did not in fact carry through on his threat to resign from the MSC International Advisory Board. See Alvin Toffler, "Upheaval Dims Hopes for Mahathir's Silicon Valley," *Los Angeles Times,* 17 November 1998, ⟨http://www.dranees.org/toffler.htm⟩ (5 March 2001).

35 "A Global Convivencia vs. The Clash of Civilizations," *Asiaweek* (30 May 1997), ⟨http://www.cnn.com/ASIANOW/asiaweek/⟩ (August 2000); "Review of *The*

Asian Renaissance by Anwar Ibrahim," *Sunday Star (Malaysia)*, ⟨http://www. ecomz.com/timeseditions/politics/anwar.html⟩ (5 March 2001); Toffler, "Upheaval Dims Hopes for Mahathir's Silicon Valley."

36 Anwar Ibrahim, *The Asian Renaissance* (Kuala Lumpur: Times Publishing Group, 1997).

37 Cited in "Anwar's New Asia."

38 See Chandra Muzaffar, "The Anwar Episode: An Analysis," ⟨http://www. jaring.my/just/ANALYSIS.html⟩ (5 March 2001).

39 Malaysia is a member of APEC (Asia Pacific Economic Co-operation), which is defined by a notion of "open regionalism." Open regionalism is driven by market integration but is institutionally informal and does not discriminate against participation by outsiders. However, Mahathir has repeatedly sought to create an East Asian Economic Group (EAEG), which would include all major East Asian countries but would exclude non-"Asian" countries like New Zealand, Canada, the United States, and Australia—all currently members of APEC. On the distinction between "open" and "closed" regionalism, see, for example, Ross Garnaut and Peter Drysdale, *Asia Pacific Regionalism: Readings in International Economic Relations* (Pymble, Australia: HarperCollins, 1994), 2.

40 Malaysia's government-sanctioned tourism campaign for 2001 features five women representing each of the major ethnic groups of Malaysia. The women are standing in front of a landscape that contains natural elements, such as the jungle and waterfalls, as well as Malaysia's urban skyline, dominated by the Petronas twin towers. The caption beneath the photograph reads: "Sense all of Asia in Mal*aysia:* Truly Asia." See Malaysia Tourism Promotion Board, *Tourism Malaysia* (1 June 2000), ⟨http://www.tourism.gov.my⟩ (1 October 2001).

41 Leo Ching, "Globalizing the Regional, Regionalizing the Global: Mass Culture and Asianism in the Age of Late Capital," *Public Culture* 12, no. 1 (winter 2000): 239.

42 All of this formed part of a larger reformasi movement. See *Berita Reformasi.*

43 Michel Foucault, *The History of Sexuality,* vol. 1, trans. Robert Hurley (London: Penguin Books, 1998), 43.

44 Frances Harrison, "What Future for Anwar?" *BBC News,* 8 August 2000, ⟨http://news.bbc.co.uk/hi/english/world/asia-pacific/newsid_870000/870834.stm⟩ (5 March 2001).

45 Anwar's supporters set up the National Justice Party (Keadilan Nasional) under the leadership of his wife, Dr. Wan Azizah Ismail, to secure his release from prison and also to serve as a platform to keep his political image alive. However, it is not nor is it likely to become a major political party in Malaysia. See Jones.

46 Tan.

47   Anwar Ibrahim was convicted by a state-appointed judge. Syariah courts are
     Muslim courts established by state governments and have jurisdiction only
     over Muslims and only over offenses committed by Muslims against the
     precepts of Islam as defined under the Muslim Courts (Criminal Jurisdiction)
     Act of 1969. *Malaysia's Legal System/History,* ⟨http://www.law.emory.edu/
     IFL/legal/malaysia.html⟩ (15 August 2001). My interviewee believed that the
     parties could have gotten away with just paying a fine in the syariah court.
     Having a trial in the civil court with all of Malaysia involved thus made the
     issue a *national* matter and not simply a Muslim one.

48   The Islamic Affairs Department operates as a kind of morality police, with
     fifty enforcement officers around the country empowered to arrest Muslims
     for transgressions against religion, including adulterers, homosexuals, trans-
     vestites, and transsexuals. Usually in response to tip-offs, officers arrest sev-
     eral gays each month, generally for being in a room together. Last year 111 men
     were arrested in Kuala Lumpur for "attempting to commit homosexual acts."
     Even when men are fully clothed together in a room, if there is a tip-off, they
     are arrested for attempting to commit homosexual acts. According to Abdul
     Kadir Che Kob, head of education and research at the Islamic Affairs Depart-
     ment, they have never arrested a lesbian: "There are no complaints, maybe
     because it is difficult to gauge who is a lesbian." See Mageswary Rama-
     krishnan, "Homosexuality Is a Crime Worse Than Murder: Interview with
     Malaysia's Morality Police," *Time (Asia),* 26 September 2000, ⟨http://www.
     time.com/time/asia/features/interviews/2000/09/26/int.malay.gay2.html⟩
     (5 March 2001).

49   "Chronology of the Case against Anwar Ibrahim," *Human Rights Watch* (No-
     vember 1998), ⟨http://hrw.org/hrw/campaigns/malaysia98/anwar-chronology.
     htm⟩ (5 March 2001).

50   The ISA is a legacy from the former British colony of Malaya. It was intro-
     duced to combat the communist insurgency in the late 1940s and 1950s and
     has survived to become one of the most effective weapons for silencing politi-
     cal dissent by the ruling government of the time. It exists anachronistically in
     relation to Malaysia's pretensions to be a modern, tolerant, and democratic
     society. Chandra Muzaffar, "Anwar and ISA Arrests," ⟨http://www2.jaring.
     my/just/ISA.html⟩ (5 March 2001); and Farish A. Noor, "Two Hundred
     Years of Colonialism Is Enough Time to Free Ourselves from Oppressive
     Colonial Laws," ⟨http://www2.jaring.my/just/ColonialismF.html⟩ (5 March
     2001), and Richard S. Ehrlich, "Malay Prisoners and the Internal Security
     Act," ⟨http://www.zolatimes.com/v2.34/malaypr.html⟩ (5 March 2001).

51   "More than 1000 in anti-Mahathir Protest in Malaysian Capital," *Berita
     Reformasi.*

52   "Chronology of the Case against Anwar Ibrahim."

53   Jonathan Fryer, "Police Remove Anwar Supporter Tien Chua," *BBC News,* 8 August 2000, ⟨http://news.bbc.co.uk/hi/english/world/asia-pacific/newsid _871000/871175.stm⟩ (5 March 2001).

54   *Free Anwar* Web site, ⟨http://www.freeanwar.com⟩ (5 March 2001). See also *Malaysiakini,* an alternative online newspaper. The site contains eighteen pages of readers' opinions on the Anwar verdict: ⟨http://www.malaysiakini. com/⟩ (5 March 2001).

55   Len Holmes and Margaret Grieco, "The Power of Transparency: The Internet, E-mail, and the Malaysian Political Crisis," ⟨http://legacy.unl.ac.uk/relational/ papers/malaysia.htm⟩ (15 July 2000).

56   Cited in ibid.

57   The official Web site of the International Free Anwar Campaign is at ⟨http: //www.freeanwar.com⟩ (18 July 2002). For a listing of fifty Web sites on Anwar Ibrahim, see *Official Anwar Ibrahim's Online Resources* Web site, ⟨http://www. geocities.com/CapitolHill/Senate/8722/sambung.htm⟩ (18 July 2002). Some of the more prominent sites are *Justice for Anwar—Reformasi,* ⟨http://members. tripod.com/~Anwarite/⟩ (5 March 2001), which contains a collection of An-war's speeches; and *Anwar Online,* ⟨http://members.tripod.com/~Anwar_Ibra-him/⟩ (5 March 2001), which includes a "news and views" archive and Anwar's letters written from prison.

58   Mageswary Ramakrishnan, "During the Anwar Trial It Was Easy to Get Lucky: Interview with Ashley Lee," *Time,* 26 September 2000, 1, ⟨http://www. time.com/time/asia/features/interviews/2000/09/26/int.malay.gayl.html⟩ (5 March 2001).

59   Yet it is important to note that fears of a crackdown against homosexuality in Malaysia following the Anwar trial are not entirely unfounded. Supporters of Malaysian Prime Minister Mahathir Mohamad have launched a movement against homosexuality—the People's Voluntary Anti-homosexual Movement (Pasrah)—calling homosexuality "a new threat to the country." Chairman of Pasrah Ibrahim Ali is also a senior member of Mahathir's ruling UMNO Party. See "Combating the Gay 'Threat,'" *Straits Times,* 22 October 1998, ⟨http: //www.ilga.org/Information/legal_survey/asia_pacific/supporting%20files/ group_against_homosexuality_form.htm#⟩ (5 March 2001). Pasrah was of-ficially established on 21 October 1998.

60   Foucault writes that the nineteenth-century categorization of sexuality and in particular the labeling of homosexuality as "perversity" also made possible the formation of a "reverse discourse," with homosexuality as a "point of resistance": "homosexuality began to speak in its own behalf, to demand that its legitimacy or 'naturality' be acknowledged, often in the same vocabulary, using the same categories by which it was medically disqualified" (178). It is interesting that Mahathir's plans for Cyberjaya and the possible censorship or

surveillance of LGQ material on the Internet also cannot be contained by that very same medium.

61 In *The Virtual Community* (London: Minerva, 1994), Howard Reingold describes virtual communities as "social aggregations that emerge from the Net when enough people carry on . . . public discussions long enough, with sufficient human feeling, to form webs of personal relationships in cyberspace" (5). On regionalism and globalization, see Ching, 237. Ching argues that regionalism is not an alternative to globalization but forms an integral part of the globalist project.

62 Ching, 244.

AUDREY YUE

Paging "New Asia":

Sambal Is a Feedback Loop,

Coconut Is a Code,

Rice Is a System

The recent emergence of Singapore as a regional New Asian center reflects how cultural policy functions as a technology of sexuality associated with institutions, practices, and discourses, as management, economics, and citizenship. "Singapore-as-New Asia" designs the nation as a cultural template for the region and directs a contradictory practice of consumption that is both Oriental and Occidental, global and particular, urban and exotic.[1] "Singapore 21" promotes the ideal Singapore society by emphasizing the preservation of family values and active participation as citizens.[2] "Dot.com the nation" restructures the media by adhering to the "nation-building role and fostering community values."[3] The congruence of government, economy, and population has produced culture as a field of "social management," as a system of training competence in order to situate and alter the forms of conduct of a citizenry.[4]

At the heart of these postcolonial, postmodern, and developmental capitalist processes of modernization is the force of "New Asia" as a homogenizing strategy of regionality.[5] The past few decades of globalization in late capitalism have witnessed the realignment of people, capital, and markets through different and disjunctive modes of deterritorialization and reterritorialization, from supra, transnational, national, intra, and virtual to the local and the everyday. Spivak's provocative metaphor of "globe-girdling" suggestively points to the global effects of regionality as a hegemonic process of unequal development to create a global presence of the information-rich at the expense of the technologically poor.[6] By emphasizing economic success through the neo-Orientalizing ideology of shared Asian values, the discursive construct of New Asia highlights the rise of a new hegemonic Asian class that exposes the geographical materialist politics of representation.

Singapore's top-down policy codes engineer techniques and produce practices that interconnect with a regional New Asian sexuality. The regulation of the Internet and the endorsement of new media and their consumption reveal how Singapore's emergent queer culture has become an ambiguous site for the exercise of power.[7] This culture problematizes the governmentality of the social by actively participating in the operative procedures of such technologies and turning them into different modalities of dissent. With modern images promoting positive role models, resistant politics highlighting an emergent minority movement, and transnationally queer identities mediating new forms of connectivity, this presence has made Singapore's subterranean gay and lesbian communities visible through and in spite of the ambiguous relationship surrounding globalization and the local policing of queer.

This essay argues that Singapore's transnational Queer'n'Asian modernity celebrates cultural citizenship through the consumption of shared Asian values and constitutes a politics that has witnessed the rise of a New Asian class. It demonstrates the formation of this culture by examining the different consumption practices of new media technologies by lesbian communities in Singapore, its diaspora, and its cyberspace. I show how the constitution of a regional sexuality, processed and navigated through cybernetic rice as a new system for representing New Asia, reveals the hegemony of New Asia as a class that is used to sustain a normalizing vision of modernity as a narrative of progress. "Paging 'New Asia' " highlights technology as a mark of the modern New Asian queer present, as a device that attends to the exigency of how a community makes itself present by calling out the stakes and challenges involved in the creation of new identities and belongings.

Introducing the Cybernetic Force of New Asia

The hegemony of New Asia is a force similar to Gibsonian cyberspace as a form of "consensual hallucination."[8] Not coincidentally, Chua also states that the Gramscian form of consensus is the key marker of the success of the

Singapore–New Asian ideology.[9] Others have accounted for Singapore-as-New Asia through its political economy and economic consumption;[10] I argue here that another way to decode the impact of such a force is through cybernetics and its system of coding and reproducing information.

Information, as a form of Virilian speed-space, after all, underpins the rapid progress of Singapore's new global informational capitalist economy. The rise of new media has witnessed the revaluation of information as data to image, exchange, and capital.[11] The theory of cybernetics helps to explain how New Asian regional sexuality is characterized by a consumption of Asian values organized in a system that restructures information as New Asian capital. Norbert Wiener's idea of cybernetics as a technoscience that explains both organic and machinic processes as parts of information systems has resulted in many developments in Western culture that have contributed to our current cyborg age.[12] By emphasizing the theorization of cybernetics as a mechanism for the organization of information based on the structure and the representation of information,[13] the trajectory I propose in this essay is to move away from the technologically deterministic or euphorically utopic tropes that have been deployed in the theorization of the cyborg.

The *cyber* of cybernetics is derived from the Greek word *kubernétés,* meaning "steersman," or *kubernan,* for "control" or "navigate." As a study of the systems for controlling the travel of information, the fundamental feature of cybernetics is its computational capacity for feedback or recursion. Feedback is the return of part of an output (receiver) to an input (sender). I examine feedback as a device that interrogates the regime of the input by its ability to alter the characteristics of an input.[14] A linear or digital system organizes information hierarchically from the top down; a nonlinear or analog system self-organizes information chaotically from the bottom up.[15] My objective is to show how "cybernetic rice" functions as both a linear and a nonlinear system that codes a New Asian regional sexuality. Exposing the structure of cybernetic rice will produce a critique of the modernization of Singapore–New Asian lesbian cultures, and allows for the emergence of a Queer ('n') Asian modernity that can account for class. The following case study attends to such a task in two stages. First, I demonstrate the rise of a transnational and diasporic Singapore–New Asian lesbian class using rice as a network for making intelligible the discourse of SAMBAL, an acronym for Singapore and Malaysian Bisexual and

Lesbian Network.[16] I examine SAMBAL as a diasporic film, *Sambal Belacan in San Francisco* (Madeleine Lim, 1997) and as an electronic mailing list (e-SAMBAL) to reveal *sambal* as a feedback loop. My aim here is to show how information travels and which tactics of recursion relate to which specific classes of lesbian cultures. I contrast this by concluding with the use of paging technologies by lesbians in Singapore to argue that the consumption of different technologies produces different identities that expose the politics of class. This politics delineates a regional New Asian sexuality steered through the cybernetic emergence of "rice" and functions as a cultural formation of transnational Queer ('n') Asian modernity. Such a formation expresses its progress by calling to task the effect of its own hegemonic force.

Sambal Is a Feedback Loop, Coconut Is a Code, Rice Is a System

Sambal belacan is very hot, very aromatic and it's shrimp paste and fresh pounded chili, red chili, and how we eat it is with squeezed lime, like you mix it with the rice and you eat it in the rice and in the food . . . *lemak* is a dish that you always eat with *sambal belacan*. . . . *Sambal belacan* is pounded chili that's not completely smooth.

The above voice-over begins the documentary *Sambal Belacan in San Francisco* (*SBSF*), an award-winning short film by American-based Singaporean lesbian filmmaker Madeleine Lim.[17] The film documents the lives of some members of SAMBAL, a support group for Singapore and Malaysian bisexuals and lesbians in San Francisco. Since 1995, SAMBAL has also been archived as a closed electronic mailing list. E-SAMBAL is the first electronic mailing list for lesbians from the Singapore-Malaysian region. At its peak, a two hundred-odd strong membership spanned Singapore and Malaysia, as well as the Singapore and Malaysian diaspora in Australia, the United States, Canada, and Japan. Like most electronic mailing lists organized around shared interests, e-SAMBAL recalls Rheingold's conceptualization of a virtual community through its primary function as a forum for community announcements, communication among its members, and diasporic outreach.[18]

Sambal belacan is a signifier for the affirmative project of Singapore lesbians in San Francisco, expressing a particular Singaporean lesbian diasporic politics through a self-conscious practice of how food can be made to code and recode. As a playful reclamation of Asian sexual stereotyping, its material signification speaks through the gendered and sexualized discourses of the relationship between migrant Asian women and food. Enough has been written on this topic and there is no need to repeat it here. Suffice it to say that the stereotypes of migrant Asian women as sexualized exotic objects and piece workers expose consumption as a contradictory practice discordant with the politics of diasporic Asian lesbian sexuality.

The film uses food (and the practices of eating and cooking) as a site for (diasporic) cultural maintenance and negotiation. In addition to the visibility project of political organizing (e.g., Pride marches, conferences, workshops), one of SAMBAL's most regular activities is the monthly potluck. *SBSF* chronicles the ritual of this practice through the labor of food preparation that culminates in a reenacted potluck sequence. Here, a voiceover reminds us of the limitations of Anderson's imagined community when food functions not just as a site of comfort, but also as a moment of contestation of disjunctive heritages, traditions, and sexual identities.[19] As a source of "home" comfort, the potluck serves its imagined community function when SAMBAL, as a group and as an acronym, expresses a shared identity organized through food as a mobile (monthly) site of belonging. In this instance, sambal belacan materializes as a sexy project of collective Singapore-Malaysian-diasporic-lesbian identity: hot, aromatic, pounded, raw, mixed.

Such practices surrounding food and eating also expose the material force of its construction. As a form of food, sambal belacan is the type of side dish that, like pickles and condiments, on its own is pungently and tastefully inedible, or so my refined taste buds constantly remind me. Rather, consuming sambal belacan requires a form of cultural capital that is acquired through the privilege of shared knowledge, in this instance, a particular discourse about the history of its heritage, the function of its materiality, and the practice of its culture. Its (culinary) potency lies in its preparation, its mix, and its mode of presentation. The film's gastronomic advice, and correctly so, is that in its orthodoxy, sambal belacan works only to the extent that it is mixed in with coconut (lemak) and served with rice.

Coconuts and rice are essentially Asian and diasporic Asian. The cultural history of coconuts exposes the quintessential forbidden delights of the stereotyped sexualized image of Asia consumed in the West, with idyllic beaches, tropical sun, and mail-order Asian brides. Coconuts, like bananas, are also codes for Westernized Asians, who are "brown on the outside and white on the inside." Enough has also been written about such signifiers as the coconut as an ideological relay for the fetish and disavowal of Asian femininity, sexuality, and ethnicity through the technology of its image and its racial science. *SBSF* recuperates this image, not by inversion or turning it inside out, but by mediating it through the Asian diaspora. Where else but in a Westernized Asia can the coconut make sense, in what Butler has eloquently termed the historicity of its force of oppression, as the postcolonial genealogy of racism (and consequently self-internalized racism)?[20] While *SBSF* narrativizes the racism experienced by its cast in San Francisco, from immigration policies to isolation in the mainstream gay and lesbian community, what the film recodes is an identity that can be expressed only through the historicity of the lemak. By making sambal belacan intelligible (or, indeed, edible), the coconut functions as a (renewed) code for a sexual politics of displacement mediated through the technology of food. The material force of the coconut produces SAMBAL as an emergent and diasporic possibility in its construction and representation by destroying its abject status through its constitution as a platform for engaging with the specificity of a diasporic New Asian lesbian politics.

Such a politics engages the West (in the film, San Francisco), the diaspora (in the film, overseas Singaporean lesbians), and the homeland (in the film, Singapore) in a feedback loop that produces and organizes information as New Asian capital. New Asian capital refers to the new economic wealth evident in the developmental rise of Asia in the past two decades. It is also characterized by cultural capital, whereby a taste around New Asia becomes a form of classification and a class emerges through the acquisition of such shared values.[21] Let's take the central motif of the film, for example, to examine how diasporic New Asian lesbian identity is constituted through a discourse of value.[22] The narrative reveals the homesickness experienced by the three lesbians through interviews and newsreel footage that recount the memories of and desires for their families in

Mobile Cultures

Singapore. The foregrounding of the family discourse, made (more) "objective" by the documentary talking-head device, exposes how the discourse of shared (family) values underpinning the ideology of New Asia functions as a hegemonic force. For the three interlocutors, diasporic Singapore lesbian identity is narrated through the irreducibility of cultural difference; the values of a San Franciscan lesbian sexuality are at odds with the values of being a good Singaporean daughter. Shared Asian family values become the neo-Orientalist motif that makes explicit the film's narrative of displacement: homesickness and daily reminders of outsiderness are constructed through the yearning for family and their homes in Singapore.

Such an instance highlights the discourse of shared Asian values as an "exchange of sacrifice and gain"[23] to reconcile the values accorded a good Singaporean daughter and a diasporic Singaporean lesbian. As suggested earlier, at the core of cybernetics is the processing of information through the ability of the machine to use the results of its own performance as self-regulating information.[24] Information denotes whatever can be coded for transmission through a channel that connects a source (homeland) with a receiver (diaspora), regardless of semantic content. Here, information does not reveal a retrieval of data or facts; rather, information is transformed to an exchange value connoted by New Asian capital. As the "negative" (psychical) condition of homesickness and displacement can arguably be "lessened" or leveled out through a positive feedback, a positive feedback can be said to be represented by an exchange of New Asian consciousness, evident in the film's thematic preoccupation with the familial discourse. This suggests that diasporic New Asian sexual identity requires the acquisition of cultural citizenship through the consumption of shared family values. Such a quest recalls the self-regulating technology of the Singapore 21 cultural policy, where citizenship is patterned out of an active process of consumption. Clearly, policy lends itself as an agent for sexuality in a cybernetic system that institutionalizes the force of New Asian consciousness in a hierarchy from top/homeland/source to bottom/diaspora/receiver. A diasporic New Asian regional sexuality is thus characterized by a belonging to Singapore-as-New Asia, and by extension, a form of New Asian cultural citizenship consisting of ascribing a value equivalence to New Asian consciousness compatible to the ideology of shared Asian (and family) values. I argue that cybernetic rice becomes the system by which the acquisition of citizenship is enabled.

Cybernetic Rice

Rice highlights a unique relationship among food, trade, and technology. A luxury crop that is preferred in Asia as superior to other grains, the technological innovations evident in the cultivation of rice have revolutionized and modernized the region.[25] Its status as a primary commodity has shaped links between countries and the development of the land, in particular, within Asia and across the world.[26] Its cultivation as staple and surplus has produced rice cultures that are characterized by "sculpturation" networks and practices.[27] From the engineering of terraces, the conduits of irrigation canals, and the changes in social structures, rice has refashioned the landscape to engender an intricate connection among technological systems, everyday life, and global trade. This connectivity resonates with how, as a metaphor, rice can be made to speak to the current contradictory forces of informational capitalism, identity production, and cultural governance.[28]

Cybernetic rice is both a linear and a nonlinear system of representing information organized around "rice" as a signifier for diasporic New Asian gay and lesbian sexuality. As a linear system of informational flows from top/homeland to bottom/diaspora, cybernetic rice reinforces the hegemony of New Asia by commodifying Asian values as New Asian capital. As a nonlinear system of informational flows from bottom/diaspora to top/homeland, cybernetic rice decenters the hegemony of New Asia by appropriating New Asian capital as New Asian body politic. This politic exposes a transnational New Asian sexuality as a diasporic class.

In the film, the serving of rice with sambal and coconut reveals the central function connoted by "rice" as a structure that makes sambal possible as a recursive or feedback device. Like the coconut, rice has functioned as a stereotype for Asians in the West. As a geographical material culture, it is both a staple food and a mode of production constituted in a regional network facilitating the exchange of ideas, food, and resources. Soja recently suggested that one way to map the governmentality of regionality is by understanding how urban agglomeration functions. He uses the ancient Greek word, *synekism,* to refer to regional settlements under a center, and to imply a form of "urban-based governmentality . . . as well as . . . an interconnected network of settlements . . . interacting within defined and defining *regional* boundaries."[29] The film reveals such a system of governmentality when belonging as (Singapore) citizens requires the taking up of New

Asian values as a sexual identity organized around regionality. Recalling the Latin root of the term, *regere*, meaning "to rule," the incorporation of shared Asian values in *SBSF* shows the centering of regionality by positioning a discursive New Asia as a regional center. As a signifier for an economy that organizes the defining social order of Asians, the hegemony of rice reveals cybernetic rice as a linear system of rendering meaning from top/ homeland to bottom/diaspora.

However, in recent years, "rice" has also been reappropriated by Asians in the West and has become an affective force for new diasporic formations. Consider, for example, the recent phenomenon of the rice boy in the West. A rice boy, or a rice rocket, is an Asian identified by his car and what he does to it. The rice boy usually drives a Japanese car, but unlike a normal performance enthusiast, he is more concerned with the image of speed than performance.[30] The rise of the rice boy is connected to the rise of the New Rich in Asia, where sustained economic growth in the past two decades has translated into a rapid expansion of consumerism as part of daily life. Chua writes that the body has emerged as the site for consumerism with "adornment as its primary modality."[31] The image of speed becomes a form of New Asian capital that expresses a resistance to the body politic of (emasculated) Asian masculinity in the West. Here, the desire for Occidental muscularity is displaced by the display of materialism: Western consumption (purchase of cars)/Eastern practice (adornment of cars), globally familiar (branding)/regionally specific (customizing), modern (urban street savvyness, road-wise)/tradition (amateur "novice" car enthusiast).

This transformed body politic is also evident in the gay and lesbian communities. The past decade has witnessed a politics of (diasporic) visibility organized around "rice." From rice pride marches and queer rice workshops to award-winning Asian gay and lesbian Web portals, "rice" has now come to connote what the online *Race Magazine* gay editors have promoted as "a total lifestyle . . . for gay Asian men by gay Asian men."[32] Its Web site address, www.riceasia.com, encapsulates the diasporic Asian queering of "rice" mediated by the displacement of people, technology, and markets. Factors such as the global consumption of difference, the role of new media in enabling new modes of Asian presence and connections, and the mainstreaming of Asian popular culture have led to the emergence of a New Asian sexual identity tied to New Asian capital. This is also evidenced by the shift from the postcolonial "rice/potato queen" sexual identity to a "sticky rice" sexual model, or what I have written of elsewhere as a sexual identity represented by the desire for Asians by other Asians in the West.[33] Such an identity politic celebrates a regional sexuality made possible by the New Asian body politic: urban, cosmopolitan, fashionable, newly exotic, adorned with the correctly acceptable Western lingo, attire, and style. As a nonlinear system, cybernetic rice highlights the (sexual) appropriation of New Asian capital as New Asian body politic. Such a politic decenters the hegemony of New Asia by reordering it through its diasporic settlements and produces a regional sexuality characterized by the emergence of a class. The following discussion of e-SAMBAL demonstrates this.[34]

E-SAMBAL: New Regionality, Sexuality, Class

E-SAMBAL's construction of its membership and the rice-accumulation strategies practiced by its members problematize the forces of regionality and globalization and support the structure of cybernetic rice as a linear and nonlinear system. These two systems underpin the emergence of a New Asian sexuality through a New Asian body politic that produces class. This politics mediates and mediatizes a regional material culture and destroys the ontological claims of the West, the homeland, and its diaspora by exposing their hegemonic constitutions.

E-SAMBAL began in 1995 as a nonautomated and private list called Singalaysian. In May 1996, a survey on membership and subscription was posted to the list, intended as an appraisal to consider the possibility of automating it due to a rapidly growing membership.[35] This survey constructed membership regionally, with two initial assumed policies. First, it is a Malaysian/Singaporean-only space. Second, it is a women-only space. Regional specificity is maintained through a strict vetting system whereby, "other than [the] initial contact person, the list mistress or regional contact cross-examines, subtly or otherwise, on behalf of SAMBAL."[36] Regionality is problematized in one post when an Australian lesbian who has lived in Malaysia for the past twenty years decided to subscribe to the list.[37] She was vetted out because she is Australian. Here, the status of being Australian highlights race as a form of classification according to not just one's country of birth, but one's line of descent. Rather than the transcendence of racial boundaries promulgated by new media enthusiasts, this instance highlights the significance of race as a necessary determinant for the reinscription or reterritorialization of a New Asian regional difference. The cybernetic force of rice highlights the discourse of New Asian regionality as a discourse of race by structuring it as a form of self-regulating governance, where the right to belong requires a claim to an Asian genealogy. Australia is clearly not (in) Asia. It also supports Soja's synekism whereby sambal emerges as a transnational Asian lesbian formation through a series of hierarchical networks capable of generating growth and order from within Asia as a "defined territorial domain" (Asia, not Australia).[38] The rejection of the Australian lesbian living in Malaysia supports an essentialist, neo-Orientalist construction of a Malaysia/Singapore spatiality through the force of its diaspora. Such a spatiality organizes a practice that is ambivalent.

On the one hand, it produces a citizenship that extends Ong's concept of flexible citizenship[39] because cybernetic rice, as the hegemonic ideology of New Asia, governs in a linear system that produces feedback hierarchically. In other words, citizenship, or belonging, is not flexible; membership is fixed by race. Rather, citizenship is fixed through an active process of Asian-identified rice reclamation or accumulation, to use David Harvey's term.[40] This reclamation is evident in the list, for example, through the postcolonial use of the Singaporean/Malaysian hybrid creolized language, Singlish. New Asian capital as information value recodes the generic status of a newbie through differential Singlish proficiencies. Here, Singlish is not a performative effect of cultural hybridity; rather, Singlish has shifted from its "unofficial" status as a spoken vernacular to a formal genre of writing stylized as a self-conscious technique of pedagogical accumulation. Its literalization foregrounds English language as a necessary device for making intelligible the parodic play with other languages (Mandarin and Malay) and other dialects (Hokkien, Teochew, Cantonese, Hakka).

Another example includes the neo-Confucian discourse of what has been termed "the responsible thing." In a series of introductory postings, members (who have recently returned from overseas) introduced themselves using the discourse of the "responsible thing" as a specific New Asian lesbian argot. "Coming back to do the responsible thing," for Evette, describes an accountability that "is to set priority of coming home first . . . think of myself later."[41] Clearly, "being true to myself" is discordant with the "Confucian" value of "filial piety." Again, the reconciliation of sexuality to the communitarian discourse of "coming home" supports the agenda of Singapore 21. These self-conscious and self-regulating practices highlight cybernetic rice as a linear structure for the accumulation and consequent acquisition of cultural citizenship in the diasporic Singapore lesbian cyberspace.

On the other hand, cybernetic rice, as a nonlinear system, also reorders informational flows from bottom/diaspora to top/homeland, producing feedback that renders meanings in a haphazard, chaotic, and subterranean manner. In such a system, the informational value of rice (New Asian capital), as the signifier for diasporic New Asian gay and lesbian sexuality, decenters the hegemonic positionality encoded by the regional center, Singapore-as-New Asia, and repositions, through feedback (New Asian body politic), the new sambal space of Singapore/Malaysia. Singaporean and Malaysian membership is reconstituted as newly Asian through the diaspora. As a loop, sambal emerges as a queer and Asian formation that is characterized by dispersion and exposes the ontologies of the homeland, the host land, and its diaspora.

Such a formation exposes the hegemony of the Occidental global queering project as well as the production of a local resistance. Take the naming strategies used in the survey as a cultural template. In question 1, when asked what "type of people [members] want/don't want on SAMBAL," 75 percent of the respondents answered that they wanted "lesbian-identified women." About 50 percent and 60 percent, respectively, responded by stating that they "don't want but (can negotiate on case-by-case)" "bisexual-identified women, women involved in hetero relationship [and] gay-positive straight women." And 80 percent stated that they did not want "people exploring" on the list, but "newborn" ("just realized she is lesbian/bisexual") lesbians and bisexuals are welcomed.[42] These naming devices ("lesbian," "bisexual," "gay positive," "newborn," etc.), as instances of the globalization of queer, are at the same time destabilized by a neo-Orientalizing strategy of retrieving the histories of Asian sexualities so that other identities such as *wasawa*, *hubungan sejenis*, or "slang" are equally valid.[43] The following post encapsulates the contradiction aptly:

Lesbian, Chinese, Slang
Sociology, Postmodernist, Foucault, Goffman
Customer Service, Insurance
Popular Culture, movies, books, music, food, Shopping malls.[44]

It is interesting to note that "slang" is the only term that fits the status of an argot. Slang is the name of the women's subgroup in People Like Us.[45] Its local specificity foregrounds its status as a New Asian lesbian identity constituted in its function as a suture that coheres the seemingly disparate identity claims connoted by the rest of the terms. The metaphorical, transitory, and unofficial status accorded to slang vocabularizes the ephemerality of a culture mediated by information and mediatized by the contradictory logics of Occidentalism, neo-Orientalism, global consumption, racial nativism, and developmental capitalism.

As both a linear and nonlinear system for organizing the specificity of a diasporic New Asian lesbian sexuality, cybernetic rice redefines the essential Asian discourse of *guanxi* (connections) by transforming its traditional familial and kinship discourse of connections to an artifice driven by a new informational structure of representing the regionality of Asia. Rather than a network enabled by families and friends, this structure is constructed by mobilizing diasporic displacement through the capital and body politic of a New Asian consciousness. Such a redefinition reconstructs New Asia as a self-conscious diasporic interface navigating the economic, social, and political specificities underpinning the material force of its capitalist development.[46] It calls to task the New Asian lesbian diaspora as a specific class.

In a recent survey on the status of privilege in Singapore, Chua and Tan note that the past three decades of economic growth have led to the emergence of a majority "new rich" middle-class culture.[47] Middle-class households enjoy monthly incomes between $3,000 and $10,000. Comfortable middle-class households have monthly incomes of $4,000 or more; tertiary-educated professionals and entrepreneurs predominate in this group. Such a classification resonates with e-SAMBAL's membership comprising mostly Western-educated, overseas-returned, tertiary-trained professionals. This is evident when e-SAMBAL was targeted in 1999 for market research by a global queer publishing house researching the possibility of providing an Asian queer Web portal based on lifestyle and a monthly income of more than $5,000.[48] Characteristics listed under lifestyle included frequency and place of overseas vacations, hobbies and weekend pursuits such as water sports, bike rides, car rallies across Malaysia, and golf. Lifestyle is expressed in the terrain of everyday material consumption where vacations, ownership of vehicles, and "luxury sports" are "positional goods" that determine and stratify class.[49] These practices reveal e-SAMBAL as a "new rich" transnational and cosmopolitan diasporic lesbian class.

This classification became evident when I began actively researching the use of paging technologies by lesbians in Singapore in September 2000. I used my guanxi connection to engage a childhood friend, who now owns and manages what is unofficially known as the lesbian alfresco pub in Singapore, as a local informant, and to help circulate in her pub an anonymous questionnaire about local lesbian beeper practices.[50] The questionnaire included personal data such as income, profession, language spoken, and educational level. The results revealed a monthly income of less than $5,000 and a predominantly Mandarin- or dialect-speaking blue-collar 20–35 age-group class. According to the Singapore Department of Statistics' table distribution of monthly household income in 1990, $5,000 is the mark that demarcates working and lower middle class from the "new rich."[51] Chua and Eng rightly argue that the working-class culture in Singapore expresses itself differently from the working-class youth subcultures in Britain, where local resistance is expressed through a politics of fashion and dress.[52] They state that a taste for designer fashion in Singapore is coded by the working class as a sign of upward mobility. My pager research reveals that working-class lesbians also aspire to such desires. All inscribe a "brand" consciousness. Those in the lower-range income group adorn themselves with Charles Jourdan, Adidas, and Dr Marten's shoes and, "if they can afford it," will wear "Gucci, Louis Vuitton and Valentino."[53]

Beeper culture in Singapore expresses the politics of class. As an accessory, they adorn the body and constitute the class of the user. The use of colors, for example, helps to single out the identity of the user in a sea of beeper ubiquity. Gold is the color of the new rich.[54]

In mainstream culture, beepers, like telephones, are a form of communication. Beepers, unlike the globality of the Internet, are more localized, more personalized, and site-specific. By *literalizing* New Asian capital as New Asian body politic, working-class lesbian culture mobilizes beepers to mediate the production of a locality in their reconstitution of a neighborhood.[55] In my membership participation in e-SAMBAL since 1995, daily and weekly posts have ranged from activist announcements (e.g., workshops, meetings, socials, fundraisers) and conference discussions (e.g., pride, safe sex, health), to requests (e.g., market surveys, classifieds). Here, class expression is tied to a global queer politics of visibility. By *appropriating* New

Asian capital as New Asian body politic, e-SAMBAL's tactics support Appadurai's disjunctive global "scapes" that are formed as a result of cultural flows.[56] Mobile cultures are produced, one transnationally, the other subculturally.

Feedback: Paging Sambal

Like many of my childhood dyke buddies who have left Singapore for the United States, I migrated to Australia in 1987, in the wake of a post-Independence generation of women who have grown up in a culture that has experienced the region's most rapid development as well as the impact of the country's infamous social engineering policies, ranging from the Great Marriage Debate to the state control of motherhood and reproduction. The policy emphasis on education and language, the state directive that required proficiency in both Mandarin and English in order to gain admission to the local university, marked the pivotal point in our young 20–30-something adult lives. Many of us failed miserably at our "Chinese as a Second Language" examinations. We were the products of a colonial government-aided school education system that valorized the English language. Mandarin, the Chinese language, and local dialects were the markers of "the others." In short, those who failed left, and those who passed stayed.

I returned routinely during my many summer breaks through the years, temporally and permanently out of sync with my friends in the United States. I cruised the streets with those who passed. One summer in the early 1990s I met L. She was carrying a pager. On the screen was a code. This was not just any ordinary pager, ordinary pagers being de rigeur accessories in a country that has the highest penetration rate of pagers (one in three owns a pager); this was a pager constantly beeping a nonsensical series of numeric mobile codes, 88 for a bar, 5281 for a restaurant, even 6634 for a hotel room. It took me a while to realize that these codes were charged in a chain of associations, not as revolutionary as December 2000 in the Philippines where anti-Joseph Estrada (SMS) messages were sent among some of the nation's 4.5 million mobile phone users, but equally as monumental. Every beep became a secret code for a place or an event: 10.2 On the way; 10.7. Arrived at destination; 533-0. Where are you?; 3347-0 Are you free tonight? Every beep was an introduction to a subterranean world where toms (butch) hung Motorolas and traded Prada and Gucci with their GFS, *femmes with colored beepers in handbags, on call. I learned to traffic in the lingo, like a recursive Morse code, as we shape-shifted from pubs to discos and cafés.*

Meantime, I became a Sambalite and SAMBAL *became my feedback loop, paging New Asia like a technology out of sync.*

Notes

1   Singapore-as-New Asia is a cultural tourist state discourse that endorses the blending of heritage with modern cosmopolitanism. It constructs New Asia "at the crossroads of the East and the West," with "a single national identity, so much so that you are likely to hear someone regard himself as a Singaporean first before a Chinese, Malay, Indian or Eurasian." See Singapore Tourism Board, *Official Guide: Singapore New Asia* (May 2000), 2–16. Its Web site highlights its regional agenda with its non-Singapore registered domain. See Singapore Tourism Board, *New Asia–Singapore: The Official Website for Tourist Information on Singapore,* 1 July 1998, ⟨http://www.newasia-singapore. com⟩ (30 May 2001).

2   Singapore 21, *Singapore 21 Website,* 1 January 2000, ⟨http://www.singapore 21.org.sg⟩ (30 May 2001).

3   Lee Hock Suan, "Digital Television: Managing the Transition," keynote address presented at BroadcastAsia 2000, Singapore Expo, Singapore, 5 June 2000, in Singapore Government Media Release, *Singapore Government Website,* 28 April 2000, ⟨http://app.internet.gov.sg/data/sprinter/pr/archives/ 2000060503.htm⟩ (18 July 2002).

4   Tony Bennett, "Putting Policy into Cultural Studies," in *Cultural Studies,* ed. Lawrence Grossberg, Cary Nelson, and Paula A. Treichler (London: Routledge, 1992), 27. On the governance of culture, see Michel Foucault, "Governmentality," in *The Foucault Effect: Studies in Governmentality,* ed. Graham Burchell, Colin Gordon, and Peter Miller (Hemel Hempstead, U.K.: Harvester Wheatsheaf, 1991), 87–104. Ian Hunter has also seminally written on education as a site for managing culture. See "Setting Limits to Culture," in *Nation, Culture, Text: Australian Cultural and Media Studies,* ed. Graeme Turner (London: Routledge, 1993), 140–63. In a similar vein, Joseph Tamney suggests that education functions as a key site for the ideological shaping of Singapore's culture. See *The Struggle over Singapore's Soul: Western Modernization and Asian Culture* (Berlin: W. de Gruyter, 1996).

5   On "Asia" as a discourse of regionality, see, for example, Rob Wilson and Wimal Dissanayake, eds., *Asia/Pacific as Space of Cultural Production* (Dur-

ham, NC: Duke University Press, 1995); Chen Kuan-Hsing, ed., *Trajectories: Inter-Asia Cultural Studies* (London: Routledge, 1998); Aihwa Ong and Donald Nonini, eds., *Ungrounded Empires: The Cultural Politics of Modern Chinese Transnationalism* (London: Routledge, 1997); Tu Wei-ming, ed., *Confucian Traditions in East Asian Modernity* (Cambridge, MA: Harvard University Press, 1996); Arif Dirlik, ed., *What Is a Rim?* (Boulder, CO: Westview Press, 1993); Ron Martin, ed., *Money and the Space Economy* (Chichester, England: Wiley, 1999); Kris Olds et al., eds., *Globalisation and the Asia Pacific: Contested Territories* (London: Routledge, 1999); Myong-gon Chu, *The New Asia in Global Perspective* (New York: St. Martin's Press, 2000).

6 Gayatri Spivak. "Cultural Talks in the Hot Peace: Revisiting the 'Global Village,'" in *Cosmopolitics: Thinking and Feeling beyond the Nation*, ed. Pheng Cheah and Bruce Robbins (Minneapolis: University of Minnesota Press, 1998), 342.

7 The Singapore Broadcasting Authority's regulation on Internet content ensures that community values, national security, and religious and racial harmony are maintained. Section 6(d) of its guidelines, "Contents which depict or propagate sexual perversions such as homosexuality, lesbianism, and paedophilia," highlights the extent of its censorship codes by positioning sexual identities as issues concerning the governance of "public morals." See Singapore Government, "Chapter 297," *Singapore Broadcasting Authority Act*, 15 March 1994 (Singapore: Statutes of the Republic of Singapore, 1994). On the Internet as a site for policing, see Terence Lee and David Birch, "Internet Regulation in Singapore: A Policy/ing Discourse," *Media International Australia*, no. 95 (May 2000): 147–69. On the legal discourse of homosexuality, see Laurence Wai-Teng Leong, "Singapore," in *Sociolegal Control of Homosexuality: A Multi-Nation Comparison*, ed. Donald J. West and Richard Green (New York: Plenum Press, 1997), 127–44. Singapore's recent IT push toward global informational capitalism has not only enabled the emergence of the city-state as the world's first digital economy; the consumption of high-tech communications technology has also led an emerging queer presence to emanate from Singapore cyberspace. Ng King Kang argues that the Internet has enabled the globalization of post-Stonewall gay-related information in the West to be available to many gay men in Singapore. See *The Rainbow Connection: The Internet and the Singapore Gay Community* (Singapore: Kang-CuBine, 1999), 5. Baden Offord's essay in this volume further supports the role of the Internet in paradoxically enabling an "unruly sexuality."

8 William Gibson, *Neuromancer* (London: Grafton, 1986), 56.

9 Chua Beng Huat, *Communitarian Ideology and Democracy in Singapore* (London: Routledge, 1997).

10 The list is too long to cite here. Some examples include ibid.; Chu; Michael

Leifer, *Singapore's Foreign Policy: Coping with Vulnerability* (London: Routledge, 2000); Shirley Geok-lin Lim, Larry E. Smith, and Wimal Dissanayake, eds., *Transnational Asia Pacific: Gender, Culture, and the Public Sphere* (Urbana: University of Illinois Press, 1999); Michael Pinches, *Culture and Privilege in Captialist Asia* (London: Routledge, 1999); Joel S. Kahn, ed., *Southeast Asian Identities: Culture and the Politics of Representation in Indonesia, Malaysia and Singapore* (New York: St. Martin's Press, 1998); Robert W. Hefner, ed., *Market Cultures: Society and Morality in New Asian Capitalisms* (Boulder, CO: Westview Press, 1998).

11 See Theodore Roszak, *The Cult of Information* (Berkeley: University of California Press, 1994); McKenzie Wark, "Infohype," in *Transit Lounge: Wake-Up Calls and Travellers' Tales from the Future,* ed. Ashley Crawford and Ray Edgar (Sydney: Craftman House, 1997), 144–47; Mitsuhiro Yoshimoto, "Real Virtuality," in *Global/Local: Cultural Production and the Transnational Imaginary,* ed. Rob Wilson and Wimal Dissanayake (Durham, NC: Duke University Press, 1996), 107–118.

12 David Jerison, L. M. Singer, and Daniel W. Stroock, eds., *The Legacy of Norbert Weiner: A Centennial Symposium in Honour of the 100th Anniversary of Norbert Weiner's Birth,* Massachusetts Institute of Technology, Cambridge, MA, 8–14 October 1994. For a history of the convergence between cybernetic science and post/modern cultural representation, see Donna Haraway, *Modest Witness@Second Millennium: Female Man Meets Onco Mouse* (New York: Routledge, 1997). For a brief but succinct development of the relationship between cybernetics and the cyborg, see Chris H. Gray, ed., *The Cyborg Handbook* (New York: Routledge, 1995).

13 Charles Francois, ed., *International Encyclopedia of Systems and Cybernetics* (Munchen, Germany: Saur, 1997). Lyotard's postmodern treatise on the death of metanarratives links the partiality of information to the crisis in science. He sees incomplete information as offering a chaotic and anarchic potential to disrupt the structure of knowledge. See Jean-Francois Lyotard, *The Postmodern Condition: A Report on Knowledge* (Minneapolis: University of Minnesota Press, 1984). Mark Poster suggests that cybernetics enables a new mode of communication, producing national identities that are multiple and fragmented. See *The Mode of Information* (Oxford: Polity Press, 1990).

14 This emphasis differs from Margaret Morse's suggestion that feedback produces interactivity by constituting a feeling of liveness, and Sherry Turkle's emphasis on how it engages the user as a second self. See Margaret Morse, *Virtualities: Television, Media Art and Cyberculture* (Bloomington: Indiana University Press, 1998); Sherry Turkle, *Life on the Screen: Identity in the Age of the Internet* (New York: Simon and Schuster, 1995).

15   Ron Eglash, "Cybernetics and American Youth Subculture," *Cultural Studies* 12, no. 3 (1998): 383–84.

16   For more information, contact SAMBAL at ⟨http://groups.yahoo.com/group/sambal⟩.

17   Madeleine Lim, dir., *Sambal Belacan in San Francisco*, Madbull Productions, United States (1997). I thank Madeleine Lim and Soo-lin Quek for enabling my access to the film.

18   Howard Rheingold, *The Virtual Community: Homesteading on the Electronic Frontier* (London: Minerva, 1994), 3.

19   Benedict Anderson, *Imagined Communities: Reflections on the Origins and Spread of Nationalism* (London: Verso, 1983), 15.

20   Judith Butler, *Bodies That Matter: On the Discursive Limits of "Sex"* (London: Routledge, 1993), 227.

21   On cultural capital, see Pierre Bourdieu, *Distinction: A Social Critique of the Judgment of Taste* (Cambridge, MA: Harvard University Press, 1984). Bourdieu differentiates cultural capital (knowledge acquired through upbringing and education) from economic capital (wealth). According to Bourdieu, the group "nouveau riche" possesses no cultural capital despite having the means to purchase the high artifacts of "culture." I argue here that the consumption practices of the New Rich in Asia produce a taste that distinguishes itself as the new hegemonic modern middle class. See Pinches; see also Chua Beng Huat, ed., *Consumption in Asia: Lifestyles and Identities* (New York: Routledge, 2000).

22   John Frow proposes the concept "the regime of value" to describe how values are discursively constructed. A regime of value refers to "a semiotic institution generating evaluating regularities under certain conditions of use, and in which particular empirical audiences or communities may be more or less fully imbricated." "Economies of Value," in *Cultural Studies and Cultural Value* (New York: Oxford University Press, 1995), 144.

23   Arjun Appadurai, "Introduction: Commodities and the Politics of Value," in *The Social Life of Things: Commodities in Cultural Perspective*, ed. Arjun Appadurai (New York: Cambridge University Press, 1986), 4.

24   Roszak, 9. See also Max H. Boisot, *Information Space: A Framework for Learning in Organizations, Institutions and Culture* (London: Routledge, 1995).

25   Francesca Bray has suggested that "rice economies" in Asia emerged through an alternative model of progress. Compared to Western models of progress that are characterized by "labor-substituting" mechanical development, Asian rice economies are characterized by "land substitution" and an orientation toward skills. *The Rice Economies* (Oxford: Basil Blackwell, 1986), 5, 115.

26   For a history of the rice trade, see A. J. H. Latham, *Rice: The Primary Commodity* (New York: Routledge, 1998).

27 For a brief examination of rice cultures, see Jacqueline M. Piper, *Rice in South-East Asia* (New York: Oxford University Press, 1993).

28 Although the metaphor of rice is not directly used in Singapore to describe the relationship between cyberculture and information technology, there has been a prominent increase in the circulation of rice metaphors in global queer cultures, on and off the Internet. This section shortly will show how this circulation has produced emergent "rice pride" queer movements in Asia and its diaspora.

29 Edward Soja, *Postmetropolis: Critical Studies of Cities and Regions* (Oxford: Blackwell, 2000), 13.

30 Rice Boy, *Rice Boy Page*, 17 September 2000, ⟨http://www.riceboy.com⟩ (27 September 2000).

31 Chua, *Consumption*, 14.

32 Rice Magazine, *Rice Magazine Online*, 1 July 2000, ⟨http://www.riceasia.com⟩ (27 September 2000).

33 Audrey Yue, "Asian-Australian Cinema, Asian-Australian Modernity," in *Diaspora: Negotiating Asian-Australia*, ed. Tseen Khoo et al. (St. Lucia, Australia: University of Queensland Press, 2000), 190–99.

34 As e-SAMBAL is a closed and private list, my respondents have stated their desire to remain anonymous. In this section, the authors' names used in the citation of e-mails are fictional.

35 At the time of the survey, Singalaysian had twenty-seven members. Of the three from Singapore, two had just recently returned from overseas studies in the United States. The only two from Malaysia had also just recently returned from the United States. The rest were diasporic members from the United States and Canada. Four were regional contacts in Australia (two in Melbourne, one in Sydney, and one in Perth). In Kris, "The Replies," 15 May 1996, private Singalaysian email, 30 June 1997.

36 Ibid.

37 Veronica, "Re: Join and Membership," 9 September 1996, private SAMBAL email, 30 June 1997.

38 Soja, 13. On such a concept of regionality, see also Stefan Immerfall, ed., *Territoriality in the Globalizing Society: One Place or None?* (Berlin: Springer, 1998).

39 Aihwa Ong, "Flexible Citizenship among Chinese Cosmopolitans," in Pheng Cheah and Bruce Robbins (1998), 134–62.

40 David Harvey, *The Conditions of Postmodernity: An Inquiry into the Origins of Cultural Change* (Cambridge, England: Basil Blackwell, 1989), 147.

41 Evette, "Re:Intro," 22 April 1996, private SAMBAL email, 30 June 1997.

42 Kris, "The Replies."

43 Faridah, "Some Names," 18 October 1995, private Singalasian email, 30 June

1997. *Wasawa* and *hubungan sejenis* are Malay terms and, according to the author, have been used interchangeably with "gays and lesbians" to refer to "same-sex having sex" or "same-sex relationships."

44 Selena, "Re:Intro," 10 May 1995, private Singalaysian email, 30 June 1997.

45 People Like Us is a gay and lesbian activist group in Singapore. They can be contacted at ⟨http://www.geocities.com/WestHollywood/3878/⟩.

46 Myung-gon Chu recently suggested that the Asian diaspora is responsible for the regional rise of New Asia and is the result of capital returning to the homeland.

47 Chua Beng Huat and Tan Joo Ean, "Singapore and the New Middle Class," in Pinches, 141.

48 Evette, "Focus Group Market Research," 16 March 1999, private SAMBAL email, 30 January 2000.

49 Chua and Tan, 138.

50 This questionnaire was distributed on 23 September 2000. Twenty-three of eighty questionnaires were returned. The questionnaire consists of categories delineating age, education, income, language/dialects most frequently used, pager model (current and old), pager code (and where they came) (numeric/ alpha-numeric), other hangout places, dress, handphones (if any), and SMS (short messaging system) code. I thank Lim Li for her assistance.

51 Cited in Chua and Tan, 140.

52 Ibid., 144.

53 Lim Li, "Re: more pager questions," 10 October 2000, private email, 30 October 2000.

54 Chua Beng Huat, "Beep Beep: Look at Me, I'm Important and Needed Urgently," *Straits Times,* 10 February 1996, 6.

55 Arjun Appadurai, *Modernity at Large: Cultural Dimensions of Globalization* (Minneapolis: University of Minnesota Press, 1996).

56 Ibid.

COMPILED BY SALENA CHOW

Bibliography

Action for Aids: The Act. *AFA Homepage*. 1 January 1997. ⟨http://www.afa.org.sg⟩ (1 November 2000).

"A Global Convivencia vs. The Clash of Civilizations." *AsiaWeek* (30 May 1997), ⟨http://www.cnn.com/ASIANOW/asiaweek⟩ (August 2000).

Adam, Barry D., Jan Willem Duyvendak, and Andre Krouwel, eds. *The Global Emergence of Gay and Lesbian Politics: National Imprints of a Worldwide Movement*. Philadelphia: Temple University Press, 1999.

Aestheticism. 27 December 2000. ⟨www.aestheticism.com⟩ (29 December 2000).

Agamben, Giorgio. *The Man without Content*. Stanford: Stanford University Press, 1999.

"Agents of Change." *Asiaweek Online* 26, no. 11 (24 March 2000). ⟨http://www.asiaweek.com/asiaweek/magazine/2000/0324/cover.4people. html⟩ (30 November 2000).

Ali, Novel. "Sulih Suara Dorong Keretakan Komunikasi Keluarga" (Dubbing Damages Family Communication). In *Bercinta Dengan Televisi: Ilusi, Impresi, dan Imaji Sebuah Kotak Ajaib* (In Love with Television: Illusion, Impression, and Imagination), ed. Deddy Mulyana and Idi Subandy Ibrahim. 338–46. Bandung, Indonesia: PT Remaja Rosdakarya, 1997.

Allison, Anne. *Permitted and Prohibited Desires: Mothers, Comics and Censorship in Japan*. Berkeley: University of California Press, 2000.

Altbooks. *SEX no Arukikata: Tōkyō Fūzoku Kanzen Gaido* [How to find your way around Tokyo's sex scene: A complete guide]. Tokyo: Mediawākusu, 1998.

Althusser, Louis. "Ideology and Ideological State Apparatuses." In *Lenin and Philosophy and Other Essays*, trans. Ben Brewster. 121–73. London: New Left Books, 1971.

Altman, Dennis. *Global Sex*. Chicago: University of Chicago Press, 2001.

——. *Defying Gravity: A Political Life*. St. Leonard's, Australia: Allen and Unwin, 1997.

——. "On Global Queering." *The Australian Humanities Review*, no. 2 (July–August 1996). ⟨http://www.lib.latrobe.edu.au/AHR/home.html⟩ (21 March 2001).

——. "Rupture or Continuity? The Internationalization of Gay Identities." *Social Text*, no. 48 (1996): 77–94.

——. "The New World of 'Gay Asia.' " In *Asian and Pacific Inscriptions,* ed. Suvendrini Pereira, special book edition of *Meridian* 14, no. 2 (1995): 121–38.

Anderson, Benedict. *Imagined Communities: Reflections on the Origins and Spread of Nationalism.* London: Verso, 1983.

Anwar Ibrahim. *The Asian Renaissance.* Kuala Lumpur, Malaysia: Times Publishing Group, 1997.

Anwar Online. ⟨http://members.tripod.com/~Anwar_Ibrahim/⟩ (5 March 2001).

"Anwar's New Asia." *Asia Pacific Management News* (29 January 1998). ⟨http://www.apmforum.com/news/apmn148.htm⟩ (5 March 2001).

Appadurai, Arjun. "Commodities and the Politics of Value." Introduction to *The Social Life of Things: Commodities in Cultural Perspective,* ed. Arjun Appadurai. 3–63. New York: Cambridge University Press, 1986.

——. "Disjuncture and Difference in the Global Cultural Economy." In *Global Culture: Nationalism, Globalisation and Modernity,* ed. Mike Featherstone. 295–310. London: Sage, 1990. Reprinted, with other pertinent essays, in Arjun Appadurai, *Modernity at Large: Cultural Dimensions of Globalization.* 27–47, Minneapolis: University of Minnesota Press, 1996. Also published in *Public Culture* 2, no. 2 (Spring 1990): 1–24.

——. *Modernity at Large: Cultural Dimensions of Globalization.* Minneapolis: University of Minnesota Press, 1996.

——. "Grassroots Globalization and the Research Imagination." *Public Culture* 12, no. 1 (2000): 1–19.

Arnaldo, Carlos A., et al. "Freedom of Expression: A Universal Optique." *Journal of International Communication* 5, nos. 1–2 (1998): 25–53.

Arendt, Hannah. *The Origins of Totalitarianism.* 2d ed. Cleveland, OH: Meridian, 1958.

"ask." *Xiao Mo* [Little Mo]. Hong Kong: Huasheng Shudian [Worldson], 1996.

Au, Alex. *Yawning Bread.* 30 November 1996. ⟨http://www.geocities.com/WestHollywood/5738⟩ (30 November 2000).

Aventure. 14 February 2000. ⟨http://newhalf.co.jp/main.html⟩ (1 July 2000).

Azuma, Hiroki. "Ontological, Advertising, 'Character.' " *Kohkoku* 41, no. 2 (March 2000): 6–8.

Bakhtin, M. M. *The Dialogic Imagination.* Trans. C. Emerson and M. Holquist, ed. M. Holquist. Austin: University of Texas Press, 1981.

Balachandran, Chandra S. "Desi Pride on the Internet: South Asian Queers in Cyberspace." *Trikone* 11, no. 1 (1996): 18–19.

Bara no sōretsu [Funeral procession of roses]. 35 mm, 105 min. Dir. Toshio Matsumoto, 1969.

Barker, Chris. *Television, Globalization and Cultural Identities.* Buckingham, England: Open University Press, 1999.

Barlow, John Perry. "Censorship 2000." 1 July 2000. ⟨http://www.nettime.org⟩ (12 July 2000).

Bauman, Zygmun. *Postmodern Ethics*. Oxford: Blackwell, 1993.

Baym, Nancy K. "The Emergence of Community in Computer-Mediated Communications." In *CyberSociety: Computer-Mediated Communication and Community*, ed. Steven G. Jones. 138–63. Thousand Oaks, CA: Sage Publications, 1995.

Becquer, Marcos, and Jose Gatti. "Elements of Vogue." *Third Text*, nos. 16–17 (1991): 69–70.

Benjamin, Walter. "The Task of the Translator." In *Illuminations: Essays and Reflections*. Trans. Harry Zohn. 69–82. New York: Schocken Books, 1955.

———. "The Work of Art in the Age of Mechanical Reproduction." In *Illuminations: Essays and Reflections*. Trans. Harry Zohn. 217–52. New York: Schocken Books, 1955.

Bennett, Tony. "Putting Policy into Cultural Studies." In *Cultural Studies*, ed. Lawrence Grossberg, Cary Nelson, and Paula A. Treichler. 23–37. London: Routledge, 1992.

Berita Reformasi. February 1999. ⟨http://www.geocities.com/Tokyo/Flats/3797/berita.htm⟩ (5 March 2001).

Berry, Chris. "My Queer Korea: Identity, Space and the 1998 Seoul Queer Film and Video Festival." *Intersections*, no. 2 (May 1999). ⟨http://wwwshe.murdoch.edu.au/intersections⟩ (20 March 2001).

———. "Seoul Man: A Night on the Town with Korea's First Gay Activist." *Outrage*, no. 159 (August 1996): 38–40.

Berry, Chris, and Fran Martin. "Queer'n'Asian on—and off—the Net: The Role of Cyberspace in Queer Taiwan and Korea." In *Web Studies: Rewiring Media Studies for the Digital Age*, ed. David Gauntlett. 74–81. London: Arnold, 2000.

Blackman, Lisa M. "Culture, Technology and Subjectivity: An Ethical Analysis." In *The Virtual Embodied: Presence/Practice/Technology*, ed. John Wood. 132–46. London: Routledge, 1998.

Blackwood, Evelyn. "*Tombois* in West Sumatra: Constructing Masculinity and Erotic Desire." In *Female Desires: Same-Sex Relations and Transgender Practices across Cultures*, ed. Evelyn Blackwood and Saskia E. Wieringa. 181–205. New York: Columbia University Press, 1999.

Boellstorff, Tom. " 'Authentic, of Course!' *Gay* Indonesians, Language Ideology, and the Metastasis of Hegemony." Unpublished manuscript, n.d.

———. "The Gay Archipelago: Sexuality, Nation, and Globalization in Indonesia." Unpublished manuscript, n.d.

———. "The Perfect Path: Gay Men, Marriage, Indonesia." *GLQ: A Journal of Gay and Lesbian Studies* 5, no. 4 (1999): 475–510.

———. "Zines and Zones of Desire: Mass Mediated Love, National Romance, and Sexual Citizenship in Gay and Lesbian Indonesia." Unpublished manuscript, n.d.

Bogue, Ronald. *Deleuze and Guattari.* London: Routledge, 1989.

Boisot, Max H. *Information Space: A Framework for Learning in Organizations, Institutions and Culture.* London: Routledge, 1995.

Bourdieu, Pierre. *Distinction: A Social Critique on the Judgement of Taste.* Cambridge, MA: Harvard University Press, 1984.

"Boys Night Out: We're Here. We're Queer. Get Used to It. Can Singapore Accept Its Gay Community?" *Time International* 157, no. 19 (March 2001): 37.

Bray, Francesca. *The Rice Economies.* Oxford: Basil Blackwell, 1986.

Bromberg, Heather. "Are MUDs Communities? Identity, Belonging and Consciousness in Virtual Worlds." In *Cultures of Internet,* ed. Rob Shields. 143–52. London: Sage, 1996.

Brunn, Stanley D., and Charles D. Cottle. "Small States and Cyberboosterism." *Geographical Review* 87, no. 2 (1997): 340–42.

Buchbinder, David. *Performance Anxieties: Re-producing Masculinity.* St. Leonards, Australia: Allen and Unwin, 1998.

Buckingham, David. "Electronic Child Abuse?: Rethinking the Media's Effects on Children." In *Ill Effects: The Media/Violence Debate,* ed. M. Barker and J. Petley. 32–47. New York: Routledge, 1997.

Buddy. *Buddy Digital Queer Society.* 1998–2001. ⟨http://www.buddy79.com⟩ (20 March 2001).

Budiman, Amin. *Lelaki Perindu Lelaki: Sebuah Tinjauan Sejarah dan Psikologi Tentang Homoseks dan Masyarakat Homoseks di Indonesia* (Men Seeking Men: A Historical and Psychological Review of Homosexuality and Homosexual Communities in Indonesia). Semarang, Indonesia: Tanjung Sari, 1979.

Butler, Judith. *Bodies That Matter: On the Discursive Limits of "Sex."* London: Routledge, 1993.

———. *Excitable Speech. A Politics of the Performative.* New York: Routledge, 1997.

———. *The Psychic Life of Power: Theories in Subjection.* Stanford: Stanford University Press, 1997.

Canclini, Néstor García. *Hybrid Cultures: Strategies for Entering and Leaving Modernity.* Trans. Christopher L. Chiappari and Silvia L. López. Minneapolis: University of Minnesota Press, 1995.

Carey, James. "Technology and Ideology: The Case of the Telegraph." In *Communication as Culture: Essays on Media and Society.* 201–30. Cambridge, MA: Unwin Hyman, 1988.

Case, Sue Ellen. *The Domain-Matrix: Performing Lesbian at the End of Print Culture.* Bloomington: Indiana University Press, 1997.

Castells, Manuel. *The Power of Identity.* Oxford: Blackwell, 1997.

Cerna, Christina M. "Universality of Human Rights and Cultural Diversity." In *Regional Systems for the Protection of Human Rights in Asia, Africa, in the Americas and in Europe,* ed. W. Heinz. 10–13. Strasburg, Germany: Friedrich Naumann Stiftung. 1993.

Chalmers, Sharon. "Lesbian (In)visibility and Social Policy in Japanese Society." In *Gender and Public Policy in Japan,* ed. Vera Mackie. London: Routledge, forthcoming.

Chambers, Iain. "The Broken World: Whose Centre, Whose Periphery?" In *Migrancy, Culture, Identity.* 67–92. London: Routledge, 1994.

Chang Zhong de Jia [*Chang Zhong's home*]. 21 February 1997. ⟨http://www.geocities.com/WestHollywood/Heights/1777⟩ (20 March 2001).

Chao, Antonia. "Embodying the Invisible: Body Politics in Constructing Contemporary Taiwanese Lesbian Identities." Ph.D. diss., Cornell University, 1996.

Chatterjee, Partha. *Nationalist Thought and the Colonial World: A Derivative Discourse.* Minneapolis: University of Minnesota Press, 1986.

Chaudhry, Lakshmi. "Virtual Refuge for Gay Muslims." *Wired* (8 May 2000). ⟨http://www.wired.com/news/print/0,1294,35896,00.html⟩ (5 March 2001).

Chee Soon Juan. *To Be Free: Stories from Asia's Struggle against Oppression.* Melbourne: Monash Asia Institute, 1998.

Chen Cong-Qi [Chong Kee Tan]. "Are You a Gay, Kuer or Tongzhi? Notes on the Politics of Hybrid Sexual Identity." Paper presented at the second International Conference on Sexuality Education, Sexology, Gender Studies and LesBiGay Studies, National Central University, Taiwan, 31 May–1 June 1997.

Chen Kuan-Hsing, ed. *Trajectories: Inter-Asia Cultural Studies.* London: Routledge, 1998.

Chen Mei-Ling, et al., eds. *Minfa Rumen* [An introduction to civil law]. Taipei: Yuedan, 1993.

Chew, Melanie. "Human Rights in Singapore: Perceptions and Problems." *Asian Survey* 34, no. 2 (1994): 933–48.

Ching, Leo. "Globalizing the Regional, Regionalizing the Global: Mass Culture and Asianism in the Age of Late Capital." *Public Culture* 12, no. 1 (2000): 233–57.

Chong Kee. "Fighting the Wrong Devil." *SiGNeL Homepage* (7 June 1998). ⟨http://www.geocities.com/WestHollywood/3878/signel.htm/⟩ (25 July 2002).

"Chronology of the Case against Anwar Ibrahim." *Human Rights Watch* (November 1998). ⟨http://www.hrw.org/hrw/campaigns/malaysia98/anwar-chronology.htm⟩ (5 March 2001).

Chu, Myong-gon. *The New Asia in Global Perspective.* New York: St. Martin's Press, 2000.

Chua Beng Huat. "Beep Beep: Look at Me, I'm Important and Needed Urgently." *Straits Times,* 10 February 1996, p. 6.

——. *Communitarian Ideology and Democracy in Singapore*. London: Routledge, 1997.

——, ed. *Consumption in Asia: Lifestyles and Identities*. New York: Routledge, 2000.

Chua, Beng Huat, and Tan Joo Ean. "Singapore and the New Middle Class." In *Culture and Privilege in Capitalist Asia*, ed. Michael Pinches. 137–58. London: Routledge, 1999.

Chua, Lawrence. "An Odd Circuit: Shu Lea Cheang's Online Road Trip." *Art Asia Pacific*, no. 27 (March 2000): 46–51.

Cicioni, Mirna. "Male Pair-Bonds and Female Desire in Fan Slash Writing." In *Theorizing Fandom: Fans, Subculture and Identity*, ed. C. Harris and A. Alexander. 153–78. Cresskill, NJ: Hampton, 1998.

Clammer, John. "Consuming Bodies: Constructing and Representing the Female Body in Contemporary Japanese Print Media." In *Women, Media and Consumption in Japan*, ed. Lise Skov and Brian Moeran. 197–219. Surrey, England: Curzon Press, 1995.

Clifford, James. "Mixed Feelings." In *Cosmopolitics: Thinking and Feeling Beyond the Nation*, ed. Pheng Cheah and Bruce Robbins. 362–70. Minneapolis: University of Minnesota Press, 1998.

"Clueless in Tokyo: Schoolgirls Exchange Sexual Talk for Money to Buy Designer Clothes." *The Economist* 339, no. 7969 (8 June 1996): 66.

Collini, Stefan. Introduction to *Interpretation and Overinterpretation*, ed. Umberto Eco. 5–29. Cambridge, England: Cambridge University Press, 1992.

Collins, Jim. "Postmodernism and Television." In *Postmodern After-Images: A Reader in Film, Television and Video*, ed. Will Brooker and Peter Brooker. 192–207. London: Arnold, 1997.

"Combating the Gay 'Threat.' " *Straits Times*, 22 October 1998. ⟨http://www.ilga.org/information/legal_survey/Asia_Pacific/supporting%20files/group_against_homosexuality_form.htm#⟩ (5 March 2001).

Conquergood, Dwight. "Rethinking Ethnography: Towards a Critical Cultural Politics." *Communication Monographs* 58, no. 2 (1991): 179–94.

Constantine, Peter. *Japan's Sex Trade: A Journey through Japan's Erotic Subcultures*. Tokyo: Tuttle, 1993.

Cornwall, Andrea. "Gendered Identities and Gender Ambiguity among *Travestis* in Salvador, Brazil." In *Dislocating Masculinity: Comparative Ethnographies*, ed. A. Cornwall and N. Lindisfarne. 111–32. London: Routledge, 1994.

Cretive Girls' Home. 15 September 1998. ⟨http:www.lunatique.org.yaoi/⟩ (5 June 2000).

Cumings, Bruce. *Korea's Place in the Sun: A Modern History*. New York: Norton, 1997.

Cvetkovich, Ann, and Douglas Kellner. "Introduction: Thinking Global and Local." In *Articulating the Global and the Local: Globalization and Cultural Studies*, ed. Ann Cvetkovich and Douglas Kellner. 1–30. Boulder, CO: Westview Press, 1997.

Cyberjaya. 2000. ⟨http://www.cyberjaya-msc.com/⟩ (5 March 2001).

Dalby, Liza. *Kimono: Fashioning Culture.* New Haven: Yale University Press, 1993.

Deleuze, Gilles, and Félix Guattari. *A Thousand Plateaus: Capitalism and Schizophrenia.* Trans. Brian Massumi. Minneapolis: University of Minnesota Press, 1987.

Deng Xue-Ren. *Qinshufa zhi Biange yu Zhanwang* [Family law's transformation and future prospects]. Taipei: Yuedan, 1997.

Department of Statistics: Malaysia. 12 October 1998. ⟨http://www.statistics.gov.my/⟩ (5 March 2001).

Deshpande, Shrinand. "Point and Click Communities? South Asian Queers Out on the Internet." *Trikone* 15, no. 4 (2000): 6–7.

Dingo. *To-Get-Her.* 24 November 1996. ⟨http://www.to-get-her.org⟩ (20 March 2001).

Dirlik, Arif, ed. *What Is a Rim?* Boulder, CO: Westview Press, 1993.

Doi, Takeo. *Anatomy of Dependence.* Trans. John Bester. Tokyo: Kodansha International, 1994.

Douglas, Susan J. *Inventing American Broadcasting, 1899–1922.* Baltimore: Johns Hopkins University Press, 1987.

Dragoncastle's Gay Malaysia. 2001. ⟨http://www.dragoncastle.net/malaysia.html⟩ (5 March 2001).

Drucker, Peter, ed. *Different Rainbows.* London: Gay Men's Press, 2000.

Dyer, Richard. "Whiteness." In *The Matter of Images: Essays on Representation.* 141–63. London: Routledge, 1993.

"East Asia Economic Summit Ends with Call for Building New Asia." *Xinhua News Agency,* 15 October 1999. ⟨http://www.xinhuanet.com/english/index.htm⟩ (5 March 2001).

"Editorial: The End of Politics: The Market Is Moving Force Behind the New Asia." *AsiaWeek,* 23 November 2000. ⟨http://www.cnn.com/ASIANOW/asiaweek⟩ (August 2000).

Eglash, Ron. "Cybernetics and American Youth Subculture." *Cultural Studies* 12, no. 3 (1998): 383–84.

Egroups.com. 2001. ⟨www.egroups.com⟩ (5 March 2001).

Ehrlich, Richard. "Malay Prisoners and the Internal Security Act." *City Times* 2, no. 34, n.d. ⟨http://www.zolatimes.com/v2.34/malaypr.html⟩ (5 March 2001).

"The End of Politics: The Market Is Moving Force behind the New Asia." *AsiaWeek* (23 November 2000). ⟨http://www.cnn.com/ASIANOW/asiaweek⟩ (August 2000).

Eng, David, and Alice Horn, eds. *Q&A: Queer in Asian America*. Philadelphia: Temple University Press, 1998.

Enteen, Jillana. " 'Whiskey Is Whiskey; You Can't Make a Cocktail from That!' Self-Identified Gay Thai Men in Bangkok." *Jouvert* 2, no. 1 (1998). ⟨http://152.1.96.5jouvert/v2il/Enteen.htm⟩ (25 July 2002).

Errington, Joseph. *Shifting Languages: Interaction and Identity in Javanese Indonesia*. Cambridge, England: Cambridge University Press, 1998.

Featherstone, Mike. "Global and Local Cultures." In *Mapping the Futures: Local Cultures, Global Change*, ed. Jon Bird et al. 169–88. New York: Routledge, 1993.

Fishel, Thamora. "Extending the Limits of Social Construction: Female Homosexuality in Taiwan." *Historical Reflections/Reflexions Historiques* 20, no. 2 (1994): 267–86.

Foucault, Michel. "Governmentality." In *The Foucault Effect: Studies in Governmentality*, ed. Graham Burchell, Colin Gordon, and Peter Miller. 87–104. Hemel Hempstead, U.K.: Harvester Wheatsheaf, 1991.

——. *The History of Sexuality*. Vol. 1: Trans. Robert Hurley. New York: Penguin Books, 1998.

Foucault, Michel. *The History of Sexuality*. Vol. 2. New York: Vintage Books, 1985.

Francois, Charles, ed. *International Encyclopedia of Systems and Cybernetics*. Muchen, Germany: Saur, 1997.

Free Anwar. ⟨http://www.freeanwar.com⟩ (5 March 2001).

Frow, John. *Cultural Studies and Cultural Value*. New York: Oxford University Press, 1995.

Fryer, Jonathan. "Police Remove Anwar Supporter Tien Chua." *BBC News*, 8 August 2000. ⟨http://news.bbc.co.uk/hi/english/world/asia-pacific/newsid_871000/871175.stm⟩ (5 March 2001).

Fuss, Diana. "Inside/Out." In *Inside/out: Lesbian Theories/Gay Theories*, ed. Diana Fuss. 1–10. New York: Routledge. 1991.

Gallard, Xavier. "Two Pages That May Help Some Families." *The Nation* (2 February 1999). ⟨http://202.44.251.4/nationnews/1999/199902/19990202/38445.htm⟩ (15 June 2000).

Garnault, Ross, and Peter Drysdale. *Asia Pacific Regionalism: Readings in International Economic Relations*. Pymble, Australia: HarperCollins, 1994.

"garrido." *Meimei Wan'An* [Goodnight little sister]. Hong Kong: Huasheng Shudian [Worldson], 1996.

Gatens, Moira. "Woman and Her Double(s): Sex, Gender and Ethics." In *Imaginary Bodies: Ethics, Power and Corporeality*. 29–45. London: Routledge, 1996.

Gayatri, B. J. D. "Indonesian Lesbians Writing Their Own Script: Issues of Feminism and Sexuality." In *From Amazon to Zami: Towards a Global Lesbian Feminism*, ed. Monika Reinfelder. 86–97. London: Cassell, 1996.

GayCapitalKL. ⟨http://members.tripod.com/gaycapitalkl/⟩ (5 March 2001).

Gerbner, George. "The Stories We Tell and the Stories We Sell." *Journal of International Communication* 5, nos. 1–2 (1998): 75–82.

Gibson, William. *Neuromancer.* London: Grafton, 1986.

Gibson-Graham, J. K. *The End of Capitalism (as We Knew it): A Feminist Critique of Political Economy.* Cambridge, MA: Blackwell, 1996.

Gilroy, Paul. "Nationalism, History, and Ethnic Absolutism." In *Small Acts: Thoughts on the Politics of Black Cultures.* 63–74. London: Serpent's Tail, 1993.

Gin Gin [Jing Jing]. *Gin Gin Wanglu Ziyuan* [Gin Gin's Internet resources], Club 1069.2000. ⟨http://club1069.com/gingins/4[1].htm⟩ (20 March 2001).

"A Global Convivencia vs. The Class of Civilizations." *Asiaweek* (30 May 1997). ⟨http://www.cnn.com/ASIANOW/asiaweek⟩ (August 2000).

Global Internet Statistics. 30 December 2000. ⟨http://www.glreach.com/globstats/index.php3⟩ (17 January 2001).

Global Internet Statistics. 2001. ⟨http://www.glreach.com/globstats/index.php⟩ (17 January 2001).

Goffman, Erving. *The Presentation of Self in Everyday Life.* London: Penguin, 1959.

Gottlieb, Nanette. *Word Processing Technology in Japan: Kanji and the Keyboard.* Richmond, England: Curzon Press, 2000.

Government of Malaysia. *Sixth Malaysia Plan, 1991–1995.* Kuala Lumpur: Kuala Lumpur Government Printers, 1991.

Graff, E. J. "Sexual Disorientation." *OUT* (September 1997): 190.

Graham, Sharyn. "Negotiating Gender: Calalai' in Bugis Society." *Intersections* 6 (August 2001). ⟨http://wwwsshe.murdoch.edu.au/intersections/default.htm⟩. (1 December 2001).

Grahn, Judy. *Another Mother Tongue: Gay Words, Gay Worlds.* Boston: Beacon, 1984.

Gray, Chris H., ed. *The Cyborg Handbook.* New York: Routledge, 1995.

Greenberg, Clement. "The Avant-Garde and the Kitsch." In *Kitsch: the World of Bad Taste,* ed. Gillo Dorfles. 116–26. London: Studio Vista, 1969.

Griner, Massimiliano, and Rosa Isabella Furnari. *Otaku: I giovani perduti del Sol Levante* (Otaku: The Lost Youths of the Rising Sun). Rome: Castelvecchi, 1999.

Grossberg, Lawrence, Cary Nelson, and Paula A. Treichler, eds. *Cultural Studies.* New York: Routledge, 1992.

Grosz, Elizabeth. "A Note on Essentialism and Difference." In *Feminist Knowledge: Critique and Construct,* ed. Sneja Gunew. 332–34. London: Routledge, 1990.

Gupta, Akhil. *Postcolonial Developments: Agriculture in the Making of Modern India.* Durham, NC: Duke University Press, 1998.

Habermas, Jürgen. *The Structural Transformation of the Public Sphere: An Inquiry into a Category of Bourgeois Society.* Trans. Thomas Burger. Cambridge, MA: MIT Press, 1989.

Hahn, Joel S., ed. *Southeast Asian Identities: Culture and the Politics of Representation in Indonesia, Malaysia and Singapore.* New York: St. Martin's Press, 1998.

Hall, David, and Roger Ames. *Anticipating China: Thinking through the Narratives of Chinese and Western Culture.* New York: State University of New York Press, 1995.

——. *Thinking through Confucius.* New York: State University of New York Press, 1987.

Hall, Stuart. "The Local and the Global: Globalization and Ethnicity." In *Culture, Globalization and the World System,* ed. Anthony D. King. 19–39. London: Macmillan, 1991.

——. *Representation: Cultural Representations and Signifying Practices.* London: Sage, 1997.

Hamano, Hoki. "Japanese Anime: Quality and Quantity." *Chuo Koron* (September 2000) ⟨http://www2.chuko.co.jp/koron/200009.html⟩ (19 April 2001).

Haraway, Donna. "Manifesto for Cyborgs." *Socialist Review,* no. 80 (1985): 65–107.

——. *Modest Witness@Second Millennium: FemaleMan Meets Onco Mouse.* New York: Routledge, 1997.

Harrison, Frances. "What Future for Anwar?" *BBC News,* 8 August 2000. ⟨http://news.bbc.co.uk/hi/english/world/asia-pacific/newsid_870000/870834.stm⟩ (5 March 2001).

Harvey, David. *The Condition of Postmodernity: An Inquiry into the Origins of Cultural Change.* Cambridge, England: Basil Blackwell, 1989.

Hefner, Robert W., ed. *Market Cultures: Society and Morality in New Asian Capitalisms.* Boulder, CO: Westview Press, 1998.

Heider, Karl G. *Indonesian Cinema: National Culture on Screen.* Honolulu: University of Hawaii Press, 1991.

Heinz, W., ed. *Regional Systems for the Protection of Human Rights in Asia, Africa, in the Americas and in Europe.* Strasburg, Germany: Friedrich-Numann-Stiftung, 1993.

Heng, Geraldine, and Janadas Devan. "State Fatherhood: The Politics of Nationalism, Sexuality, and Race in Singapore." In *Nationalisms and Sexualities,* ed. A. Parker, M. Russo, D. Sommer, and P. Yaeger. 343–364, New York: Routledge, 1992.

Heng, Hiang Khng Russell. "Tiptoe out of the Closet: The Before and After of the Increasingly Visible Gay Community in Singapore." In *Gay and Lesbian Asia: Identities and Communities,* ed. Peter Jackson and Gerard Sullivan. 81–97. New York: Haworth Press, 2001.

Hinsch, Bret. *Passions of the Cut Sleeve: The Male Homosexual Tradition in China.* Berkeley: University of California Press, 1992.

Hodge, Robert, and Gunther Kress. *Social Semiotics.* Ithaca, NY: Cornell University Press, 1988.

Bibliography

Holden, Todd Joseph Miles. " 'I'm Your Venus'/'You're a Rake': Gender and the Grand Narrative in Japanese Television Advertising." *Intersections* 3 (January 2000). ⟨http://wwwsshe.murdoch.edu.au/intersections/issue3/holden_paper1.html⟩ (10 October 2000).

Huang Yu-Xiu. "Sexual Equality Before the Law." *Funü Xinzhi,* no. 146 (1994): 4–6.

Hung, Lucifer. "Identity Politics Ends/and Its Own Lack: From the Interaction within Taiwanese Cyberspace to the Dynamics/Visibility of Queer Politics/Discourse." Paper presented at the second International Conference on Sexuality Education, Sexology, Gender Studies and LesBiGay Studies, National Central University, Taiwan, 31 May–1 June 1997.

Hunter, Ian. "Setting Limits to Culture." In *Nation, Culture, Text: Australian Cultural and Media Studies,* ed. Graeme Turner. 140–63. London: Routledge, 1993.

Iemvonmet Thienchai. *Standard Thai-English Dictionary.* Bangkok: Ruamsam, 1990.

"I.K.U. Press Info." *I.K.U.* (12 June 2000). ⟨http://www.I-K-U.com⟩ (24 August 2000).

Immerfall, Stefan, ed. *Territoriality in the Globalizing Society: One Place or None?* Berlin: Springer, 1998.

International Gay and Lesbian Rights Commission (IGLHRC). *Action Alert: Bigotry and Censorship Masquerade as Protection of Youth,* 23 August 2001 ⟨http://www.iglhrc.org/word1/ne_asia/Korea2001Aug.html⟩ (3 October 2001).

Ioshihara, Rieko. *Ai no kusabi* (The Wedge of Love). 2 vols. Tokyo: Rieko Ioshihara/Magazine Magazine, 1992–94. Italian translation *Il cuneo dell'amore* (Milano: Yamato Video S.R.L., 1995).

"Is Optimism about the MSC Justified?" *Bits & Bytes: MSC.Comm.* ⟨http://www.mdc.com.my/msc.comm/html/b_n_b01.html⟩ (5 March 2001).

Itoi, Kay. "Rising Daughters." *Newsweek* 135, no. 14 (3 April 2000): 40–45.

"It's Normal to Be Queer." *The Economist* (6 January 1996): 68–70.

Iwabuchi, Koichi. "Idealess Japanisation or Purposeless Globalisation? Japanese Cultural Industries in Asia." *Culture and Policy* 7, no. 2 (1996): 33–42.

Jackson, Peter A. "An American Death in Bangkok: The Murder of Darrell Berrigan and the Hybrid Origins of Gay Identity in 1960s Thailand." *GLQ* 5, no. 3 (1999): 361–411.

——. "An Explosion of Thai Identities: Global Queering and Reimagining Queer Theory." In *Culture, Health and Sexuality* 2, no. 4 (2000): 405–424.

——. "Kathoey> <Gay> <Man: The Historical Emergence of Gay Male Identity in Thailand." In *Sites of Desire/Economies of Pleasure: Sexualities in Asia and the Pacific,* ed. Lenore Manderson and Margaret Jolly. 166–90. Chicago: University of Chicago Press, 1997.

——. "The Persistence of Gender: From Ancient Indian *Pandakas* to Modern Thai *Gay-Quings.*" In *Australia Queer,* ed. Chris Berry and Annamarie Jagose, special issue of *Meanjin* 55, no. 1 (1996): 110–20.

——. "Tolerant but Unaccepting: The Myth of a Thai 'Gay Paradise.' " In *Genders and Sexualities in Modern Thailand,* ed. Peter A. Jackson and Nerida M. Cook. 226–42. Chiang Mai, Thailand: Silkworm Books, 1999.

Jackson, Peter, and Gerard Sullivan, eds. *Gay and Lesbian Asia: Identities and Communities.* New York: Haworth Press, 2001.

Jacobs, Sue-Ellen, Wesley Thomas, and Sabine Lang, eds. *Two-Spirit People: Native American Gender Identity, Sexuality, and Spirituality.* Chicago: University of Illinois Press, 1997.

Jagose, Annamarie. *Queer Theory.* Melbourne: Melbourne University Press, 1996.

Jameson, Fredric. "Notes on Globalization as a Philosophical Issue." In *The Cultures of Globalization,* ed. Fredric Jameson and Masao Miyoshi. 54–77. Durham, NC: Duke University Press, 1998.

——. "Postmodernism, or the Cultural Logic of Late Capitalism." In *Postmodernism: A Reader,* ed. Thomas Docherty. 62–92. Hemel Hempstead, U.K.: Harvester Wheatsheaf, 1993.

Jenkins, Henry III. *Textual Poachers: Television Fans and Participatory Culture.* New York: Routledge, 1992.

Jerison, David, L. M., Singer, and Daniel W. Stroock, eds. *The Legacy of Norbet Weiner: A Centennial Symposium in Honour of the 100th Anniversary of Norbet Weiner's Birth.* Massachusetts Institute of Technology, Cambridge, MA, October 1994.

Jnanavira, Dharmachari. "Homosexuality in the Japanese Buddhist Tradition." *Western Buddhist Review* 3 (1999). ⟨http://www.westernbuddhistreview. com/vol3/homosexuality.htm/⟩ (15 July 2002).

Jones, Carla. "Watching Women: The Domestic Politics of Middle-class Femininity Formation in Late New Order Indonesia." Ph.D. diss., University of North Carolina–Chapel Hill, 2001.

Jordan, David K. "Changes in Postwar Taiwan and Their Impact on the Popular Practice of Religion." In *Cultural Change in Postwar Taiwan,* ed. Steven Harrell and Huang Chün-chieh. 137–60. Taipei: SMC Publishing, 1994.

Justice for Anwar—Reformasi. ⟨http://members.tripod.com/~Anwarite/⟩ (5 March 2001).

Kahn, Joel S., ed. *Southeast Asian Identities: Culture and the Politics of Representation in Indonesia, Malaysia and Singapore.* New York: St. Martin's Press, 1998.

Kai Tuo, Fan Shuteng Workshop [Gongzuo Xiaozu]. "Taiwan 1997 Wanglu Shiyong Diaocha Huodong" [The 1997 Taiwan Internet use survey]. Fan Shuteng Wanglu Diaocha Gang [Yam Online Survey Net]. July 1997. ⟨http://taiwan.yam.org.tw/survey⟩ (20 March 2001).

Kamui K. "*Bronze* Fan Page." 1996. ⟨kamui_kun.tripod.com/Zetsuai/zindex. html⟩ (4 January 2001).

Kavi, Ashok Row. "An Indian Original." Interview by Sandip C. Roy. *Trikone* 8, no. 3 (1993): 5–7.

Khanaye Doost. ⟨http://www.geocities.com/khanaye_doost/welcome.html⟩ (5 March 2001).

Kinsella, Sharon. *Adult Manga: Culture and Power in Contemporary Japanese Society.* Richmond, England: Curzon Press, 2000.

——. "Cuties in Japan." In *Women, Media and Consumption in Japan,* ed. Lise Skov and Brian Moeran. 220–54. Surrey, England: Curzon Press, 1995.

——. "Japanese Subculture in the 1990s: Otaku and the Amateur Manga Movement." *Journal of Japanese Studies* 24, no. 2 (1998): 289–316.

Kirshenblatt-Gimblett, Barbara. "The Electronic Vernacular." In *Connected: Engagements with Media,* ed. George E. Marcus. 21–65. Chicago: University of Chicago Press, 1996.

Kleinwaechter, Wolfgang. "The People's 'Right to Communicate' and a 'Global Communication Charter.'" *Journal of International Communication* 5, nos. 1–2 (1998): 105–21.

Kodaka, Kazuma. *Kizuna.* Tokyo: Seiji Biblos/Daiei, 1994. Italian translation *Kizuna* (Milano: Yamato Video, 1995).

——. *Kizuna.* 6 vols. to date. Tokyo: Biblos, 1992–.

Kolko, Beth E., Lisa Nakamura, and Gilbert B. Rodman, eds. *Race in Cyberspace.* New York: Routledge, 2000.

Komatsu, Anri. *Nyūhāfu ga kimeta "watashi" rashii ikikata* [Deciding to be a newhalf and live like myself]. Tokyo: KK Ronguserāzu, 2000.

Kondo, Dorinne. *Crafting Selves: Power, Gender, and Discourses of Identity in a Japanese Workplace.* Chicago: University of Chicago Press, 1990.

"Korean Internet Users Tallied at 20.9 Million." *Korean Herald News,* 20 April 2001. ⟨http://www.koreaherald.co.kr/SITE/data/html_dir/2001/04/17/200104170032.asp⟩ (1 May 2001).

Kramer, Gavin. *Shopping.* New York: Soho Press, 2001.

Krampen, Martin. "Phytosemiotics." In *Frontiers in Semiotics,* ed. John Deely, Brooke Williams, and Felicia E. Kruse. 83–95. Bloomington: Indiana University Press, 1986.

Kugle, Scott. "Internet Activism, Internet Passivism." *Trikone* 15, no. 4 (2000): 10–11.

Latham, A. J. H. *Rice: The Primary Commodity.* New York: Routledge, 1998.

Lee Hock Suan. "Digital Television: Managing the Transition." Keynote address presented at BroadcastAsia 2000 Singapore Expo, Singapore, 5 June 2000.

Lee Kuan Yew. *From Third World to First.* New York: HarperCollins, 2000.

——. "Interview." *Time Australia* 18 April 1994, 16.

Lee, Terence, and David Birch. "Internet Regulation in Singapore: A Policy/ing Discourse." *Media International Australia,* no. 95 (May 2000): 147–69.

Leifer, Michael. *Singapore's Foreign Policy: Coping with Vulnerability.* London: Routledge, 2000.

Leong, Laurence Wai-Teng. "Singapore." In *Sociolegal Control of Homosexuality: A Multi-Nation Comparison,* ed. Donald J. West and Richard Green. 127–44. New York: Plenum Press, 1997.

"Lesbian and Bi Women's Forum." *Bibian.* ⟨http://www.silkroad.ne.jp/bibian⟩ (7 June 2000).

Leupp, Gary. *Male Colors: The Construction of Homosexuality in Tokugawa Japan.* Berkeley: University of California Press, 1995.

Lim, Madeleine. "Chatting with Madeleine Lim." *Sintercom.* 14 July 1997. ⟨http://www.sintercom.org/sp/interview/madeleine.html⟩ (11 November 2000).

Lim, Shirley Geok-lin, Larry E. Smith, and Wimal Dissanayake, eds. *Transnational Asia Pacific: Gender, Culture, and the Public Sphere.* Urbana: University of Illinois Press, 1999.

Lindsay, Jennifer. "Speaking the Truth: Speech on Television in Indonesia." In *Media Discourse and Performance in Indonesia and Malaysia,* ed. Ben Arps. Athens: Ohio University Press, forthcoming.

Liu, Lydia H. *Translingual Practice: Literature, National Culture, and Translated Modernity—China, 1900–1937.* Stanford: Stanford University Press, 1995.

Lovink, Geert. "Interview with Shu Lea Cheang." 30 December 2000. ⟨http://www.nettime.org⟩ (30 December 2000).

Ludlow, Peter. Introduction to "Self and Community Online." In *High Noon on the Electronic Frontier: Conceptual Issues in Cyberspace,* ed. Peter Ludlow. 311–316. Cambridge, MA: MIT Press, 1996.

Lunn, Stephen. "The Big Mo Wins in Japan." *The Australian,* 9 November 2000, media sec., p. 13.

Lyotard, Jean-Francois. *The Postmodern Condition: A Report on Knowledge.* Minneapolis: University of Minnesota Press, 1984.

Mahathir, Mohamad. "Dr. Mahathir's World Analysis." *Mainichi Daily News,* 15 February 2000. ⟨http://www.mainichi.co.jp/english/mahathir/13.html⟩ (5 March 2001).

Mahathir, Mohamad, and Shintaro Ishihara. *The Voice of Asia: Two Leaders Discuss the Coming Century.* Trans. Frank Baldwin. New York: Kodansha International, 1995.

Maier, H. M. J. "From Heteroglossia to Polyglossia: The Creation of Malay and Dutch in the Indies." *Indonesia* 56 (1993): 37–65.

Maira, Sunaina. "Identity Dub: The Paradoxes of an Indian American Youth Subculture (New York Mix)." *Cultural Anthropology* 14, no. 1 (1999): 29–60.

Maier, H. M. J. "From Heteroglossia to Polyglossia: The Creation of Malay and Dutch in the Indies." *Indonesia* 56 (1993): 37–65.

"Malaysia Stands by Anti-sodomy Law." *International Lesbian and Gay Association*, 13 June 1999. ⟨http://www.ilga.org/Information/Legal_survey/Asia_ Pacific/supporting%20files/malaysia_stands_by_anti.htm⟩ (5 March 2001).

Malaysia Tourism Promotion Board. *Tourism Malaysia Website* (1 June 2000). ⟨http://www.tourism.gov.my⟩ (1 October 2000).

Malaysiakini. ⟨http://www.malaysiakini.com/⟩ (5 March 2001).

Malaysian Gay and Lesbian Club. ⟨http://webnection.com/mglc⟩ (18 July 2002).

Manderson, Lenore, and Margaret Jolly, eds. *Sites of Desire, Economies of Pleasure: Sexualities in Asia and the Pacific.* Chicago: University of Chicago Press, 1997.

Mankekar, Purnima. *Screening Culture, Viewing Politics: An Ethnography of Television, Womanhood, and Nation in Postcolonial India.* Durham, NC: Duke University Press, 1999.

Mann, Chris, and Fiona Stewart. *Internet Communication and Qualitative Research: A Handbook for Researching Online.* London: Sage, 2000.

Marchetti, Gina. "Counter-Media and Global Screens: Recent Work by Shu Lea Cheang." Paper presented at the annual meeting of the Society for Cinema Studies, Chicago, March 2000.

Markley, Robert, ed. *Virtual Realities and Their Discontents.* Baltimore: Johns Hopkins University Press, 1996.

Martin, Emily. *Flexible Bodies: The Role of Immunity in American Culture from the Days of Polio to the Age of AIDS.* Boston: Beacon Press, 1994.

Martin, Fran, and Chris Berry. "Queer 'n' Asian on the Net: Syncretic Sexualities in Taiwan and Korean Cyberspaces." *Critical InQueeries* 2, no. 1 (1998): 67–94.

Martin, Ron, ed. *Money and the Space Economy.* Chichester, England: Wiley, 1999.

Marvin, Carolyn. *When Old Technologies Were New: Thinking about Electric Communication in the Late Nineteenth Century.* New York: Oxford University Press, 1988.

Massumi, Brian. *A User's Guide to Capitalism and Schizophrenia: Deviations from Deleuze and Guattari.* Cambridge, MA: MIT Press, 1996.

Matsui, Midori. "Little Girls Were Little Boys: Displaced Femininity in the Representation of Homosexuality in Japanese Girls' Comics." In *Feminism and the Politics of Difference*, ed. S. Gunew and A. Yeatman. 177–96. Boulder, CO: Westview Press, 1993.

Matzner, Andrew. "Thailand: Paradise Not (On Human Rights and Homophobia)." *Transgender in Thailand.* 1998. ⟨http://home.att.net/~leela2/ paradisenot.htm⟩ (3 May 2000).

Maurer, Bill. "A Fish Story: Rethinking Globalization on Virgin Gorda." *American Ethnologist* 27, no. 3 (2000): 670–701.

Maygra. "Re: [*AMLA*] Mainstreaming slash (was looking for perspective)."
16 April 2000. ⟨http://groups.yahoo.com/group/amla/message/3283⟩
(4 March 2001).

McLean, R., and Robert Schubert. "Queers and the Internet." *Media Information Australia,* no. 78 (1995): 77–80.

McLelland, Mark. "Essay Review of *Queer Japan.*" *Sexualities* 3, no. 1 (Spring 2000): 150–53.

——. "Male Homosexuality and Popular Culture in Japan." *Intersections,* no. 3 (January 2000). ⟨http://wwwsshe.murdoch.edu.au/intersections/issue3/mclelland2.html⟩ (21 October 2000).

——. *Male Homosexuality in Modern Japan: Cultural Myths and Social Realities.* Richmond, England: Curzon Press, 2000.

——. "No Climax, No Point, No Meaning? Japanese Women's Boy-Love Sites on the Internet." *Journal of Communication Inquiry* 24, no. 3 (2000): 274–94.

——. "Out and About on Japan's Gay Net." *Convergence* 6, no. 3 (2000): 16–33.

McQuire, Scott. "Electrical Storms: High Speed Historiography in the Video Art of Peter Callas." In *Peter Callas: Initialising History,* ed. Alessio Cavallaro. 30–47. Sydney: Dlux, 1999.

McVeigh, Brian J. "Commodifying Affection, Authority and Gender in the Everyday Objects of Japan." *Journal of Material Culture* 1, no. 3 (November 1996): 291–312.

——. "How Hello Kitty Commodifies the Cute, Cool and Camp: 'Consumutopia' versus 'Control' in Japan." *Journal of Material Culture* 5, no. 2 (July 2000): 291–312.

Mehta, Michael, and Dwayne Plaza. "Pornography in Cyberspace: An Exploration of What's in USENET." In *Culture of the Internet,* ed. Sara Kiesler. 53–67. Mahwah, NJ: Erlbaum, 1997.

Mendes, E. P. *Asian Values and Human Rights: Letting the Tigers Free.* Ottawa: Human Rights Research and Education Centre, 1996.

Miller, Daniel, and Don Slater. *The Internet: An Ethnographic Approach.* New York: Berg, 2000.

Miller, Neil. *Out in the World: Gay and Lesbian Life from Buenos Aires to Bangkok.* New York: Random House, 1992.

Miyazaki, Rumiko. *Watashi wa toransujendā* [I am transgendered]. Tokyo: Neo-raifu, 2000.

Miyoshi, Masao. "A Borderless World? From Colonialism to Transnationalism and the Decline of the Nation-State." *Critical Inquiry,* no. 19 (summer 1993): 726–51.

——. "'Globalization,' Culture, and the University." In *The Cultures of Globalization,* ed. Fredric Jameson and Masao Miyoshi. 247–70. Durham, NC: Duke University Press, 1998.

Miyuki. "*Zetsu ai* Fan Page." ⟨www.geocities.com/Tokyo/Shrine/3303/z-index.
html⟩ (4 January 2001).

MJ Johnson. "Re: [amla] Genders: Back to Nuriko (FY spoilers, sortof)." 12 July
2000. ⟨http://groups.yahoo.com/group/amla/message/6228⟩ (4 March 2001).

———. "Re: [amla] Seme behavior." 4 May 2000. ⟨http://groups.yahoo.com/group/
amla/message/4278⟩ (4 March 2001).

Moeran, Brian, and Lise Skov, eds. *Women, Media and Consumption in Japan.*
Surrey, England: Curzon Press, 1995.

"More Than 1,000 in Anti-Mahathir Protest in Malaysian Capital." *Berita Reformasi,* 19 February 1999. ⟨http://www.geocities.com/Tokyo/Flats/3797/
eng0219a.htm⟩ (5 March 2001).

Morse, Margaret. *Virtualities: Television, Media Art and Cyberculture.* Bloomington: Indiana University Press, 1998.

Morris, Rosalind C. "A Ban on Gay Teachers: Education and Prohibition in the
'Land of the Free.'" *Social Text* 15, nos. 3–4 (1997): 53–79.

———. "Three Sexes and Four Sexualities: Redressing the Discourses on Gender
and Sexuality in Contemporary Thailand." *Positions* 2, no. 1 (1994): 15–43.

Morton, Donald. "Birth of the Cyberqueer." In *Cybersexualities: A Reader on
Feminist Theory, Cyborgs and Cyberspace,* ed. Jenny Wolmark. 295–313. Edinburgh: Edinburgh University Press, 1999.

———. "Global (Sexual) Politics, Class Struggle, and the Queer Left." *Critical In-
Queeries* 1, no. 3 (May 1997): 1–30.

Multimedia Supercorridor. ⟨http://www.mdc.com.my⟩ (5 March 2001).

Murray, Alison. "Let Them Take Ecstasy: Class and Jakarta Lesbians." In *Female
Desires: Same-Sex Relations and Transgender Practices across Cultures,* ed.
Evelyn Blackwood and Saskia E. Wieringa. 139–56. New York: Columbia Uni-
versity Press, 1999.

Muzaffar, Chandra. "Anwar and ISA Arrests." *International Movement for a Just
World,* 21 September 1998. ⟨http://www2.jaring.my/just/ISA.html⟩ (5 March
2001).

Nagarajan, Mala. "SAGrrls and Desidykes: Women on the Internet." *Trikone* 15,
no. 4 (2000), 8.

Naked Earth. 12 April 1999. ⟨http://www.nakedearthcomix.com⟩ (15 September
2000).

Nanda, Serena. *Neither Man nor Woman: The Hijras of India.* Belmont, CA:
Wadsworth, 1990.

Nardocchio, Elaine F., ed. *Reader Response to Literature: The Empirical Dimension.*
Berlin: Mouton de Gruyter, 1992.

Ng, Irene. "Do Gays Have a Place in Singapore?" *Straits Times,* 27 May 2000, n.p.

Ng King Kang. *The Rainbow Connection: The Internet and the Singapore Gay
Community.* Singapore: KangCuBine Publishing, 1999.

Nguyen, Dan Thu, and Jon Alexander. "The Coming of Cyberspacetime and the End of Polity." In *Cultures of Internet,* ed. Rob Shields. 99–124. London: Sage, 1996.

Noor, Farish A. "The Other Malaysia." *Malaysiakini,* 30 September 2000. ⟨http://www.malaysiakini.com/archives_column/farishnoor_column3092000.htm⟩ (5 March 2001).

Oetomo, Dédé. "Ketika Sharon Stone Berbahasa Indonesia" (When Sharon Stone Spoke Indonesian). In *Bercinta Dengan Televisi: Ilusi, Impresi, dan Imaji Sebuah Kotak Ajaib,* ed. Deddy Mulyana and Idi Subandy Ibrahim. 333–37. Bandung, Indonesia: PT Remaja Rosdakarya, 1997.

Official Anwar Ibrahim's Online Resources. ⟨http://www.geocities.com/CapitolHill/Senate/8722/Sambung.htm⟩ (18 July 2002).

Official Web site of the *International Free Anwar Campaign.* ⟨http://www.freeanwar.com⟩ (18 July 2002).

Offord, Baden. "The Burden of (Homo)sexual Identity in Singapore." *Social Semiotics* 9, no. 3 (1999): 301–16.

Okada, Toshio. "Before Japanese Creators Become Extinct." *Chuo Koron,* September 2000. ⟨http://www2.chuko.co.jp/koron/back/200009.html⟩ (19 April 2001).

Olds, Kris, et al., eds. *Globalisation and the Asia Pacific: Contested Territories.* London: Routledge, 1999.

Ong, Aihwa. "Flexible Citizenship among Chinese Cosmopolitans." In *Cosmopolitics: Thinking and Feeling beyond the Nation,* ed. Pheng Cheah and Bruce Robbins. 134–62. Minneapolis: University of Minnesota Press, 1998.

——. *Flexible Citizenship: The Cultural Logics of Transnationality.* Durham, NC: Duke University Press, 1999.

——. "State vs. Islam: Malay Families, Women's Bodies, and the Body Politic in Malaysia." In *Bewitching Women, Pious Men: Gender and Body Politics in South East Asia,* ed. Aihwa Ong and Michael G. Peletz. 159–94. Berkeley: University of California Press, 1995.

Ong, Aihwa, and Donald Nonini, eds. *Ungrounded Empires: The Cultural Politics of Modern Chinese Transnationalism.* London: Routledge, 1997.

Ong, Aihwa, and Michael G. Peletz, eds. *Bewitching Women, Pious Men: Gender and Body Politics in South East Asia.* Berkeley: University of California Press, 1995.

Out in Malaysia. ⟨http://www.outinmalaysia.com⟩ (5 March 2001).

Ozaki, Minami. *Bad Blood.* Tokyo: Margaret Comics, 1992.

——. *Bronze.* 11 vols. to date. Tokyo: Margaret Comics, 1993–.

——. *Captain Tsubasa.* N.p., n.d. YAOI *dōjinshi* fanzine.

——. *God.* Tokyo: Margaret Comics, 1992.

——. *Zetsu ai 1989.* 5 vols. Tokyo: Margaret Comics, 1989–1992.

Pai Hsien-Yung. *Crystal Boys* [*Niezi*]. Trans. Howard Goldblatt. San Francisco: Gay Sunshine Press, 1995.

Palmer, Spencer J. *Korea and Christianity.* Seoul: Seoul Computer Press, 1986.

Patton, Cindy. "Stealth Bombers of Desire: The Globalization of 'Alterity' in Emerging Democracies." Trans. Zhuang Ruilin. *Working Papers in Gender/ Sexuality Studies,* ed. Center for the Study of Sexualities, National Central University, Chungli, nos. 3–4 (1998): 301–23.

Patton, Cindy, and Benigno Sánchez-Eppler, eds. *Queer Diasporas.* Durham, NC: Duke University Press, 2000.

Penley, Constance. "Feminism, Psychoanalysis and the Study of Popular Culture." In *Cultural Studies,* ed. Lawrence Grossberg, Cary Nelson, and Paula A. Treichler. 479–500. New York: Routledge, 1992.

People Like Us. *PLU Homepage.* 15 July 1999. 〈http://www.geocities.com/ WestHollywood/3878〉 (30 November 2000).

Phillips, David J. "Defending the Boundaries: Identifying and Countering Threats in a Usenet Newsgroup." *Information Society* 12, no. 1 (1996): 39–62.

Pinches, Michael. *Culture and Privilege in Capitalist Asia* (London: Routledge, 1999).

Piper, Jacqueline M. *Rice in South-East Asia.* New York: Oxford University Press, 1993.

Podhisita Chai. "Buddhism and Thai World View." In *Traditional and Changing Thai World View.* 25–53. Bangkok: Chularlongkorn University, 1985.

Pointon, Susan. "Transcultural Orgasm as Apocalypse: Urosukidoji: The Legend of the Overfiend." *Wide Angle* 19, no. 3 (1997): 41–63.

Poster, Mark. *The Mode of Information.* Oxford: Polity Press, 1990.

Povinelli, Elizabeth A., and George Chauncey, eds. *Thinking Sexuality Transnationally. GLQ,* special issue, 5, no. 4 (1999).

Pritchard, Sarah. "Asian Values and Human Rights." Paper presented at the Australian and New Zealand Society of International Law Colloquium, University of New South Wales, March 1996.

Qiu Miaojin. *Eyu Shouji* [The crocodile's journal]. Taipei: Shibao, 1994.

"Queer Asian Pacific Resources." In *Journal Articles of Interest for Gay, Bi, Lesbian, Transgender Asian/Pacific People* (29 December 1997). 〈http://www.geocities. com/WestHollywood/Heights/5010/articles.html〉 (30 June 1998).

Queer Jihad. 〈http://www.well.com/user/queerjhd〉 (18 July 2002).

Rafael, Vicente L. *Contracting Colonialism: Translation and Christian Conversion in Tagalog Society under Early Spanish Rule.* Ithaca, NY: Cornell University Press, 1988.

Ragawa, Marimo. *New York New York.* 4 vols. Modena, Italy: Marvel, 1999–2000.

Rajchman, John. "Diagram and Diagnosis." In *Becomings: Explorations in Time, Memory and Futures,* ed. Elizabeth Grosz. 42–55. Ithaca, NY: Cornell University Press, 1999.

Ramakrishnan, Mageswary. "During the Anwar Trial It Was Easy to Get Lucky: Interview with Ashley Lee." *Time*, 26 September 2000. ⟨http://www.time.com/time/asia/features/interviews/2000/09/26/int.malay.gay1.html⟩ (5 March 2001).

——. "Homosexuality Is a Crime Worse Than Murder: Interview with Malaysia's Morality Police." *Time (Asia)*, 26 September 2000. ⟨http://www.time.com/time/asia/features/interviews/2000/09/26/int.malay.gay2.html⟩ (5 March 2001).

"The Rationale behind the Media Review." *Straits Times Interactive*, 6 June 2000. ⟨http://www.straitstimes.asia1.com.sg/singapore/sin17_0606_prt.html⟩ (6 June 2000).

Rattachumpoth, Rakkit. "Dispelling Myths/Myth vs. Reality." *The Nation* (15 January 1998). ⟨http://202.44.251.4/nationnews/1998/199801/19980115/21062.html⟩ (15 June 2000).

——. Foreword to *Lady Boys, Tom Boys, Rent Boys: Male and Female Homosexualities in Contemporary Thailand*, ed. Peter A. Jackson and Gerard Sullivan. xiii–xx. New York: Haworth, 1999.

Rheingold, Howard. *The Virtual Community: Homesteading on the Electronic Frontier*. London: Minerva, 1994.

Roach, Mary. "Cute Inc." *Wired* 7, no. 12 (December 1999). ⟨http://wired.com/wired/archive/7.12/cute.html⟩ (25 July 2002).

Robins, Kevin. "Cyberspace and the World We Live In." In *The Cybercultures Reader*, ed. David Bell and Barbara M. Kennedy. 77–95. London: Routledge, 2000.

——. *Into the Image: Culture and Politics in the Field of Vision*. London: Routledge, 1996.

Rofel, Lisa. "Discrepant Modernities and Their Discontents." *Positions: East Asia Cultures Critique* (forthcoming).

——. "Qualities of Desire: Imagining Gay Identities in China." *Thinking Sexuality Transnationally. GLQ*, ed. Elizabeth A. Povinelli and George Chauncey, special issue, 5, no. 4 (1999): 451–74.

Rose, Frank. "Pocket Monster." *Wired* 9 (September 2001), 128–35.

Rose, Nikolas. "Identity, Genealogy, History." In *Questions of Cultural Identity*, ed. Stuart Hall and Paul Du Gay. 128–50. London: Sage Publications, 1996.

Roszak, Theodore. *The Cult of Information*. Berkeley: University of California Press, 1994.

Roy-Chowdhury, Sandip. "Coming Out, Coming Home." *India Currents* 14, no. 6 (2000): 36–40, 68.

Rutt, Richard. "The Flower Boys of Silla (Hwarang): Notes on the Sources." *Transactions of the Korea Branch of the Royal Asiatic Society* 38 (1961): 1–66.

Sadistic. ⟨http://www2.networks.ne.jp/~foo/SDSTC/⟩ (14 June 2000).

Said, Edward W. *Orientalism*. London: Routledge and Kegan Paul. 1978.

Sanrio Co. Ltd. *Hello Kitty Special Feature*. ⟨http://kitty.sanrio.co.jp/characters/kitty/kitty.htm⟩ (20 November 2000).

SayangAbang. ⟨http://www.roy.com/64821⟩ (18 July 2002).

Schiller, Herbert I. "The Global Information Highway: Project for an Ungovernable World." In *Resisting the Virtual Life: The Culture and Politics of Information,* ed. James Brook and Iain A. Boal. 7–33. San Francisco: City Lights, 1995.

Schleiner, Ann-Marie. "Open Source Art Experiments: Lucky Kiss." 26 November 2000. ⟨www.nettime.org⟩ (26 November 2000).

Schodt, Frederik. *Dreamland Japan: Writings on Modern Manga*. Berkeley: Stone Bridge Press, 1996.

ScooterX. "[amla] Re: read any good manga? (translated comics)." 17 July 2000. ⟨http://groups.yahoo.com/group/amla/message/6327⟩ (4 March 2001).

Seidler, Victor. "Embodied Knowledge and Virtual Space: Gender, Nature and History." In *The Virtual Embodied: Presence/Practice/Technology,* ed. John Wood. 15–29. London: Routledge, 1998.

Seiji Biblos. 4 January 2001. ⟨www.biblos.co.jp/beeep/index.htm⟩ (4 January 2001).

Sen, Armartya. "Human Rights and Asian Values: What Lee Kuan Yew and Li Peng Don't Understand about Asia." *New Republic* 217, nos. 2–3 (1997): 33–41.

Sen, Krishna. *Indonesian Cinema: Framing the New Order*. London: Zed Press, 1994.

The Sex Warriors and the Samurai. Prod. Parminder Vir, dir. Nick Deocampo. 25 min. Formation Films Production for Channel Four, 1995. Videocassette.

Shari, Michael. "Welcome to Internet Island." *Business Week,* 1 February 1999, 37.

Shaw, David F. "Gay Men and Computer Communication: A Discourse of Sex and Identity in Cyberspace." In *Virtual Culture: Identity and Communication in Cybersociety,* ed. Steven G. Jones. 133–45. Thousand Oaks, CA: Sage Publications, 1997.

Siegel, James T. *Fetish, Recognition, Revolution*. Princeton, NJ: Princeton University Press, 1997.

SiGNel. *SiGNel Homepage*. 15 March 1997. ⟨http://www.geocities.com/WestHollywood/3878/signel.htm/⟩ (25 July 2002).

Signorile, Michelangelo. *Queer in America: Sex, the Media, and the Closets of Power*. New York: Anchor, 1994.

Silver, David. "Looking Backwards, Looking Forwards: Cyberculture Studies 1990–2000." In *Web.Studies: Rewiring Media Studies for the Digital Age,* ed. David Gauntlett. 19–31. London: Arnold, 2000.

Silvio, Teri. "Drag Melodrama/Feminine Public Sphere/Folk Television: 'Local Opera' and Identity in Taiwan." Ph.D. diss., University of Chicago, 1998.

——. "Reflexivity, Bodily Praxis, and Identity in Taiwanese Opera." *Thinking Sexuality Transnationally. GLQ,* special issue, 5, no. 4 (1999): 585–603.

Singapore 21. *Singapore 21.* 1 January 2000. ⟨http://www.singapore21.org.sg⟩
   (30 May 2001).
Singapore Broadcasting Authority. *Singapore Broadcasting Authority.* 8 July 1998.
   ⟨http://www.sba.gov.sg⟩ (28 December 2000).
Singapore Government. "Chapter 297." *Singapore Broadcasting Authority Act.*
   15 March 1994. Singapore: Statutes of the Republic of Singapore, 1994.
Singapore Government Media Release. *Singapore Government Website.* 28 April
   2000. ⟨http://app.internet.gov.sg/data/sprinter/pr/archives/2000060503.
   htm⟩ (18 July 2002).
Singapore Tourism Board. *Official Guide: Singapore New Asia.* Singapore: Silk
   Route Publications, May 2000.
———. *New Asia–Singapore: The Official Website for Tourist Information on Sin-
   gapore.* 1 July 1998. ⟨http://www.newasia-singapore.com⟩ (30 May 2001).
Sintercom. *Sintercom Homepage.* 1994. ⟨http://www.sintercom.org⟩
   (30 November 2000).
Slevin, James. *The Internet and Society.* Cambridge, England: Polity Press, 2000.
Soja, Edward. *Postmetropolis: Critical Studies of Cities and Regions.* Oxford: Black-
   well, 2000.
Sondheim, Alan. *Being on Line: Net Subjectivity.* New York: Lusitania Press, 1997.
Song, Byung-Nak. *The Rise of the Korean Economy.* Hong Kong: Oxford Univer-
   sity Press, 1990.
Spigel, Lynn. *Make Room for TV: Television and the Family Ideal in Postwar Amer-
   ica.* Chicago: University of Chicago Press, 1992.
Spivak, Gayatri. "Cultural Talks in the Hot Peace: Revisiting the 'Global Village.'"
   In *Cosmopolitics: Thinking and Feeling beyond the Nation,* ed. Pheng Cheah
   and Bruce Robbins. 329–50. Minneapolis: University of Minnesota Press, 1998.
Sproull, Lee, and Semer Faraj. "Atheism, Sex, and Databases: The Net as a Social
   Technology." In *Culture of the Internet,* ed. Sara Kiesler. 35–51. Mahwah, NJ:
   Erlbaum, 1997.
Staff. "The Marketing of Adolescence in Japan: Buying and Dreaming." In
   Women, Media and Consumption in Japan, ed. Lise Skov and Brian Moeran.
   255–73. Surrey, England: Curzon Press. 1995.
———. "Okatu Culture Set for Extinction?" *Kobe Shimbun,* 7 November 2000, 19.
Steedly, Mary Margaret. *Hanging without a Rope: Narrative Experience in Colonial
   and Postcolonial Karoland.* Princeton, NJ: Princeton University Press, 1993.
Stewart, Ian. "Second Jail Term for Anwar." *South China Morning Post,* 9 August
   2000. ⟨http://scmp.com⟩ (15 August 2000).
Stocker, Timothy. "The Future at Your Fingertip." 4 October 2000. ⟨http:www.
   tkai.com/press/001004_independent.htm⟩ 20 September, 2001.
Storer, Graeme. "Performing Sexual Identity: Naming and Resisting 'Gayness' in
   Modern Thailand." *Intersections: Gender, History and Culture in the Asian*

Context, 2 (1999). ⟨http://wwwsshe.murdoch.edu.eu/intersections/issue2/Storer.html ⟩. (7 July 2000).

Sullivan, G., and L. W. Leong, eds. *Gays and Lesbians in Asia and the Pacific: Social and Human Services.* New York: Harrington Press, 1995.

Sullivan, Gerard, and Peter Jackson, eds. *Gay and Lesbian Asia.* New York: Haworth Press, 2001.

Summerhawk, Barbara, Cheiron McMahill, and Darren McDonald, eds. *Queer Japan: Personal Stories of Japanese Lesbians, Gays, Bisexuals and Transsexuals.* Norwich, VT: New Victoria Press, 1998.

Sussex Technology Group. "In the Company of Strangers: Mobile Phones and the Conception of Space." In *Technoscapes,* ed. Sally R. Munt. 205–233. London: Continuum, 2001.

Suvir and Arvind. Editorial. *Trikone* 1, no. 1 (1986): 1.

Takarajima. *Ura Tōkyō kankō* [Backstreet Tokyo sightseeing]. Tokyo: Takara-jimasha, 1998.

Takemiya, Keiko. *Kaze to ki no uta* (The Song of Wind and Trees). Tokyo: Take-miya Keiko/Sogakukan/Herald, 1987. Italian translation *Il poema del vento e degli alberi* (Milano: Yamato Video S.R.L., 1997).

——. *Kaze to ki no uta.* 9 vols. Tokyo: Shogakukan, 1998–99.

Tamney, Joseph. *The Struggle over Singapore's Soul: Western Modernization and Asian Culture.* Berlin: W. de Gruyter, 1996.

Tan Beng-Hui. "Moving Sexuality Rights into the New Millennium." *Women in Action* 1 (1999). ⟨http://www.isiswomen.org/wia199/sex00006.html⟩ (15 August 2000).

Tang, James T. H., ed. *Human Rights and International Relations in the Asia-Pacific Region.* New York: Pinter, 1995.

Templer, Robert. "Lennon v Lenin." *Age Good Weekend* (17 October 1998): 52–57.

Terry, Jennifer. "The Seductive Power of Science in the Making of Deviant Sub-jectivity." In *Posthuman Bodies,* ed. Judith Halberstam and Ira Livingston. 135–61. Bloomington: Indiana University Press, 1995.

Thadani, Giti. "No Lesbians Please: We Are Indian." *Trikone* 9, no. 2 (1994): 6.

Tirrell, Lynne. "Derogatory Terms: Racism, Sexism and the Inferential Role The-ory of Meaning." In *Language and Liberation,* ed. Christina Hendricks and Kelly Oliver. 41–88. New York: State University of New York Press, 1999.

Tobin, Joseph J. *Re-made in Japan: Everyday Life and Consumer Taste in a Chang-ing Society.* New Haven: Yale University Press, 1992.

Toffler, Alvin. "Upheaval Dims Hopes for Mahathir's Silicon Valley." *Los Angeles Times,* 17 November 1998. ⟨http://www.dranees.org/toffler.htm⟩ (5 March 2001).

Tomes, Kimberly SaRee. "Shu Lea Cheang: Hi-tech Aborigine." *Wide Angle* 18, no. 1 (August 1995). ⟨http://jhupress.jhu.edu/demo/wide_angle/18.1tomes.html⟩ (30 December 2000).

Tremewan, Christopher. "Human Rights in Asia." *Pacific Review* 6, no. 1 (1993): 17–30.

Tsang, Daniel C. "Notes on Queer'n'Asian Virtual Sex." In *Asian American Sexualities: Dimensions of the Gay and Lesbian Experience,* ed. Russell Leong. 153–62. New York: Routledge, 1996. Also published in Donald Morton, ed. *The Material Queer* (Boulder, CO: Westview, 1996), 310–17.

Tu Wei-ming, ed. *Confucian Traditions in East Asian Modernity.* Cambridge, MA: Harvard University Press, 1996.

Turkle, Sherry. *Life on the Screen: Identity in the Age of the Internet.* New York: Simon and Schuster, 1995.

TV's FORUM JAPAN. ⟨http://www.geocities.com/WestHollywood/Village/9111/⟩ (17 July 2000).

United Nations High Commissioner for Human Rights. "International Covenant of Civil and Political Rights." *United Nations Homepage.* 25 November 2000. ⟨http://www.unhchr.ch/html/menu3/b/a_ccpr.htm⟩ (1 December 2000).

Utopia. *Utopia Homepage.* 13 December 1995. ⟨http://www.utopia-asia.com⟩ (25 July 2002).

van Esterik, Penny. "Repositioning Gender, Sexuality, and Power in Thai Studies." In *Genders and Sexualities in Modern Thailand,* ed. Peter A. Jackson and Nerida M. Cook. 275–89. Chiang Mai, Thailand: Silkworm Books, 1999.

Vanita, Ruth, and Saleem Kidwai. *Same-Sex Love in India: Readings from Literature and History.* New York: St. Martin's Press, 2000.

Vikram. "Cybergay." *Bombay Dost* 7, no. 1 (1999): 8–13.

"Voice of Asia? Or of Racism and Retribution." *Free Malaysia,* 7 December 1999. ⟨http://www.freemalaysia.com/political/voice_of_asia.htm⟩ (5 March 2001).

"Visto Terms of Agreements (TOS)." *Visto Corporation.* 24 May 1999. ⟨http://www.visto.com⟩ (3 January 2001).

Vithalani, Jay. "Passport Princesses." *Bombay Dost* 7, no. 1 (1999): 17, 25.

Vitiello, Giovanni. "The Fantastic Journey of an Ugly Boy: Homosexuality and Salvation in Late Ming Pornography." *Positions: East Asia Cultures Critique* 4, no. 2 (1996): 291–320.

Wachman, Alan M. *Taiwan: National Identity and Democratization.* Armonk, NY: M.E. Sharpe, 1994.

Wahyuni, Hermin Indah. *Televisi dan Intervensi Negara: Konteks Politik Kebijakan Publik Industri Penyiaran Televisi* (Television and State Intervention: The Political Context of the Television Broadcasting Industry Public Decrees). Yogyakarta: Penerbit Media Pressindo, 2000.

Wakefield, Nina. "Cyberqueer." In *The Cybercultures Reader,* ed. David Bell and Barbara M. Kennedy. 403–15. London: Routledge, 2000.

Wang Ru-Xuan. Introduction to *Fan Qishi zhi* Yue [A date on which to oppose discrimination]. Taipei: Tongzhi Gongzuo Fang, 1993.

Wark, McKenzie. "Infohype." In *Transit Lounge: Wake-Up Calls and Travellers' Tales from the Future,* ed. Ashley Crawford and Ray Edgar. 144–47. Sydney: Craftman House, 1997.

Warner, Michael. Introduction to *Fear of a Queer Planet: Queer Politics and Social Theory,* ed. Michael Warner. vii–xxxi. Minneapolis: University of Minnesota Press, 1993.

Watanabe, Tsuneo, and Jun'ichi Iwata. *The Love of the Samurai: A Thousand Years of Japanese Homosexuality.* London: Gay Men's Press, 1989.

We Are Family. *We Are Family Homepage.* 27 August 2000. ⟨http://www.geocities. com/WestHollywood/Heights/7288/⟩ (30 November 2000).

West, Donald J., and Richard Green, eds. *Sociolegal Control of Homosexuality: A Multi-Nation Comparison.* New York: Plenum Press, 1997.

Wheeler, Deborah L. "Global Culture or Global Clash: New Information Technologies and the Islamic World—A View from Kuwait." *Communication Research* 25, no. 4 (1998): 359–77.

White, Merry. "The Marketing of Adolescence in Japan." In *Women, Media, and Consumption in Japan,* ed. Lise Skov and Brian Moeran, 255–73. Surrey, UK: Curzon Press, 1995.

Wieringa, Saskia E. "Desiring Bodies or Defiant Cultures: Butch-Femme Lesbians in Jakarta and Lima." In *Female Desires: Same-Sex Relations and Transgender Practices across Cultures,* ed. Evelyn Blackwood and Saskia E. Wieringa. 206–29. New York: Columbia University Press, 1999.

Williams, Carolyn. "Identity Politics in the Postmodern." In *Gay and Lesbian Perspectives IV,* ed. Robert Aldrich and Garry Wotherspoon. 28–40. Sydney: University of Sydney, 1998.

Williams, Linda. *Hard Core: Power, Pleasure, and the "Frenzy of the Visible."* Berkeley: University of California Press, 1989.

Wilson, Ashleigh. "Unbridled Innocence." *The Australian,* 12 October 2000, media sec., p. 18.

Wilson, Rob, and Wimal Dissanayake, eds. *Asia/Pacific as Space of Cultural Production.* Durham, NC: Duke University Press, 1995.

——, eds. *Global/Local: Cultural Production and the Transnational Imaginary.* Durham, NC: Duke University Press, 1996.

Wockner, Rex. "Malaysian Prime Minister Disparages Gays," *International News* 304, 21 February 2000. ⟨http://www.longyangclub.org/toronto/news.htm#4⟩ (5 March 2001).

Wolmark, Jenny, ed. *Cybersexualities: A Reader on Feminist Theory, Cyborgs and Cyberspace.* Edinburgh: University of Edinburgh Press, 1999.

Wong, Adeline, and Brian Chia. "E-com Legal Guide Malaysia." *E-Com Legal Guide.* ⟨http://www.bakerinfo.com/apec/malayapec.htm⟩ (5 March 2001).

Yang Hyon-Ah. "Hankuk Kajokpop-eso Omoni-nun Odiso Iss(Oss)-da?" [Where is (not) the mother in Korean Family law]. In *Mosong-ui Namron-gwa Hyonshil: Omoni-ui Song, Sarm, Jongchesong* [Discourses and realities of motherhood: Mothers' gender, livelihood, and sexual politics], ed. Kim Yong-Hee, Jong Jin-Song, and Yun Jong-ro. 117–36. Seoul: Hanam, 1999.

Yang, Linda. "Virtual Space and the Flow of Sexual Discourse." Paper presented at the second International Conference on Sexuality Education, Sexology, Gender Studies and LesBiGay Studies, National Central University, Taiwan, 31 May–1 June 1997.

Yang, Mayfair Mei-Hui, ed. *Spaces of Their Own: Women's Public Sphere in Transnational China.* Minneapolis: University of Minnesota Press, 1999.

Yaoi a Laboratory. ⟨http://www.lilac.cc/~maco/⟩ (16 June 2000).

Yensabai, Chad. "Gay: Sisan Thi Taektarng" [Gay: A different color]. In *Krungthep Turakij.* (21 October 1999). ⟨http://xq28.hypermart.net/different. html⟩ (12 May 2000).

Yoshimoto, Mitsuhiro. "Real Virtuality." In *Global/Local: Cultural Production and the Transnational Imaginary,* ed. Rob Wilson and Wimal Dissanayake. 107–18. Durham, NC: Duke University Press, 1996.

Yue, Audrey. "Asian-Australian Cinema, Asian-Australian Modernity." In *Diaspora: Negotiating Asian-Australia,* ed. Tseen Khoo et al. 190–99. St. Lucia, Australia: University of Queensland Press, 2000.

Yuki, Shimizu. *Love Mode.* 7 vols. to date. Tokyo: Biblos, 1996–.

Zhang Zhiben and Lin Jidong, eds. *Zui Xin Liufa Quanshu* [The latest edition of the six legal codes]. Taipei: Da Zhongguo, 1996.

Contributors

CHRIS BERRY is Associate Professor in the Film Studies Program at the University of California, Berkeley. He was Visiting Professor at the Korean National University of the Arts in Seoul in both 1997 and 1999. He has written widely on sexuality and East Asian cinema, including his book *A Bit on the Side: East-West Topographies of Desire* (EMPress, 1994) and a recent article in *Jump Cut* on Zhang Yuan's *East Palace, West Palace.*

TOM BOELLSTORFF received his Ph.D. from Stanford University in 2000 and has been working with gay and lesbian Indonesians since 1992. He has taught at Stanford, UCLA, and UC Irvine. His forthcoming book is entitled *The Gay Archipelago: Sexuality and Nation in Postcolonial Indonesia.*

LARISSA HJORTH is a writer and artist lecturing in Visual Art History at The Victorian College of the Arts, and in Critical Studies and Design History at Swinburne University of Technology, Australia. She has written for *Art Asia Pacific, Like* magazine, *Broadsheet, Art and Australia,* and *Paletten.* In 2000, she completed an Australia Council Studio residency in Tokyo.

KATRIEN JACOBS is Assistant Professor in New Media at Emerson College. She studied at University of Maryland, College Park, where she wrote a Ph.D. thesis on dismemberment myths in 1960s and 1970s performance art. She has published several articles on pornography and new media art in journals such as *Wide Angle* and *Cultural Studies.* She is working on a book about Internet porn and digital art entitled *Erotic Peepzones: Performers, Peepsters and Digital Drifts.*

OLIVIA KHOO is Lecturer in Film at the University of New South Wales, Australia. She is also completing a Ph.D. in the Department of English with Cultural Studies at the University of Melbourne. Her research interests include Asian exoticism and regionalism and contemporary representations of diasporic Chinese femininity. She has published in *Continuum, Intersections,* and *Hecate,* and in *Diaspora: Negotiating Asian Australia.*

FRAN MARTIN is Lecturer in Cinema Studies at La Trobe University, Australia. Her book, *Situating Sexualities: Queer Representation in Taiwanese Fiction,*

Film, and Public Culture is forthcoming from Hong Kong University Press (2003), and her anthology of ten of her own literary translations, *Angelwings: Contemporary Queer Fiction from Taiwan,* is forthcoming from the University of Hawai'i Press (2003). Her work has appeared in journals including *Positions, GLQ, Intersections, Communal / Plural,* and *Chungwai Literary Monthly.*

MARK J. MCLELLAND is a Postdoctoral Fellow in the Centre for Critical and Cultural Studies at the University of Queensland. He is the author of *Male Homosexuality in Modern Japan: Cultural Myths and Social Realities* (Routledge-Curzon 2000) and coeditor of *Japanese Cybercultures* (RoutledgeCurzon 2002). He has also written many book chapters and journal papers exploring the intersections between gender, sexuality, and new technologies in Japan.

DAVID MULLALY is currently completing a combined degree at the Australian National University in Canberra. His research is focused on gender/sexuality in Thailand.

BADEN OFFORD teaches Cultural Studies and is a Principal Researcher in the Centre for Law, Politics, and Culture at Southern Cross University, Australia. His forthcoming book is titled *Homosexual Rights as Human Rights: Activism in Indonesia, Singapore and Australia.*

SANDIP ROY grew up in Calcutta and now edits *Trikone* magazine in San Francisco. His work has appeared in anthologies including *Q&A: Queer in Asian America, Contours of the Heart: South Asians Map North America, A Part Yet Apart: South Asians in Asian America, Men on Men 6,* and *Chick for a Day.* He writes regularly for *India Currents* and *India Abroad.* He also works with Pacific News Service and hosts a radio show, UpFront on San Francisco's 91.7 FM.

VERUSKA SABUCCO graduated in 2000 in Sociology at LaSapienza University in Rome with the thesis, "A Gender-Confused Genre. Una proposta di studio della fiction slash come genere." She is the author of *Shonen Ai* (Castelvecchi Editore, 2000) and is a freelance writer and reviewer for magazines and Web sites. Currently she is the curator, editor, and the head of press office and marketing departments of the Italian Boy's Love comic series "Boy+Boy."

AUDREY YUE is Lecturer in Cultural Studies at the University of Melbourne, Australia. Her essays on Hong Kong cinema, queer theory, and diaspora cultures have appeared in *New Formations, Inter-Asia Cultural Studies, Journal of Homosexuality, Journal of Australian Studies, Meanjin,* and *Asian Journal of*

Communication. Her chapter contributions appear in *The Horror Reader* (Routledge, 2000), *Multicultural Queer: Australian Narratives* (Haworth Press, 2000), *Floating Lives: The Media and Asian Diasporas* (University of Queensland Press, 2000), and *Diaspora: Negotiating Asian-Australia* (University of Queensland Press, 2000). She currently researches on sexual and cultural identity in New Asia.

Index

accumulation: flexible, 23; pedagogical, 255; rice, 254, 255

activism, 105, 189, 202, 206, 213; activist groups, 93, 214; coalitions and collaborations, 116, 191; grassroots, 12, 189; in India, 12, 180–81, 188; in Indonesia, 32; movements, 88, 180–81, 189, 192–93, 195; organizations, 32, 212, 249; Pride march and parade, 40, 192, 253; in Singapore, 12, 141, 152; in South Korea, 98; in Taiwan, 104; visibility project, 249. *See also* community; gay men; identity; Internet; lesbians

ACT-UP, 192

Agamben, Giorgio, 42

agency, 21, 24, 26–27, 40, 44; sexual, 202; theories of, 23. *See also* globalization

AIDS, 3, 35

allegory, 203

Allison, Anne, 78, 216–18

Althusser, Louis, 44

Altman, Dennis, 6, 87–88, 169, 236 n. 4

ambivalence, 11, 158, 160–62, 166–75

Anderson, Benedict, 249

androgyny, 231

anime, 70–71, 166, 170, 210, 213; dubbed, 73, 75; and fantasy, 208; and industry, 206; and porn, 206; subtitling of, 73. *See also* audience; films; manga

Another Mother Tongue, 6

anthropology, 210; in Indonesia, 28

Appadurai, Arjun, 3, 4, 5, 88, 173, 201, 210, 259

appropriation, 3, 13–14, 71, 87, 124, 160, 162, 170, 174, 213, 254; as cultural sampling, 213; fetishistic, 173; and reappropriation, 174; transgressive, 161

Arendt, Hannah, 24

articulation, 45, 51 n. 47, 105, 134, 140

Asia, 11, 14, 222, 224, 230–31, 235, 245, 252, 260, 260 n. 1; and queer culture, 2, 13, 22, 26, 222. *See also* region

Asian values, 24, 133–34, 147, 150, 153 n. 2, 227, 229, 246, 251–53. *See also* family; identity; ideology; region; sexual identity; sexuality

Asian Renaissance, The, 230

Au, Alex, 136, 140, 144–48, 150–51

audience, 8, 42, 72, 120, 164, 205–6, 213, 215, 234; readership, 212; viewers, 202, 205, 212, 219. *See also* fans; identification; reception; spectatorship

aura, 170

authenticity, 21, 25, 27, 40–42, 44–46, 192

avatar, 213

Azuma, Hiroki, 170–71

Bakhtin, Mikhail, 127 n. 19

Barker, Chris, 173

Barlow, John Perry, 215

Bauman, Zygmunt, 152

Baym, Nancy, 10–11

Becquer, Marcos, 89

belonging, 43, 46, 74, 133–34, 152, 246, 249, 251–52

Benjamin, Walter, 42, 44–46, 170

Berry, Chris, 8, 11–13, 14, 87–114, 124

bisexuality: of Indian men in Fiji-Australasia, 182; in South Korea, 95; of women in India, 191

body politic, 42, 252–53, 257–59

Boellstorff, Tom, 7, 9, 14, 21–51

boy love. *See* manga; romance

Buckingham, David, 166

Buddhism, 91

Budiman, Amen, 35

broadcasting, 9. *See also* regulation

bulletin boards (BBS), 2, 14, 16 n. 8, 56, 61, 94, 97, 100–101, 105; and member of the same sex (MOTSS), 100–104, 114 n. 37

butch-femme, 31. *See also* lesbians; sexual identity

camp, 168

capital, 3, 202, 204, 235, 250–53, 255–56, 258–59

capitalism, 3, 4, 26, 40; developmental, 245, 257; digital, 204; global, 3, 202; informational, 12, 247, 252; late, 23, 78, 87, 245. *See also* globalization

Carey, James, 9

Carrey, Jim, 39

Castells, Manuel, 133, 138–40

censorship. *See* regulation

Cerna, Christine M., 136

chat, 2, 64, 100, 212

chat rooms, 15, 61, 101, 183–84, 201, 213; Internet Relay Chat (IRC), 100, 183–84; lines, 234. *See also* Internet

character dolls, 11, 14, 158, 163–65, 171; changing roles of, 160; *Dokodemo-Issyo*, 170; as fad, 163; *Hello Kitty*, 158, 162–64, 166, 168–70, 172, 174–75, 178 n. 32; humor in, 164; *Kiki Lara*, 165; and landscape cultures, 159, 161–62, 164, 169, 172–73; and love, 171; *My Melody*, 165; *Pokemon*, 170; *PostPet*, 158, 164, 170; *Sanrio*, 1, 158, 164; *Tare Panda*, 165. *See also* culture; kitsch; phones

Cheang, Shu Lea, 10, 14, 201–19

Ching, Leo, 231, 235

Christianity, 91–92; in Indonesia, 33

chronotope, 151, 157 n. 50

Chua, Beng Huat, 246–47, 253, 257–58

Chua, Lawrence, 204–5

civil society, 135, 140

class, 30–31, 87, 194–95, 246–47, 252–53; in India, 187; in Indonesia, 33, 35; in Japan, 9, 164; new rich, 257–58; in Singapore, 11, 258–60; in South Korea, 9; in Taiwan, 9; in Vietnam, 3

classifieds, 103. *See also* electronic mail; Internet

citizenship, 122, 133, 151, 245; as accumulation, 255; as consumption, 251; cultural, 12, 246, 251, 256; flexible, 23, 255

coconut, 252. *See also* code; cultural history; food

codes, 77, 159, 161, 168, 173, 208, 214, 247; and beeper, 259–60; and censorship, 261 n. 7; and coder (android), 203, 211, 216; Japanese language as, 56; and policy, 246; sexual, 159; in short messaging service (SMS), 2. *See also* pagers; regulation; short messaging service

colonization, 116. *See also* globalization

commodification, 3, 4, 26, 201

commodity, 2–3, 6, 173, 213–14. *See also* culture; materialism; rice

communications, 13, 39, 102, 141–42, 145, 149, 162, 168, 171, 175, 178 n. 32, 183, 187, 195, 211, 249, 258; electrical, 9; in Indonesia, 37; intercultural, 6, 133; interpersonal, 11; and mass media, 116, 205; as system, 10; theory, 11; tool, 13. *See also* technology

community, 1, 2, 9, 11, 13–14, 25, 36, 40, 43, 94, 96, 106, 140, 184, 186–89, 190–91, 193–94, 201, 203, 205–6, 211–13, 214, 218, 210, 224–26, 229, 233–35, 246; imagined, 28, 36–37, 43, 249; values, 245. *See also* activism; fans; gay men; Internet; lesbians; transgenderism

computer games, 70, 72

computer-mediated communications (CMC), 8, 10–11, 14, 87–90, 213

computers, 87, 162, 204; at home, 164; handheld, 162; and lesbian, gay and queer use in South Korea, 96, 98; and lesbian, gay and queer use in Taiwan, 96, 98; and male activity in Taiwan, 97. *See also* Internet

consumerism, 159, 161, 173–74, 253; and customer profiling, 205; and fetishism, 206

consumers, 11, 54, 87, 121, 124, 159–60, 164, 167, 170, 175, 192–93, 202, 204, 219

consumption, 2, 12, 159, 162, 164, 167, 169, 173, 210, 245, 247, 251, 253, 257

Confucianism, 90, 110 n. 16, 134–35, 255. *See also* Asian values; ideology

consensus, 246

convergence, 13, 40

Cornwall, Andrea, 60

cosmopolitan, 222, 254, 258

Crocodile Diary, 105

cross-cultural exchange, 6, 7, 12, 27, 75, 82, 210

cross-dressing, 59–60, 169; as female role-players (*onnagata*), 54; as male role performers (*otokoyaku*), 54

Crystal Boys, 92

cultural difference, 4, 6, 7, 181, 251

cultural history, 12, 250

cultural identity. *See* hybridity; identity

cultural policy, 12–13; as technology of sexuality, 245, 251. *See also* governmentality; regulation cultural studies, 210, 218

cultures, 1, 2, 5–6, 8, 15, 28, 41, 71, 87–88, 105–6, 116, 136, 167, 173, 192, 202, 211, 219, 235, 246, 252; as collective formations, 88; and counterculture, 213; popular, 161, 164–67, 169, 171, 173, 216, 253; as scapes, 211; as social management, 245. *See also* Internet; manga

cuteness, 158–61, 164–65, 169, 173; and childhood, 167; and merchandise, 166; and place of females, 168; and sexuality, 172. *See also* character dolls

Cvetkovich, Ann, 5

cyberboosterism, 142

cybercafés, 183, 190

cyberculture, 8, 10, 185, 247

cyberfeminism, 216; VNS Matrix, 219

Cyberjaya, 222–24, 227–28, 234–35

cyberlaw. *See* Internet; regulation

cybernetics, 12, 246–47, 251; designer wear, 201; system, 251; theory, 247. *See also* feedback; information; rice

cybersex, 212, 218

cyberspace, 2, 10, 12–13, 141, 152, 174, 202, 205, 208, 223, 246, 256; anonymity in, 89; autonomy in, 125. *See also* Internet; online community

cyber-squatting, 204

cyborgs, 216, 247

Deleuze, Gilles, 208; and becoming, 211–12; and image, 220 n. 15. *See also* minorities

desire, 7, 23, 212; same-sex, 169, 235

deterritorialization, 245

dialogic relationships, 34, 137, 152, 155 n. 15

diaspora, 1, 2, 7, 12, 14, 181, 183, 246, 251, 254–55; limitations of, 183; and politics of visibility, 253

Different Rainbows, 1

disjuncture, 3, 4, 41

displacement, 2, 13, 250, 253, 257

divide, 190–91; as linear system, 247; media, 10, 22, 234; revolution, 183, 189; signature, 228; slavery, 204. *See also* new media; technology

Douglas, Susan, J., 10

dubbing, 8, 9, 14, 22, 24–28, 37–45, 50 n. 36, 50 n. 39; on video, 203. *See also* subject-position; translation

e-commerce. *See* online community

electronic discussion group. *See* listservs; mailing lists

electronic mail, 8, 9, 64, 103, 141, 144, 158, 162–63, 183–84, 188, 190; and access, 182; and address, 63, 184, 194; and counseling, 185; as personals, 184; surveys on, 13; as wireless receiver, 162. *See also* listservs; mailing lists

Empire, 4

Etheridge, Melissa, 35

ethnic absolutism, 29

ethnicity, 29, 183, 250; online, 8; as trans-ethnicity, 43. *See also* identity

ethnography, 12; as encounter, 27

family, 135–36; as shared values, 251; and values, 147, 245

fans, 70, 73–74, 76, 77–79; and fandom, 12, 70–71, 73–74, 78; and guided fan fiction, 70, 73, 79, 82, 84 n. 10; and subtitling cooperatives, 74. *See also* audience; community; Internet; magazines; manga; reception; translation

fantasy, 58, 65, 82, 124, 211, 213

Faraj, Semer, 116

fax machines, 8

feedback, 247–48, 251–52, 256, 262 n. 14; as loop, 250, 256, 260

femininity, 162, 173, 216, 218, 250

films: *Ai no kusabi*, 74; *Bara no sōretsu* (*Funeral Possession of Roses*), 68 n. 26; *Blade Runner*, 201, 203; Bombay cinema, 214; *Cruising*, 35; festivals, 180, 203, 205; *Fire*, 191; *Fresh Kill*, 206; *Gigantor*, 58; *High Tech Rice*, 1; *IKU: A Japanese Cyber-Porn Adventure*, 14, 201–19; industry in Indonesia, 37; *Jungle Taitei* (*Kimba, the White Lion*), 71; *Kaze to ki no uta*, 74; *Kusatta Kyōshi no Hōteshiki*, 73, 82, 84 n. 12; *La Blue Girl 4: The Perverted World of the Haunted Sword*, 207; *My Best Friend's Wedding*, 35; *The Naked Earth*, 206; *New York, New York*, 84 n. 12; *Sambal Belacan in San Francisco*, 248–49; *Satree Lek* (*The Iron Ladies*), 123; Seoul Queer Film and Video Festival 1997, 103; *Tetsuwan Atom* (*Astro Boy*), 71; *The Wedding Banquet*, 35

food, 249, 250, 252. *See also* coconut; rice

Foucault, Michel, 25–26, 178 n. 28, 205, 231, 243–44 n. 40
Frankfurt School, 165

Gatens, Moira, 119
Gatti, Jose, 89
Gay and Lesbian Asia, 1
gay men, 8, 20, 30–31, 35, 37, 40–41, 43–46, 53, 117, 119, 122–24, 138, 145, 183, 192; and Asian male (GAM), 1; *Bombay Dost*, 192; *Chodonghoe*, 92; *Companions on a Journey*, 181–82; and de/sexualization of Asian man, 2, 16 n. 8; as framework, 33; and genetics, 12, 14, 115–16, 125; *Humrahi*, 189; *Humsafar Trust*, 182, 186, 192; in India and South Asia, 180, 182–83, 187, 191; in Indonesia, 7, 31–32, 34; in Japan, 53, 59, 68 n. 26, 212; *Khush Toronto*, 193; in Malaysia, 224, 231, 234; and marriage, 92; as public culture, 211; *SALGA*, 182; South Asians in West, 183; in South Korea, 95; and support groups, 189; in Taiwan, 95; *Trikone*, 181, 187, 190; *Trikone-Tejas*, 182; in Vietnam, 3. *See also* activism; community; Internet; sexual identity; subject-position
gender, 32, 41, 165, 167, 172, 174, 181, 211; and computer use in South Korea, 96; as difference, 216; as difference from Western norms in Japan, 173; as identity, 60, 174; as nonconformist and nonconfirming, 159, 162; normative, 118, 211; as performances and roles in Japan, 54, 119, 159, 160–61, 166, 168–69; politics of, 225; and politics of sex work in Taiwan, 103. *See also* hegemony; identity; sexual identity; transgenderism
genealogy, 255
Gerbner, George, 145
Gibson-Graham, J. K., 26
globalization, 4, 5, 6, 9, 14, 21, 27, 40–41, 45, 52, 202, 224, 230, 254; cultural, 3, 4, 6, 14, 87–89; as cultural Americanization, 4–5; as cultural domination of West, 4; as cultural flow, 4, 14; as cultural homogeneity and homogenization, 88, 105; as cultural imperialism, 105, 173; and development of gay and lesbian issues in Singapore, 141; feminist critiques of, 26; of gayness, 3, 195; as globe-girdling, 245; as new order, 211, 231; as

queering, 26, 40, 104; and sexual agency, 201; and sexual identities, 235; of sexual and queer cultures, 2, 104, 256; studies and debates of, 3–5; as unequal development, 245. *See also* capitalism; global queering; identity; Internet; sexual identity
global queering, 3, 6, 7, 11, 14, 27, 87, 105–6, 169, 181, 201, 223, 256. *See also* activism; Altman, Dennis; capitalism; community; gay men; homosexuality; Internet; lesbians; sexual identity
glocalization, 7, 8, 13–14, 17 n. 23
Goffman, Erving, 160
Gottlieb, Nanette, 52
governance, 135, 148, 152, 252, 255. *See also* governmentality; regulation
governmentality, 246, 252. *See also* regulation
Graff, E. J., 138
Greenberg, Clement, 165–66
Guattari, Félix, 4
Guggenheim Museum, 204

Hall, Stuart, 3, 117
Hamano, Hoki, 170
Haraway, Donna, 108 n. 6
Hard Core: Power, Pleasure and the "Frenzy of the Visible," 210
Harvey, David, 255
hegemony, 4, 125, 233, 246, 252–53, 256
Heng, Russell H. K., 140
hermaphrodites, 123
heterogeneity, 3, 5, 89
heteronormativity, 40, 53–54, 116, 120, 122, 124–25, 134, 168; as heterosexism, 211; as heterosupremacy, 119–21
heterosexuality, 136, 163, 165–66; compulsory, 53; framework, 159; mainstream, 63
History of Sexuality, The, 25. *See also* Foucault, Michel
Hjorth, Larissa, 11–12, 14, 158–79
Holden, Todd, 160
home, 204, 250–51
homogenization, 3, 4, 14, 173
homophobia, 116, 147
homosexuality, 3, 8, 70, 163, 180, 212; in films, 35; in India, 9, 187, 192; in Indonesia, 29, 31, 33, 35, 36; as love, 169; in magazines, 35; in Malaysia, 222–25, 227–28, 231–32; as medical category or pathology, 35, 231;

and national politics, 233; as resistance identities, 139, 147; in Singapore, 133–36, 140, 145–46, 150; as Western stereotype, 28. *See also* gay men; Ibrahim, Anwar; regulation; romance; sexual identity; sodomy

human rights, 40, 147, 211, 233; in Indonesia, 24, 30; International Gay and Lesbian Human Rights Commission, 187; in Singapore, 135–37, 144–45, 149, 151–52; as site of intervention, 133

hybridity, 4, 89, 161, 201, 211, 255

Ibrahim, Anwar, 8, 222–25, 229–34. *See also* homosexuality; practice; sexuality

identification, 88, 95–96, 139, 163–64, 166, 168, 174; and gender, 162; as self-identification, 2, 25, 202; sexual, 104, 106, 162. *See also* audience; identity; reception; representation

identity, 5, 7–8, 13–14, 25, 27, 36, 44, 53, 88, 136, 138, 161, 165, 171, 210, 246; cultural, 6; as myth, 211; as production, 252; politics, 61, 133, 139, 254; and queer groups, 183; as site of intervention, 133. *See also* activism; community; ethnicity; gender; Internet

ideology, 43–44, 125, 135, 137, 139, 159, 231–32, 246, 251, 255; Eurocentric, 4, 5, 8. *See also* Asian values; Confucianism

image, 1, 42

imaginary, 46, 201, 205; as social imagination, 211

Inanavira, Dharmachari, 178 n. 28

Indonesia, 28, 38–39, 43. *See also* dubbing

information, 1, 2, 13, 61, 64, 65 n. 5, 74, 78–79, 88–89, 95–96, 100, 103–4, 137–38, 144, 149, 183, 185–89, 195, 206, 213, 215, 222, 228–29, 234, 245, 247, 252, 255, 257; as capital, 247, 250; as data, 203, 205, 217, 227, 247; as exchange, 247, 251; interface, 2, 13, 27, 148, 257; and technology, 1, 223, 226, 229–30, 232, 234–35

intellectual property, 228. *See also* Internet; regulation

Internet, 8, 10–14, 27, 52, 64, 70, 72, 89, 93, 99, 121, 133, 137, 141, 143, 146, 149, 152, 170, 181, 187, 192–93, 202, 211, 213; and access, 106, 117, 192, 228; as alternative forum space, 55, 101, 109–10 n. 13, 117, 136, 141, 142, 188, 193; anonymity on, 106, 188; censorship of,

203, 215, 227–28; as communications, 10, 137, 142, 206, 212, 215; and community, 11, 14, 53, 72–74, 78, 102, 104, 107, 141, 143, 186, 190, 193, 196, 202–3, 218, 224, 233–35, 248; as entertainment, 64–65; gay, lesbian, and queer activism and, 117, 133, 141, 146, 148, 181–82, 187, 192–93, 195–96, 206; gay content on, 53, 180; and global reach, 52, 73, 144, 185; in India, 184, 190–91, 194; as information provider, 98–99, 184, 225–26; in Japan, 1, 11, 52, 55, 64, 65 n. 3, 164, 170, 221; in Malaysia, 224, 225, 227, 233–35; and politicization of sexuality, 64, 206, 215; and pornography, 67 n. 23, 184, 203, 206, 214, 218–19; and queer cultures, 116, 212; and service providers, 134, 193, 214–15; in Singapore, 1, 12, 14, 137–38, 141–43, 149, 152; in South Korea, 1, 8, 89, 94–95, 100, 105; in Taiwan, 8, 89, 94–95, 100, 103–5. *See also* activism; chat; electronic mail; globalization; information; listservs; mailing lists; new media; phones; web

interracial desire, 205. *See also* cross-cultural exchange; sexual identity

interpellation, 44

interviewees, 226, 232; Ashley Lee, 234; Anji, Madhuri, 187–88; Bhavesh, 186, 188–89, 193, 195; Darta, 21, 36; Kavi, Ashok Row, 185–86, 192–94; Kugle, Scott, 189; Kumana, Geeta, 191; Nagarajan, Mala, 188, 194–95; Puar, Jasbir, 188; Thadani, Giti, 192; Vaid, Urvashi, 194; Vikram, 190–92

Islam, 21, 24; in Indonesia, 33–34; in Malaysia, 232, 235–36 n. 1, 242 n. 47

Jackson, Peter, 87–88

Jacobs, Katrien, 10, 12, 14, 201–21

Jagose, Annamarie, 202

Jameson, Fredric, 4

Japan: childhood in, 167; gift giving in, 169; social etiquette in, 162

John, Elton, 35

Jolly, Margaret, 7

Kellner, Douglas, 5

Khoo, Olivia, 8, 12, 14, 222–44

Kinsella, Sharon, 70, 72, 167, 168–69, 171, 173–74

kitsch, 165–66; and pop/trash, 159. *See also* character dolls

Kleinwaechter, Wolfgang, 141
Kramer, Gavin, 158

Lee, Kuan Yew, 134
Leong, Laurence Wai-Teng, 134–36, 141
lesbians, 8, 122, 192; *Aanchal Organization*, 185; *Chodonghoe*, 92; *Counsel Club*, 187; and dance party advertisements in Japan, 158, 172; as global culture, 8; in India, 187, 191; in Indonesia, 7, 21–27, 30–32, 35, 37, 40–41, 43–46; in Malaysia, 224, 255–56; *Pink Triangle*, 225; *SALGA*, 182; *Sappho*, 185; in Singapore, 135, 143, 145, 248–50, 256–57; *Singapore and Malaysian Bisexual and Lesbian Network*, 247–48; in South Korea, 95; and support groups, 160, 191, 224–25; in Taiwan, 95, 105; *Trikone*, 181, 187, 190; *Trikone-Tejas*, 182; *Women Zhijian*, 92; *Yellow Kitties*, 1. *See also* activism; community; globalization; Internet; sexual identity
Lim, Madeleine, 144, 248
listservs, 2; electronic discussion groups, 182, 187, 189; lists, 226; *Desidykes*, 182, 194; *4AsiaGays*, 225; *Gay Bombay*, 183, 186–87, 189–91, 196; *Gay Delhi*, 189; *Khush*, 182, 188, 191, 193; *Malaysian Lesbian Network*, 225; *SAGrrls*, 182, 188, 194; *Singaporean and Malaysian Bisexuals and Lesbians*, 225, 248, 254–60; *Women Who Love Women*, 224. *See also* electronic mail; Internet; mailing lists
local, 5, 7–8, 13–14, 34, 46, 87–88, 95, 104–5, 141, 205, 211, 215, 245, 257; as face-to-face, 9; as ethnolocal, 28–29; as indigeneity, 31, 40, 45, 89; as neighborhood, 29, 205, 258; as site of production and contestation, 235; as translocal, 29, 36; as vernacular, 162, 255
locality, 14, 41, 117, 258
Lovink, Geert, 218–19

magazines, 32–35, 40, 45, 48 n. 20, 116, 180; *Advocate*, 1; *Aestheticism*, 74–75; *Aibao*, 92; animation, 55; *Asiaweek*, 146–47, 230; *Bombay Dost*, 180, 188; *Buddy*, 92; *Da Vinchi*, 59; fanzines, 54, 70, 74, 85 n. 14; *Femina*, 35; *G&L*, 92; *Good Weekend*, 3; in Indonesia, 32; in Japan, 52; *June*, 55–56, 72; *Kartini*, 21, 35; *Nation*, 124; *Pafu*, 55; *Pent-house*, 212; *Queer Japan*, 66 n. 7; *Rice Magazine*, 253; *Time*, 1–2; *Together*, 92; *Trikone Magazine*, 180–81
mailing lists, 73, 75–76, 79, 85 n. 18, 213, 224, 235. *See also* electronic mail; listservs
Malaysia, 222; Cyberjaya, 222–24, 227–28, 234–35; Wawasan 2000, 226, 228. *See also* multimedia; regulation
Manderson, Lenore, 7
manga, 14, 54–55, 70, 76–77, 165–66, 169–70, 213, 216; *Ai no kusabi*, 73; and anime-connection, 71; *Captain Tsubasa*, 72; *Fake*, 73, 84 n. 12; and fan translation, 73; *Gundam Wing*, 77, 79; history and origins of, 70–71; *Kizuna*, 73, 77; *Love Mode*, 76, 79–80, 86 n. 31; reader-produced, 79; *Saint Seiya*, 72; sex between beautiful boys and men in YAOI, 58; sex in YAOI, 57–58; *Shōjo* manga, 54–55, 70–74; subgenres of, 73; *West End*, 79; Western women's rewriting of YAOI, 12, 76, 79–83; YAOI, 10–11, 13–14, 52–56, 58, 64, 70–72; YAOI fan fiction, 74–75, 78–79; YAOI fan web pages, 73–74, 76, 84–85 n. 13; *Zetsu ai/Bronze*, 73–74, 76–77, 84 n. 12; *Zetsu ai manga*, 73. *See also* audience; fans; films; Internet; magazines; reception; web
Mann, Chris, 12
Marchetti, Gina, 204, 206, 211
Martin, Fran, 8, 11–13, 14, 87–114, 124
masculinity, 173; as alternative in Indonesia, 31; of Asians in West, 253; of male queers, 119; as social prestige, 124
Massumi, Brian, 220 n. 15
materialism, 201, 249–50, 253–54
matrix, 202, 216, 218–19
Matsui, Midori, 54
McLelland, Mark, 11–14, 52–69, 169, 173, 213, 215
McVeigh, Brian, 168–69
media, 22, 24, 27, 33–37, 40–41, 44–46, 134, 169, 215; in Asia, 22; in Indonesia, 21, 34–35, 39. *See also* globalization; information; multimedia; new media; technology
mediascapes, 1, 116, 160. *See also* Appadurai, Arjun
message boards, 73, 101
Miller, Daniel, 117

minorities, 193; and Deleuze, 211; and groups, 2, 201; as model, 194; sexual and gender, 23

Miyoshi, Masao, 4

modernism, 165, 166

modernity, 2, 6, 22, 42, 113 n. 29, 128 n. 38, 135, 160, 174, 222, 225, 246; of Queer'n'Asian, 246–48

Modernity at Large: Cultural Dimensions of Globalization, 211

modernization, 159, 229, 245, 247

Mohamad, Mahathir, 222–23, 225, 227–30, 235

Morris, Rosalind, 119–20

Morton, Donald, 66 n. 7, 87–88

Mullaly, David, 12, 14, 115–29

multimedia, 2, 226; as industry, 228

Multimedia Convergence Act, 227

Multimedia Super Corridor in Malaysia, 1, 223, 226–29

Multimedia University in Malaysia, 223

nation, 45, 211, 224, 245; and boundaries, 1, 36, 201, 210; and celebrities in Japan, 54; and culture and language in Indonesia, 28–29, 38–39, 42–43; Singapore-as-New-Asia, 245

National Gay and Lesbian Task Force, 194

nationalism, 41; in Malaysia, 8; and nationalist metaphors in Indonesia, 36, 38, 39, 46; scholars of, in Indonesia, 28

network, 2, 4, 13, 26, 72, 117, 142, 144, 193, 201, 210, 212, 215, 218, 252, 257; as circuit, 204; as sites for struggle, 204. *See also* rice

newhalf, 11, 13, 52, 62, 68 n. 37; *Deciding to Be a Newhalf,* 59–60; as intermediate sex, 53, 59, 64; *Living Like "Myself,"* 59; Matsubara Rumiko, 59; network of, 53; as occupational category, 60; as site of identity, 60; and transgendered men in sex industry, 53, 59. *See also* transgenderism; web

Newly Industralized Economies, 87

new media, 1, 2, 9, 10–14, 138, 141, 170, 201, 202–3, 205–6, 246, 253–54; social effect and function of, 8–10, 15; as technology, 171, 206. *See also* communication; Internet; media; multimedia

newspapers, 34, 40, 118; *Australian,* 230; *Sunday Star,* 230

Ng, King Kang, 142, 261 n. 7

NTT Inter-Communication Center (NTT-ICC), 204

Occidentalism, 257

Offord, Baden, 12, 14, 133–57

Ong, Aihwa, 255

online community, 2, 8, 164, 182, 184, 193, 201, 203, 205, 210, 224, 228, 235; and sexual communities, 214; transactions, 228. *See also* community; ethnicity; identity; Internet; magazines; pornography; race; regulation; sexuality; subjectivity

ontology, 41, 216, 256

Orientalism, 257

Out in the World, 6

pagers, 8, 11, 248, 258–60

Permitted and Prohibited Desires, 216

PFLAG, 186

phones, 12, 160, 187, 247; mobile (cell), 8, 11, 14–15, 27, 63, 69 n. 44, 158, 160, 162, 164–65, 171, 174, 204; and sex, 205

political economy, 12, 247

popular culture. *See* culture

pornography, 12, 58, 100, 135, 201–2, 206, 208, 210–11, 214–15, 218–19; as art, 219; and children, 56, 65; conventions of, 202–3, 208, 219–10; in domestic sphere, 65; and globalization, 216; online, 13, 193, 213; pleasure in, 210, 216; production of, 201, 214. *See also* activism; culture; films; Internet; representation

postcolonialism, 5, 37, 41, 50 n. 39, 245, 250

postmodernism, 12, 135, 159, 166–67, 245

Power of Identity, The, 139

practice, 2, 64, 175, 245–46; as consumption, 246; embodied, 13; sexual, 31, 53, 134, 201, 229, 233; social, 201. *See also* consumption; sexual identity

prostitution, 103. *See also* gender; sex

public sphere, 225

Q&A: Queer in Asian America, 1

Queau, Philippe, 144

queer culture, 1, 63–64, 83 n. 1, 203; and art, 202; among Asians, 27, 95, 113 n. 29, 125, 133–34, 149, 152, 184, 193, 196, 203; as concept and discourse, 23, 87, 126 n. 2, 201, 208; and gay and lesbian studies, 202; as identity, 66 n. 7, 134; as lifestyle, 66 n. 7; as

queer culture (*cont.*)
politics, 24, 258; as queerscapes, 211; as stigma, 122–23; as theory, 53, 104, 133, 138, 140, 155 n. 17, 202. *See also* activism; Asia; community; culture; identity; Internet
Queer Diasporas, 7
Queer Theory, 202
questionnaires, 12, 93–95, 98, 104, 164, 210, 216, 225, 258; online, 8; and race, 194, 254–55; and racial nativism, 257; and racism, 250. *See also* ethnicity; identity; Internet

Race in Cyberspace, 11
Rainbow Connection, The, 142
Rajchman, John, 211–12
Rattachumpoth, 116, 118–19, 125
reception, 25, 41, 44, 120; as heterosexual viewing, 205; as misreading, 76, 79; as picture-reading, 82; and reader-oriented theorists, 75; Western, 71. *See also* audience; consumption; manga
region, 1, 5, 210, 231, 235, 245, 253; Asian, 5, 28, 134, 182, 257; and children, 58; politics of, 12, 246; and regional boundaries, 252, 255; as regionalism, 14, 224, 230–31, 235, 241 n. 39; and regionality, 245–47, 254–55; and representation, 27, 43, 64, 124, 134, 141, 159, 161–62, 164, 166–69, 174, 225, 250; of self, 136, 160; and self-naming strategy, 106, 123; as strategy, 140; and women in Japanese pornography, 216. *See also* activism; gender; identity; pornography; regulation
regulation, 1, 13, 246; as censorship, 12, 173, 217, 219; censorship laws in Japan, 173; cyberlaw in Malaysia, 12, 227–29, 234; Internal Security Act in Malaysia, 232; of media and broadcasting, 38–39, 226; online, 214; as policymaking, 215; of self, 205; of sexuality and homosexuality, 90, 134–35, 231. *See also* cultural policy; governmentality; Internet; pornography
Rheingold, Howard, 248
rice: and boys, 253; as commodity and material culture, 252; and cybernetics, 246–47, 248, 251–58; and diasporic queering, 253; and informational value, 256; as network, 247; as stereotype, 252. *See also* accumulation; culture; identity; materialism
Roach, Mary, 166

Robins, Kevin, 10
Rofel, Lisa, 4, 7
romance, 41, 54. *See also* homosexuality; manga
Rose, Frank, 162
Roy, Sandip, 9, 12, 14, 180–99

Sabucco, Veruska, 10, 12, 14, 70–86, 213
same-sex relations, 173, 178 n. 28. *See also* consumption; desire; gay men; homosexuality; lesbians; queer culture; transgenderism
Sasano, Michiru, 175
Schleiner, Anne-Marie, 213
Schodt, Frederik, 54, 57, 71, 73, 75
Scott, Ridley, 201
sex: commercialization of, 13; as industry, 63–64; and morality in Japan, 173; as subversion, 172; and work, 103, 194
sexual identity, 1, 6, 119, 137, 143, 164, 174; and Anglo-American assumptions, 5, 65; cyber-queer, 126; diasporic, 2, 13, 136, 147, 225, 246, 250–53, 257; gay, in China, Indonesia, and Thailand, 7, 26, 128 n. 38; gay, Western, 6, 212; and Japanese subversion of Western classifications, 52; lesbian, gay, and queer, in Korea, 104; lesbian, in Japan, 163; and rice and potato queens, 253; as sexual difference, 161, 168–69, 171; and sexual politics, 166, 169; as sticky rice, 253; as taboo, 165. *See also* activism; community; gay men; global queering; homosexuality; identity; Internet; lesbians; practice; representation; sexuality
sexuality, 2, 5–9, 23, 26–27, 35, 63, 103, 147, 165, 170, 174, 202, 210, 212, 218, 225; in Asian diaspora, 249, 251; in childhood, 166; in Japan, 14, 163, 167; lesbian, gay, and queer, 21, 203, 235; in Malaysia, 229, 235; New Asian, 142, 180, 218, 246–48, 250–51, 254, 256–57; nonnormative, nonconformist, and deviant, 23, 53, 106, 159, 215; queer and Asian, 23, 27; in Singapore, 133, 135–36, 140–44, 148–49, 152; as site of intervention, 133; study and analyses of, 8, 24–25, 90; as Western category, 8, 32. *See also* activism; Asia; community; culture; gay men; homosexuality; identity; Internet; lesbians; practice; queer culture; region;

representation; sexual identity; transgenderism

Silver, David, 8, 10

Singapore, 21, 245, 251, 256; as authoritarian police state, 136, 146; Broadcasting Authority Act, 135, 142, 154 n. 6, 261 n. 7; Department of Statistics, 258; Dot.com the nation, 245; Great Marriage Debate and sexual reproduction, 136, 259; Internal Security Act, 147. *See also* Asia; Asian values

slash, 54–55, 58, 70, 83 n. 3; *Star-Trek*, 58; *X Files*, 58. *See also* community; fans; Internet

Slater, Don, 117

Slevin, James, 133, 137–38, 143, 149

short messaging service (SMS), 162, 259. *See also* code; phones

social theory, 24

sodomy, 8, 222, 225, 229, 231, 233–34. *See also* Ibrahim, Anwar

Soja, Edward, 252, 255

Sondheim, Alan, 141

South Korea, 90–91, 93. *See also* activism; Berry, Chris; gay men; global queering; homosexuality; identity; Internet; lesbians; queer culture; sexual identity

spectatorship, 12. *See also* audience; reception

Spigel, Lynn, 9

Spivak, Gayatri, 245

Sproull, Lee, 116

Stewart, Fiona, 10

Stone, Sharon, 25, 39, 42

Stonewall, 2, 90, 117

subculture, 3, 52, 90–91, 108 n. 12, 162, 164, 167, 169, 174, 259. *See also* community; fans; Internet

subject-positions, 22, 25, 27, 29, 32, 33, 36, 40, 43, 46, 122. *See also* identity; sexual identity; subjectivity

subjectivity, 23, 25–26, 34, 37, 40–41, 88, 159, 168–69, 175, 211. *See also* identity; Internet; sexual identity; subject-position

surveillance, 47 n. 7, 203, 205, 229. *See also* regulation

Sussex Technology Group, 160

syncretization, 89, 91, 105–7, 113 n. 29

Taiwan, 90–91. *See also* activism; Berry, Chris; gay men; global queering;

homosexuality; identity; Internet; lesbians; queer culture; sexual identity

Takarazuka Revue, 54

technology, 9, 13, 14, 90, 100, 104, 107, 117, 141–42, 170, 189, 202, 205, 210–11, 225–27, 235, 246, 248, 250, 253, 260; as communication, 158, 218; as multimedia, 9, 116–17, 222; new, 160, 164, 174, 223, 228; speed of, 2, 204, 208. *See also* communication; computer-mediated communications; information; Internet; media; new media

telegraph, 9

television, 8–9, 24, 37–40, 42, 70, 72. *See also* audience; media; reception

telnet, 2

Those Fluttering Objects of Desire, 205

Tobin, Joseph J., 78

Toffler, Alvin, 229–30

Tomes, Kimberly SaRee, 205

transgenderism, 60; and constructions of female body, 206; in India, 194; in Indonesia, 28, 29–33, 47 n. 15, 48 n. 17, 48 n. 18; intersexual, 60; in Japan, 58–59, 169; in Malaysia, 47 n. 15; and Nataf, 208, 217; in Philippines, 47 n. 15; in South America, 60; in South Korea, 95; in Thailand, 47 n. 15, 117–18, 120, 122, 124–25; transsexual, 59. *See also* community; newhalf; subject-position; transvestitism

translation, 7, 22, 26–27, 29, 36, 40, 44–46, 50 n. 39, 74, 76–77, 82, 93, 120, 160, 171, 201; cultural, 12, 43; as cultural anxiety, 39; as subversion, 168; and transmissibility of culture, 42. *See also* fans; manga; transmission

transmission, 8, 36; cultural, 12, 133, 137–38, 144, 147–48, 151–52

transnationalism, 10, 12, 14, 46, 117, 201–3, 206, 208, 210–11, 215, 218–19, 224, 226, 235, 245, 247–48, 252, 255, 258; transborder, 205; transcultural, 7. *See also* globalization

transvestitism, 10, 26, 53. *See also* newhalf; transgenderism

Tremewan, Christopher, 135

van Esterik, Penny, 119

virtual reality, 12, 73, 105–6, 117, 196, 206, 212, 215, 245. *See also* community; Internet; regulation

Index

virus, 3, 181

Voice of Asia, The: Two Leaders Discuss the Coming Century, 227

Wakefield, Nina, 117
web, 1, 12, 14–15, 56, 100, 102–3, 137, 213; and access, 182; *Action for Aids: The Act*, 143; and art, 204; *Bombay Dost*, 185; *Brandon*, 205; *Buy One Get One*, 204–5; *Catnap*, 57; *Creative Girls' Home*, 55–56; *Dosamo*, 101; *Electronic Frontier Foundation*, 215; *Free Anwar Campaign*, 233; *Gay Bombay*, 188, 193, 195; *gayDelhi.com*, 185; *gay India*, 189; and graphics, 73; *Home Delivery Newhalf System*, 62; *khushnet.com*, 185, 188; *Newhalf Health Adventure*, 61–62; *Newhalf Net*, 63; pages and sites, 73, 225, 234; *Panopticum Interface*, 205; "*People Like Us*," 143; *Queernet*, 101; *Rainbow*, 97; rings, 53; *Ruby in the Skye with Sitrine*, 212; *Sadistic*, 57; *Saki's Room*, 215; *Sappho's Daughters*, 97; *SiGNel*, 143; *Sintercom*, 143; *Trikone*, 183–84; *Utopia*, 1, 143; *Virtual Gaybar Elizabeth*, 61; *Visto.com*, 214; *We Are Family*, 143, 149–51; *World KiSS Project*, 213; *www.gay.com*, 183–84; *www.riceasia.com*, 253; *Xq28*, 115, 119–25; *Yaoi Intelligence Agency*, 55; *Yawning Bread*, 140, 144–48; *Zetsu ai/Bronze*, 73. *See also* Internet

Wheeler, Deborah L., 141
When Old Technologies Were New, 9
White, Merry, 167
whiteness, 174, 160–61. *See also* ethnicity
Wiener, Norbert, 247
Williams, Carolyn, 140
Williams, Linda, 208–9
women, 8, 160, 225. *See also* gender; lesbians; queer culture; representation

Yang, Mayfair, 225
Yue, Audrey, 11–12, 14, 245–65